Anna Tilden,

UNITARIAN CULTURE,

and the

PROBLEM *of*

SELF-REPRESENTATION

Anna Tilden,

UNITARIAN CULTURE,

and the

PROBLEM *of*

SELF-REPRESENTATION

Sarah Ann Wider

THE UNIVERSITY OF GEORGIA PRESS

ATHENS AND LONDON

© 1997 by the University of Georgia Press
Athens, Georgia 30602
All rights reserved
Designed by Betty Palmer McDaniel
Set in 10.5 on 12.5 Minion by G & S Typesetters
Printed and bound by Braun-Brumfield, Inc.
The paper in this book meets the guidelines for
permanence and durability of the Committee on
Production Guidelines for Book Longevity of the
Council on Library Resources.

Printed in the United States of America
01   00   99   98   97   C   5   4   3   2   1

Library of Congress Cataloging in Publication Data
Wider, Sarah Ann.
Anna Tilden, Unitarian culture, and the problem of self-representation / Sarah Ann Wider.
p.   cm.
Includes bibliographical references and index.
ISBN 0-8203-1900-7 (alk. paper)
1. Tilden, Anna.   2. Unitarians—United States—Biography.
3. Spouses of clergy—United States—Biography.
4. Self-evaluation—Case studies.   I. Title.
BX9869. T58W53   1997
289.1'092
[B]—dc20   96-34259

British Library Cataloging in Publication Data available

For my mother, Mary C. Wider,
and
my daughter, Faith Elizabeth

Contents

Acknowledgments

As projects end, we trace beginnings. By what means do we travel back to our point of departure? Where did our thoughts begin?

For this work, the images are clear. The Houghton Library: standing in the bridge at the card catalog, looking for Emerson's ordination sermon and finding instead the description of the Tilden-Gannett manuscripts. A peculiar slant of light in the Massachusetts Historical Society as the otherwise smooth pages of Ezra Stiles Gannett's journals yielded pressed flowers from Anna Tilden's grave.

Away from these sources, the mind acknowledges others. Kay Johnston and Margaret Maurer, whose conversations simply and generously opened new thought for me. Linck Johnson, colleague and fellow Americanist, whose interest in the "other" nineteenth centuries meets and matches my own. Wes Mott, Joel Myerson, and David Robinson for the long-distance support that sustains a work over time.

Based as it is on unpublished manuscripts, this work looks to its source in those aptly named special collections and rare-book rooms. The Anna Tilden and Ezra Stiles Gannett manuscripts as well as the Harriet Martineau and Tilden family correspondence are quoted by permission of the Houghton Library, Harvard University. The Houghton has been an incomparable place for my work, and to its staff I say a resounding "thank you." The Ezra Stiles Gannett journals and letters and the letters from Henry Ware Jr., Anna Tilden, William Ellery Channing, and from the Federal Street Church are quoted by permission of the Massachusetts Historical Society. Their Gannett collection has been invaluable and the staff unfailingly cheerful over my many requests. The Tilden genealogy is quoted by permission of the New England Historic Genealogical Society, a place in which, no matter how unwieldy the material, the work was always defined by ease. For help with the William Channing Gannett collection in the Department of Rare Books and Special Collections at the University of Rochester Library, I thank Mary Huth, who alerted me to the fragmentary "Some Recollections of My Children," one of the few pieces of Tilden's writing from the 1840s. To Michael R. Gannett, I extend heartfelt thanks for his generosity in sharing Tilden materials with me, giving substance to his great-grandmother's last days, and joining image to word. The steady gaze of the daguerreotype speaks with the frankness of her prose. In 1989, I edited Tilden's sermons for publication in *Studies in the American Renaissance,* edited by Joel Myerson (University Press of Virginia). My discussion of Unitarianism in this book is both source and product of the work behind my entry on Unitarianism in the *Encyclopedia of Transcendentalism,* edited by Wesley T. Mott (Greenwood Press, 1996). I thank both editors and publishers for their cooperation.

In a project that required traveling, the Colgate University Research Council in a very real sense kept me on the road. Research became much easier under Research Council grants and a Picker Fellowship that graciously has been extended over the necessary number of summers. Another support added a different kind of ease to my travels. Whether sharing the daily commute or deciphering an epitaph in Mount Auburn cemetery, my aunt Doris Stantial entered into this project with a flamboyant curiosity that turned humid summers into a great gleeful adventure. The writing itself began during a rare rainy October at the John Peters Inn in Blue Hill, Maine, and its progress logged with Rick and Barbara Seeger's yearly inquiries about the project's latest point.

When these pages come to print another reader will hear the echo of several seasons. Reader of competing paragraphs, peruser of provisional prose and revisionary thinking, my husband Bruce has shared and even enjoyed the incomparably messy process we call writing.

Anna Tilden, the subject of my work, sought to understand and be understood. Her process of understanding became the focus of the work, and her phrase "rightly understand" could well be said to be a life's work. As solitary as our research often is, there are a few who share the task with us even when they least expect it. Tilden's phrase in fact speaks of sisters: she looked for someone "like a sister" who would "rightly understand" her. To my own sister Susan, fellow traveler, I recall our many conversations where "exactly" spoke for us. My father, Henry, will see his own fascination with observers and their accounts actively at work in these pages. And to my mother, Mary, who introduced me to the great excitement of the wondering mind, I offer this book. In your own life, you have embodied the scholar's passion, an expansive curiosity that finds ever more to pursue, that discovers in any project several more, and that knows no work ends but only opens another beginning.

Anna Tilden,

UNITARIAN CULTURE,

and the

PROBLEM *of*

SELF-REPRESENTATION

Introduction:
The Biography of the Unknown Life

On Christmas Day, 1846, one of the most popular narratives of the nineteenth century was drawing to its close in a Boston minister's home. An
"angel in the house" was dying. Mother, wife, redeemer, friend, she had
given her life for her husband and children. Only thirty-five years old,
Anna Tilden Gannett had come to the end of her life on the path traveled so
frequently by her female contemporaries. A book-hungry adolescent who
read Hume and Paley every morning before breakfast, a schoolteacher who
viewed her duties with high seriousness, a wife who made it her goal to become "worthy" of her husband, she gradually learned to "die to self" and
"live for others." In short, she became a priestess sacrificed in the "cult of
domesticity," accomplishing her "last, best work" through her death.

The story is an undeniably familiar one. The young woman whose intellectual promise is thwarted by marriage; the individual who comes so close
yet falls so short of developing a self defined in, and on, her own terms. For
every Margaret Fuller, there are dozens of Anna Gannetts, women who
accommodated themselves to their society's conventions. We have long
learned to privilege the convention breakers, to celebrate their independence and praise their adherence to an apparently single-minded principle.
It fits so readily into that favorite narrative from the patriarchal past: the individual triumphs over society, thus earning its, and our, acclaim.

For the women who took up the roles their society defined for them,
criticism has been less generous. Ann Douglas's treatment of "the sentimental" in *The Feminization of American Culture* (1977) delineates the case
only too clearly. Women like Catharine Beecher or her sister Harriet Beecher
Stowe who, as Douglas sees it, bought into their society's ideal of domesticity inevitably betrayed their own cause. They engaged in a battle that could
only mean loss: women were confined to the home playing the simply
repetitive, simply limiting role of wife, mother, sister. Douglas's version
subscribes wholeheartedly to an overpowering "cult of true womanhood"

in which the woman's power was always executed by "influence" and always signified a debased cultural value.

The limitations of this approach have been amply taken up by recent studies. Jane Tompkins's discussion of sentimentality in her book *Sensational Designs: The Cultural Work of American Fiction, 1790–1860* (1985) calls attention to the conventions of our criticism and how they shape our interpretation of the women we study. She looks again at what has been dismissed as "sentimental fiction" and enables her readers to see strategy where others have seen kitsch. Arguing that critics have too readily judged nineteenth-century women writers by standards intrinsically biased against them, Tompkins seeks to recover the standards by which these writers judged their own work. What she finds is that their works did not so much attempt to preserve the status quo, as Douglas had argued, but rather projected a social order that had never yet existed. She looks at women's published writings, fiction and nonfiction, to show how these writers used the conventions of the society to transform it. In marked contrast to the nostalgia Douglas sees in these texts, Tompkins finds a powerful rhetoric of persuasion designed to shape a future radically different from the past.[1]

Interested in both the affect and effect of nineteenth-century sentimental writing, the critics in Shirley Samuels's collection *The Culture of Sentiment: Race, Gender, and Sentimentality in Nineteenth-Century America* (1992) explore the double-edged nature of embodied sympathy. Looking at the varied uses to which the methods of sentiment could be put, these essays address the uneasy balance between radical revision and complicitous conservation. The collection also extends the discussion of sentimentality beyond the antebellum period to include works from both the early and late parts of the century. With the discussion opened to a greater variety of writing, different questions are foregrounded and different texts emerge. The questions, by now, should be familiar (questions of race, class, and gender), although the texts remain less so (the autobiographical writings of Zitkala-Sa, the fiction of Lydia Maria Child or Pauline Hopkins). Examining sentimentality as "a set of cultural practices designed to evoke a certain form of emotional response," the collection illustrates the ways in which "sympathy" participated in creating the very "social, political, racial and gendered meanings" it also called into question (4–5).

Tompkins's book and Samuels's collection focus on published writers, both male and female. Their project is less to recover "forgotten" women writers than to discuss the politics of such "forgetfulness." Other critics—

scholars such as Nina Baym, Cathy Davidson, Joanne Dobson, Mary Kelley, Joyce Warren—have made it possible to study the women so well known in the nineteenth century, so recently forgotten by "us." These writers— writers such as Catharine Sedgwick, E. D. E. N. Southworth, Fanny Fern— have now begun to receive critical attention. Where the voice of the white, middle-class woman was effectively silenced by mid-twentieth-century criti- cism, the African American woman writer was both silenced and erased. A rich tradition of autobiographical writing, poetry, and fiction is now being recovered and studied. William Andrews, Joanne Braxton, Frances Smith Foster, the editors of Oxford's Schomburg Library of Nineteenth-Century Black Women Writers: their work illuminates the finely crafted and power- fully subversive authority created by writers who, in Foster's words, felt strongly the "responsibility of speaking out and into history."[2] With the Schomburg series, the Rutgers American Women Writers series, and the Oxford Women Writers Project reprinting works that have long been out of print, and with essays like those collected in Joyce Warren's *The (Other) American Traditions* and with studies like Frances Smith Foster's *Written by Herself*, we have been given the texts to read and new ways of reading the texts.[3]

In the past ten years, critical studies have increasingly turned their atten- tion to the variety of novels written by women in the late eighteenth to the mid-nineteenth century. These studies embrace a variety of methods, reflecting numerous concerns that the late twentieth century has brought to light. Much of the work has been that of recovery: the sheer task of find- ing the novels written by women, finding the publishers to reprint them, essentially making it possible to read the works that were once so well read. This work has gone hand in hand with another type of recovery: writing about women writers who were never fully "forgotten" but who were nonetheless marginalized. Ellen Moers in her groundbreaking study *Liter- ary Women* began, one might say, the "whole procession," enabling us to reconsider works by women writers whose names we still knew. Nina Baym taught us to name what we did not know. In her 1978 book *Woman's Fic- tion*, Baym presented the reader with dozens of American women writers who were virtually unknown to the late twentieth century.[4] Patricia Meyer Spacks, Elaine Showalter, Rachel Brownstein, Ellen Moers, Sandra Gilbert, and Susan Gubar continued this work of rereading and recovery: Gilbert and Gubar focusing on the woman writer, Showalter and Spacks on the representation of the female protagonist, Brownstein on the reader.[5]

What remains more problematic is the unpublished work of nineteenth-century women. Nancy Cott's *The Bonds of Womanhood*, published in 1977, prepared the ground some years ago, but the work has gone more slowly. What was needed was a thoroughgoing recovery of both the writers and the genres that had been marginalized. The connection between who these writers were and in what form they wrote is not coincidental. Diaries, journals, letters: women who did not consider themselves writers and who did not write for a public audience turned to the genres most accessible to them. Part of daily life, reflecting its rhythms, each form offered the individual a chance to re-form her days through her words, to make meaning out of otherwise unnoted tasks. And like the daily work they recorded, these forms have regularly been overlooked by the twentieth century. Until recently, only the letters and journals of already "famous" individuals have received critical attention. Letters were deemed "interesting" if written by Thomas Jefferson or John Adams. Journals merited critical study as long as they were Emerson's or Thoreau's, but when it came to the private writings of nineteenth-century women, acceptance stopped short. Writing about the self was essentially understood to be writing about "man."

Recent work in feminist criticism, however, has directed close and careful attention to women's autobiographical writings. Defining a rich area of inquiry, these studies have brought to light "new" (that is, forgotten) texts and have virtually written them into a larger audience's attention.[6] Work on women's autobiography can indeed claim that signal privilege of doing its thinking on the (cutting) edge. Sidonie Smith, Françoise Lionnet, Estelle Jelinek, Margo Culley, Felicity Nussbaum, Joanne Braxton: the list goes on, each writer speaking for the multiple perspectives that can be brought to bear on autobiography.[7] *Auto, bios, graphe*—the self, the life, the writing: we have not yet exhausted the possible permutations in bringing this word together with the work called by its name. As Margo Culley comments, "The most pressing concerns of contemporary scholars—genre and gender as culturally inscribed; the construction of the self within language systems; the referentiality of language itself; the nature of subjectivity, authority, and agency; the problematics of making meaning and making history; theories of time, memory, and narrative—all absorb critics of autobiography" (*American Women's Autobiography*, 3). Culley's list of theoretical concerns could indeed be said to write the "autobiography" of literary study in the past two decades, but as some readers may note, many of these scholarly questions are inconsequential in other contexts. Pressing concerns "press" unequally; where critics are "absorbed," other readers remain unimpressed. The life stories of women are not one, nor are they definitively told by the issues within which scholars choose to frame them. Culley reminds all of her readers that by foregrounding the differences of particular individuals, the study of "women's autobiography" can readily avoid the danger of "critical absorption" in the narrow interest writ large as a universal concern.

The structure for many of these recent studies speaks directly to this recognition of difference. Recent work on African American women's autobiographical writing, for example, takes as its point of departure the numbers of women writing and the ways in which autobiography, from its inception, functioned as a genre for effecting fundamental change. Essay collections abound, and indeed frame the field, from Jelinek's early *Women's Autobiography: Essays in Criticism* to Culley and Hoffmann's *Women's Personal Narratives* to Culley's *American Women's Autobiography*. Collections such as Shari Benstock's *The Private Self: Theory and Practice of Women's Autobiographical Writings* and Bella Brodzki and Celeste Schenck's *Life/Lines: Theorizing Women's Autobiography* have begun to do the hard work of, as Brodzki and Schenck's subtitle so neatly puts it, "theorizing women's autobiography" by drawing on a multiplicitous group of women. But these studies focus only on published materials or works by published writers. We still need to hear the voices of women who daily crafted themselves, their surroundings, their family and kin in the prose of their autobiographical writings.[8] The Personal Narratives Group, affiliated with the Center for Advanced Feminist Studies at the University of Minnesota, has opened a prospect on a new world. In its *Interpreting Women's Lives* (1989), the contributors look at writer and reader, at the methods by which the individual shapes experience into expressed meaning and interprets the meaning as it is shaped. In addition, *Women's Studies Quarterly* and the *Women's Studies International Forum* devoted special issues to women's autobiographical writing (1989 and 1987, respectively). Focusing on diaries, letters, and oral histories, these collections concentrated on forms used or created by women who did not define their projects as literary. Many did not define their writing or storytelling as a "project" at all. Personal narratives, like diaries and letters, rarely stake out a claim for themselves; they do not promise the "coherence" we ascribe to other texts.

For those scholars working on women's autobiographical writings, attention has largely been directed toward defining and describing the various

genres included in the category "autobiographical." Even when the term
genre has been abandoned as inadequate because too restrictive, as it has
been by the Personal Narratives Group, emphasis remains on the "narrative
forms" in which women present their life stories. Some of these autobiographical forms have themselves been appropriated as models for feminist
criticism: life history makes its way much more readily into the "critical essay" than it did twenty years ago.[9] And in her 1989 essay in *Women's Studies
Quarterly,* Cynthia Huff maintains that the diary itself is a fit image for
feminist criticism. In its resistance to closure, its predication on a diverse
assemblage of material, it speaks against a totalizing vision of "truth" or
"knowledge" and reminds readers, by its very shape, that all knowledge is
constructed.[10]

The study of personal narratives is clearly at the heart of a feminist project. As the women who collaborated in the production of *Interpreting
Women's Lives* write, "The recovery and interpretation of women's lives
have been central concerns of feminist scholarship from the earliest pio-
neering works to the present. Listening to women's voices, studying women's
writings, and learning from women's experiences have been crucial to the
feminist reconstruction of our understanding of the world" (4). Their emphasis on the "use" to which their work can be put forms an interesting
parallel to the earlier "legitimation" of autobiography written by women.
The author justified her written "life" by trusting that it would be useful
for others. What differentiates the nineteenth century from the twentieth
might well be represented as an issue of manners. Nineteenth-century
women "hoped" for good effect; twentieth-century women claim its centrality. To that end, work has been directed toward new ways of reading autobiographical texts. Since letters and journals, oral accounts and life histories do not play by the same rules as the novel or essay, they cannot be read
as if they were what they clearly are not. Much of the emphasis on new ways
of reading brings together several texts—the diaries of women on the Nebraska or Kansas or California frontier, diaries of working women, conversion narratives of Puritan women. Writings seen as similar by circumstance
are read together, and from this reading emerges a representative (i.e., gen-
eralized) text to which certain techniques of reading can be applied.[11]

Generalizations have, for the most part, been admirably cautious. Few
want to—or would—be accused of claiming a "universal" experience for
any group of women, whether in late-nineteenth-century Nebraska or in
the 1960s rural South. However, comparative studies allow virtually no way

around the fragmentation of individual diaries and their writers. Combining texts in a single study may well make visible a form that has been overlooked, but this approach also obscures individual selves behind the studied form. The focus is on texts as representative of genre rather than on a particular self and its strategies of self-representation.

What is absent from recent studies of women's autobiographical writing is the sustained consideration of one unknown woman's life. Laurel Ulrich's *A Midwife's Tale* is the outstanding exception with its careful reading of Martha Ballard's diary. Ulrich's success may well have made others less eager to approach the whirl of words individuals spin around themselves. However, such studies are well worth the time, for they offer their readers a way of negotiating the distance between different experiences. A life read on the terms it generated, borrowed, revised, rejected is a life that readily reminds its reader that generalizations are conveniences, not truths, that individuals may be judged "representative" of a particular group but are finally distinct individuals. Their "identity" is not simply, and certainly not fully, expressed by their representative status.

My tale of Anna Tilden makes no claim to being "representative," although it makes every claim for the richly textured world in which self-representation occurs. I give attentive consideration to one individual in particular. Studying the words she wrote, I seek, not to make her representative of a particular group, but to explore the complexities of the representations she created for herself. She does not stand for nineteenth-century ministers' wives, merchants' daughters, sermon listeners, or novel readers. The focus instead is on dilemmas of self-representation: creating a credible persona whose voice is recognized and authority acknowledged. Examining her writings and the forms they took, I structure a study that emphasizes a particular life yet cannot be called a traditional biography.

Critics have recently pointed out the limitations of the time-honored style of biography with its "spotlight" approach to a single individual. Focusing exclusively on its subject, biography presents a life by isolating it. The individual stands alone. His (generally) life is separated carefully from the lives of his contemporaries. Even when others figure largely in the biography, the "spotlight" rarely shifts off the "main subject" and never for long. Other lives are presented as subsidiary to his; his life is made central to theirs. As Liz Stanley points out, such an approach necessarily distorts the life. No life is lived with such intense concentration on the self. Every life yields its unaccentuated moments. We are rarely the center of attention, nor does being at this center have to be the raison d'être of biography. There are other ways to write (and perhaps right) a life. To this end, biographers have recently begun to experiment with new methods for writing lives. Carolyn Heilbrun's call to consider the stories of women of *all* ages; Meryn Stuart's emphasis on the biographer's role in the life she writes; Liz Stanley's attention to the biographer's process, maintaining that this process must appear as an integral part of the written product; Kathleen Barry's concern with recontextualizing the seemingly exceptional individual: each invention directs the reader toward the new field of study that we now call feminist biography.[12]

What follows is a narrative study of self-representation, one form that this new biographical work might take. Anna Tilden directly connected the process of writing with the difficult task of discerning identity. She kept a journal, she said, "to have a clearer idea of what *I am.*"[13] What she was emerged from what she wrote, and what she wrote stemmed from the words that defined her days. Tilden crafted various personae in her letters and journals, adapting different models of self-representation for her self. Drawing on the available resources, she tried out the character(s) offered in sermons and novels. Her writing was predicated on listening and reading, and to that end, I direct my reader's attention to the sermons she heard and the novels she read.

This is more, however, than the study of influence. While Tilden's life structures the book, her self is freed from exclusive attention. Tilden is not simply, or always, at the center. The chapters read with a rhythm that alternates between a close reading of her reading and a close reading of her response. She occasionally "disappears" from the discussion as did the female protagonists in the novels Tilden so heartily admired. In part, her apparent absence reminds us of the marginalization practiced on certain genres and their writing readers. In part, it calls into question studies governed by the assumption that a center demands a periphery. Restructuring the construct of the center, I experiment with a model of multiple, nonconcentric circles. The center is arbitrary and certainly not single. What proves interesting is the way in which overlapping circles of numerous centers intersect.

Freeing biography from the great man's model, I maintain that writing about *the* life means *any* life. Looking at various points of intersection, I seek to discern the particular story together with the stories of which it was a part and to which it contributed. To make known the unknown, I first turn to what my readers require. Anna Tilden needs "introduction": the first chapter offers the life of this unknown woman. Designed for the reader, it is not intended as a "definitive" account of her life. It is, first and foremost, an introduction. The next chapters offer a complex weave of writers and readers, speakers and hearers. To measure the models Tilden appropriated, we must first see their sources. One chapter studies sermons; the other, novels. In both, Tilden's response frames the discussion, but the texts themselves are allowed their moment in the center. What the intersections of sermon, novel, and listener/reader reveal is the problematic limitations of verbal constructs. Worlds built out of words create powerful illusions of reality, but the illusion is readily altered by lived experience. Tilden's crisis of faith is a case in point. It defines another center through her revision of the "old centers" and their well-known models. She edited out their limitations, built on the strengths, and used their conventions to license her "plain speaking." As writing reader, she turned author in her letters reassembling pieces from various models. In this process of re-collection, she engages in an ongoing definition of authority in which she finally claims authority as her own. Tilden's letters provided her with the form in which she could authorize herself. She was eyewitness and a trusted source of knowledge for her correspondents. She was counselor, verifying advice through her own experience. She was responsive observer, detailing material according to her correspondent's interest.

Before turning to the life and its work, I want briefly to describe Tilden's autobiographical writings. If we read them by the older models designed for published work and published writers, we fail as readers. We cannot place them if we inadvertently misplace the writer. A woman like Anna Tilden poses an interesting problem and an ideal subject for feminist biography. She has not been included in our list of the nineteenth century's remarkable women, nor was she acknowledged as such in her own century. Viewed through the framework of an earlier model of biography, her life hardly seems noteworthy, simply one more repetition of domesticity. She was no Margaret Fuller, no Harriet Martineau. She devoted none of her life to social reform. She constructed no closely argued analyses of economic systems. Neither was she a Harriet Beecher Stowe or a Lydia Maria Child. She never published a word that she wrote, nor was she known as a writer. In the public eye, she was known as a minister's wife, neither more nor less.

Beyond the public eye, she wrote, and wrote extensively: letters, sermon notes, journals—hundreds of thousands of words.[14] Her first extant writings

date from 1824, when she was not quite thirteen years old. Following a
common practice of the time, she kept notes on the sermons she heard,
recording the name of the minister, his text, and as much of his sermon as
she could remember. The entries read like a roll call of prominent Unitarian ministers: William Ellery Channing, Ezra Stiles Gannett, Henry Ware,
senior and junior, William Furness, Frederic Henry Hedge, Ralph Waldo
Emerson. She listened as Boston Unitarianism defined itself and duly recorded its progress. She continued this practice of note taking for at least
seven years, eventually sewing her notes into a single, pocket-sized book.[15]
That her crafting was self-conscious appears on the first page. She begins
her book of sermon notes with the ordination of Ezra Stiles Gannett. The
date of official connection to the new minister, colleague of the renowned
and beloved Channing, marks the beginning of her sermon note taking.
Whether she kept notes before this date is unknown. When she sewed the
separate pages together is likewise uncertain, but her book's opening words
speak meaningfully in retrospect. The minister who was counselor to her
mother, "brother" and "friend" to herself and her sisters, the individual
who would eventually become her husband, is the first subject of her attention. In her words, Channing delivered an "excellent discourse" for his
colleague's ordination. She gives nothing but the biblical text from which
Channing preached. The choice was indeed provocative: "Behold, I send
you forth as sheep in the midst of wolves: be ye, therefore, wise as serpents,
and harmless as doves" (SAR 1989, 17). As she remarked at the end of many
of her entries, she hoped that these remembered sermons would do her
"much good."

In late adolescence, Tilden turned to another popular means for self-
improvement. Beginning her first journal on New Year's Day, 1827, she announced in her opening sentences the role she envisioned for her daily entries. Echoing the comments she recorded in her sermon notes, she trusted
that journal keeping would do her "a great deal of good." The journal itself
may well have been a New Year's gift. By no means luxurious, the book was
nonetheless purchased, not homemade. The front and back covers are a
marbleized paper, standard fare for the blank books sold at stationer's
shops. Much larger than the sermon notes, these pages measure 6½ by 10½
inches. There are 175 pages with forty, sometimes fifty, lines of writing to a
page. The entries are daily, and Tilden worked diligently to maintain that
structure. Even when she admits that a week's entries were written in retrospect, she retained the distinction of days. This running record covered a

period of significant change: her father's year-long trading voyage, her grandmother's death, her family's change of residence, the extension of her family to include both an invalid cousin and the church's colleague minister Ezra Stiles Gannett. Written from January 1827 through mid-September 1828, the journal was a place in which she remembered conversations, described the ordinary routine and the extraordinary events that disrupted the daily pattern. She recorded the books she read and the people she saw. She discussed the news within her community—death, departures, the Harvard achievements of her cousins and their friends—but rarely included the news beyond her household. She defined the world by her experience. The journal was also the place in which she voiced her opinion, speaking her identity into a separate existence. And it eventually became the place in which she learned to silence herself.

This journal ends abruptly in September 1828, most probably because of severe difficulty with her eyesight at this time.[16] Whether she returned to journal writing before the spring of 1834 is unknown. If she did, these journals have been lost or destroyed. The next extant journal dates from 1834–35. Like its predecessor, it also was designed for self-improvement but with a different emphasis. Faulting her previous journals for their attention to "every petty event," she dedicated this endeavor to a more closely defined purpose. In the opening entry she explained why, after several years of silence, she once again turned to this form: "It is many years since I have kept any thing like [a] Journal, but I now think I shall again commence one, not like those I have formerly written, an account of every petty event, but there are times when I think it may do me good to see my own thoughts and feelings expressed, I may then have a clearer idea of what *I am*" (20 April 1834). This journal covers a period of severe crisis. Uncertain whether she believed in God, unable to feel certain of the "truth" of Christianity, burdened by her family's financial difficulties and her own distaste for the teaching position she had taken, she wrote, not as in 1827 to correct her faults, but literally to reconstruct a self that had collapsed. Through expression, she sought to discover what her identity in fact was.

In appearance, this journal forms a marked contrast to its 1827–28 predecessor. A far plainer affair, perhaps reflecting the family's straitened economic circumstances, it is homemade, not purchased, sewn together with no cover. If it was begun with an eye to economy, its writer did not always keep up her end of the bargain. Unlike pages in the closely written 1827–28 journal, pages in the second journal are left blank. The entries are sporadic.

The pressure of time appears starkly in the entries themselves: Tilden wrote only on Sunday, the one day free from her work as a schoolteacher.

Both the 1827–28 and 1834–35 journals were undertaken as a means for self-improvement. Tilden keenly identified the form with formation of character. Entries provided a private place for self-examination. Chastisement was frequently the response, complete with stated resolves for how the next day or week would differ from the last. The journals written at home were designed for herself as reader, and as such she felt free to criticize herself but not always free to express herself openly. Fearing other readers, she practiced the art of self-interruption. Silencing a thought before she wrote it, substituting blank lines for individuals' names, and finally silencing herself altogether, she left thoughts unfinished and journal pages blank. In Boston, the journal increasingly became a record of what she could not risk saying. The genre, however, offered more than a course in silencing the self. It was, after all, a flexible form that served readily for self-examination but could as readily be adapted into a travel book or a letter. During her absences from Boston, her journals no longer announced their purpose as self-improvement. When she left for England in 1837, she began a new journal. She turned to this book for companionship, for comfort, and for the sake of memory. Describing places that she most likely would never see again, she recorded her days with the detail that would keep this one brief period of her life present. Like the 1827–28 journal, the travel record is given a more formal appearance. It also was a book purchased for the purpose, and on the first page she designated it as "*Journal No. I.*" She wrote on one side of the page only, leaving the facing page available for later comments. She amended entries after they were written, adding information from the guidebooks she consulted or commentary on the events of the day. The travel record is apparently her longest venture in journal writing, but this cannot be confirmed in fact. Only one volume remains; however, at different points it refers its reader to volumes 2 and 5. The single volume covers only three months of her nineteen-month stay, and thus the journal may well have extended to several volumes.

Although the journal could be adapted to several uses, only when it functioned as a letter did she write without reservation. In her day, the letter was a clearly accessible form. Tilden would have been expected not only to write letters but to have learned *how*, a skill that meant shaping a correspondence as well as writing an individual letter. The instructional books known as "letter-writers" were in abundance, and Tilden could hardly have missed out on this essential element in an early-nineteenth-century education.[17] Letters also figured prominently in Tilden's reading. She read the advice books of her day, framed as correspondence for "young ladies."[18] She also read travel literature formed once again on the letter. By her adulthood, letter reading was as common a practice as novel reading; only in the former case, she could turn author. Writing to her husband, she used the letter for persuasion. She used her writing to blur the boundaries of time and to erase distinctions of space. When separated from her mother and sisters, she called her letters "journals." They were designed to collapse the distance between herself and her correspondents. Writing out certain moments in minute detail, she sought to include her absent family members in her daily experience. The descriptions ring with the present tense, offering the illusion of "now" to her far-distant readers. Her sense of audience was acute. Tailored to the specific interests of her readers, these letters reflect a keen sensitivity to the individual or individuals who would read them.

For Tilden, the letter served numerous purposes. Of the eighty-three known letters, most are letters of length, written to her husband, mother, or sisters to justify, persuade, or re-create. They often take the shape of what she called "letter journals," written over a period of time, each sitting marked by its date and taking the form of a journal entry. There are, however, shorter variations of this genre: letters acknowledging gifts, notes of farewell, letters arranging social visits. That these letters mattered to the family is suggested by their meticulous preservation. Envelopes were kept, as were the pressed flowers occasionally enclosed. Each letter's date is written on the envelope, and often some brief remark indicates the significance of the letter itself.

A journal for her family, a method of persuasion, a place to struggle with one's faith: the letter accommodated the particular need of a particular occasion. In the case of her spiritual crisis, the letter provided a safe way of expressing ideas she could not voice openly. Choosing the letter over the conversation, she settled on this written form of expression because it preserved privacy without forfeiting response. Given the inadmissible nature of her thoughts—doubting God's existence and questioning immortality—she avoided the immediacy of conversation. At the same time, she longed to break the isolation created by her self-imposed silence. The letter filled both needs. Through it, the writer solicited a response from outside herself but protected herself from what this response might be.

While Tilden's early letters provided protection, her later letters offered freedom. Distanced from immediate response, she used her side of the correspondence to present a singular, independent self that remained fully

CHAPTER ONE

Daughter, Sister, Mother, Wife: The Self in Search of Expression

Born in 1811, Anna Linzee Tilden[1] grew up in a household that would quickly pass from genteel prosperity to struggling respectability. Her father, Bryant Parrott Tilden (1781–1851), was a merchant, caught in the once profitable but by the 1820s highly unpredictable China trade. Her mother, Zebiah Cravath Brown (1783–1842), practiced a domestic economy that would have inspired Catharine Beecher. With limited funds and unlimited uncertainty about their permanence, Zebiah Tilden managed her household of ten, sometimes more, with the creative frugality that produced the illusion of plenty, at least until her daughter's midadolescence. By the late 1820s the Tildens could no longer disguise the discrepancy between the daily cost of living and the meager income available to them. The economic world had changed radically, and Bryant Tilden had been on the wrong side of Fortune's wheel.

The Tildens' story was by no means uncommon. In this period of economic instability, fortunes that had been won in the years following the Revolutionary War were readily lost in the boom-bust cycles that defined the new nation's economy. Bryant Tilden's father, Joseph Tilden (1753–1800), had turned a handsome profit in his trading ventures. A privateer in the Revolutionary War, he learned his trade well. Capitalizing on the lucrative rum triangle, he traded New England lumber for West Indies molasses, apparently with no qualms about the consequences of his work. For him, it simply meant prosperity. By 1787 he was wealthy enough both to own his own vessel and to begin buying land in Boston. At the time of his death at sea in 1800, he owned a significant amount of property on Batterymarch Street in addition to his house with adjacent land on Milk Street.[2] With all debts paid, he also left the sizable sum of $49,604.73.[3] The bulk of it went to his wife; the rest was divided among his six children, a handsome inheritance for each.

The children ranged in ages from the twenty-one-year-old Joseph to the youngest daughter, Caroline, born after her father's death. Bryant Tilden, the second-born son, was eighteen when his father died. Since he was not yet of age, his property was held in guardianship until 24 July 1802, his twenty-first birthday. A year later he married Zebiah Brown. By this time, he had taken his father's trade as his own. His world, however, was not his father's. His ventures were much more speculative, buying sugar in Brazil, for example, to sell at a profit in Europe. His choice of goods suggests the very real difficulties facing the New England shipping industry in the early part of the nineteenth century. The northern United States had few of its own goods to export. Even the timber trade, by which Joseph Tilden had earned so much of his fortune, had slowed considerably by the time his son undertook his own voyages. And with the problematic blockades of the War of 1812 and the continued interruption of trade with Europe throughout the decade, it is no wonder that Bryant Tilden could not match his father's success. He had chosen the wrong occupation.

It was his older brother Joseph who had made the shrewder decision by staying on land and involving himself in the Lowell textile mills. But even this expanding industry faced hard times in the 1820s. Joseph Tilden weathered the economic difficulties well, for his work was not simply centered in Lowell. He also served as president of Boston's Columbian Bank from 1824 to 1837 and as vice president and eventually director of the ever successful Massachusetts Hospital Life Insurance Company.

From his niece's perspective, "Uncle Joseph" was "one of the best of this world," the individual who stopped by almost every day while her father was away on his lengthy trading voyages. He bought theater tickets for his brother's daughters, knowing that such an expense would be well beyond their means. His only daughter Susan, by then married to Samuel Torrey, was something of an idol in her younger cousin's eyes. She was both exemplar and benefactress—a "fine woman," in Tilden's words, and one who seemed genuinely concerned about the family's financial dilemmas. Susan Torrey's two younger brothers, George and Charles, were unquestionably favorite visitors in the Tilden household. Anna Tilden's 1827–28 journal notes their frequent visits with pleasure. Her cousins brought news from Harvard, books from the Boston Athenaeum,[4] and the prospect of a lively and thought-provoking conversation. This journal reveals just how much Tilden enjoyed conversation and how highly she valued the immediate exchange of ideas that accompanied it.[5] Whether listening to her father and the minister review the morning's sermon during Sunday dinner or participating in a discussion about the role of reading in women's lives, Anna Tilden described her happiest days as those filled with good conversation.

The Tilden household never lacked for conversational opportunities. When Tilden began her first journal on 1 January 1827, her entries recorded days punctuated by numerous visitors. Her father had just departed for Pernambuco, and well-wishers stopped in to see what support they could offer in his absence. In addition, there was a group of young people roughly Tilden's age who frequently came to see Tilden and her sisters. Conversation in the house during the day gave way at night to evening parties. Boston's "season" was under way, and although the Tildens were by no means part of the most fashionable circles, they still held a place on the periphery. Their house was located on Otis Place, a street that could claim reflected elegance by its proximity to the fashionable Tontine Crescent in Franklin Street. Designed by Thomas Bulfinch to be one of the showpieces of Boston, this curved street presented a stately facade of sixteen connected brick houses. At the central point, an arch opened into the appropriately named Arch Street.[6] Otis Place ran parallel to Arch Street, turning at the bottom almost to connect with it.

Tilden clearly enjoyed this proximity, the chance to walk these streets as if they were her own and the chance to join the fashionable evening entertainments that literally were held right around the corner. In early January 1827, Tilden recorded frequent invitations as well as her mother's concern about the propriety of attending so many parties. She wrote, "Tomorrow the girls are going to cousin Susan Torrey's but I do not know as I shall go, for I have been out two evenings this week, and Mother says that she does not think that it looks well for me to go out so much, however I shall be content at home if I do not go" (2 January 1827). Although Tilden asserts her willingness to miss Susan Torrey's evening gathering, the next day's entry suggests what her first choice in fact was: "This morning I went out with E[lizabeth] Tucker, and down to Grandmothers with her, Grandmother was very pleasant and talked to me about going to cousin Susans, So I said that I should either go myself or send to her for leave." The grandmother's words were convincing. Tilden's entry records a favorable response from her mother; Tilden and her sisters went to the Torrey's that evening.

Circumstances changed markedly in February with the death of her grandmother. The family went into mourning, and their very change of dress revealed yet another marked change that Tilden would soon confront.

Tilden noted that all the grandchildren would wear the same type of mourning dress except her sister Sarah and her cousin Louisa, who had both spent more time with their grandmother. Restricting the full mourning to only two grandchildren made good economic sense as well, given the number of children in the family. Tilden was one of eight children: seven daughters and a son.[7] Fewer new garments of clothing would be required; expenses could thus be kept minimal. Mrs. Tilden borrowed what she could; family members did the sewing themselves. The only purchases Tilden mentions were gloves and some muslin.[8]

These small measures of economy, however, could not substantially alter their worsening financial situation. By the end of April the Tildens could no longer afford their house on Otis Place. On 21 April, Tilden learned for the first time that their domestic situation was on the point of changing. They would either stay in the house and take in their minister, Ezra Stiles Gannett, as their boarder, or they would move to the parsonage on Berry Street. But even with Gannett's payment for room and board, the house on Otis Place would remain unaffordable, and so in late May the family moved to a house on the corner of Berry and Federal Streets, right next to the church.

For Tilden these changes were highly troubling. She disliked the prospect of moving *and* of living with the minister. How much her dislike was related to their change in socioeconomic status is unclear. Her remarks give little indication of what she found the most troubling in their move, whether it was the loss of the house in which she had lived since birth, the alteration of the family structure to include Gannett, or the open announcement of economic distress. Her comments focus solely on her response: "pretty soon after I heard this news I *took to crying* and *kept it up foolish or not*" (21 April 1827). And a month later: "I have done very wrong to make *so much fuss* about *him* [Gannett] and the *house*" (22 May 1827). She kept the reasons for her reaction to herself.

A year later, Tilden would declare herself reconciled to the change, though the entries suggest a somewhat different story. While she had initially designated "temper" as one of the faults she hoped journal writing would help her eradicate, it was only after their move and as their financial situation worsened that Tilden's entries were increasingly punctuated by references to it. Her inability to remain "in temper" was frequently connected with another flaw she perceived in her character. She chastised herself with some regularity for her failure to use time wisely. In these self-reproaches she more often than not mentioned that yet again she had spoken hastily and with discontent. She was both out of time and out of temper.[9]

Her days had in fact changed substantially, requiring a far different schedule than had been the custom on Otis Place. There, she and her sisters had set aside hours for study; domestic chores were only infrequently mentioned and in fact seemed defined mostly by fancy needlework rather than by sewing. Her day's routine remained close to the rhythm of her days at school.

Her own formal schooling had ended sooner than she would have liked. Together with her older sisters Isabella, Catherine, and Sarah, she had attended William Emerson's school for young ladies in Boston in the early 1820s. She remained a pupil through 1824, the last year of the school when William was in Germany and brother Waldo continued the school by himself. She looked back fondly on her years in the Emersons' classes. As she watched Waldo Emerson show promise in his new line of work in the ministry, she followed his progress in her journal and recorded his sermons in her notes. "Oh what a good young man he is," she exclaimed after an afternoon's conversation with him (30 June 1827). She was always "delighted" to hear him preach (17 January 1828) and announced herself kindly disposed toward anyone who liked Waldo Emerson. Meeting William Furness, Unitarian minister and lifelong friend of Emerson's, she commented, "He likes Mr. Waldo and therefore I could not help liking him" (18 June 1828). She had nothing but praise for her teachers and affection for her fellow students. After leaving the Emersons' school, she and her sisters Catherine and Sarah (Isabella would marry in 1825) attended one of the many other private schools in Boston, but their attendance came to an end as the family's financial difficulties grew increasingly severe. Although Tilden makes no reference to a specific school in her 1827 journal, it seems likely that she had been in regular attendance shortly before she began writing. Particularly in the early entries, she makes several references to the girls she knew at school. She in fact defined herself by the group of students of which she had been a member. They were her "set of girls," and when they were no longer daily companions, she followed their activities as best she could, noting a marriage here, a journey there, and longing for a friendship in which conversation would be entirely frank, where each individual would be "rightly understood."[10]

The circumstances of her life brought the nature of such friendships sharply into question. With her family's increasing financial difficulties came the inevitable decline in social standing. The Tildens could no longer afford to send their older daughters to school; the daughters in turn could no longer afford the same friendships. It was largely a question of money figured through the element of time. Tilden's days by mid-1827 were apportioned in a vastly different way than they had been at the Emersons' school. There, the hours were divided between reading Hume's history of England, studying moral philosophy, and writing essays on topics the Emersons borrowed from their days at Harvard.[11] As a student, Tilden was in the midst of girls her own age, separated from their domestic duties, defined in each others' eyes not by what they did at home but by their reading, their questions, their conversations.

Away from school in her new circumstances on Berry Street, Anna Tilden's days took on a very different quality. They were regulated by the household routine, an endless cycle of tasks whose very nature meant that the work would never be finished. The sewing alone was a staggering prospect. There were not only the numerous articles of clothing she sewed for herself—petticoats, drawers, dresses, nightgowns—but clothing for her father and brother and younger sisters. In early 1827, the Tildens could still afford a seamstress for the larger items such as outer garments, but as the year progressed and Bryant Tilden's voyage looked less and less likely to be successful, the daughters took over the work that had originally been done by others.

For Anna Tilden, the work was costly and on more than one count. The increased amount of sewing invariably decreased the amount of time left for reading. In journal entry after journal entry, Tilden recorded her displeasure over sewing, most predictably when her sisters asked her to help them with their work. Although she took pride in sewing shirts for her father, such comments were the exception and not the rule. More typical is the following remark: "Soon after breakfast I sewed and was mending etc. all the morning till after one, besides not being any too good natured" (17 December 1827). What separated sisters at home from sisters at school was this fact of work, a work that was required by economic, not intellectual, necessity.

It is uncertain whether Tilden associated their increased sewing with their decreased social status. Three years later, however, society's judgment clearly heightened her uneasiness when, under the direction of their sister Catherine, the older Tilden sisters started their own school. In this case, Tilden directly connected their work of teaching with their loss of standing. The work of sewing was somewhat different. For one thing it was far more

easily kept private. Opening a school undeniably announced their economic situation; the extent of one's sewing could well remain an unpubli-
cized event.

At the earlier point in Tilden's life, the difficulties with domestic work
were of a different order. Sewing took too much time away from her reading. It also rendered useless what time she had. Although her hours of work
were far different from those of a seamstress, the physical realities of the
work took their predictable toll. As her sewing increased, Tilden more frequently mentioned trouble with her eyes. On 29 September 1827, Tilden
noted in her journal, "In the evening I sewed the shirt onto the waist of my
white gown, and put it into the wash. I can't use my eyes much in the
evening they are so weak." Six weeks later, the situation was much the
same: "I did not read any in the evening, my eyes are not very well, and it
seemed most prudent for me not to" (16 November 1827). The following
summer she once again records difficulty with her eyesight: "In the evening
worked some but my eyes are not strong enough to use them much and I
am obliged to be careful" (15 August 1828). Three weeks later, shortly before
the journal breaks off, Tilden voices frustration over what she *cannot* do:
"Latter part of the afternoon and evening wrote in [journal], after attending to Zibby—but my eyesight is so bad that I can't do half as much in
the evening as I want to—" (5 September 1828). By late September, the
difficulty had become serious enough to require medical attention. In a letter of November 1828, Tilden's mother called Anna her "poor blind girl,"
noting that her daughter was confined to a darkened room, since exposure
to more than the slightest amount of light was painful. How long the problem remained this severe is unknown. There are very few extant writings
between 1828 and 1832. The only clue comes from Tilden's sermon notes.
There is a five-month silence between 7 September 1828 (a week before her
last journal entry) and 22 February 1829, when the notes resume. Since
Tilden studiously avoided mentioning specific details about herself in these
notes, it is unclear exactly when she was able to return to her sermon note
keeping. Nor do we know how long she was confined to the house or how
long she was unable to read, or for that matter, to sew.[12]

Little is known of Tilden's life between 1828 and 1832. There may have
been other journals no longer extant. When she began a new journal in 1834,
she referred to the journals she had kept earlier in her life, but whether she
meant more than her 1827–28 journal is unclear. What does emerge in the
writings from 1832 is just how difficult the four years had been. In a letter of

2 September 1832, she told her minister that for three years she had been struggling with her faith. No longer certain that she believed in immortality, let alone in God, she traced the beginning of her doubts to 1829. She said little about what prompted this questioning of faith. She only assured her minister that her doubts were wholly of her own making: they had not been caused by any outside influences. In other words, she had neither been reading the wrong books nor talking to the wrong people.

Her only extant writings from 1829, the year when her doubts began, are the sermon notes. They suggest that what she heard from the pulpit only increased her uncertainty. She reported sermons on the evidences of Christianity in which the evidence did not quite add up; sermons on "true religion" in which God "could destroy [the world] in an instant" while humanity was nothing but "the worm which crawleth in the dust."[13] What Tilden remembered from these sermons was hardly comforting. By her rendering, God was as inescapable as death. The individual who could believe both in God's mercy and in his own worth prospered, but the individual who doubted either, and particularly the latter, fared quite differently. Isolated from her fellow worshipers, she was left alone with the knowledge of her failed faith.

Tilden's early adulthood was defined by division: what she showed to others, what she kept to herself. Intertwined with the economic upheaval within her family, her crisis of faith articulated her crisis of self-definition. The struggle had begun as early as 1827 and built gradually toward its most intense moment in the winter of 1835. Within that eight-year period, Tilden's life changed radically. In 1827 she still thought of herself as a student, seeking friendships with people her age and looking forward to a life of "usefulness" in which economic necessity formed no apparent part. In 1835, she was a schoolteacher, disliking her role, disliking the public acknowledgment of her family's straitened circumstances, and disliking herself most of all for such thoughts.

The course of Tilden's life in these years is notably similar to the pattern described by Nancy Cott in her discussion of women's religious experience during the Second Great Awakening.[14] Cott argues that young unmarried women were profoundly affected by the socioeconomic changes in the early part of the nineteenth century. As the center of manufacture shifted from home to factory, roles within the household fundamentally changed. With productive labor increasingly located outside the home, it became more difficult for women to define themselves by their specific contribution to the household economy. As Cott shows, the difference divided mothers from daughters. Married women retained their identity of "mother." Their work shifted to the care and education of young children. They still administered the household, although this work focused less on what was produced and more on what was consumed. Unmarried daughters, however, could not shift their tasks so readily; unlike their mothers, they had no equivalent work for them within the household. They now primarily consumed goods rather than produced them. And many families could not afford a household of consumers. Once essential members of domestic manufacture, unmarried daughters were, so to speak, out of a job, their previous identities a useless item in a new market. Pointing to this period of economic change, Cott highlights the crises of self-definition experienced by young women and suggests that the resolution of the crises came through a combination of new faith and new work. Daughters left home to work in the factories or to enter domestic service. At the same time, they turned to evangelical Christianity with its clearly defined image of significant selfhood. The conversion experience offered a new identity in the image of new birth and a new family in the community of the church.

The young women studied by Cott typically left home to find work. They became the acclaimed "factory girls" of Lowell and Lawrence and were typically drawn from families who lived in the farming regions of Massachusetts and New York. They were daughters of farmers, not merchants; the products of the village, not the city. For Tilden, work outside the home was never a real possibility. With family prosperity still a distinctly recent memory, the Tilden daughters were kept at home to do the "genteel" work available to them. Unlike the young women of Cott's study, Tilden did not leave the home when the household economy changed. Her work, first sewing and then teaching, occurred within its walls. The real mark of her displacement lay in the fact that her work was not primarily an example of "moral" usefulness but of economic necessity.

This single difference altered the very nature of her family and of her place within it. In the late 1820s, before the worst of their financial difficulties, Tilden held to the belief that sewing for the family or taking care of her younger sisters was the contribution expected of her and by which she could define herself. By the mid-1830s, when she and her sisters essentially became the only support for the family, her security slipped dramatically. Plagued by the fear that she simply did not contribute enough to the family finances, she wondered in her journal just what reason she had to live.

"What have I to live for," she asked, and she responded with a sobering answer, "My parents have children enough, better than I am who will love and take care of them" (28 September 1834). She came to see herself as superfluous, someone who could barely earn her keep. In her own eyes, she was just one daughter among too many.

Had Tilden been part of the evangelical tradition, she might well have resolved her crisis of self-definition through conversion. Her Unitarian background, however, prevented such possibilities. She could not distance herself from her economic situation by dividing her old life from her new. Raised in the tradition of liberal Christianity, Tilden lived in a world that was highly skeptical, and in fact dismissive, of the new identity conferred by conversion. Both of Tilden's parents were members of the Federal Street Church, the bastion of Unitarianism. William Ellery Channing, prime apologist for the Unitarians, was the senior minister; Ezra Stiles Gannett, one of the founders of the American Unitarian Association, was his colleague. Under their preaching, Tilden learned to distrust the conversion experience by which young women in the evangelical tradition defined their identities.

In its place Unitarian ministers preached "probation." For them, the word evoked a series of trials, an ongoing process by which an individual's character was determined. It offered a very different alternative to the scenes of life-riveting revelation portrayed by their orthodox counterparts. Dismissing the validity of the sudden change implied by conversion, Unitarian ministers argued that the only real change in an individual's identity came through relentless hard work. Conceiving the individual's life as an ongoing course of self-improvement, they emphasized "character" and the painstaking process of forming it. Progress was invariably slow: self-examination was a difficult discipline. Ministers were quick to remind their congregations that bad habits were all too easily acquired and all too readily retained. Discouragement was inevitable: so much to do, so little time in which to do it. A lifetime, in fact, was hardly long enough to accomplish the formation of a "true Christian character." But here is where the ministers played their strongest card. Individuals who were truly engaged in the process of self-improvement finally did not have to worry about the element of time. Where mortality left off, immortality began. As consolation for the hard and unending work in this life, ministers offered their congregations the "hope of Heaven"—an afterlife in which individuals continued to work toward perfection.

That Tilden was highly influenced by her ministers' sermons is evident everywhere in her writings. The words from the pulpit informed how she represented herself, how she envisioned others, how she interpreted her life. They stood at the center of her crisis in the early 1830s and shaped her understanding of what such a crisis meant for her own "character." She had early dedicated herself to "self-improvement." In the opening entry of her first journal, begun auspiciously on New Year's Day, she gave self-improvement as her reason for writing. "This is the first time I have kept a regular journal," she commented, "and I hope that it will do me a great deal of good, and enable me to correct many of my faults, especially my temper which is much too hasty" (1 January 1827). Recording what her ministers counseled, she crafted models for herself. Her mother was the perfect example of patience, her older sister Catherine of usefulness; her younger sister Zibby and her cousin Cornelia filled the role of the admired, patient sufferer. Her models were not simply drawn from her ministers' sermons, however. She read and read voluminously. Her world was peopled as much by characters from novels as by exemplars from sermons. Whether the title character in Maria Edgeworth's novel *Belinda* or Hope Leslie and Esther Downing from Catharine Sedgwick's *Hope Leslie,* these fictions provided yet more patterns of the "good woman" she aspired to be.

By her own account she fell far short of any of her model characters. Comparing herself with the exemplary figures of the sermons, she increasingly came to identify herself by the ways in which she differed from them. Her task of self-improvement had become the work of self-denial. To emerge as the desired exemplar, she first needed to submerge the characteristics that seemed inextricably part of her self. Where the exemplary figures were patient and long-suffering, she was quick tempered and ill natured. Their virtues defined her vices. Her "old" self was a collection of attributes she increasingly sought to eradicate. When she began her 1834–35 journal, her search for a new identity was apparent. She worked to create a new self that was defined by its opposition to the old. She dissociated herself from her past writings. Dismissing her earlier journals, she commented that this piece of writing would not be like the others, "an account of every petty event," but a far more serious endeavor. She turned to writing to gain a clearer understanding of herself, to see her "own thoughts and feelings expressed." Looking at the words she wrote, she would see the reflection of herself.

This desire for self-expression—to see her "thoughts and feelings expressed"—speaks most forcefully for the many ways in which she had
learned to silence herself. As early as 1828 she had come to realize that curb-
ing her temper meant curtailing her frank expression of ideas. No matter
that she prized "frankness" as a highly desirable quality. Her own practice
of this self-defined virtue consistently resulted in criticism. Expression,
thus, turned inward as she took on the tasks of "self-examination and self-
discipline" advocated by her minister. A glance at the 1829 sermon notes reveals how much of her attention was captured by ministerial injunctions
to discipline the self to silence.[15] By 1832, suffering in silence had become
Tilden's daily work. Holding within her the secret that could not be said,
she kept her religious doubts solely to herself, until finally all she could
hear was the voice of unending uncertainty. Reflecting her ministers' "doctrine of probation," she mirrored an image never displayed in the sermons.
In their "hope of Heaven," all she saw was a dubious immortality and a
questionable God (SAR 1989, 35).

When she at last broke her silence, it was to her minister. She wrote him
a letter apologizing for her failings yet challenging him to make sense of the
inconsistencies within the doctrine he preached. It was the beginning of a
long correspondence, the extension of the conversations that had long been
part of the Tilden household. After the Tildens moved to Berry Street in
1827, Gannett essentially became part of their family. Tilden's mother
looked to him as confidant; Tilden and her sisters termed him "brother" or
"uncle." He had become an integral part of their family, which made it yet
more difficult for Tilden to approach him with her crisis of faith. She refused to tell any of her family members about her doubts, maintaining that
such self-revelation would be more painful than she could bear. Even with
Gannett, it was painful enough. She feared losing his respect; she assumed
that her "confession" would in all probability confer upon her an entirely
new, entirely undesirable identity. Her one hope, she said, lay in the possibility that he would understand her. She hoped against hope that he would
take her doubt in good faith and work with her to answer the questions
raised by the central tenets of Unitarianism.

What became apparent over the two years of their correspondence was
just how different Tilden's questions were from Gannett's answers. Thanking him for a sermon he had loaned her, she regretted that it was not the
"comfort" she had hoped it would be. She wondered at times if he did understand the nature of her difficulty. He offered further elaboration on the

proofs of God's existence and the evidences of Christianity, taking his Sunday sermons out of the pulpit for her benefit, but she had little need of more argument along this line. She was perfectly satisfied that the arguments for Christianity made perfect sense. Her problem lay in perception. Although she could acknowledge the "truth" of Christianity, she had no experience of this truth other than a theoretical assent. In her first letter to Gannett, she had written, "My difficulty lies not in the *want of proofs*, but in not being able to fasten these proofs with the conviction of *realities* upon my own mind" (2 September 1832). What she hoped he could do was explain to her how she might cultivate proof until it turned into conviction.

Their correspondence in fact cultivated something quite different. Her willingness to confide in him elicited a reciprocal response from Gannett. He increasingly turned to her to discuss his own self-doubt as well as his uncertainty about whether he should ever marry. Interested in one of his parishioners, the widowed Phoebe Bliss, he talked with Tilden about his dilemmas of relationship. The congregation, in turn, began to talk about their minister and Anna Tilden. Writing to him in late January 1835, she explained what he had questioned as her abrupt change in "manner" toward him. She wrote,

> I have been placed in a most unpleasant situation. Owing to our intimacy with you, different members of our family have been exposed to many remarks, and for several months I have been a subject of conversation to all who have visited here intimately, and to many strangers. I find the world has been completely deceived, and I felt that I ought not by word, look or action be the means of continuing the many and repeated observations, which have been, and are constantly made about *you* and myself. Now this is the simple reason for any intentional change in manner which you may have noticed in me. (26 January 1835)

In the letter she emphasized his relationship to her family, calling him an "affectionate, able and *ever kind brother*." From what she said, however, his behavior toward her had not been entirely "brotherly." The congregation was talking, but given the nature of his conversations with her, she could only assume that his romantic interest lay elsewhere and that he in turn assumed that hers did as well.

A month later she adopted a markedly different tone. Sending him a letter she promised would be her last, she announced that their friendship was at an end. "That connexion," she wrote, "*is dissolved* between us" (25 February 1835). There was, however, another connection that she wanted to secure. Enclosing a lengthy passage from her journal and an equally lengthy discussion of one of his sermons, she declared herself a candidate for church membership. She was "not so far from the right opinions as [she] had feared." She felt that she had at last resolved her doubts and that she was ready to become an "acknowledged Christian."

The two types of "connection" at work in this letter contrast sharply. Looking forward to the public acknowledgment of a formal relationship, she at the same time openly admitted that her private relationships would radically change. Announcing that her friendship with Gannett was at an end, she also described her relationship with her family members as one based on disguise. She hid her true feelings from them. Where they saw "good spirits and cheerfulness," she experienced emotions that were quite the opposite. Her only consolation was that her counterfeit happiness would reassure her mother and sisters. "I am sure it will be *wicked* in me to voluntarily continue a source of trouble to my family," she wrote, "and as *they* will not know it is a mask I am wearing, they will be satisfied." Creating an image of profound isolation, Tilden structured a new identity for herself. Based on self-denial, it took the ministers at their word, adopting the silent sufferer as its model.

What exactly had happened in that month between Tilden's letters of 26 January and 25 February is unclear. There is only one journal entry from the period, the entry included in Tilden's February letter to Gannett, and it conceals more than it reveals. In language that speaks as revelation but withholds its content, she turns to her journal to learn once more "what I am":

> It is rather more than one month since I have written in this book, and oh what an *eventful* month it has proved to me! Little did I dream that all which has been *uttered* by me would ever have been done, but the *truth is told!* and shall I regret it? I have broken many resolutions, I have been fearfully tossed and agitated in my own mind, I have suffered, oh! more than words can ever tell! And now shall my suffering my experience, be of no avail, God forbid that it should be so. Oh may I learn, and be willing to take instruction from the past, and may all that has happened make me better, make me a Christian. (15 February 1835)

At this point in the entry, she wrote a rededication of herself to the work of self-improvement, this time convinced that God would be on her side. She then reminded herself that her faith was not as errant as it had seemed. Closer to the "right opinions" than she had suspected, she anticipated that her difficulties would soon be at an end. Her phrasing is as curious as her solution is familiar. She writes,

> I think that now when I examine my heart and mind that I am not so far from the right opinions as I had feared even very lately, and I now look forward with delight and gratitude that I shall as I trust be released from a trial that has disheartened and discouraged me for years. I trust that by strict self discipline such as I have the *utmost* and *hourly* need of and such as I have not yet practiced I may be worthy in the course of a few months to become an acknowledged Christian.

Returning to the conventional call to self-discipline, she at the same time indicates that such discipline was untried by her. She seemingly trusts its efficacy implicitly. It will, she assumes, produce the desired result. "Trust" is the operative term in this passage. Her actions are guided by her suppositions. She "thinks" that her beliefs are close to the acceptable ones. Acknowledging that her difficulties are not yet over, she nonetheless "trusts" that they will be. She acts on faith.

This is the closest to a conversion experience that Tilden's religious tradition would allow. In this declaration of intent, she sought to define a new identity for herself. As she continued to think about what this unpracticed form of self-discipline would be, she completely revised the premise with which she had begun this journal. In April 1834, she had thought that expression might well be the key to understanding herself. The very act of writing down her "own thoughts and feelings" would create a clearer image of herself. Almost a year later, she advocated a quite different approach:

> And now what in particular must I try to amend this week,—not to *express* and not to have discouraging views of life I must be willing to live, and try to do all the good I can by my example to others. I must not encourage thoughts of ==== that affair is settled, they have acted honourably I trust that I have also.——I can help to drive away thoughts by strenuously avoiding conversation upon the subject and I can avoid this in many different ways.——*Thirdly,* keep from *fretting, complaining,* and *comparing.*

Setting herself up to become an exemplary figure, she predicates this act on a mechanism of self-censorship. She must "drive away thoughts," avoid conversation on certain subjects (undoubtedly her relationship to Gannett), keep from "fretting, complaining, and comparing": in a phrase, "not to *express.*" She does not, however, silence herself altogether. At the end of the entry, she keeps the prospect of journal writing open but provides a particular set of constraints under which such writing would operate. "Turn to *this* journal *often,*" she tells herself, "and see if I am rightly trying to be a Christian." Although writing is permitted, it is of a piece with the earlier injunctions. If the journal becomes a place in which to see her reflection as a "Christian," and if her definition of Christian is based on what the individual cannot say, then her prose becomes analogous to the mask she told Gannett she had donned for her family.

Tilden's use of this journal entry suggests just how far she would mask her language. She sent a substantial portion of this passage to Gannett in her late February letter. Tellingly, she did not copy out the entire entry. She let him see only a part. What she reserved for her eyes alone were her particular plans for self-discipline. She would not share with Gannett the specific nature of this newly vowed plan; she would not tell him that part of her work was to avoid all thoughts of him. She provided him with only the most general, most acceptable of statements about her recent assurance of faith. The details of her projected action as well as the details of her reasons for ending their friendship are omitted. She makes her statement, gives no explanation for her new positions, and prefaces the papers she sent to Gannett with a note to suggest that she was not particularly interested in an immediate response. On the envelope she had written, "The *whole* to be read when quite at *leisure.*"

Although she had encouraged Gannett to take his time in responding, his response was swift. Upon receiving her letter, he wrote back at once. His answer was not entirely to her point. His initial letter (he would send two at the same time) said absolutely nothing about her admission to the church. And it received little attention in the letter he sent to accompany his first. Other concerns than her long crisis of faith were on his mind. He in fact offered her his own solution to this crisis, a solution that made short work of her newly announced separate self. In one of the strangest marriage proposals in history, Gannett responded to Tilden's request for church membership by proposing that she marry him. He had experienced, he told her, an "almost instantaneous revelation" in which he had seen "the folly and guilt of [his] past life" and recognized the possibility of redemption through her love.[16]

Her crisis of faith now took on an exceedingly interesting dimension. While she announced a Unitarian corollary to conversion that separated her from man and united her to God, he claimed one that united man to woman and placed God in some vague relation to them both. Doubting his good faith, she at first questioned his motives. Did he consider her so irretrievably lost that he must turn martyr and sacrifice himself? Was he acting out of a misplaced sense of pity for her? Did he really understand who she was?

His letters from this period are not extant. And perhaps such letters never existed. He may have answered her in person rather than by letter. In either case, whether through written or spoken conversation, she was persuaded by what he had to say. Addressing him as her "dearest friend" in a letter of 7 March 1835, she abandoned the solution of separation she had proposed three weeks earlier. Her admission to the church was delayed on "general principles" until June. Their engagement was announced in the same month. They married in October, and so the familiar story goes. The woman on the verge of autonomy is once again co-opted back into the system.

But is that the story Tilden's life tells? It could be argued that her marriage effectively curtailed her first attempts at self-definition. She exchanged autonomy for dependence. In letters written in the months before their marriage, there are indications enough to suggest that Tilden readily became yet another victim of the "cult of true womanhood." She often adopted a tone of deference toward Gannett. She would try to be "worthy" of him, she promised. She asked him for guidance. Early in March she wrote to him, "I want you to tell me what I must do to become better . . . how I shall improve my mind that it may more nearly comprehend the beauty and the strength of yours" (7 March 1835). She clearly saw her intellect as inferior, clearly heightened his excellence by emphasizing her ordinariness. She took this identity one step further, casting herself as the child, with Gannett as her teacher and father. She wrote, "I shall be a better child. . . . If *you* will be the teacher . . . I will be the *apt pupil*" (30 May 1835). From the individual suffering silently behind her mask of "good spirits and cheerfulness," she had become the child trying to be good. The persona she created for herself as she contemplated marriage is unquestionably disturbing.

So was the other persona she had earlier created for herself in her letters and journal. In either case, the image of the mask works well to describe not simply what is at work behind her representations of herself *but* what our critical assumptions have been and how they have masked our understanding of the identities women created for themselves. Read through the lens provided by Ann Douglas in *The Feminization of American Culture,*

Tilden's life becomes another step downward: intellectual rigor capitulating to debased religiosity, the opportunity for power lost in a perjured influence. While Douglas's position raises thought-provoking questions about the nature of women's intellectual work in the nineteenth century, the foregone conclusion of capitulation remains problematic. Rethinking the category of the "sentimental," Nina Baym and Jane Tompkins forcefully address these questions, allowing us to see far more about sentimental culture. Its discourse created a reality imaginably close to the reader's experience. It offered the possibility of real power, a power the individual herself could experience within her daily life. The circumstances limiting the fictional characters mirrored her own. And yet within those circumstances, no matter how confining or limiting, the fictional protagonists could and did pursue a decided course of action. In Baym's assessment, participants in sentimental culture took a sharp-eyed view of reality. No "sentimentalists," they understood what could *and* could not be done.[17]

As twentieth-century readers, our doubts undoubtedly linger. We distrust the virtue made of necessity, a second-best when the whole structure appears to be flawed. But again, our doubts reveal their own limitations. Our backward glance almost invariably simplifies; the interpretive frame presents an undeniably clear picture, but the clarity comes at the cost of complexity. Where Douglas sees self-defeating models in the process she calls feminization, Baym and Tompkins present narratives of women empowered precisely through the elements Douglas termed impotent. Tilden's choices, however, were not the ones we have represented. The order we impose, the preferences we voice, measure the concerns of our own times but do not always allow us to see beyond them.

Tilden's changing self-representations offer ample proof that the societal conventions were not simply self-defeating nor were they easily empowering. Whatever a society's—theirs or ours—evaluation of a "self," the particular individual speaks another kind of story. What Tilden herself wrote is far different from what our debates about sentimental culture say. Tilden represented many selves in her writing. Some she rejected out of hand; others she claimed and abandoned only to reclaim at some later point in her life. Each self-representation arose from her work within a particular set of circumstances, and each set of circumstances provided the possibility for a revisioning of the self, at times radical, at times subtly nuanced. For Tilden, remaining single offered no clear path toward independence; it imposed as many limitations as did marriage. Self-determination, as we have defined it, did not rest on one side or the other of the marriage equation. In Tilden's Unitarian world, it meant something markedly different.

The different selves created by Tilden challenge our views—if we let them. Reflecting the unwieldy process of self-representation, they illustrate the always mixed nature of self-definition. No "self" is permanent; each reflects a particular moment. To borrow the words of another nineteenth-century woman who variously represented herself, "It is always thus with the new form of life; we must learn to look at it by its own standard." [18] Margaret Fuller's comments speak volumes for our reading of Tilden's life. Hers is no either-or story. Neither defeated nor liberated by her circumstances, she worked with what she was given, navigating her way through the conventions, crafting working solutions that the next change of circumstance would require her once again to revise. Hers is the narrative of continual alteration; the self of one year was not the self for another.

In the spring of 1835, during the several months before her marriage, Tilden created the disturbing "child" persona chiefly to carry the weight of what she found even more troubling. She cast herself as a child precisely because she feared marriage. Whenever she called herself "child," the comparison either prefaced or concluded a reference to her profound uncertainty about becoming a wife. She was clearly uneasy at the prospect. It plunged her into a world of judgment. Would she be a "good" wife to her husband *and* to his congregation? The role of the minister's wife figured largely in her writings. In marrying a clergyman, she became part of his ministry, her duties marked out by certain expectations about how she would dress, act, converse. There would be little privacy in their marriage, and as she told Gannett in the spring of 1835, "I do so dislike to be talked about" (29 April 1835). [19]

In the months before their wedding, Tilden repeatedly expressed anxiety over the new identity offered by marriage. On the one hand, it freed her from economic dependence on her family, in turn freeing them from some portion of the financial burden under which they labored. It also provided her with a clearly defined course of "usefulness." As the minister's wife, she would be expected to involve herself fully with the Sunday school, numerous charitable activities, and not least of all the "ministry" of parish visiting. Where she had earlier feared that she had no real use in her world, she was now provided with the prospect of undisputed "social usefulness" (30 May 1835). It was a mixed blessing. The role defined for her became increasingly problematic in her eyes precisely because of how clearly it had already been defined. Expectations were firmly in place, held by individuals with whom she had had only the slightest contact. She had been simply one parishioner among many. She was now the exemplary figure held up as the model for others to emulate. Given her earlier despair over ever matching the exemplars she had adopted as her own, it comes as no surprise that to be thrust into the exemplary figure of the minister's wife was distinctly troubling.

The problem may well have rested primarily with the fact that she had no part in defining her new role. And if the early years of her marriage had been lived within the boundaries of helpmate to the parish minister, Tilden's hardest work might well have been to take self-denial to its terribly logical conclusion and become the individual she clearly felt she was not. However, the first years of marriage offered Tilden a different part than the one she had initially expected. Rather than settling into the role of adjunct in her husband's parish ministry, she played a very different variation on that theme. Instead of her quiet, unassuming, but duly noted activities in the parish, Tilden's task required all the forthrightness and decisiveness she had earlier praised in others.

Less than six months after their marriage, Gannett suffered a severe mental and physical collapse.[20] The difficulties were not unexpected: he had long confided in both William Ellery Channing and Tilden about his profound self-doubt. Both had encouraged him in his work, reminded him of his usefulness, praised him for the power of his ministry. But to Gannett's ears, their encouragement echoed falsely against the verdict he repeatedly rendered against himself. In his own tribunal, he invariably tried himself and was found wanting. He was "too ignorant, too indolent, & too wicked" (letter to Tilden, 23 May 1836). Judging himself incompetent for the ministry, he held out little hope that he could do anything else.

The earliest record of his self-criticism dates from his years at Harvard. It grew into a recurrent refrain in journals and letters. From the beginning of his ministry at the Federal Street Church, he feared that he was doomed to failure. His situation was undeniably difficult. As Channing's colleague, he would inevitably be subject to comparison with the most popular Unitarian preacher of the day. Gannett experienced daily what Tilden herself found the most disconcerting about marriage: living according to the clearly defined, sharply circumscribed expectations of others. From his ordination in 1824, Gannett labored to become the exemplary minister, responding to every perceived criticism with a vow to greater self-discipline and immersion in more work—launching yet another lecture series, or Sunday school plan, or worship service. He worked relentlessly, warned by his colleagues and congregation alike that his work might well cost him his health, if not his life.

It did indeed almost cost him his sanity. By early April 1836, Gannett was no longer able to fulfill his parish duties. Sent to Leicester, Massachusetts, to rest, he chafed at his forced idleness. "I must go back to Boston or relinquish my ministry," he wrote to Tilden in late April (25 April 1836). His doctor, as well as his wife and his congregation, held a quite different opinion. Writing to Joshua Clapp, the person with whom Gannett was staying, Dr. Jacob Bigelow assessed his patient's situation in the following way: "Mr G. from excessive and long continued exertion of mind has fallen into a state of great nervous prostration [and] weakness which shows itself in alternating fits of despondency and excitement, amounting at times to partial alienation of mind" (5 April).[21] The prognosis did not improve. Two weeks later, Bigelow suggested that Gannett enter "some asylum, either at Hartford[,] Pepperell or Charlestown" (21 April). At the end of the month, Gannett's congregation offered him, without reservation, a year's leave of absence with pay. Initially convinced that he could not accept their generosity, he finally acquiesced and accepted the offer in early June.

The summer saw little improvement in his mental health, and in August his doctor advised a European tour. Gannett sailed in October. It was, almost to the day, his first wedding anniversary. He sailed alone, for Bigelow felt that were Tilden to accompany him, Gannett would simply continue to focus on his difficulties. Bigelow wanted his patient literally to leave his old life behind him: he was to take nothing of his Boston identity with him, neither his sermons nor his wife. Gannett clearly felt uneasy with this approach and was no sooner out of sight of land when he began recording his despair in his journal. England brought no change in his outlook. He had been referred to the care of Francis Boott, well known for his work with cases such as Gannett's, but even Boott began to despair of his patient's life.[22] Writing to Channing in November, he recommended that, if at all possible, Tilden be sent to join her husband. It was not clear how long Gannett would live.

The letter arrived in early January, and Channing accordingly passed on his news to Gannett's wife. Displeased by this indirect communication, Tilden registered her complaint with Channing but quickly proceeded to what she viewed as the more important consideration. For her, there was no question as to whether or not she would go. The only matter was to arrange her affairs quickly enough so that she could leave on the next ship bound out of New York for London. The decisiveness with which she acted and the efficiency with which she made the necessary arrangements won her unqualified praise. In the eyes of her acquaintances she was rapidly becoming an exemplary figure, a model for the congregation, to be added to their repertoire of good examples. For herself, she had found a way of working within the conventional expectations to construct an identity independent of disguise.

The first year of marriage brought Tilden markedly different possibilities for self-definition. Given Gannett's increasing inability to make decisions, she gradually took over the economic decisions for the household. She also played an instrumental role in convincing Gannett to accept the church's proffered leave of absence. And with Gannett's absence, first in Leicester and then in London, she gained an independent existence that was nonetheless grounded in relationship. She unquestionably described herself as "wife," but the terms of her role had changed. In contrast to her envisioned task of fitting obediently into her husband's life and his congregation's expectations, she faced circumstances in which Gannett became the individual upon whom all eyes rested. She was at once aligned with the congregation, consulted by them, and considered part of their attempt to provide Gannett with the best care possible. At the same time she escaped their expectations of how a minister's wife should become part of her husband's ministry. Since Gannett's parish activities were so clearly suspended, Tilden could reformulate "social usefulness" in her own way. With Gannett out of the picture, she could define her work for herself.

This work was largely, though by no means entirely, centered on counseling Gannett himself. Reversing roles, she became minister to him. Reminding him of certain aspects of their faith, she essentially preached her own sermons in her letters. They presented a doctrine forged out of her own experience. Reminiscent of her earliest comments to Gannett on her crisis of faith, they privileged experiential knowledge. What she wrote to him came out of ideas she felt had the "conviction of realities." She had little use for proofs independent of experience.

When she sailed for London in January 1837, her self-representations had changed markedly from two years earlier. Gone were the references to masks and children. She in fact was much less inclined to characterize herself at all. In her letters to Gannett after his departure for London, she wrote with the frankness she had earlier silenced. Whether reporting the news from Boston or her assessment of a recently published book, she spoke her mind freely. And she encouraged him to respond with similar candor. Her tone did not change with a change of correspondents. After leaving Boston, she wrote to her mother and sisters. Her letters served multiple purposes — to keep them informed of Gannett's health and of her own, to describe in loving detail the scenes in England and on the Continent that she knew her family would never see. But the letters seemed primarily a way of maintaining her distinct place in a community of women. She wrote to her mother and her sisters, not her brother or her father. And she urged these women to trust her word alone; only she could give the truth about Gannett's condition.

He was still far from stable when she arrived in London in February 1837. Her journal describes numerous incidents in which Gannett, upset by a seemingly trivial event, became increasingly agitated. Tilden would then work patiently to calm him, reassure him, talk through the ways in which the problem could be solved. In many cases, her best efforts achieved no result, and she called Dr. Boott, who readily came to talk his patient out of his distress. Boott finally advised that they leave London. In Tilden's words, the city held too many complications. There were "such an immense number of objects to visit — so many friends to see" (journal entry, 24 February 1837). By her assessment this host of expectations — of seeing the "right" places and visiting the "right" people — was only adding to Gannett's distress.

They traveled first to France, a joyless two weeks in which they both felt uneasy. Gannett was troubled by his indecisiveness, unable to say when exactly they should go to Italy and what exactly they should see in France. When they arrived in Italy, however, their response was quite different. Both were delighted with the chance to immerse themselves in thoughts of ancient Rome. Tilden wrote to her mother, "We perfectly luxuriated among ruins, *statues* and *paintings,* it is the most interesting place I have seen — Such a field for thought — such stores for the future and such recollections of the past" (31 May 1837). In Rome, they also found the landscape more familiar owing to George and Anna Ticknor's hospitality.[23] Staying with them, they experienced what nineteenth-century Americans loved about traveling abroad: a foreign country safely framed by their own society.

In late May, Tilden and Gannett left Italy. From Rome they headed north to cross the Alps through the Simplon Pass. Detained by a late spring storm, Tilden reveled in the delay. A week later she wrote to her mother, "I never am so well as when among the mountains" (31 May 1837). Setting up residence in the resort town of Vichy, Tilden and Gannett remained there through the summer. Unable to obtain rooms in one of the many hotels, they rented a small cottage in the country. Both agreed that they could not have found a happier solution. They were close enough to town to allow Gannett to follow the regimen of the water cure faithfully; yet they were freed from the social ritual of spa life. Their days were characterized by simplicity and freedom: "drinking—bathing—walking—reading—writing—working—and riding" (6:29). In his journal, Gannett wrote, "These six weeks have given me also a season of quiet which I needed for my mind. I have been led to reflection and meditation, and I hope permanent benefit will be the consequence. I rejoice on every account that I came to Vichy" (6:70).

There were indeed many reasons for him to rejoice in their stay. By the time they left Vichy, Tilden was pregnant. Delaying their return to the States until after the child was born, they settled in London, traveling for an extended period to Scotland as well as making the obligatory visit to Wordsworth at Rydal Mount and to Scott's house at Abbotsford. For Tilden, the months before her child was born were punctuated as much by uneasiness as by joy. In her letters home, she chided her family members for being remiss on their side of the correspondence. In December, she invited them to follow her example and write letters a few lines at a time. In her words, every word from home was "precious" (10 December 1837). A month later she was so ill as to be unable to keep up even her side of the correspondence. And when her daughter, Catherine Boott Gannett, was born in early April 1838, Tilden would be confined to bed for nearly three months. The complications following childbirth delayed their return to the United States until late July.

Childbirth would eventually prove fatal. Tilden died at age thirty-five, eleven years after her marriage. Her unmarried sisters Catherine, Mary, and Maria lived well into their seventies. And yet her childbearing years had seemed to extend some promise of real hope. She gave birth to three children, daughter Catherine in 1838 and two sons, William in 1840 and Henry in January 1842. While every birth held its anxious moments, the severity of the immediate danger apparently lessened. Bedridden for three months after her daughter's birth, she was confined for six weeks after the second birth and three weeks after the third. Health, however, was a fleeting experience. Although none of the extant family papers mentions specific physical problems, clues of difficulty are everywhere present. Letters written by Gannett to Tilden were addressed under care of a doctor. These letters lamented their separation, but Tilden admitted it was for the best. She was, she told Gannett in one letter, "more run down" than she realized, and in the country, away from Boston and parish duties, she found herself in "better health" with "more freedom from pain" (28 June 1839).

There are few writings from these years. Only a handful of letters date from the eight-year period before her death. In part, the decrease can be attributed to the proximity of her family. She no longer wrote to bridge the distance of several thousand miles. And with the births of her children and her periods of illness, another reason for her silence comes readily to mind. It is all too likely that what once went into writing now went into caring for others, a caring that has traditionally gone unrecorded. In the letters that survive, Tilden returned to creating new personae for herself or returned to older versions of her character. She wrote in the "voices" of her infant children. She assumed the tone of apologetic wife, lamenting her husband's absence yet convinced that he would find the household too distracting were he with them. And she continued to speak in her voice of the late 1830s — forthright, frank in its criticism, eager in its desire for response. But mostly there was silence.

Far more can be said about Gannett's life. He regularly kept his journal, remained actively involved with the Unitarian publication, the *Christian Examiner,* published a number of his sermons, and continued to worry over how his words were received. His story is the easier to tell; its shape is not only familiar but is fully embodied by the words he wrote and the words written to and about him. With Tilden, the case is much different. Her words are few. When Gannett mentioned her in his journal, he generally recorded her day's activities without comment. From his account, it would hardly seem that her health was even an issue. Although he was aware that she was not as "strong" as she might be, it appeared to be no different from the intermittent periods of illness he knew she had experienced before their marriage.

And thus her death, when it came, was unexpected both to himself and to his congregation. In early September 1846, Gannett reported his pleasure and relief at Tilden's renewed "strength." "We have returned home well," he wrote in his journal, "and find all well. Let us be grateful, tranquil, and dutiful." What can be gleaned from his journal accounts suggest that Tilden spent the fall in relatively good health. His references to her indicate an active schedule uninterrupted by illness:

> 3 Oct . . . Anna out for dinner.
> 17 October . . . drinking tea with Anna.
> Thanksgiving 26 November . . . no one else at dinner, but we had a very pleasant meal and afternoon. . . . Indeed it was one of the pleasantest Thanksgiving's I have spent for many years—more like the days of my childhood. (vol. 40)

The happiness would not last. In less than a month, Tilden would be dead. Gannett's journals are markedly silent; they give no indication that he saw any cause for concern. Ten days before her death, he noted that she had attended one of Louis Agassiz's lectures at the Lowell Institute. Two days before her death, she helped her husband read proof for the next issue of the *Christian Examiner*.[24] Her fourth pregnancy remained the unspoken fact of that autumn. It is present only in the relief Gannett expressed over Tilden's apparent strength. Whatever the appearance, the reality of Christmas Day was far different. Tilden died in childbirth; the child itself was stillborn. In his congregation's words, her death was a "sudden and distressing dispensation."[25]

Distress was profoundly the measure of her final days. Though sudden, the death followed its own protracted course, bending time out of proportion for those who watched Tilden die. Writing to their father a few days after Tilden's death, sisters Kate and Zibby described the painful reality. Zibby wrote, "I trust that during the greater part of the time her distress was not so excruciating as it appeared, for I am told that in convulsions the patient is unconscious—& it seems to me as if Thursday [the day before she died] from 6 in the morning till 6 in the evening was one long convulsion." The only consolation came at the very end when the last moments took a calmer shape. In Catherine's words, "Our dear Nanny after apparently constant suffering thro those two anxious days, peacefully breathed her last, as if sinking to rest in Mother's arms."[26]

In the letters of consolation that followed, Tilden would be remembered as "a noble-hearted woman, a person of character, of courage."[27] The woman who in 1834 had despaired of being "liked" and who felt she was not "agreeable enough to be wanted in society" had become not only the light of the home but the close friend of many, both inside and out, of her husband's congregation. To Harriet Martineau, she was "dear Anna," thought of with "tender love," extended the "warmest sympathies." To her sister Mary, she was a woman known for her "courage and determination," and to Zibby, the younger sister to whom Anna had been "little mother," she was irreplaceable: "Who was so necessary to their family as Anna? how faithfully she has performed her various duties—how steadfastly she has met her many heart wearing demands. All depended upon her. The sincere mourning felt for her by all who knew her, the many tributes of gratitude & affection expressed by those whom we should have thought scarce knew her, prove her true excellence and loveliness."[28] Gannett, in the first sermon he preached after her death, remembered her as an individual characterized by "patient thought" (quoted in William Channing Gannett's *Ezra Stiles Gannett*, 423). In her last years, "patient thought" may perhaps have taken the place of impatient questioning, but if so, the change was marked by silence. One of her last letters offers a fleeting, disquieting suggestion. In the summer of 1840 she had written to her husband, "Perhaps one of these days I shall leave off fretting" (2 August).

Tilden's life offers its reader a puzzling tangle of published texts, public events, and private response. Reading this life requires a revision of time. Rather than moving steadily forward through Tilden's life, we step back, focusing on a crucial period in which Tilden shaped and reshaped the selves she represented. In the late 1820s, the years of Tilden's late adolescence, sermons framed her weeks; novels defined her days. Each offered a particular version of character, and each set limits against which Tilden struggled.

To understand her written work, we need to look closely and separately at both sermon and novel. Chapter 2 discusses Tilden's use of the sermonic culture of Boston and concludes by looking at the ways in which she transformed the ministers' words into a daily record of who she was and how she was perceived. Chapter 3 examines the novels Tilden read and her journal responses to them. Appropriating the fictional conventions of misunderstood character and sympathetic reader, Tilden sought to make peace with the ministerial exemplars by framing them within fiction, but as Chapter 4 illustrates, Tilden's weave of religious crisis, narrative resolution, and desired reader's response emerged only painfully after years of intricately tangled efforts of self-expression. Tracing these threads back to their origins in the sermons and novels of her late adolescence, the following three chapters expand Tilden's life to contain her thought.

CHAPTER TWO

Exemplary Lives: In Pursuit of
the "True Christian Character"

Tilden's image of herself as the "fretting" wife echoes her earlier self-representation as the discontented and ill-tempered daughter. The girl who engaged in the hard work of self-reform continued the apparently endless task when she became the minister's wife. Her "tools" remained the same: she turned to the sermons delivered by her husband and his colleagues. Tilden's highest praise for a sermon was that it was "calculated to do much good." The minister's words succeeded if the congregation could indeed practice what he preached. Few Unitarian ministers would have disputed her opinion. The "religious principle," they reminded their listeners week after week, was known for its "activity." Sermons were to be enacted, their illustrations to be lived. When ministers provided their audiences with models of exemplary behavior, they presented them as a pattern for their listeners' lives. Time and again they exhorted their congregations to follow the "example of Christ" and pattern their lives after his. They lavished "good examples" upon the listeners, peopling their daily lives with insistent reminders of the "Christian character." [1]

Tilden took the ministers at their word. As early as 1828, she was worrying that she did not set a "good example" for her younger sister, Zibby. Citing herself for her "faults" of "temper" and "selfishness," she looked to herself and saw a character in need of reform. Her life was far from "exemplary." There were too many inconsistencies, too many failed attempts at "being good." By her own estimation, she did not possess one of those "lovely Christian characters" that she praised in others (1 May 1834). She was too "hasty"; she expressed her feelings too bluntly; she resented the "duties" that interfered with her own interests. Looking to those around her—whether to her minister, her mother, or her sisters, older *or* younger—she found an array of the qualities she herself lacked. Surrounded by such a cloud of witnesses, all she could hope for was some small degree of success. In the world she described to herself, she was clearly dwarfed by the virtues of her companions.

Both the 1827–28 and 1834–35 journals are punctuated by "good examples." A week rarely passed without an entry that celebrated an individual for his or her, particularly her, virtue. Wherever she turned, there were people to praise for their "fortitude," "patient suffering," "self discipline," "benevolence." She knew the language well and drew on the familiar sermonic phrasing to describe the subjects of her admiration. What she heard from the pulpit shaped her view of those around her as well as her judgment of herself. In addition to her daily journals and extending well beyond them, Tilden recorded sermons in separate entries that she eventually sewed together in a book of sermon notes.[2] Covering seven years and hundreds of sermons, these notes are filled with exemplary figures designed by the ministers for their listeners' emulation. Tilden practiced her own version, translating the ministers' illustrations into the individuals she portrayed in her journals. Every day offered its model of Christian character, and behind every model stood the "supreme example" of Jesus, whose perfection set the standard against which individuals measured their self-worth. It was hardly surprising that Tilden found so little to recommend herself. Judged by the standard that emerged from her journals and sermon notes, she was a wayward aspirant.

UNITARIAN SELF-CULTURE:
EMERSON'S PRINCIPLE AND TILDEN'S ACTION

Tilden's practice of taking notes on the sermons she heard was a time-honored one. As part of their weekly religious discipline, churchgoers preserved Sunday's words for their weekday use. Early New England churches were even known to accommodate the listener by providing writing desks for the note takers.[3] Tilden's earliest notes date from 1824, when she was not yet thirteen years old. She continued the practice for at least seven more years.[4] Returning home from church week after week, she would write down as much of the sermon as she could remember. Her goal was to produce as exact a copy of the sermon as possible. She began each entry by identifying the minister and then giving the biblical text of his sermon. In some cases this constituted the entire entry, but more frequently the entry included some portion of the minister's sermon. Her first thought was to present the central idea of the sermon; her next, to re-create as precisely as possible the way by which the minister reached his point. She wanted more than the central idea of the sermon. His illustrations, anecdotes, biblical quotations, exact wording: the closer the approximation of her notes to his sermon, the better.

In taking these notes, Tilden saw her role more as transcriber than interpreter. She recalled the sermon but did not seek to revise it. Yet as faithfully as she attempted to keep her notes, interpretation, of course, formed a part of them. Memory inevitably turned interpreter. Its selectiveness wrote a version of the sermon the minister may well not have preached. What she remembered from a sermon on any given Sunday was more likely to reflect the particular concerns on her mind than the general plan of the minister's argument.

The ministers themselves took little issue with this form of subjectivity, and in fact, they encouraged it. Their concerns lay in other directions. Any recollection of the sermon was clearly better than none at all. According to the most popular Unitarian devotional guide of the day, it was an all too frequent occurrence for the listener to forget the sermon wholesale. In his *Formation of the Christian Character,* Henry Ware Jr. cites a common "complaint" among listeners, a common horror for ministers. Individuals protested that they could not remember the text of the sermon, let alone its substance. Too many listeners left the church with no recollection of what they had just heard. This was not the only danger, however. A too precise memory could be as troublesome as its complete absence. Ministers worried that verbatim recall meant nothing more than a chance for the listener to display his or her power of memory. What they feared was a hermetically sealed recollection in which the listeners failed to apply the remembered words to their own lives. Although, for instance, Ware endorsed the practice of sermon note taking, calling it a "very commendable and useful custom," he nonetheless cautioned his readers against turning their sermon notes into a "mere effort of memory and trial of skill." Reminding them of their "duty of self-application," he urged them to use their sermon notes as a guide for daily living. If properly used, they would enable the individual to measure "his actual attainments" against the "standard" created by the minister's words.[5]

The stakes were high, and not only for Tilden but for her ministers. In regular attendance at the Federal Street Church, Tilden heard the Sunday side of the ongoing defense of liberal Christianity against its orthodox critics. She was well positioned: with sermons from William Ellery Channing and Ezra Stiles Gannett, she could not have been closer to the source of American Unitarianism. By the late 1820s, the battles were long-standing. While the war over divine and human nature continued to rage, the Sunday emphasis from liberal pulpits increasingly singled out the individual believer's particular work. A peculiar slant of self-denial appeared in these sermons, a slant that may in part reflect the ministers' uneasiness in the face of theological battles that were fought but never finished.[6]

Although the dissent from Calvinism extends well back into the eighteenth century, the turn into the nineteenth century provided a hallmark moment for a literal split between the Christians who would call themselves "liberal" and those they would define as "orthodox." When minister Henry Ware Sr. was chosen in 1805 to fill the Hollis professorship at Harvard, a declaration in favor of liberal Christianity had clearly been made. As it would be defined over the next two decades, the set of beliefs we know as Unitarianism would come increasingly to focus on the definition of human nature and its implications for the nature of the divine. The ministers' work emerged in the context of debate. What late-eighteenth-century Calvinism created, early-nineteenth-century liberal Christianity sought to dismantle.

The eighteenth century had given momentum to the importance of human agency. The doctrine of innate depravity fell far short of the potential for human action everywhere evidenced. While New Light Calvinism had downplayed the incomprehensibility of God, it nonetheless foregrounded the necessity of a divinely governed human nature. Retooling the conversion experience so vital to its Puritan forebears, it paved the way for one of the most powerful drawing cards of nineteenth-century evangelical Christianity. By way of conversion, the individual enjoyed a dramatic reorientation of his or her abilities. Those who received grace were radically empowered toward the work of progress in this world.

What remained at the heart of this Christianity, whether the reserved expression in certain Boston churches or the evangelical flamboyance preached by Lyman Beecher, was the concept of divine agency. No matter what the individual achieved after conversion, he or she remained dependent on God's particular intervention. Although packaged more attractively, the individual was still depraved, still in absolute need of God's grace. Human nature remained entirely dependent on a salvation that came only through the act and fact of Christ's death and resurrection. Innate depravity, however, did not play equally well in all parts of Boston, and for those

who termed themselves "liberal," priding themselves on the free inquiry
their designation implied, a radical revisioning of religious terms was not
only desirable but necessary.

In an age that believed a moral law organized the universe and termed
this law "moral" precisely because it was rational, the old God of the Calvin-
ists was clearly outworn. No good God would damn infants to hell; no reasonable deity would perform a magic redemption through one being. As
Channing would wittily point out, the old God belonged to an old age. The
Calvinist deity was neither moral nor godly, appearing as he did to act on
whim in a wrathful vengeance that would seem anything but reasonably
just. With a moral law regulating the universe, with human beings well able
to observe and keep that law of their own volition, the need for conversion
paled under the Unitarian light of human intellect. Emphasizing the excellence of God's human creation, an excellence that one man (Adam) could
not eradicate, the liberal Christians promoted a religion based on reason.
Human beings were divinely imprinted with the power of virtue: good action was their province. The major question, then, was how to realize potential, how to take the power and use it to further the progress the moral
law had legislated for the universe. The answers came in the Unitarian insistence on human perfectibility. Human life was defined as a course of
improvement. Every thought, every action, was to be directed toward perfecting the character with which a benevolent God had endowed each individual. A heaven on earth became possible, not through some miraculous
second coming by an intervening deus ex machina but by the hard work of
human effort.

The appeal of such thinking is evident, as are its vulnerabilities. In the
Unitarian schema, individuals could truly work out their own salvation;
they were no longer dependent on a whimsical or willful God who chose
some and rejected others. At the same time, the human-centeredness of
such thought invariably opened the liberal Christians to charges that their
system was hardly "religion" and was, in fact, only marginally moral. Orthodox ministers attacked their liberal counterparts for relegating God to
the periphery and placing human reason at the center. As they were sure
to remind their listeners, such reason might mean nothing more than
rationalization. Unitarian ministers met such criticism with a vengeance.
Arguing a superior morality, Channing had launched his "moral argument against Calvinism" in his 1819 ordination sermon for Jared Sparks.
Point by point, he ticked off the answers to the criticism: liberal Christianity's concept of God was freed from the taint of a wrathful deity; liberal

Christianity's concept of humanity placed responsibility squarely with the individual. No one was to blame but the individual himself if he failed to meet his God-given potential.

Rejecting the reliability of a single moment of conversion, Channing and his colleagues preached another form of Christian labor, one they argued was far more demanding than anything grounded in depravity could be. *Self-culture* was the operative term; *probation*, the word defining the doctrine. In place of Christ's effect, they put his example. No one was saved by a bloody sacrifice, but all people could be saved if they took Christ's life as a model for their own. Framing this exemplary life as a period of probation, the Unitarians crafted a doctrine that would meet any criticism of self-delusion or indulgence. As David Robinson has shown, the Unitarians increasingly emphasized the concept they called self-culture. In his groundbreaking study of Emerson's debt to Unitarianism, Robinson writes, "The repeated turn to the word 'culture' or 'cultivation' in Unitarian sermon and devotional literature reveals a conception of the soul based upon the organic analogy of germination, development, and fruition. 'Culture,' as it was used by Ware and other Unitarians, still carried most of the horticultural associations originally connected with the word" (*Apostle of Culture,* 9). The ministers' listeners were advised to be fastidious in their work, uprooting the weeds from this garden (somewhere between Eden and Paradise) called character. The work was exacting. In the words of Henry Ware Jr., "This is only a state of trial, preparatory to a final state. . . . Principle is to be tested. Character is to be tried. The soul is to be thus *educated.* By rightly bearing the trials, rightly enduring the temptations, rightly struggling with obstacles, it improves its virtue . . . or failing this, sinks and perishes in the desert" (*Works,* 3:410).

The means to the end of self-culture were numerous, and ministers presented them as undeniably difficult. Individuals labored, world without end. The work of probation knew no bounds—here or hereafter. The sermonic version of heaven promised the listener all eternity for the formation of character. As the one parishioner named Anna Tilden so markedly shows, the listener took her ministers' sermons to heart through her careful recollection of the head. What the minister said was collected and recollected in journal entries and sermon notes, articulating the standard by which to judge herself.

Tilden clearly used her notes as just such a measuring device. Intently interested in applying the sermons to her own situation, she filled her notes with the "good" and "bad" individuals that peopled the ministers' sermons.

Recalling their examples, she sought to define a pattern for her own behavior. Each illustration provided her with one more model. The figures in her sermon notes served a single end—the formation of character.

Tilden's practice fit closely with the minister's intent. As Ware told his ministerial students at the Harvard Divinity School in 1829, the purpose of the sermon was "to *influence and form* [*the listeners'*] *characters*" (*Works*, 2:180).[7] And the simplest way to direct the sermon toward this goal was to provide the congregation with numerous illustrations. Preachers were well aware that their listeners were much more likely to act on the sermon if it contained clear and memorable examples of individual behavior. One of Emerson's early sermons (no. 19) provides a case in point. Written in May 1828, it takes individual action as its topic. Its position is distinctly "Emersonian." The emphasis of the essays appears readily in Sermon 19 with its subordination of individual personality to universal law.

Emerson counseled his audience to look closely at themselves and gave them ample opportunity for doing so. He crowded his sermon with examples. These hypothetical individuals fall neatly into two categories: the admirable and the questionable. The "bad" examples far outnumber the "good." There are several black sheep in Emerson's fold: the person who tells seemingly innocuous lies, the inaccurate scholar, the dishonest bargainer, the intemperate drinker. On the other side, Emerson presents a number of individuals whose behavior is, at least in its sermonic representation, unimpeachable. He even brings in the founding fathers and, in particular, the participants in the Boston Tea Party. Illustrations dominate the first part of the sermon, and Emerson himself felt the need to explain why they were even more prolific than usual. He pleaded difficulty. What he hoped to accomplish in his sermon was no mean feat, for he was up against a "practical error . . . so common and so pernicious" that it was all too likely his listeners had never learned to notice it (*Sermons*, 1:181).

From Emerson's point of view, this "pernicious error" was doubly significant. It jeopardized the formation of the individual's "character," which was, as he told his congregation, "the whole object of the moral and material creation" (1:182). And it paradoxically gave the individual an unwarranted sense of self-importance. Particular action weighed light in Emerson's balance, and the error he hoped to correct was the tendency to view action as a self-evident sign of an individual's character. Maintaining that the effect was always subordinate to the cause, he argued that what the individual did mattered far less than why he or she did it. His concern was not with the act itself but with the motive behind it. He told his congregation, "It is the great, the main conclusion of religion that in the eye of God not the *actions* but the *principles* of moral beings are regarded" (1:179). Distinguishing the effect of an action from the reasoning behind it, he argued for a careful reexamination of where the importance of action actually lay. Reminding his listeners that particular actions were inevitably short lived, he asked them to shift their focus. What they did would be forgotten. No matter how important any action seemed at the time of its completion, it in fact was of relatively minor significance. He bluntly reminded his listeners, "If you imagine you were called into being for the purpose of taking a leading part in the administration of the world—in order to guard one province of the moral creation from ruin, and that its salvation hangs on the success of your single arm—you have wholly mistaken your business. Creep into your grave, for the Universe hath no need of you" (1:182). Providing a lesson in humility, Emerson cut the individual down to size, the proverbial six feet of the grave. In place of self-importance, he offered his hearers another focal point for their lives. The only hope of permanence lay in the principles behind the actions. They alone were unchanging.

Playing the transitory nature of action off against the unchanging character of principle, he structured his examples to highlight the distinction. In isolation, actions were not what they seemed. When looked at by themselves, they were unreliable, providing an appearance that could well be misleading. In Emerson's view, an action was clearly not its own interpretation. Near the beginning of the sermon, Emerson presented a pair of contrasting examples to show his listeners how necessary interpretation was. Instructing them to disregard their initial impression of particular actions, he offered them two illustrations, one of an ostensibly "good" action, the second of an apparently insignificant one. In the first case, he cited an act of charity. What would normally be praised as an example of selfless behavior becomes something quite different in Emerson's description. The benefactor benefits none other than himself. Emerson reminds his congregation that an individual's "gift of a dollar" can in reality do little for the recipient.

> When you give a dollar to a starving beggar, what good have you done? You have appeased his hunger for a little hour, and given bread to himself and his famished child, until the evening;—perhaps you have lit the fire on his frosty hearth, or covered the straw on which he lies from the cold. But with the morning sun, his misery returns, and

again, for pity's sake, he is begging, from door to door, for a crust. To
him, your kindness has done little; it is to *yourself* the good was done.
As long as you exist, you shall be the better for that action. The performance of that action has given a portion of strength to the noblest
fibre in your moral frame. (1:180)

His example goes straight to the difference between the effect of an action
and its motive. The beggar remains a beggar despite the individual's action,
and were the individual to congratulate himself on what he had done for
the poor, he would simply be deluding himself. The lasting benefit remains
with himself alone. The only permanent effect, Emerson asserts, stems
from the compassion that prompted the gift. It, in short, strengthens one
more virtue within the giver's character.[8]

From charity, Emerson turns to truth, but this time with an example of
how an ostensibly trivial action wreaks havoc for the individual. Giving his
listeners a tangle of history that few would care to unravel, he turns a
scholar's uncorrected error into his ruin.

It is of very little consequence whether Asaraddon or Tigranes was the
name of the fiftieth king of Syria, but if you, knowing it to be Asaraddon, say it was Tigranes, you have done a great and indefinite evil. To
whom?—to the world? no, but to yourself. You have violated a solemn
law within you, which you are sensible ought never to have been violated. If with an intention to deceive, you have uttered a falsehood,—
you have rebelled against yourself, you have begun to unsettle all the
foundations of goodness in your nature. (1:180)

The misidentification of an obscure and long-forgotten ruler seems an unlikely candidate for a breach of principle, but in Emerson's example, the
smallest untruth gains an importance far beyond its immediate effect. What
might simply be construed as a bit of laziness on the historian's part—the
decision to ignore a mistake that seems hardly worth the words to correct
it—becomes a major transgression. The substance of the issue pales before
the principle. Emerson's example makes this point by its very nature. The
extreme contrast between the bit of historical trivia and the violated solemn
law is in effect its own argument.

In the end, Emerson's sermon reads as a call to principle, not action. Although he carefully guards himself against misinterpretation by assuring
his audience that an individual's actions remain important, his focus is

elsewhere. Letting the actions take care of themselves, he privileges the life of the mind. Principle is its nourishment, and if tended properly, it creates a painless separation of the individual from both his or her apparent achievements and failures.[9] Encouraging his hearers to "take hold on imperishable principles," he adopts the ministerial first person to show them their reward: "It seems to me in obeying them, in squaring my conduct by them, I part with the weakness of humanity, I exchange the rags of my nature for a portion of my maker's majesty" (1:183). One step closer to divinity, Emerson's principled individual is immune from the changes that surround him. In this, his final illustration of the sermon, Emerson offers his listener his preferred model of earthly perfection.

What the minister offered and what the individual received were often two quite different things. Such discrepancy might well be credited to the process of self-application: the listeners take from the ministers' sermons what applied most immediately to their lives. In the case of Emerson's sermon, the illustrations indeed proved memorable, but their implications for the listener were somewhat different than for the speaker. Tilden heard this sermon the second time it was delivered. Having completed it on 7 May, Emerson used it first at the Brattle Street Church on 11 May, and then a week later at the Federal Street Church.[10] Tilden was in the congregation, and her notes leave no doubt as to which sermon Emerson preached. She remembers certain phrases almost word for word. The illustrations are vividly drawn in her notes and clearly bear the stamp of their Emersonian original. And although the illustrations dominate her entry, they do not overshadow the point they were intended to represent. Tilden's emphasis closely parallels Emerson's. Her conclusion is not precisely Emerson's, but she registers no departure from his major premise. In its entirety, the entry reads as follows:

Mr W. Emerson in the morning from Romans—
   The principles not the consequences of our actions are the most important. A man may tell a falsehood, or deceive from politeness, or in some little matter, and if you tell him that it is wrong, he will say, it is only a little thing, what effect can it have on others? he should ask what effect it has himself, he has weakened and violated the sacred principle of truth which he ought to have in his soul. One may give away a dollar in charity to a poor man, how long will the effect of this act of kindness last? it may save the poor man and his child from

hunger for one day, it may light a fire on his cold hearth, but the next morning he is again obliged to beg from door to door—the principle which called forth this good deed was a noble one, and may be of lasting benefit to the individual, though the consequences of his kindness were of so short duration. What an enkindling idea is it that the same principle of generosity from which a little child may act, is the same which our Heavenly Father exerts. We attach much importance to trifling circumstances, such as what is our personal appearance? in what town or city we live, and other things of slight nature occupy our time and our thoughts, what advantage shall we derive from having been so engaged, when we are in another world? then we shall hardly be able to believe we have done so, when our disembodied spirits are measuring the depth and breadth of God's wisdom—

In every hour that passes we have opportunities of exercising eternal principles— (SAR 1989, 41–42)

At first glance, Tilden's notes give a fairly close approximation of Emerson's sermon. Her opening sentence about the primacy of principle succinctly restates Emerson's major point, and her last sentence follows Emerson's nearly word for word. Emerson concluded his sermon, "No hour of life elapses, without giving opportunity for the exercise of eternal principles" (1:184). Tilden changed the negative construction and wrote, "In every hour that passes we have opportunities of exercising eternal principles." The illustrations are remembered in marked detail, particularly in the example on charity. Here she recalls not only the general tenor of the illustration but the specific images Emerson had used to flesh it out: The fire on the "cold hearth" (Emerson had written "frosty hearth"), the hunger appeased for one day but no longer, the individual reduced again to begging from "door to door." These details reappear with little change in Tilden's version.

There are, of course, differences. Tilden omits several illustrations from the early portion of Emerson's sermon and conflates others. The individual guilty of intemperance and the Revolutionary War figures who stand on the "*principle of Freedom*" (1:181) do not appear in her notes. The erring scholar is also missing; however, in this case Tilden has combined two instances of deception into one. Emerson's first example of untruthfulness— the individual who excuses himself for a "little deception of benevolence or of politeness" (1:179) matches perfectly with Tilden's initial illustration.

However, she alters the conclusion drawn from this illustration, borrowing Emerson's phrasing from the later example where he referred to the scholar's benign lie as a "violation" of Truth's "solemn law" (1:180). Tilden substitutes "sacred principle" for "solemn law" but, like Emerson, associates the broken law with an individual failing. Several other small differences are readily apparent. Where Tilden wrote "disembodied spirits," Emerson used the phrase "disembodied minds." Tilden's "enkindling idea" and Emerson's "kindling excitement" are quite similar; only Tilden compared the child's "principle of generosity" directly with God's. Emerson used a slightly less ambitious comparison. He simply compared the child to an archangel (1:183).

Tilden's version, however, differs by more than these relatively small changes of word and reference. Her recollection is much more forgiving than Emerson's original. Where he talks about "all the foundation of goodness" being "unsettled" by the individual's single act of deception (1:180), she speaks simply of absence, the principle "he ought to have in his soul." Emerson uses absolutes; Tilden qualifies them. Much less sanguine about the guaranteed effect of a principle, she limits his claim that the almsgiver's improvement continued for a lifetime. In her phrasing, "the principle . . . may be of lasting benefit"; in Emerson's version, the profit was certain. Emerson had written, "As long as you exist, you shall be the better for that action." But while Tilden lessened the stakes in one area, she heightened them in another. Placing limits on the effect of an action, she removed any restraint from the effect of the individual. She credited the individual with a power that Emerson most emphatically insisted was not in the individual's possession. In her version, the individual's falsehood "weakened and violated the sacred principle of truth." Emerson argued that this was exactly the kind of control the individual did not have. Regardless of his actions, he could not weaken principle, only himself.

The speaker and the listener finally interpreted individual action from very different points of view. Where Emerson painstakingly attempted to separate the listener from the life of everyday action, Tilden found a validation of the here and now. Like Emerson she referred to certain daily concerns as "trifling circumstances," but her conclusion about what these trifles meant led her back into this world. Even here, the two parted company, for Tilden's experience of everyday life differed markedly from Emerson's representation. He moved from the question of personal appearance and physical location to individual accomplishment and its concomitant fame.

When you shall be nourishing the powers of an angel's intellect, and
exploring the height and the depth and the length and the breadth of
the wisdom and the knowledge of God,—then, when you look back a
moment at the scenes of your infancy and this poor earth which was
your cradle,—will it really seem to you of consequence, whether you
were dressed in silk or in mats; whether you lived on one side or another of the globe; or whether you staid there, one or two summers
more or less?

Or will you remember with the same vanity, as now, all that your
hands performed; the house that you built; the money that you earned;
the honours which you attained; the pages which you wrote; your extensive influence, your charitable acts? No; these will pass away and be
insignificant—these will depart into utter oblivion; but the principles
which these actions brought into exercise will survive this unmea-
sured duration—in immortal youth. (1:183)

Reducing the individual's life on earth to "infancy"—a stage he clearly sees
as the least desirable—Emerson reminds his congregation, or at least some
portion of it, that from the perspective of eternity, their accomplishments
are hardly worth noting. What men, here functioning as a decidedly gendered term, identify as the height of achievement Emerson assures them
will inevitably be forgotten. Writing, building, money making, and money
giving: all "will depart into utter oblivion," he says. Women's work fares
little better. Infancy, typically the care of women, is no more than a preliminary stage, something that is best left behind, together, presumably, with
the caretakers. This is, of course, only by implication, for Emerson draws
no direct distinction. His dividing lines are simply the conventional constructs of the day. His comparisons are drawn with an eye to freeing his listeners from the activities of this world.

The freedom he describes, however, would not have held an equal appeal
for all members of his audience. It would have been exceedingly difficult for
the female listener to slot herself into the "honors" Emerson described.
They belonged to a world quite separate from her own experience. Tellingly,
Tilden omitted this section. What in Emerson's sermon was the climactic
example was for her a distinctly forgettable illustration. It did not apply to
her, and thus her section on assessing the importance of "trifling circumstances" is shorter and remains clearly tied to her own experience. The two
"circumstances" she cites—personal appearance and where one lives—
had direct application to her life.

Her 1827–28 journal suggests that both had, at certain points, occupied much of her attention. Scattered throughout the 1827–28 journal are various reports of how others viewed her appearance. It was an issue that clearly made Tilden uncomfortable. She writes that after fixing her hair "plain as a quakeress," she was told she looked like a shorn sheep. At another time, she records her confusion at the compliments paid her during tea.[11] While her tone in these passages remains humorous, the other issue, that of where one lived, elicited a more open note of despair. Early in 1827, the Tildens faced their move from the house Tilden had lived in since childhood. She was disturbed by the prospect of this change and reports her initial reaction: "Pretty soon after I heard this news I *took to crying* and *kept it up foolish or not*" (21 April 1827). Tilden heard Emerson's Sermon 19 a year after her move. By that time she had settled into the new house on Berry Street and, in fact, found their new living arrangements preferable to the old. Her initial fears over the change from one house to the next—what it would mean to have their minister living with them, how she would feel in a house for which she had no fondness—all these had been laid to rest by the intervening year. Thus, Emerson's comment on the unimportance of place added the moral to her own experience and took precedence over the examples to which he had given greater emphasis.

What is missing from Tilden's description is Emerson's position on individual action. His point goes unheard—or at least unrecorded. He advised his audience to think less of their actions. Every example served as a call to humility. His reminders of human insignificance are incessant:

We are very apt to overrate the importance of our actions. (1:181)

We lose ourselves in the details of this prejudice till we become blind to the absurdity that we are making the everlasting progress of the Universe hang upon the by-laws of a Missionary Society or a Sunday School.
    Let us think of ourselves more humbly. (1:181–82)

Do not suffer yourself to be blinded by an overweening conceit. (1:182)

None of these phrases is recorded in Tilden's notes, and for good reason. In the context of her daily life, she had little opportunity for thinking too highly of her own activity. She experienced a situation completely separate from the one Emerson described. Her fear was not that she would fall prey to pride of accomplishment but that she would have little opportunity for acting at all. She hoped to do "some good" somewhere, but her journal entries attest to the fact that her greatest worry was that she finally would not lead a "useful" life. What she longed for was some opportunity to engage in the work of this world. From her vantage point, the Sunday school looked like a godsend and not, as in Emerson's comment, an "absurdity." [12] In hearing his sermon, she changed his emphasis to fit her own situation. What he intended as a call to principle she interpreted as a call to action. The thought that "every hour" gave the individual a chance for useful action—"opportunities for exercising eternal principles"—was indeed an attractive idea for a young woman who questioned the value of her daily routine.

FROM CAUTIONARY TALE TO CHRISTLIKE PERFECTION: TILDEN'S SERMON NOTES AND THE MINISTERS' SERMONS

Tilden's entry for Emerson's sermon is typical of the notes as a whole. The examples that peopled her sermon notes were, more often than not, defined by their actions. It was not that the ministers, or even Tilden herself, did not recognize the primacy of principle but that distinct actions were far more memorable than disembodied abstractions. The ministers' individuals move through her notes with a certain animation. They are caught in the act, and the verdict is not always favorable. For every "good example" in her notes there are many more negative ones. The negative example, in fact, prevails. What Tilden most frequently remembered from the sermons were the cautionary tales, the stories of individuals whose mistakes had cost them their good character. In part, these negative examples succeeded by virtue of their shock value. When, for instance, Ezra Stiles Gannett preached a sermon on Christian idolatry, Tilden's notes attest to the power of his seeming paradox. She remembered three of his examples, each in detail. [13]

Together with the shock of an unexpected connection, the negative example combined elements of fear and horror. Although Unitarian ministers protested strongly against the rhetorical fireworks of their evangelical opponents, they nonetheless worked out their own version of sermonic flamboyance. It was perhaps a more genteel terror, but the prospects painted by the ministers were often designed to make their audiences feel exceedingly uncomfortable. Witness Emerson's chilling statement, "the Universe hath no need of you." The listener's perspective offered little relief. Here is Tilden's description of one of Gannett's promising young men gone bad: "Take for

instance a young man who is brought up well but has not paid much attention to his religious principles[,] he has good talents. He goes forth into the
world where every one esteems him and his opinion is sought for by all the
wise and the virtuous at last he mixes with bad companions and is led away
by them because his character was not early founded upon Christianity and
he dies a good example only of admonition and warning" (SAR 1989, 24).
Ruin, warned the minister, threatened even those with a good—but not
good enough—upbringing. The detail of Tilden's memory is interesting.
She clearly could not fit herself directly into the minister's example. She had
little prospect of going "forth into the world," and it was highly unlikely
that her opinions would be of interest to "all the wise and virtuous."
Nonetheless the image was a powerful one for her. Whether, at age fifteen
when this entry was written, she still found it relatively easy to imagine herself into a life she could never live or whether she was here thinking more of
the male cousins and friends she saw on the threshold of the public world
remains unknown. But in either case, the minister's example of the ruined
young life came home to her with a powerful warning. It seems no coincidence that, given examples like these, her later concern over her own relation to religious principles became a central issue in her life.

The minister's negative examples were not always as specific as the above
detail of a young man's ruin. In an entry from 1829, Tilden gives a picture of
an "insincere Christian" based on the state of mind rather than the course
of action: "Is he a sincere Christian who though he may make the precepts
of Jesus his rule of conduct in many cases, yet allows himself to be passionate, who lays no restraint upon his angry feelings, and is excited and disturbed by the slightest opposition, his ungoverned feelings may disturb the
quiet and harmony of a family" (SAR 1989, 64). In this case, the individual's
actions remain unspecified. It is enough to refer to "angry" and "ungoverned feelings" and their effect on other family members. This passage
may well have affected Tilden with particular force, for in her own family
she held the reputation of the one in need of self-control. Time and again
family members cautioned her about her "temper." Time and again she
told herself that she must "govern" her temper and control her feelings. According to her memory of this sermon, the stakes were indeed high. She
wrote, "Those who do not obey this warning voice of Jesus cannot enter the
kingdom of heaven, they will bring upon themselves woe, unutterable woe,
in eternity! and all this they may be saved from by their own exertions"
(SAR 1989, 64). Those who disobeyed were barred from heaven. If they did

not heed the warning, they were damned by their own failure. Salvation
was self-determined and a pointedly difficult work. Although particular action in this example remained unspecified, the solution for the individual's
failings required uncompromising activity. To restore "quiet and harmony"
to a family, the individual was expected to "exert" him- or herself. Self-
restraint was the most demanding of tasks, requiring an unbroken and unending effort.

While negative examples dominate Tilden's sermon notes, there are numerous instances in which praiseworthy individuals were presented for the
audience's admiration and, it was hoped, emulation. The most common
context for the "good example" comes in an individual's response to death
or suffering. Tilden's notes give several examples of an ideal "Christian resignation." An individual (in Tilden's examples, most frequently a mother)
faces the death of a loved one (most often her infant) with the calm assurance of God's goodness.[14] In the case where the individual himself was the
victim, an uncomplaining acceptance of death was again the hallmark of
the sermonic model. In an entry from March 1828, Tilden records a text-
book-perfect pattern for the dying Christian: "I will tell you of one who is
not the work of imagination but the outlines are furnished by facts—There
was a young man who bid fair to do well in the world who had all that heart
can desire, he was seized in the midst of his youth and high expectations, by
the hand of sickness, what now should support him? he had the Hope of
Heaven and was happy—he was willing to relinquish his earthly enjoyments great and numerous as they were, he trusted in his God and found
comfort—" (SAR 1989, 40). In contrast to the earlier example of the ruined
young man whose death was a warning to all, this passage offers the model
of Christian success. Despite an unexpected—and for all appearances, ter-
minal—illness, the individual retains his happiness in the good old-fash-
ioned way. Clearly trained in the school of self-denial, this example can
"willingly" forgo the pleasure of this world when presented with the
prospect of an all too imminent future life. The "hope of heaven" is all he
needs, and he lives, a perfect example for, it would seem, every listener's experience. And just in case the hearers protested that their minister's sermons presented an unattainable ideal, the minister, as in this case, would
provide a pointed preface to his illustration. His examples, he assured his
listeners, were not simply the "work of [his] imagination" but borrowed
from actual experience.[15]

Whether facing death or some milder form of worldly disappointment,
the "good examples" of Tilden's notes share an uncanny "calmness." They

meet any situation with unshakable equanimity. In her entries, such individuals are notably silent. Where the negative example is characterized by his actual speech, the good example never speaks for him- or herself. Commentary, in this context, functions only as rationalization. Individuals speak in these sermon notes either to justify their erring behavior or to level complaints against God's will. Silence is thus held up as a virtue; the individual should be "self-conquered."[16] In marked contrast to the "passionate" individual whose feelings destroyed the "harmony of the family," the good Christian had little to do with passion and even less to do with the daily difficulties that called forth an unchecked expression of feeling. Tilden's description ran as follows: "One who is not excited by passing events, but is equable and calm, who exercises himself in finding out and performing his duty to man and God, who is benevolent and pious."[17] Piety consisted in calmness; benevolence, in a duty performed equably, that is, without complaint.

To achieve this good character was no easy task. Tilden's notes frequently mention exactly what the work entailed. Self-discipline, self-examination, self-control—such were the duties expected of the individual, and it is clear, from her descriptions, that this work was never done. Rarely a Sunday passed without a sermonic reminder that self-examination was of paramount importance and that daily discipline could never be relaxed. In her memory, an intense self-scrutiny was the only method to safeguard one's character from seemingly minor mistakes. And even the closest watch on the self could not guarantee complete success. A "faithful" examination of the self inevitably turned up more areas in need of improvement, more duties that had been neglected, more "small sins" that unconscionably had been overlooked.[18]

While this relentless practice of measuring the soul offered the individual a bleak prospect on the self, it also dictated a not entirely comfortable relationship with others. Tilden records a sermon of Gannett's in which he instructed his listeners to serve as moral watchdogs for those around them. She writes, "Have you a brother, a sister a friend, tell them of their errors, do not be afraid of exposing yourself to censure, you may do them lasting good" (SAR 1989, 63). Here was a situation in which "good" individuals could safely break their silence. Gannett told his audience that it was their duty to speak out when their words would serve as a reprimand to someone else. What sanctioned this "outspokenness" was another form of self-denial. It could not jeopardize the individual's character because it was firmly grounded in sacrifice. In such situations the individual might well be called upon for all the self-control he or she could manage. Regardless of one's feelings, duty took precedence. The immediate consequences for the speaker were hardly cheering. Criticism rarely meets with grateful acceptance. The person who reminded others of their errors could expect censure in return. Such words would, more likely than not, separate the speaker, at least temporarily, from his or her closest companions. It thus comes as no surprise that the "good example" was also identified with a certain "independence of character." Given the separation experienced by the critic, he or she might well feel the need of such "independence." It offered one antidote, if not an entirely satisfactory one, to the isolation that would result from "good" action.

There was, however, no question whether such action should be performed. Labeled as a duty in Tilden's notes, it was a requirement for the individual who hoped to achieve or maintain a good character. And in the event that the individual was tempted to say nothing, there were numerous admonitions against such ill-advised silence. From Tilden's notes, it is clear that the silence of the patient sufferer was one thing. His or her self-sacrificing counsel was quite another. Having recorded the minister's instructions to his congregation, she did not fail to include his reminder about why they were not to be disobeyed: "Our duty to our family is great, we know not the influence a single word or act, may have upon it. As members of society we are bound to set a good example, we may so save a soul from death. By all your dread of misery and sin, by all your love for the virtue of yourself and others, by all your desire of happiness hereafter, I beseech [you] do what in you lies to turn another from the error of his ways and save a soul from sin" (SAR 1989, 63). The stakes were high. An individual's good example could mean salvation for someone else and perhaps for the individual as well. If the duty was neglected, the prospect looked bleak for both individuals. Failure to "set a good example" might well close the gates of heaven. The erring individual would continue along his unremarked, misguided path, and the undutiful bystander, by virtue of his sin of omission, would lose the chance for a happy immortality.

In Tilden's notes, both possibilities were always present. Whether by direct contrast or unstated implication, the comparison of "good" and "bad," of exemplary and undutiful behavior, is constant. Her method of comparison is fairly predictable. Bad examples are set against good, and once the contrast has been made, the notes may well turn to a series of questions in which the listener was asked to measure herself against each figure and see on which side she fell. This is clearly the structure in her notes for Emerson's Sermon 19 where she begins with the negative example of the individual who covers his lie under the name of "politeness," moves to the "good example" of the charitable act, and ends with a group of questions in which the pronoun has pointedly shifted from third to first person: "A man may tell a falsehood. . . . One may give away a dollar in charity . . . and other things of slight nature occupy our time and our thoughts, what advantage shall we derive from having been so engaged, when we are in another world? then we shall hardly be able to believe we have done so" (SAR 1989, 41–42). By the end of the entry, the note taker's activity has shifted from observation to judgment. This method of comparison is common in her notes, and when a good example appears, it more often than not has been preceded by its contrasting counterpart. There is, however, one consistent exception to this structure. In the sermon notes focused on Jesus, direct contrast disappears.[19] He is set apart, a self-sufficient illustration requiring no comparison. He is the example of examples.

In her notes, Jesus is a solitary figure. He is most frequently portrayed on the cross, physically set apart from others. His silent suffering increases the separation, creating a charmed circle around him. When he breaks his silence, he speaks only in the interest of others. In the following passage from a sermon Tilden heard on 7 September 1828, the "ideal" Christ embodies the familiar attributes of Christian character. Uncomplaining and selfless, he provides the lesson for his followers:

> What a lesson is presented to our hearts by the scene of Christ's crucifixion. Let any among you who has the least imagination follow our Master to the mount of Calvary, there we see the innocent suffering,—and suffering without a murmur or complaint escaping from his lips, and even in his last moments praying for his persecutors. What a lesson of benevolence and disinterestedness! Surely it is our duty to cast selfishness far away, if we acknowledge such a Master. When he suffered and died for Strangers, shall we not sacrifice our comfort for the benefit of friends. (SAR 1989, 45)

Christ appears as the perfectly self-sacrificing figure. He substitutes prayer for complaint; others, for himself. His behavior earns the highest Unitarian praise. He represents both benevolence and disinterestedness. The Christ of anger, the figure who threw the money changers out of the temple, and the Christ of despair who cried from the cross, "My God, my God, why has thou forsaken me," are noticeably absent from her notes. In her version, Christ stands apart from others, distinguished by his exemplary character.

For Tilden, it was enough simply to write the phrase "the character of Christ." There was no need to elaborate or explain. His virtues comprehended all virtue; his life defined perfection. In only one entry does she separate this all-encompassing virtue into its various components. Dating from March 1829, it provides a checklist of desirable attributes:

> What is the example which Jesus gave to us by his death? of Compassion[,] "weep not for me but for yourself"[;] of filial tenderness, "Mother behold your son" giving her a home and a protector; of Sympathy, by saying to him who was crucified by his side, "this night thou shalt be with me in Paradise"[;] of Forgiveness and mercy[,] "Father forgive them, they know not what they do"[;] of Trust in God, "Father into thy hands I commend my Spirit"[;] of consistency of character, showing the same calmness in the hour of his death, as in the whole of his life. (SAR 1989, 46)

In other "good examples" what would be action is here Scripture. The biblical quotations serve as the evidence of Christ's virtue. Unlike his imperfectly human counterparts, he is allowed his own voice, a voice that consistently turns the focus from the speaker to some part of his audience. Consistency, in fact, is the hallmark. Combined with Christ's unwavering "calmness," it establishes the height of the Christian character. It also places the means of salvation within the individual's own hands.

In this passage, the Crucifixion provides a frame in which to assemble the composite of Christ's character. In an earlier entry, the role of his death had been rendered yet more specific. Tilden wrote, "I do not know the words of this fine sermon, but the idea that it leaves on my mind is this— that we are not saved merely by Christ's dying for us . . . but by the example which we have in him and his holy precepts, we are enabled to make ourselves better for another world" (SAR 1989, 39). Reminiscent of the entry in which a "good example" meant the difference between eternal happiness or misery, this passage makes salvation dependent on the individual's own labor. Christ's death brings his life into sharp relief, setting it apart as the perfect model for the formation of Christian character.

Tilden's hesitancy at the beginning of this entry comes as no surprise. The doctrine of salvation was a tricky question in Unitarian theology.[20] Unitarian ministers rejected the notion of a God who would accept a bloody sacrifice as some supernatural equivalent of individual sin. But the doctrine of salvation could not be dropped altogether, for in its absence, it became exceedingly difficult to distinguish religion from ethics. To maintain their claim to Christianity, the Unitarians needed to secure an unassailable place for Christ in their theology. They found it in the concept of salvation by example. Turning Christ into the emblem of perfection, they guaranteed his centrality to the individual's life. If indeed, as Unitarian ministers assured their congregations, human life on earth was a state of probation in which each person slowly perfected his or her character, then Christ, the perfect example, could never be far from the individual's mind. An individual's success in this life and the next depended on how closely he or she matched the standard set by Christ.

The character of Christ formed a popular topic among Unitarian ministers, but with no minister was it such a favorite as with Henry Ware Jr. Describing Ware in what remains a landmark study of nineteenth-century Unitarianism, Daniel Howe identifies the popular Boston minister as a Unitarian pietist.[21] Ware was known for his interest in the devotional life of his parish, and his focus on Christ proved to be simply one facet of his larger project on Christian character. Ware devoted eleven sermons to defining the place of Jesus in Unitarian Christianity, publishing them in a separate volume in 1825 under the title *Discourses on the offices and character of Jesus Christ.* Running through such roles as "Jesus the Mediator" and "Christ the Judge of the World," he ended the volume with a sermon entitled "The Example of Our Lord."[22] It gives one of the most succinct illustrations of just what "perfection" meant in a Unitarian world.

In his praise for Jesus, Ware returned time and again to an image of unfailing calmness. Christ, we are told, possessed the qualities that made life "tranquil" (*Works,* 4:145). He "exhibited . . . a calm, equal, and unwavering contentment" (4:147). He displayed a "quiet temper," an unbroken "serenity" (4:149) no matter how troubling or painful the circumstances. Ware asked his audience, "Is there anything more lovely than his equable and long suffering gentleness." There was clearly no room for a dissenting response. What recommended Christ was his capacity to suffer obediently and quietly. In Ware's description, the Christlike virtues were bound together by a single thread of unvarying calm. Even when Christ spoke out, even when he asked that "the cup pass from him," his voice remained one of "unrepining and tranquil submission." Singling out what Ware called the "prominent features in [Christ's] human character," he provided his audience with an image of obedient endurance. The list reads like a litany of self-silencing activities: "his invariable gentleness, his untiring benevolence, his ready forgiveness, his humility and condescension, his meekness and patience, his cheerful contentment, his activity in duty, his fortitude in suffering, his unreserved trust in divine Providence, his holy submission to the divine will" (4:145). Unlike the Christ in Tilden's sermon notes, Ware's figure is given no voice. His virtues might be said to speak for themselves, and in some instances, any direct comment would in fact undermine the attribute. "Meekness" traditionally is mute. And so it goes with the other qualities. "Cheerful contentment," "fortitude in suffering," "humility and condescension": words endanger these characteristics, for if proclaimed by the person who reputedly possesses them, they are immediately called into question.[23]

Read back against Tilden's sermon notes, Ware's description suggests just how consistent a character Christ was for the Unitarian establishment. There were, of course, dissenters. In a sermon written in May 1830, Emerson suggested that the perfection of Jesus might well be time-bound. Given a cumulative notion of human progress, Emerson indicated that what had passed for perfection in Jesus's lifetime would no longer be considered the peak of human achievement. Interestingly enough, Jesus is referred to primarily as "Jesus" in this sermon; he is "Christ" only once.[24] Emerson was not alone. William Furness's *Remarks on the Four Gospels,* published in 1836 and revised two years later and retitled *Jesus and His Biographers,* emphasized a specifically "historical Jesus."[25] Attempting to remove what he felt were intrusive traces of divinity from the figure of Jesus, Furness argued for a character that, if perfect, was also humanly accessible. In a period of great Unitarian debate, his book sparked much discussion. Tilden records a divided reaction to the book: "What shall I say of it, as yet I hardly know. Humanitarians must be delighted with the work. But I cannot wholly agree with him. Some expressions startle, offend me."[26] Feeling that she should praise the book out of loyalty to the author, who by that time was a close family friend, she nonetheless disliked the representation of Jesus. She was not alone. Reporting a conversation with William Ellery Channing, she noted that he, much to her relief, shared her reservations about Furness's argument.[27]

Like Ware, Channing preferred a Jesus who remained decidedly "Christ." In a sermon titled "The Character of Christ," he argued that this "character" was "wholly inexplicable on human principles" (*Works,* 304). His virtues, taken together, were marked by their "divine original" (302); they could not have arisen by human effort alone. Nor could they be surpassed. In Channing's view, Christ's character "as an example . . . has no rival" (302). There was no way to improve on his "benevolence," "sympathy," "serenity," and "tranquillity" (306). What Tilden reported in her notes is borne out emphatically in Channing's words. "Calmness" was one of the most valued attributes whether it appeared in Tilden's memory or in Ware's and Channing's sermons. A pointed comment against their evangelical opponents, this praise for poise sounds the keynote of Unitarian virtue. And it proved to be the epitome of Christ's perfection. Channing writes,

> The truth is that, remarkable as was the character of Jesus, it was distinguished by nothing more than by calmness and self-possession. This trait pervades his other excellencies. How calm was his piety! . . . His benevolence, too, though singularly earnest and deep, was composed and serene. . . . Not only was he calm, but his calmness rises into sublimity when we consider the storms which raged around him, and the vastness of the prospects in which his spirit found repose. I say, then, that serenity and self-possession were peculiarly the attributes of Jesus. (306)

Beneath each of Christ's separate virtues, Channing found a common ground. What elevates the "excellent" into the "sublime" was none other than calmness. Contrasting the chaos around Christ with the "serenity" he displayed, Channing pointed to the difference between Christ and his followers. While Jesus acted with unwavering composure, his all too human counterparts rarely reached such heights of tranquillity. Tellingly, Channing referred to this ability as "self-possession," a virtue that appeared only by faithfully practicing the duties of self-control, self-discipline, and self-examination. Tilden's trinity of essential duties provides a useful reminder here. For all their emphasis on Christ's perfection, Unitarian ministers did not want to turn their praise into an impassable barrier for their congregations. As example, Christ was to be imitated and not simply adored.

Such was the ministers' hope, but they readily understood that perfection was not always enticing. Well aware that Christ's excellence might inspire as much despair as hope among their listeners, they worked diligently to lead individuals away from the discouragement that inevitably resulted from a comparison between the self and Christ. Channing took up this issue directly in a sermon pointedly titled "The Imitableness of Christ's Character." His opening remarks clearly defined his purpose: "I wish, in

this discourse, to prevent the discouraging influence of the greatness of Jesus Christ; to show that however exalted, he is not placed beyond the reach
of our sympathy and imitation" (311). Channing wanted to make Christ
"approachable," for only then could this "unrivalled example" serve some
practical use in individual lives. And given Channing's ardent belief in the
individual's capacity for improvement, Christ's perfection came dangerously close to undermining the whole project. It provided nothing but a
barrier if it remained humanly inaccessible. The difficulty for Channing
was to make Christ's character common and attainable without turning
Christ himself into simply one man among many.

Channing walked a fine line between human aspiration and appropria-
tion. What he wanted was for his audience to take Christ's life as their
model and apply themselves studiously to developing the virtues he exem-
plified. What he feared was that in the process Christ might become no
more than human. In this sermon he carefully worked to preserve the difference. At some points it was as simple as open declaration: "I believe him
to be a more human being. In truth, all Christians so believe him"
(312). In other places, where his discussion verges on an unbounded celebration of human potential, he returned in the end to a description of Jesus that underscored his difference from humanity. In a passage that ostensibly affirms Christ's humanity, Channing carefully draws attention to his
special connection with divinity: "This was the greatness of Jesus Christ.
He felt, as no other felt, a union of mind with the human race, felt that all
had a spark of that same intellectual and immortal flame which dwelt in
himself" (315). Christ's very ability to recognize his common bond with
humanity placed him beyond it. The "union" he felt was not one of identity but of comprehension. He contained what he understood but was not
bounded by it. What the individual had was a "spark." Christ possessed the
"flame."

Wanting to keep Jesus as a "more than human being," Channing sought
to provide his audience with a model that could be adopted but never surpassed. He said, however, relatively little on just what it meant to take
Christ as one's example. He provided the argument that it could be done,
but not the directions on how to do it. As far as a theological division of labor among Unitarian ministers, the issue of practice was clearly Ware's
province. His sermon entitled "The Example of Our Lord" has a very different locus from Channing's "Imitableness of Christ's Character." Ware
was much more interested in showing his audience how to take Christ as
their pattern. He assured his listeners that Christ's virtues were of the most

practical variety. "Look unto Jesus and learn of him" becomes the refrain of the sermon.

Asserting that Christ's example could provide a "literal pattern" for the individual's life, he urged his audience to think immediately of Christ's response no matter what their situation. "Why not literally make him our Pattern?" he asked. "Why not, in every season, 'look to him'; think how he did in a similar situation; what dispositions he indulged on similar occasions; how he would conduct himself, and how feel, in circumstances like our own? Is not this practicable? Would it not greatly assist us? Would it not often deliver us in perplexity and error?" (*Works*, 4:144). Insisting on the practical nature of this imaginative leap from the individual to Christ, Ware devised a plan with serious consequences for the individual's identity. Individuals might well lose themselves in Christ, for it was clear that their conduct should closely approximate his. But the imitation did not end there. Ware counseled his listeners to take not only their actions from Christ's example but their emotions as well. His character determined theirs. It provided a framework for the individual, for every individual's, experience. No portion of one's life was exempt. In Ware's view, this frame was uniquely designed to meet the need; it was, he told his listeners, "most wisely and kindly adapted to our situation and wants." And, he argued, it would produce the happiest of conclusions: "If faithfully applied to our lives . . . there is no good feeling which it might not perfect, no amiable virtue which it might not form, no suffering which it would not enable us to bear, no temptation which it might not help us to subdue" (4:146).

Ware here celebrates the "power of example." An example such as Christ's could radically alter an individual's life. Reminiscent of Tilden's notes on the meaning of Christ's death, it too identifies the example with the means of salvation. Good feelings are "perfected," amiable virtues formed, suffering endured, and temptation subdued: it looks indeed like a Unitarian heaven on earth. And yet Ware's method is not an entirely benign one. The continual reference of the self to Christ is a particularly insidious form of subordination. The governing assumption in Ware's system is that an individual's initial, untrained response to any situation will be the wrong one. Only by replacing their immediate reactions with the response of someone other than themselves can individuals hope to build a "good character." Ware in effect prescribes a path that inevitably narrows all individuals to a single, unvarying identity. Given a model to which there could be no exception, difference becomes deviation, a fault to correct rather than a distinguishing mark of the self.

HENRY WARE JR.'S AUDIENCES: THE FATE OF THE GOOD EXAMPLE

Creating this singly defined individual was in large measure Ware's pastoral project. And while Christ remained the model of perfection, Ware did not hesitate to translate that pattern into the lives of his sermonic figures. Recognizing, as did Channing, that listeners might well be alienated by too heavenly a pattern, he designed his figures to reach the listeners where they lived. In the event they had trouble imagining Christ's response to their particular situations, he offered human analogues of Christlike virtue. Although these figures might well turn out simply to be versions of the same character, he offered a variety of circumstances to draw his listeners unfailingly to the same conclusion.

Ware knew his technique well. He was a skilled reader of audience and carefully designed his sermons to fit their occasions. He developed this strength over the course of several years of unquestionably successful preaching at Boston's Second Church. He in fact is credited for bringing an ailing church back to life. When he assumed the position of pastor in 1817, church membership was in decline, church attendance poor. By 1829, when he turned over his ministry to his younger colleague, Waldo Emerson, the church was enjoying something of a renaissance. It had become one of Boston's most vital parishes.[28]

Ware's success was not due solely to his pulpit performances. His listeners gave good report of both his sermons and their delivery, but he was not considered a master of oratory as was Channing. Although he was not renowned for his pulpit manner, he nonetheless possessed the "one thing needful"—an earnestness of tone that spoke directly to his listeners' interest in an immediately practicable Christianity. Speaking of one of his lectures, Tilden comments, "In the evening I went to lecture with Father and Catherine, it was upon the Jewish religious rites, and an excellent one it was. Mr Ware has a very interesting and pleasing manner in delivering a lecture, there is nothing stiff or formal about it."[29] An even more enthusiastic report came from a former student and eventual colleague, Chandler Robbins. Recalling one of Ware's end-of-the-year lectures, Robbins describes an experience as close to conversion as most Unitarians ever came: "The memory of that discourse and that night will go with many of us to our graves. . . . No words from mortal lips ever affected me like those."[30]

Ware's reputation was firmly established by the mid-1820s, and when his poor health forced him to resign an active parish ministry, Harvard's

Divinity School was delighted to offer him its newly established professorship of Pastoral Care and Pulpit Eloquence. Essentially created for him, it brought together all the elements that Ware associated with successful ministry. Well aware that congregations did not live on sermons alone, he split his attention between courses in sermon composition, discussions of pulpit manner, and strategies for bringing the sermon home, literally, to the listener. Pastoral visits held a central place in Ware's definition of the minister's work. In his inaugural address for his Harvard professorship, he took the duties of the minister as his topic. A minister was both preacher and pastor, and Ware's project was to show the integral connection between the Sunday sermon and its weekday effects. In Ware's estimation, a sermon succeeded only insofar as the congregation put it into practice. Reminding his audience, a group composed largely of ministers and prospective ministers, that the sermon had one purpose above all others, he went straight to the heart of his project. "Preaching," he told them, "is instruction and exhortation addressed to a promiscuous audience of men and women of every rank, order, and age, with the view, as I have said, to *influence and form their characters*" (*Works,* 2:180). Ware made no attempt to gloss over the difficulty of the work. For his words to take effect, the minister faced a complicated process of sermon composition. No matter how well the preacher knew his form, or how many new topics he could generate, his method lay in a painstaking process of shaping a discourse out of his parishioners' lives. Pastoral visits were thus an essential part of sermon composition. During them, the minister learned the needs of his congregation and distilled his topics from them. But a well-chosen topic was only part of the task, for its success depended largely on the minister's choice and development of his examples. Borrowed illustrations, "flashy common-places," "periods . . . rounded only to be harmonious": such "tricks of speech," as Ware called them, were wholly unacceptable. What he advocated was a reliance on the material directly available to the minister from his listeners' lives. Ware pictured his ideal minister returning to his study from his many pastoral visits armed with numerous examples that would "give an air of reality and suitableness to the whole method of [his] discussion" (2:184). By giving his listeners an image of themselves, the preacher could hope to affect directly the character of those he addressed.

For Ware, the greatest difficulty in sermon composition lay in the composition of the congregation itself. Given the variety within the minister's audience, he would be hard pressed to speak to every listener. Each sermon would inevitably fall on a certain number of deaf ears. Although Ware used this disadvantage to emphasize the importance of pastoral visitation, his description must nonetheless have seemed daunting to any minister, whether aspiring or experienced. Presenting the congregation as a "group of men and women of every rank, order, and age," he continued, "And who does not know the extreme, the almost insurmountable difficulty, of so addressing a promiscuous assembly, that all shall understand and be affected? Such are the varieties of situation and education, of intelligence, disposition, and habit, of modes of life and thought, experience and trials, moral advancement and religious attainment, that a preacher may speak most instructively to some, while to others he is talking unintelligibly and idly" (2:180). Ware's list of differences is enough to convince any speaker of his marginal chance for success. To construct a sermon that spoke equally at all points to each member of the audience was an impossibility. The best a minister could hope for was a sermon that spoke alternately to the numerous audiences within his congregation.

In his own parish sermons, Ware clearly recognized the variety of audiences within a single congregation. Flinging his rhetorical net as wide as he could, he attempted to speak to every listener at some point in his sermon. This is notably the case in a sermon delivered in 1828. Asked to give the yearly fund-raising address for the Female Humane Society in Marblehead, he preached a sermon appropriately titled "The Duty of Usefulness."[31] It was well received and appeared in print a few months later in the *Liberal Preacher,* one of the popular religious journals of the day. Its initial audience, the listeners in the Marblehead church, was composed of many constituencies. The members of the society would naturally have attended. And with them would have come various family members: sisters, daughters, aunts, and husbands. The latter would have constituted the largest group of men in the audience, but men with no relation to the society would also have been present. Ware's reputation preceded him, and his popularity was great enough to attract even those who had little interest in the organization on whose behalf he spoke. Certainly the local ministers would have been expected to be there, as would the locally reputed "philanthropists." Ware's audience was a decidedly mixed group, and he did his best to include an example to meet every listener's needs.

He began by mandating "usefulness," which in this case meant involvement in some form of charitable activity.[32] After quoting several passages from the New Testament, he assured his congregation that there was no exception to Christ's or Paul's commands:

> "Love thy neighbor as thyself." "Whatsoever ye would that men should do unto you, do ye even so unto them." "Let no man seek his own, but every man another's welfare."
>
> Here, you observe, there is nothing optional. It is not left to a man's opinion, or judgment, or convenience, or interest. But it is bound upon him as a duty. The authority which makes it a duty to be honest, makes it also a duty to be generous; and no more leaves it to a man's choice whether he may be benevolent, than whether he may be just. (*Works*, 3:158)

Ware reminds his congregation that in this world of Unitarian self-culture, free will appears in a very particular form. The major issue is determined beforehand: the individual must engage in charitable activity. As Ware comments, there is no other option. The only choice, then, is how to perform one's duty of benevolence. To make this "choice" seem less restrictive, Ware offered his listeners several illustrations. In his first group of examples, he presented a trio of possibilities, describing for his audience the "man of influence," the "man of leisure," and the "man of wealth." The order of these examples is no coincidence. Given the fund-raising nature of the event, the man of wealth earns the most attention, although the man of leisure comes in a close second. If, as the old adage goes, time is money, then Ware's emphasis is well taken. He has plenty to say to the individual with time on his hands, but it is only with the man of wealth that Ware pulls out all his rhetorical stops. It is clear that he will bend his rules of sermon composition to accommodate "flashy common-places" and well-rounded phrases when he thinks they are necessary. His words to the wealthy are characterized by a series of rhetorical questions. They build, one question upon the next, and are not so much question as exclamation: "Why should he squander on himself sums which are adequate to the support of a multitude? Why gratify himself only, when he might gratify thousands?" (3:171). The questions continue, growing longer as Ware draws out the contrast between benevolent and self-indulgent expenditures. Looking closely at the rich man's wealth, Ware paints a bleak prospect of his final purchase. "Why leave behind him," he asks, "no monument of his privileged existence, except his tombstone?" (3:171). In Ware's description, the tombstone is all that remains of the self-indulgent rich man. Regardless of the words engraved on it, it speaks only one message to those who care to read it. It is simply a reminder that the deceased was "rich and worthless" (3:171). Ware then moves on to a tour de force of exhortation, beginning with a series of sentences marked by the formulaic "Let him remember," "Let him study," "Let him think." As if this may not be enough to capture the wealthy man's ear, he turns to a yet more emphatic construction. He begins his sentences "I exhort" and concludes his comments to the rich man with a generous quotation from the apostle Paul.

Ware's men of the world dominate the first part of the sermon's application, but they are not the only examples Ware provides. When he concludes his comments on the man of wealth, he turns to other examples of usefulness and in so doing makes a telling change in his mode of address. He speaks *of* the men of influence, leisure, and wealth. In citing them as examples, he uses third person and does not address them directly. Referring to the man of leisure, he writes, "Why will *he* be satisfied to eat, and drink, and lounge away a trifling existence" (3:171; emphasis mine). For the man of wealth, he comments, "If such a one hears me, I speak to him as to an accountable creature of God" (3:172). In both cases, Ware allows his audience a certain distance between themselves and their minister's example. Individuals can choose, or not, to identify themselves with the figures Ware presents. This is decidedly politic on Ware's part. There would be no better way of alienating the "poorer" members of his audience than by presuming that they were all men of leisure, influence, and wealth. At the same time, the individuals who may truly match Ware's description could be made exceedingly uncooperative if the more discomfiting second person were used to force the connection between the identity of the example and that of the listener.

Ware's choice is a wise one, safeguarding his audience as it does from a too close association with these prominent examples. And it is also the most prudent one, given what he could safely assume about his audience. There was no guarantee how many, if any, men of wealth or leisure or influence would be there. There was every certainty that the women of the society would, and while he would not speak exclusively to them, he would use their presence as a means of inescapably including the remainder of his audience.

In the last section of the sermon, Ware's frame of reference shifts. He announces this directly, bringing full attention to his listeners' response. With the concluding biblical injunction to the man of the world, he turns in a new direction: "But there are still others to be considered, who reckon themselves to be persons neither of influence, leisure, nor wealth, and are, therefore, ready to believe that the duty of usefulness has no application to them. '*I* can do no good,' is the language which such a one would employ; 'what is there that I can effect in my unimportant station and with my limited powers?'" (3:172). Setting aside his examples of public and widely noted authority, he introduces a new category. What about the person of "unimportant station" and "limited powers"? Where does *she* fit into Ware's duty of usefulness? At this point there is little question of which pronoun to use. Ware's phrasing in theory could be said to include lower-class men, but in practice it probably did not. It was unlikely that they would have been in the audience.

Unlike his earlier examples, his model here is explicitly female. In the next paragraphs he cites two biblical examples. Both illustrate Ware's point that no act of benevolence is too small, and both center, not surprisingly, on women. The first refers to the woman who, shortly before Christ's death, purchased the costly ointment and symbolically "anointed" Christ for burial (Mark 14:3–9). Ware reminds his audience that in response to his disciples' criticism, Jesus defended her action. Ware writes, "Our Lord's commendation was, 'She hath done'—not a great act, but—'*what she could*'" (3:173).[33] His second example is borrowed from the story of the widow's mite (Luke 21:1–4). "Do you not remember," he asks his congregation, "that the widow's mite was accepted?" (3:173). At this point in his sermon, Ware turns his attention to a very particular section of the audience. His examples speak directly to a woman's experience, whether a member of the Female Humane Society or an interested friend or relative. "There is a sphere in which you are not insignificant," he tells them. "You are a friend, a neighbor, a member of a family; one of a small circle, in which your example is seen and your actions felt" (3:173). His description conjures up images of home. Here is the domestic sphere, woman's province, in which individual action is defined by personal relations. While the man of wealth founded universities, the women present an "example" to family and friends.

When Ware shifts his definition of audience, he also changes his form of address from indirect to direct. No longer in the public world, he substitutes the more personal second person for the impersonal third. At the initial point of transition, he continues to use third-person pronouns. As with the earlier examples, he introduces his figures with an impersonal and unspecified "them." This impersonal third-person existence lasts no more than a sentence, however, for in this case, the example is given a chance to speak. The words are reminiscent of the speeches made by the "bad" examples in Tilden's notes. The individual speaks only to question the applicability of Ware's words: "'*I* can do no good,' is the language such a one would employ." Ware's response to this hypothetical protest turns his discussion into a form of conversation. Dropping the use of third person altogether, he adopts the more familiar mode of address and speaks to his listeners as both a singular and collective "you." "And remember that the question is not, whether you do *much*," he tells his congregation, "but whether as much as you can" (3:173). He then cites the woman whom Jesus praised for doing "what she could."

The examples in this section of the sermon stand in marked contrast to the earlier men of the world. Although Ware maintains that the difference is more in degree than in kind, his descriptions say something quite different. When he moves from the public to the private sphere, the action shifts accordingly. And so do the rewards. The man of leisure "aspire[d] to praiseworthy deeds"; his counterpart of wealth hoped to build a monument that would "make his name familiar and dear as long as earth shall stand" (3:171). Such were the desires of public figures. Individuals of "unimportant station" looked forward to a very different prospect. They had no hope of becoming a "visible benefit," well known to the public eye. Their contribution was more appropriately described as "invisible." It was characterized by quietness. It was unobtrusive, just the type of activity that angels record but men fail to notice. Ware encouraged his audience to perform "a slight favor," to "give a kind hint, a seasonable word of advice, a silent nod of encouragement, a gentle look of reproof" (3:173). These deeds were for the most part silent, consisting as they did of gestures that required no words. And they fit perfectly with the nineteenth century's model of "womanly" behavior. Such tasks were just the sort of work envisioned for the household: the "slight hint" to the husband, the word of advice to the son, the look of reproof to the child—a very different labor indeed from the man of leisure who "advocated and carried forward" the "arts, the sciences, the cause of humanity, of civilization, of truth, of religion" (3:170). Ware, of course, had no intention of privileging one contribution over the other. If anything, he gave greater importance to the quiet and invisible work traditionally performed by women. It came closer to the Christlike ideal of calmness; it embodied the "spirit of Jesus." It was "the very thing you most need," he told his audience, "calm, unimposing, persevering usefulness" (3:174).

But it was praise at high cost, and the final example in his sermon speaks eloquently about the fate of the good example. This illustration is none other than the Female Humane Society itself. He presents its members as his last, best example, what he hopes will be his most effective appeal to his audience. He returns to his third-person method of description, but in this case, he does not let his audience fit themselves in where they will. He defines their place for them. The women of the society are set apart in one category; the rest of the audience, in another. He keeps the two clearly separate. The society members are unequivocally "they." The rest of the audience is as distinctly "you." The opening of Ware's illustration makes the division clear. He writes, "The ladies of the society on whose account we have come together, present to you an example, and afford to you an opportunity, of well-doing, such as may illustrate our subject, and ought to call forth our charity" (3:173–74). This particular example serves a dual purpose. The women form the perfect illustration of Ware's announced topic of usefulness. But unlike the other examples, they make it possible for the listener to engage in action immediately. "They ought to call forth our charity," Ware comments, and at the end of his example he becomes yet more specific. He asks his listeners for money; in his words, to "throw together, this evening, a sum which would afford essential relief to many" (3:176). The individuals who are directly addressed at this point, largely the men in the audience, are given a readily visible work to do. And one can imagine the rustle throughout the audience as various individuals reached into their pockets and produced some part of the requested sum.

The example that called forth such action remained characteristically silent. Proper church etiquette dictated no less, for as part of the congregation, the society members were listeners, not speakers. Yet another law of social convention dictated the society's silence. While they were free to run their own meetings, members of the society were not free to speak in public. When it came to fund-raising, the society could not operate solely from within. Not only would it have been deemed highly inappropriate for women to solicit funds directly, but the means of such solicitation were barred to them as well. The most common form of fund-raising would have been an appeal from pulpit or platform. Public addresses were the easiest way of generating a relatively large sum of money. But there were certain restrictions on speakers. In the United States of the 1820s, convention decreed that women did not speak in public.[34] When women had something to say, protocol dictated that a man step in to say it for them. Of course, the woman's voice inevitably got lost in the translation. And most probably her words as well. When, for example, Ware spoke for the Marblehead Female Humane Society, he was clearly not expected to consult with the members of the society in advance. He was the guest speaker, with perfect freedom to speak to the occasion as he saw fit.

Ware ends his sermon with an example that literally would have embodied his ideal of "calm, unimposing usefulness." In all likelihood, the members sat together and thus would have constituted a visible presence for the rest of the audience. They clearly presented the epitome of silent virtue. They did not speak on their behalf; they did not actively champion their cause but let their example be spoken by someone else. The situation parallels Ware's biblical examples in which Christ sanctions a woman's otherwise overlooked or dismissed activity. As with their biblical counterparts, the work of these women was subject to criticism. Was their work with the poor acceptable, or did it take them too far from the domestic sphere? Ware attempts to lay such criticism to rest, addressing the men in the audience and soliciting their approval. "Who would not" he asks, in the safe realm of the third person, "be gratified to know that his wife, or his sister, or his daughter, was engaged in such ministrations of love?" And in case there was any doubt left in his male listener's mind, Ware "gratified" his listener's taste with the familiar image of the angelic woman. She was "occupied in the work of Heaven . . . indeed an angel—'a ministering angel'" smiled upon and greeted by "unseen messengers of Heaven" (3:175).

In large part what made such work an acceptable occupation for women was the invisibility of its workers. The work got done, but the women were not seen doing it. Even when Ware described the activities of the Humane Society, he kept the members themselves conveniently out of his prose. In the following passage, the women disappear as soon as Ware gets them into the homes of the poor. "They enter the apartment, and the scene changes. A comfortable bed is placed beneath the sufferers' aching limbs. Clean and warm clothing covers them, affording a luxury as efficacious as medicine. Little comforts, which the sickly fancy craves, and which poverty can seldom know, are placed by the bedside" (3:174–75). The good deeds are accomplished, but the worker is not seen in her action. She is replaced by the passive construction. Beds, clothing, comforts appear as if by some divine sleight of hand. The individual who is responsible for them is noticeably unmentioned. She reappears later in Ware's paragraph as the "ministering angel," one step closer to the "unseen messengers" who are her fellow laborers. Her future clearly does not lie in that public world where benevolent action won society's admiration.[35]

Ware's image of the unseen worker spells out the fate of the woman whose life had become an example for others. Silent and invisible in her daily work, she was made visible only by another's words—words designed to maintain her silence. The minister's words guaranteed that her appearance of perfect calm remained unbroken. She was a perfect fiction, her real life shaped according to an ideal called "heavenly." And the listener was expected to maintain her life according to the pattern of this "good example." It was for many a life-shattering process. When restructured into the embodiment of an ideal, the real life of an individual became exceedingly narrow. She lived as a representation of virtue, or one particular aspect of it. Silent and unchanging, she was confined to a single character. Her life was supposed to tell only one story. It was an all too familiar one. She was "mild and unobtrusive," soft spoken if speaking at all. Pain of some variety inevitably formed the center of her identity—her own illness, the deaths of loved ones, some particular trial to be borne. Praised for the serene resignation with which she met her difficulties, she was expected to be patient and uncomplaining in her suffering. She patterned her identity on a Christ who was never hasty, never angry, always ready to set his needs aside in deference to another's.

Some version of the exemplary life appeared every week in the minister's sermons. It was a staple of the popular fiction of the day, and was under frequent discussion in the popular religious journals. The ideal was inescapable. What, then, was its effect on the audience? It would, of course, largely depend on where the individual stood in relation to the example. For the men in Ware's audience, the sermon might well have seemed a perfectly acceptable division of labor. They contributed money to enable the women to continue their charitable work. As proprietors, they funded propriety. Their gift was received with an unspoken guarantee given by the physical symbol of the silently present benevolent society. For the women in the audience, there was a more complicated set of possibilities. The differences are perhaps best illustrated in the section on the men of the world. Ware offered the listener the opportunity of imagining himself into the lasting fame of the "public benefactor." But this possibility was clearly gender-dependent, for to imagine herself in the role of a public benefactor, the woman would have to imagine herself male. When Ware spoke of the men of wealth and leisure, women most likely thought of husbands and brothers. And when Ware used the Marblehead Female Humane Society as his final example, the members were directed to be more intent on their minister's words than on themselves. For those women who were not society members, there may have been a strong impulse to join. In the world Ware gave them, it was better to disappear in the work of heaven than to be relegated to "ornamental accomplishments" (3:161).

THE EXEMPLARY CHARACTERS IN TILDEN'S 1827–1828 JOURNAL

Although Anna Tilden was not in Ware's audience in Marblehead, her journal comments reveal how strongly she felt the pull of these exemplary lives. She longed to prove herself useful and sought a pattern by which she could reshape her identity. Her ministers' sermons provided the readiest source. What they said is clearly visible in what she had to say about those around her. Her descriptions often read like a piece of a sermon.[36] The connection is hardly surprising, given her attentiveness to sermons and familiarity with the devotional literature of the day. She knew all the arguments about the importance of "forming a Christian character." She knew what the "exemplary" figures looked like in her ministers' sermons. And she knew that she did not fit the description.

In her daily life, she had ample opportunity for observing any number of "good examples." They provided her with weekday sermons. Like the minister composing his discourses from real life, Tilden drew first on the experiences that characterized her daily routine. In her portrait of the Christian character, suffering formed the most prominent feature. Death, illness, disappointment—what binds the separate examples in her journal together is their shared experience of distress. Whether mourning for the death of a loved one or living with their own poor health, the figures in Tilden's journal suffer, and in good nineteenth-century fashion, they suffer patiently. In an entry from March 1827, Tilden exclaims, "Oh what a pattern Aunt Mary is of fortitude and Christian resignation."[37] Fortitude was a key word of praise in Tilden's vocabulary. She used it to describe individuals whose immediate response to bad news was calm acceptance. For instance, after her grandmother's death, she praised her aunts for the "propriety and calmness" with which they heard the news. Tellingly, she credits their behavior to the "good example" placed before them in their mother's life.[38]

From her grandmother's death Tilden saw one type of fortitude, but death did not always come at the end of a long life. It claimed young as well as old, but in either case the exemplary response was the same. Reporting on the unexpected news of her cousin Henry Brush's death, Tilden records the mother's reaction: "Father told aunt after dinner who bears this great affliction with a Christian spirit and with much fortitude." Cornelia, the daughter in this family and a figure who plays a major role in Tilden's 1827–28 journal, had in this crisis one advantage over her mother. An invalid herself, she lived in continual preparation for her own death and thus could approach the death of others with the familiarity she had learned from her own experience. Imagining how Cornelia would respond to her brother's death, Tilden writes, "We think that Cornelia will feel it more on her Mother's account than her [own], as the prospect of her ever having her health restored is so slight." The mother faced a greater loss, since both children seemed doomed for an early death. Yet for both mother and daughter, the approach to grief was the same. Tilden concludes her comment on her aunt's and cousin's reactions to death with a phrase borrowed straight from the minister: "They may both I am sure find comfort and consolation in our blessed religion" (29 March 1828).

Response to death served as one of the major proofs of Christian character. The individual who faced death with calm acceptance, who exclaimed over the ways of God without questioning them, illustrated the "Christian spirit" for which Tilden praised her aunt. Although the death of a close relation would undoubtedly affect the individual profoundly, the depth of its effect would be known to the sufferer alone. Those around her would catch only glimpses of the reality behind the behavior. They might discern the extent of her grief in a remark dropped carelessly in conversation or in the controlled calmness of her appearance. Characterized as silent and patient, she stood as a symbol of unwavering faith, an example of trials borne in quiet pain. She lived behind a mask, but a mask that was transparent. The fortitude of the sufferer displayed the severity of the loss; the greater the patience, the greater the burden.

Response to death took on yet another dimension when the individual herself was on the verge of dying. Those for whom life seemed near its end were in the perfect position to practice "resignation." A case in point is Cornelia, the invalid cousin who responded with perfect equanimity to her brother's death. Prepared to die at any moment, she provided Tilden with a constant, in-house example of the suffering Christian. Commenting on

Cornelia's perpetual illness, Tilden described her with unvarying praise. The entries emphasize the extent of her suffering and the equanimity with which she endured it:

"I never saw any one bear bodily pain better."
(14 March 1828)

"how much she suffers and with how much patience!"
(1 April 1828)

"poor girl how much she suffers and how patiently."
(3 July 1828)

As a member of the Tilden household in the 1820s, Cornelia fit into the family as yet another daughter. Tilden refers to her as a "sister," and yet it is not as sister alone that Cornelia acquired a prominent place in the family. She served as a living example, a means of instruction for the other daughters. Seen by Tilden as someone who would, in all probability, never recover her health, she offered a lesson through her life. After several months of illness, she was "perfectly resigned to leave this world." Tilden underscores this perfection by immediately drawing attention to how Cornelia viewed her situation. Free from fear or despair, she seemed, in Tilden's words, "in one of the calmest and happiest states of mind I ever knew." At this point, Cornelia stands alone in Tilden's mind as the single best example of patient suffering. Taking Cornelia as a pattern for her own life, she writes, "I hope that I shall know when I am to die, and that I may be as ready to as Cornelia is" (26 November 1827).

Four months later, at the beginning of April, Tilden returned to the same theme. Confronting the apparent hopelessness of Cornelia's situation, Tilden responded by elevating the sufferer into an example from which all her family might learn: "Cornelia came down this evening, she had a very ill turn, Dr Gorham was sent for but did not come as it was not at all probable that he could do her any good, poor girl how much she suffers and with how much patience! her sickness may do us all much good, it shews us most plainly the necessity of preparing for our great change before sickness comes upon us" (1 April 1828). Mid-twentieth- and perhaps even late-twentieth-century readers might well take more note of the doctor's refusal to come than of Tilden's comments on Cornelia's patience. With the recent work on women's health in the nineteenth century, we are learning to read the variety of meanings behind a phenomenon labeled "hypochondria" by an earlier generation.[39] Tilden, of course, saw something very different in Cornelia's invalidism. In her version, Cornelia provided an example not simply for one individual but many. Unlike the passage from December, this entry extended Cornelia's power beyond the single individual. Here, her situation is cited as something that "may do us all good." Tilden moves quickly from the bleakness of Cornelia's prospects to the benefit that may result from them. The contrast is telling. In this situation of "competing goods," good health is clearly the loser. Pitted against what the doctor cannot do is the very real good that can be accomplished through Cornelia's example. The very hopelessness of her situation offers its observers a clear and urgent lesson. To meet illness with the patience of a Cornelia, the individual must turn her attention to preparation. Otherwise, sickness would catch the individual with ill-formed habits of resignation.

Such preparation was not restricted to the experience of illness. While Tilden attempted to imagine herself into Cornelia's position, imagination played no part when it came to the severe financial difficulties her family faced in the late 1820s and well into the 1830s.[40] The upheaval caused by her family's at best limited, at worst uncertain, income provided her with ample opportunity for practicing a true "Christian resignation." The year 1827 was a particularly difficult one for the Tildens. It opened with the father's departure on a lengthy trading voyage. At this point the family was already struggling to remain solvent. Tilden's first entry in her journal speaks directly to their difficulties. Thinking about what her father's absence meant, she defined three duties for herself and for the rest of her siblings. She writes, "I am sure that we all ought to feel it our duty, and pleasure to be as good as we can, and as little expense, and trouble to our dear parents as possible" (1 January 1827). In this situation, the most tangible way of "being good" was to be of "little expense."

It turned out to be the duty that defined the year. During 1827, Zebiah Tilden, together with her daughters, made every attempt to limit their expenses. It was a duty that was not altogether pleasant. Their move from the more fashionable Otis Place to Berry Street had been difficult for all concerned. Becoming part of their minister's household proved to be another problematic venture. Although by the end of the year Tilden celebrated Gannett's presence in their family, her first response was strongly negative. This move to the Berry Street parsonage was one more advertisement of failed fortune. The exact arrangements are not known, but the implication was clear. The Tildens were a family whose financial needs were met in part by the church.

There were also smaller measures of economy. If their uncle, the successful Lowell merchant, gave them theater tickets, a careful accounting occurred to see which of the daughters most deserved the night's entertainment.[41] There was no question of purchasing more tickets to enable all of them to attend. And, of course, further tuition for school was an impossibility, except for the only son, Bryant. Three years earlier Tilden, together with her older sisters, had been students at William and Waldo Emerson's school in Boston.[42] Such "luxuries" for the older daughters were no longer possible. Although both Catherine and Sarah, at ages nineteen and seventeen respectively, were clearly beyond the period when young women were expected to attend school, fifteen-year-old Anna might well have been given another year of formal schooling. But the money was not there. And the little they could afford went for the youngest daughters' (age eleven and six) early schooling and son Bryant's preparation for Boston's Latin School. Instead, Tilden and her sister Sarah did their best to continue their studies on their own. The time for such activity was limited. Given the amount of sewing they needed to accomplish in a day, study was restricted to the early morning hours when the light would have been too poor for needlework. Typically, they read some section from Hume's *History of England* before breakfast. Other selections included Kenrick's *Exposition of the Gospels* and Paley's *Natural Theology*. This was certainly not the only reading of the day, for they followed the common practice of designating someone to read while the others sewed. Early and late morning reading, however, were placed in different categories. Before breakfast Tilden and her sister studied history or biblical criticism; after breakfast during the main work of the day, they listened to novels.

Tilden frequently complained that there was not enough time for their early morning reading. She lamented their slow progress; diligently set aside a number of pages to be read each day; registered her determination that they would be able to work according to their plan. Her hopes were rarely realized except for one brief portion of the summer when she visited her aunts in Waltham. Away from the daily routine of her household, she was free to set her own schedule and follow it. She notes with pleasure the fact that she was able not only to finish one segment of her history but to make a detailed abstract of it. She comments, "I wrote in my history nearly

would be either immediate or uncomplaining: "He has not sold his sugar, and of course he is disappointed, but all is for the best and in the hands of a kind Father who judgeth wisely for us all. I pray that whatever may happen to us[,] we and my dearest Mother may be enabled to hear it as we ought and with submission. We must all think of what Mr G. told us last night, and be above caring for the world, with the consciousness that we are doing what is right" (19 December 1827). Tilden here explores just what is expected from the "excellent example." As with the earlier passage, her first response is to affirm that "all is for the best," but in this case she refers directly to God. He is the "kind Father" whose actions will make right her own father's apparent failure. Her father, in fact, curiously disappears from the passage, for the "we" she refers to in connection with her mother is most probably herself and her sisters. She prays for submission, and it is no coincidence that her next thought is to remember her minister's words.

With her sisters and mother, she had attended his weekly vestry lecture the previous night. In it Gannett had presented yet another variation on the theme of Christian consolation. In Tilden's journal entry for this day, she gives a short account of Gannett's topic: "Mr G. explained to us part of the 8 chapter of Romains [*sic*], and he spoke of the comfort contained in it to Christians, he made the troubles and ills of this life appear light indeed, when we think of the joys of Heaven. One moment in Heaven shall pay us for all our sorrow and misfortunes here" (18 December 1827). Gannett's text was most probably Rom. 8:18, in which Paul reminded his listeners that the present pales in comparison with the future. Paul told his audience, "I consider that the sufferings of this present time are not worth comparing with the glory that is to be revealed to us." In Tilden's memory, Gannett comforted his listeners with the "joys of Heaven." While these were not specified by Tilden, it is clear that the divine compensation would more than make up for present difficulties. While cargoes of sugar did not necessarily pay off, the "Hope of Heaven" apparently would. And the exchange of sorrow for joy was not simply a one-for-one equivalent. "One moment in Heaven" reimbursed the individual for all his or her suffering on earth.

Gannett's words could not have been more familiar. They reiterated the standard version of religious compensation, a version proclaimed to be the only effective comfort for the sufferer. Tilden worked diligently to apply her minister's theology to her own situation. She translated his dismissal of present problems into a comment on her own sense of conflict. She was torn between "caring for the world" and a "consciousness of right." This conflict manifested itself in her growing awareness of her family's declining status. She was increasingly troubled by what this decline would mean in the eyes of others. Her comments about her sister Catherine's involvement in charitable activities became more frequent as if to maintain the distance between her family and "the poor." At the same time, she tried valiantly to read into each instance of self-denial a "consciousness of the right." When it was no longer possible for the Tilden daughters to frequent evening entertainments, she readily asserted a preference for staying home. She writes that duty had indeed become pleasure, "There is a party at S. Blakes to night which we have declined. I do not feel much if hardly any regret in not going to these parties. My home is one of the best that ever was" (17 December 1827). A year earlier she had begged her mother not to restrict the number of parties she could attend. Here, she expresses a calm acceptance of a markedly different position. More than satisfied to stay at home, she relegates social engagements to an item hardly worth further consideration. However, she does continue to think about the changes in their daily routine. A week later she carefully reports the "right" decision she and her sisters had made in not going out for the evening. At the point of leaving the house, they had remembered that, in Tilden's words, "in coming home, we might be subjected to unpleasant feelings." They decided to remain at home instead. The decision resulted in a twofold gratification. Not only did they experience the conventional sense of having done the "right thing," but their uncle, Joseph Tilden, the wealthy sometime benefactor of the family, happened to be present at the time. Tilden was pleased that he witnessed their choice. "I am glad of it," she wrote, "for he will see that for the sake of pleasure we did [not] incur unnecessary expense" (10 December 1827). What others thought of her mattered tremendously, and she sought to transform her misfortune into a means for gaining the "good opinion" of others.

Throughout this period, Tilden's direct comments on the family's distress illustrate all the distinguishing characteristics of a "good example." When she described her father's return, she portrayed it as a moment that preserved calmness despite the overwhelming uncertainty they all shared. "Never did I witness so silent a meeting," she writes, "and hardly ever one where there was more feeling, there was scarcely a word spoken on either side." This description, at least initially, was intended to evoke the strength of her family's endurance. This was fortitude of the hardiest variety, and yet Tilden, unlike her ministers, could not maintain the perfection of her illustration. After listing the difficulties that had punctuated the year of her father's voyage, she ends with another mention of how silent their reunion was. "All things together the meeting between us was silent indeed" (30 December 1827). Here, another reason for silence enters the scene. Their quietness meant not simply, or even primarily, acceptance of the situation but a tense recognition that their difficulties, far from being resolved, were only beginning.

These difficulties were indeed extensive. Six months after his arrival home, Tilden's father experienced a period of severe depression. Unable to find work and uncertain about the feasibility of another voyage, he apparently felt increasingly alienated from those around him. In July, Tilden comments, "He says he has no home or friends and is miserable poor man" (11 July 1828). In such situations, her journal entries are indeed a pattern of calmness. She registered no despair, made no complaint. Her exclamation "poor man" seems to fit closely with the Christlike ideal of "disinterested affection." When confronted by the general picture of her family's distress, she successfully captured the tone of an almost perfect Christian resignation. However, during specific moments when she found herself directly involved, not simply an observer and commentator but an active participant, resignation did not come as easily. There are numerous entries in which she called herself to account for being impatient when a situation interfered with her interests. She rarely spelled out the details of such occasions, telling herself that she did not need to rehearse them over and over again. She knew the minutiae of each event all too well. And there may have been the added benefit of a self-imposed silence. In her recollection, she could at least put into practice the calmness she had failed to bring to the experience itself. Even in her journal, she occasionally caught herself just on the point of openly expressing her dissatisfactions.

Her complaints center largely around the restricted time she had for reading. The impossibility of further schooling seems to have been a particularly hard reality for Tilden. Commenting on a visit by her brother's teacher, she begins to write out her own desire but suddenly silences such an open (at least to her eye) expression of her wishes. She writes, "Mr Cleveland Bryant's school master called and stayed some time, he is a very pleasant man indeed. I do wish that— there I won't write what I do wish—I may be sorry that I have but nevertheless I do wish it." (30 May 1828). "I do wish that—": she interrupts herself before completing the sentence. She leaves her "wish" unstated but does not go so far as to retract it. She will "wish it" whether she feels sorry or not. Given the context, it seems likely that the unspoken desire had something to do with her own education. Her brother was at the point of entering one of Boston's best schools. For Anna Tilden, there would, of course, have been no question of attending the Latin School or English High School; however, there were any number of schools open to girls of her age.[44] But while the money was carefully set aside for Bryant, it was not available for Anna. Little wonder that she concludes this entry, "Father has still nothing to do and what is there much worse than [that]." The last phrase is crossed out. It was an all too apparent announcement of her immediate discontent with her own situation, a situation that she, at least for the moment, could not say was "for the best."

For Tilden, resignation became an almost impossible labor. She frequently records her impatience with situations that required an abrupt change of plans. One of these all too common occurrences is reported early in her first journal. The situation was a familiar one within the household. Isabella, the oldest sister, at this point married and pregnant with her second child, wrote to her mother with a request for help. The urgency of her need was unquestioned, and the decision of who would go depended on which of the sisters could most easily be spared from Mrs. Tilden's household. Anna was chosen, and although she had no objection to helping her sister, she had little desire to go until her own "work" was finished. From what her journal entry suggests, she made little effort to conceal her displeasure at the prospect of leaving before she was ready. The entry opens, "I was not very good natured today." The reason is soon apparent, as is the difficulty she faced in arguing that her own activities should take precedence over her older sister's. What Tilden wanted to complete was certainly part of the domestic routine, but its urgency was distinctly personal. Nearing the end of a novel, she wanted to finish it. And apparently she made clear that at that moment, reading took—or should take—priority. She won her point. Her mother let her finish the book before she left for her sister's. Yet it is clear that in the configuration of Christian character, her behavior was hardly exemplary.

The entry itself betrays a curious allegiance to both sides of the situation. Divided into two paragraphs, it gives two versions of the same story, each with a different emphasis.

I have not been very good natured today. Kate & Sarah have been laughing at me, they said *reading novels* would not do for me. I was

reading Children of the Abbey and very much [wanted] to finish it because Isabella sent for one of us to go up there, and I wanted to get
through with it before going.[45]

In the afternoon Isabella sent down a note saying that she wanted
Mother or one of us to go and pass a few days with her, as Mr B[rown]
had gone to Beverly, so as I could be spared the best, I went after
finishing Children of the Abbey, one of the most fascinating books I
ever read. (26 January 1827)

She begins by admitting her poor conduct but then justifies her behavior.
This justification, however, takes away as much as it gives, seeming to trivi-
alize the very activity that it defends. All she wants to do, she claims, is "to
get through with [the book] before going." Downplaying any interest in
the book itself, she presents the situation as simply a matter of finishing one
task before moving on to the next. Such is clearly not the case, and the continuation of the entry suggests as much.

In the second paragraph, Tilden gives another version of the story with a
decidedly different moral. Repeating Isabella's request, she matter-of-factly
takes up the question of why she was chosen over her other sisters, Sarah
or Catherine. Drained of all reference to her initial reaction, it reads as a
simple account of the details of this particular day. The final detail, however, casts an interesting light back on the previous paragraph. She goes to
Isabella's, she fulfills her duty, but only after finishing the novel. And she
does not simply finish the book as one more item on her list of things to do
but because she cannot, or rather, because she does not want to, put the
book down. It was "one of the most fascinating books," she remarks, quite
different from her earlier comment about wanting to simply "get through
it." Contrary to what her sisters said, reading novels "does" very nicely for
Tilden, although her behavior clearly contradicts the "good example" of
obedience, which, as the ministers said, was the fundamental principle of
religion.

Judging by the 1827–28 journal, Tilden did not count herself among the
"obedient." The descriptions of her daily activities more often than not
are accompanied by an apologetic reminder that she did not perform her
duties as "pleasantly" as she ought. In fact, the "ought" is a constant companion for Tilden. Some version of it echoes through the majority of
her days.

I am not always so good natured about it as I ought to be. (22 March 1827)

I have not been so kind and obliging as I ought to have been. My temper I ought to learn to subdue and I hope I shall. (8 August 1827)

I was not so aimable [*sic*] and good tempered as I feel and know I ought to have been. (12 October 1827)

What she calls her "temper" appears most noticeably in situations in which she is expected to do something for someone else. Here is where her nature fails to be "good." A case in point occurs in an entry from 14 March 1827. Together with her sister Catherine, she protested an afternoon visit to their ailing Uncle Joseph. Her mother had requested that the three of them go together, but, as she wrote, "Catherine and I made more objections than we ought." Tilden singled herself out for the greatest blame: "I know myself in particular behaved very bad about it." In consequence, Mrs. Tilden stayed home; the two daughters went, and Tilden learned a not quite exemplary lesson of obedience. As with the request to spend time with Isabella, she was careful to explain her behavior: "My objections to going were not that I did not want to see Uncle, but I thought it would shorten our walk." As in the earlier example, a conflict arose between what she wanted to do and what others wanted her to do. She was careful, at least in these entries early in her journal, to maintain that her resistance should in no way be interpreted as a dislike of those around her. It was not that she did not want to see her uncle but that she wanted a longer walk; not that she did not want to visit Isabella but that she wanted to finish her book first. She configured the situation as a conflict between two essentially desirable activities. The importance she gave to one did not necessarily signify the unimportance of the other. This was her private explanation: a desire to do both but on her own terms. Whether her mother and sisters were privy to the same understanding is not clear. Did Tilden explain her reasoning to them as she did to herself? Or did her reasons remain apparent to herself alone? Writing them into a journal entry, she could bring the event to a more satisfactory conclusion. Her re-presentation supplied the missing pieces of the context—her motives and what was going through her mind when she acted as she did.[46]

Tilden's approach should not be confused with rationalization. Her commentary does not always stack the deck in her favor. In the entries, she was less concerned with justifying her actions than with explaining them. What she wanted was to be, in her words, "rightly understood" (20 October 1827). What she feared was a misinterpretation based on incomplete evidence. Even in the example of her protested visit to her uncle, she did not let her explanation have the last word. After explaining her reasons for objecting to the visit, she concluded with a reminder of what her objections cost. Through a comedy of errors, she and her sister gained the longer walk she had wanted. Their uncle was not in when they arrived, and in the absence of their mother they were free to continue their walk. But for all the time they gained, the walk was not what Tilden had hoped: "Owing to what had passed I did not have near so pleasant a walk as I should have had." She learned her lesson. Had she been cheerfully obedient to her mother's request, she could have done her duty and enjoyed her walk. Yet the lesson ends on a disconcerting note. The language of duty enters the realm of pleasure. She "should" have had a more enjoyable walk. Her last words leave the "correct" conclusion unstated. Do we, and did she, take for granted that the sentence ends with an unspoken moral about the benefit of doing one's duty? What follows the "should" in this case? Does the sentence in its entirety read something like this: "I did not have near so pleasant a walk as I should have had, had I not raised objections to visiting my uncle." Or does the absence of a pious reminder about obedience provide a way of protecting the self while still implying its criticism?

Protecting the self was not a skill that Tilden was encouraged to perfect. In a culture that singled out self-denial as the highest virtue, any self-saving devices readily fell victim to the dominant ethic of self-sacrifice. Even in the short period covered by Tilden's first journal, the entries show evidence of her growing tendency to conflate her interests with "selfishness." In the first year of the journal, she offered explanations for her outbursts of "temper." By late 1827, the explanations are fewer; self-blame, greater. In an entry from December, she writes, "My conscience reproached me for my cross behavior today," but she offers no comment on what made her "cross" or on how this behavior was manifested (10 December 1827). The conflict between her work and others' demands on her time remains apparent. What changes is her response to such pressure. Commenting on a task done grudgingly, she offers no explanation for her resistance. Instead, the entry highlights her "wrong-doing" and its consequences—both experienced and anticipated. Her commentary reads as a full endorsement of conventional arguments for obedience: "I did some sewing which Sarah wished me to, but not so pleasantly as I ought, I must overcome both my temper and selfish feelings, for if I allow them to gain the mastery over me, it will be unpleasant not only to myself but others also" (24 November 1827). In this passage, "temper" goes hand in hand with "selfishness." The expression of one implies the presence of the other. Such expression yields an "unpleasantness" that, if not checked, threatens to affect not simply the speaker but also the listeners. Tilden's injunction to herself reads as a dutiful reminder to think of others before herself. Her own experience of "unpleasantness" is not the focus here. That is a given. What matters in this framework is how her behavior affects others. She does not try to explain her behavior; she simply accepts it as wrong and writes herself a reason for readily acquiescing to her sister's requests. The reason was well within her vocabulary of "good character." Her sermon notes provided ample warnings about the danger of indulging "selfish feelings."[47]

What becomes increasingly apparent in the course of this journal is just how far Tilden judged herself to be from the "good examples" around her. She lacked Cornelia's patience. She could make no claim to the silent endurance portrayed by her mother. She even fell short when measured against her younger sister, whose "self-discipline" represented yet another characteristic she did not have. Although she admired her minister's "spiritual-mindedness," it nonetheless seemed a trait unlikely to take root in her days, crowded as they were with sewing and visiting and taking care of her younger sisters and studying with her older sisters. While Gannett expressed "opinions" that "make him more spiritual" (15 August 1828), the expression of her opinions yielded a result quite the reverse. In the journal entries, her speech is closely connected to her comments on temper. She frequently portrayed herself as an eager listener, someone who enjoyed conversations even if she had no speaking part in them. But when she called attention to herself as speaker, her words, more frequently than not, appeared in the context of her failed "good nature." Caught by the examples from the ministers' sermons, her spoken words allied her with the cautionary tale of the bad example. Searching for a more accurate description of her behavior, she pinned the telling detail on the expression of her opinions: "I don't hardly think that good natured is the right word to use, it is that if I don't like a thing I talk too much about it and not in a pleasant tone, not that I am really downright cross" (9 March 1828). In contrast to the belligerence implied in being "downright cross," Tilden presents her problem as one of untimely expression. She talks too much and in the wrong way.

Such assessments did not come unattended. Lurking behind the description of her present self was the image of the identity she might attain. The solution lies in her phrasing: she must talk less and then only in a "pleasant tone." If her words were too hasty and too many, then the solution came in the form of a cultivated silence. Such behavior was as unnatural to her as "resignation." Her first impulse was to speak out. Her early journal entries expressed unqualified praise for the "candid" and "frank" young men who contrasted so sharply with the ministers' silent sufferers. But it was clear that when she attempted to practice the forthrightness she admired, her outspokenness was deemed highly unbecoming for a young woman of her age. Gradually she learned to change her behavior, not simply from her observation of the exemplary characters around her but also at the urging of her family and minister. The experience was a painful one. In late spring of 1828, several entries bespeak her discomfort. The following three passages provide a representative sampling:

> Catherine told me something about my manner of speaking and acting, I felt bad and did not behave well. I sat alone with no lamp in the study. (26 March 1828)

> We had a long talk in the evening upon government of children, ===== said that they did not think I am as good as I used to be and which made feel very badly I cried and they were very kind to me.[48] mean to try and not answer back it may do me good. (26 May 1828)

> Last night and to night after I have gone upstairs I have felt pretty badly, but I do think that what has been said to me will at least do me no harm and it may do me good. (1 June 1828)

Each case centers around a criticism of her behavior. In the first, Catherine talked to her sister about her "manner of speaking." Tilden's response is cryptic but telling. Her "bad" behavior was tied to the pain she felt at Catherine's reprimand. "I felt bad and did not behave well." Had she not been hurt by Catherine's words, she would not have given her sister yet more cause for criticizing her "manner of speaking and acting"; for the phrase "did not behave well" read "spoke back to Catherine in no uncertain terms." The aftermath is silence. She sits alone in the dark.

Behind the criticism recorded in each of the passages rests the assumption that Tilden will become a silent, though perhaps not happy, listener. The third passage suggests that she did in fact adopt a new approach to the critical comments she heard in the parlor. Rather than responding, she retreated, isolating herself from others. She removed herself from a situation in which she would be tempted to express herself and in consequence kept her thoughts and feelings out of circulation. By herself upstairs, she could "feel pretty badly" without saying what she felt. Even within the journal entry itself, she says no more about her feelings, as if to write about them were to run once again the risk of a "too hasty" and "unpleasant" expression.

She clung to the hope that some benefit would arise out of what had thus far been a painful process of silencing herself. Placed in the position of sufferer, she turned to the familiar formula for reassurance. "It may do me good" is the phrase that acts as counterpoint to her lament of failed duty. Above all, she must try not to "answer back." Told by the minister, represented in the second passage by the double blank lines, that she is not "as good" as she used to be, she finds it impossible to remain absolutely silent. Her response, however, is cast in an acceptable form. Her tears are taken as contrition and met with a kindness that seems peculiarly directed toward encouraging a particular mode of behavior. In response to Gannett's "kindness," she resolves to remain silent in the face of criticism. A scheme of rewards and punishments is at work here. Speaking out meets with disfavor; silence earns approval. And approval was clearly a tempting hope, particularly when the source was the minister. She specifically mentions how much Gannett's praise would mean to her and uses his opinion as a motive for self-improvement. Were she "better," he would esteem her more highly. Criticizing herself for neglecting the "cultivation" of her mind, she had earlier written, "I wish Mr G had a better opinion of me than I think he has, though perhaps I deserve it not. I must try and try to become better and then I may possibly be raised in the esteem of those I like" (8 December 1827). Even though Gannett is singled out, it is clear that her interest did not end with his approval alone. She wanted acceptance, and not simply from one individual. Faced with the choice of speaking her mind or receiving praise from others, she sacrificed her voice to their approval. Longing to be greeted with admiration, she attempted to fit herself into the models of exemplary character described in her journal.

Success did not come easily. In issues of "character" she found herself faring poorly. The longed-for ministerial approval was elusive. In its place

CHAPTER THREE

In Search of an Audience: The Reader and Her Work

Judging herself inadequate at the age of seventeen, Tilden saw a bleak future portrayed from the pulpit. The sermonic model of the "true Christian character" provided a seemingly inescapable role that Tilden struggled to assume. The ministers' words, however, were by no means the only ones available to her. Another alternative for imagining character existed in the popular domestic fiction of the day. Tilden was a devoted reader, contributing her share to the novel's popularity. Her journal entries are punctuated by references to novels. In contrast to the sermons she recorded so dutifully in her notes, novels offered a different method of application. Where the sermons provided a standard against which she measured herself, the novels suggested a narrative in which she could live. They ostensibly told her story; all that was lacking was a reader.

The figure absent from the minister's sermons was, of course, the figure of herself. The young, marriageable, but unmarried daughter held only the slightest place in the minister's imagination.[1] His exemplary women were mothers and invalids, figures that Tilden knew and figures who were integrally a part of her household but finally identities to which she could lay no claim. Domestic novels, however, took the unmarried daughter as their subject. Centered around her life, they made visible what failed to appear in the sermons. The young woman, loyal to her family, principled in a steady virtue, was singled out for attention. She moved through the pages of these novels with the heartening reassurance that such lives mattered and were in fact essential to the strength of the community.

Her story was one any young unmarried daughter might desire, particularly if circumstances were demanding and family life riddled with difficulty. What Tilden found in these fictions were daughters who successfully bridged the abyss between the demands of the failed father and the sufferings of the sainted mother. Tilden needed to look no further than her own father's financial ruin and mental collapse to frame the connection. Fiction mirrored reality, and she in turn hoped the reverse might come true. Revising the fiction she read into the days she lived, she sought to replace judgment with understanding. Character remained the central question, but the operating terms were different. The ministers upheld an unwavering standard; the novelists offered a model defined by generous interpretation.

NOVEL READINGS: EDGEWORTH, SEDGWICK, AND TILDEN

Judgment was, nonetheless, a significant issue involving both the writer and her work and at the same time implicating the reader. The narrative's acceptance in part depended on the author's character. The work was only as good as the life, and an exemplary life might well license momentary "indiscretion" in the work. Both of Tilden's favorite novelists, Maria Edgeworth and Catharine Maria Sedgwick, were praised for their faultless lives. They lived by a clearly defined duty and won society's blessing for the form their duties took. Both were highly praised "dutiful daughters" to increasingly demanding fathers. Sedgwick nursed her father in his final illness and was instrumental in his resolution of religious difficulties. Having already turned to Unitarianism herself, she in turn brought William Ellery Channing to her father's bedside, where conversation relieved his spiritual distress.

Edgeworth worked as her father's assistant. Noted for his ideas on childhood education, Richard Lovell Edgeworth attained a position of prominence in the late eighteenth century. Calling on his daughter's abilities as a writer, he marshaled her talents to suit his ends. Her first work had in fact been done at her father's bidding: a translation of Madame de Genlis's *Adèle and Théodore*.[2] In the late 1790s she worked closely with him on their jointly authored *Practical Education*. The new stories she included in the second edition of *The Parent's Assistant* were written with her father's work in mind.[3] In 1805, her father essentially called a halt to her novel writing by suggesting she work with him on a "*useful* essay" in place of her "pretty stories & novelettes."[4] As respectful of paternal authority as any of the "good daughters" in her novels, Edgeworth accordingly set aside her work and involved herself in her father's project. The result, published in 1809, was a volume entitled *Essays on Professional Education*, a commentary on a young man's preparation for his chosen profession. For Edgeworth, the work must have been a troubling project at best. As she studied and wrote about the professions in which she could take no direct part, this discussion offered something like a vicarious participation in lives she would never live. Once finished with the book, she used the material in novels such as *Patronage,* her study of the young man's path to success—or failure. With her father's death in 1817, she turned yet again to his project, finishing his memoirs for publication in 1820.

In their own lives, Edgeworth and Sedgwick embodied the admired principle of daughterly duty. Neither married; both turned counselor to their siblings' households. And each in turn created fictional daughters whose principled activity was governed by their inwardly defined conviction of "right." In their novels, Sedgwick and Edgeworth offered a particular script to their late-adolescent readers. Playing several variations on a single theme, they privileged the character of independent mind. Typically she was a lover of solitude, someone who valued study and readily relinquished the distractions of society. She read, she conversed, she formed her ideas of virtue based on a model far superior to the standards set by her society. She made herself accountable solely to the "Highest Authority" and risked human displeasure in the service of a divine cause.

Translated into the specific construct of a plot, the female protagonist faced situations in which she was forced to choose between socially accepted behavior and "right action." The choice was never difficult. She would visit the poor, care for the invalid, defend the social outcast regardless of its social impropriety. Her excellence lay in her ability to see a problem and seek its remedy even when her action created conflict with established authority. Whether the spurious authority of a political manipulator or the flawed authority of a benighted state, the female protagonist refused to accede to its dictates.

One authority alone, however, posed painful difficulties for the fictional daughter. In novels filled by deviously malicious or simply misguided leaders, fathers fared little better than their public counterparts. Paternal authority was shown to be deeply flawed. In a world where mothers were either dead and maligned or living and powerless, the daughter became the sole means of hope. She alone could act and act rightly. Her principled action was often misinterpreted but always vindicated. In the end, she redeemed the father and restored the mother, all the while matching her actions to her own understanding of how a life should be lived. And in each case, her fictional life closed with a marriage prospect but with no emphasis given to marriage as an accomplished fact. Until the final pages, she remained the

young unmarried woman whose vision finally brought justice to a complicated world.

From the late 1820s to the mid-1830s, Tilden increasingly defined herself
as a character in search of a reader. Looking for the individual who would
"rightly underst[and]" her, she sought someone who, like the reader of domestic fiction, would know what care the interpretation of appearance required. She imagined an individual "like a sister" who knew her intimately
as a peer. But unlike the sibling relation, this friend was not part of the family narrative but stood outside it. The person would listen without censor-
ing; Anna could "talk . . . upon any subject [she] pleased" (20 October
1827). At the same time, Tilden did not envision a purely acquiescent listener. Her expectations included frank evaluation, but with an honesty that
never questioned the worth of the individual herself. Evaluation, in Tilden's
model, was fundamentally an affirmation of value. The evaluating listener
clearly respected the character under consideration and was deeply interested by her actions and by the thoughts behind them. Such was Tilden's
profile of the desired friend, and as such, a mirror image of the sympathetic
reader created by the domestic novelists.

By her early twenties, when Tilden began revising her interpretation of
herself, she had a long history of novel reading behind her. Judging by her
journal entries from 1827–28, Tilden read novels whenever she could. Time
was, of course, the great consideration, for other tasks took precedence.
Reading biblical commentaries and studying history; sewing, whether plain
or fancy work; visiting, with its endless and daily rounds of calling on
neighbors: these were the activities that relentlessly demanded attention.
That Tilden did not always pay attention where attention was due is clear
from her journal entries. The time spent reading novels was typically borrowed time in which she "should" have been reading history or taking care
of her sister's children. During one particularly novel-rich period, five different novels are mentioned in the journal within a time frame of two
weeks. In the entries between 15 January and 2 February 1827, Tilden was
engrossed by Maria Regina Roche's *Children of the Abbey*; she reread Maria
Edgeworth's *Belinda* while waiting for the second volume of *Children* to be
returned to the circulating library, and she began reading Edgeworth's
Patronage, still waiting for the second volume of the gothic novel. She
finished the first volume of Catharine Sedgwick's *Redwood*, obtained the
second volume of *Children* and finished it, and began reading Edgeworth's
Harrington.

The entries for this period frequently acknowledge that Tilden was reading fiction while neglecting many other activities. On 15 January she writes, "The greatest part of today I have been reading Children of the Abby [*sic*]." The next day she finished the first volume at the expense of Hume: "I finished Children of the Abby instead of reading Hume as I ought to have done."[5] That evening she began rereading *Belinda* and recorded that she was "almost if not quite as much interested in it the second as the first time." During the next two days she continued reading *Belinda*, checked the library for the second volume of *Children*, and finally received it on the 20th. On 26 January she was working diligently to finish the novel, having in the meantime finished the first volume of *Redwood* and begun *Patronage*, a book she liked "exceedingly."

Roche's gothic novel, as noted earlier, was the book that captured so much of her time and interest. This was the novel that postponed her visit to her sister Isabella and prompted her own twice-told story in the journal. In the first version, she finished the novel because she "wanted to get through with it." In the second, she finished it because it was "one of the most fascinating books" she had read. Each version speaks to a single constraint on her reading: time. At her sister's, her time for reading would undoubtedly have been diminished, and since she had not found it easy to get the second volume of *Children*, the thought of returning the book before she was "through with it" was by no means a pleasing prospect. She wanted to finish the book before tending to her sister's children, even though, as she acknowledged, the baby was "one of the dearest little creatures [she] ever saw." She indeed won her small victory, finishing the novel before she left for her sister's. For the first three days of her visit, she records no reading, but on the fourth day her habits of home return. Her sister sets out by herself on a round of visits and errands because Tilden "wanted to stay and read."

In this case the novel was *Harrington*, another of Maria Edgeworth's works. In the year and a half covered by this journal, Tilden read more fiction by Edgeworth than by any other author.[6] The choice is by no means surprising, for Edgeworth was the novelist most celebrated in Unitarian circles. Her books were praised in the *Christian Examiner*. She was lauded as a writer whose project was dear to the hearts of the ministry: she told stories in the interest of forming her reader's character. This interest took her reader from cradle to grave. Writing for a variety of audiences, Edgeworth left no portion of life unexamined. Most famous for her children's stories, she was a household presence well into the second half of the century. Her six volumes of *The Parent's Assistant: or, Stories for Children* were standard reading, as were the stories in the numerous volumes and sequels to *Early Lessons*. In early adolescence, children could be expected to read from her *Moral Tales for Young People* or *Popular Tales*. For late adolescence and early adulthood, there were novels such as *Patronage* and *Belinda*, the novels Tilden mentioned and apparently read, at least in the case of *Belinda*, more than once. Edgeworth saw these novels as appropriate for a wide-ranging audience, as applicable to the young unmarried daughter as to the long married father. In addition, she thought of her Irish novels — *The Absentee, Castle Rackrent, Ennui,* and *Ormond* — as part of an ongoing social criticism. She used fiction to shame the Anglo-Irish landlords into meeting their Irish responsibilities.

In the Tilden household, Edgeworth's novels were valued highly enough to be purchased, rather than borrowed. When Tilden, for instance, reread *Belinda,* it is clear that the book was one readily available in the house. The same is true of *Harrington,* a book she picked up at her sister's. In all probability, Edgeworth was an author with whose words Tilden was thoroughly familiar. Although no records of household possessions exist, *The Parent's Assistant* and *Moral Tales* could readily be expected to have been part of the family's library.[7] Her own response to Edgeworth was consistently favorable: every mention of Edgeworth's work was punctuated by praise.

Equally high in Tilden's esteem were the novels by Catharine Maria Sedgwick. Tilden read *Hope Leslie* twice, once while visiting her aunts in Waltham and six months later when she was again back in Boston. The first reading took her a mere two days. She began reading the book on June 24 and finished it on June 26. When she read it again, she borrowed her minister's copy for the reading class she was then attending. Her comments bespeak her enjoyment: "It is a very pleasant way of passing the afternoon" (14 January 1828).

As with her interest in Edgeworth, her enjoyment of Sedgwick offers no surprise, for Sedgwick was directly involved in the Unitarian movement and often allied her fiction with the work of its ministers.[8] Disillusioned by the Calvinism of her childhood, Sedgwick turned to Unitarianism largely because of William Ellery Channing's influence. She called him a "minister of consolation from the throne of mercy,"[9] and when she returned from Boston to Stockbridge after her father's death in late January 1813, she initiated a correspondence with Channing that would last until his death and include several visits in his home. When in 1821 she moved to New York, she joined the newly formed First Unitarian Society, the church that six years later sought to woo Ezra Stiles Gannett away from Channing's Federal Street Church. Given Sedgwick's friendship with Channing and her interest in his church, Tilden may well have been acquainted not simply with the novels but with the novelist. By the mid-1830s when Tilden wrote to Gannett about reading Sedgwick's latest publication, the tone of her comments spoke with the familiarity of a personal acquaintance.[10]

Sedgwick was frequently compared with Maria Edgeworth and was in fact called "a religious Edgeworth" by one of her reviewers. The comment refers to her novels themselves and not to any of her announcedly religious fictions. She herself would probably have approved of the designation, for even in her more secular novels, the emphasis fell squarely on what she called the "religious principle" and its importance in the formation of character. Her stories most frequently took the form of critique. In *A New England Tale* (1822), her first published work, she used fiction to criticize the effects of Calvinism. In her second novel, *Redwood* (1824), she turned her attention to individual liberty and the threat posed by the Shaker community. Her next work, *Hope Leslie* (1827), examined the same issue but set it within Puritan New England. In each case, the most beneficial religion was the one that was the least defined. Sedgwick's virtuous characters revere God in nature, celebrate the argument from design in every sunset they see, read their Bibles faithfully, and profess no allegiance to particular sects. They embody the ideas by which Unitarian Christianity defined itself, but keeping with its nonsectarian thrust, Sedgwick never mentioned the word "Unitarian" in her novels. As she commented in the preface to *Redwood*, "Our anxiety is only for the great truths of our common religion, not for any of its subdivisions."[11]

Edgeworth's and Sedgwick's novels dominated Tilden's reading. Sounding like Edgeworth's virtuous daughters, Tilden criticized the "frivolity" of certain, unnamed books. She preferred, so she said, to read works that directed "one's thoughts to the *Highest Power*" rather than those "full of mere foolish love & scenes like that" (5 March 1828). Sedgwick and Edgeworth clearly eschewed such scenes in their work. And even Roche, in the more suspect genre of the gothic, guarded her heroine against "foolish love" by rarely allowing her lovers a scene together. Her protagonist's love was saved from the fate of fools by being so closely circumscribed by daughterly duty.

Tilden's preferences in fiction were undeniably admirable by the standards of her day. The books listed in her 1827–28 journal almost perfectly match the list Lydia Maria Child would publish four years later in *The Mother's Book* (1831).[12] Listed in the novels appropriate for fifteen- and sixteen-year-olds were Sedgwick's *Redwood* and *Hope Leslie* and Edgeworth's *Belinda* and *Patronage*. Also listed among Child's recommendations are all of Scott's Waverley Novels as well as Irving's *Sketchbook*. Irving, however, is nowhere mentioned in Tilden's journal, while Scott, at this point, received only dutiful attention. Apparently preferring his poetry to his prose, she did record some interest in "The Lay of the Last Minstrel," but when it came to Scott's fiction, her responses were far from enthusiastic. After beginning *Red Gauntlet,* she thought she might find it interesting, but in no case did she turn to one of Scott's novels as a book of her own choosing. Whether she found his love scenes too "foolish" or his subject matter too distant she does not say, but by the record of her reading, her preferences were clear. She turned first to fiction in which the main characters were young, unmarried women.

That she turned first to fiction is everywhere apparent in her journal entries. Whether in the days spent finishing the novel she had only recently begun or in her responses of pleasure this reading yielded, Tilden found it difficult to resist the temptation of fiction. In the pages of her journal, however, she did attempt to weight her reading toward the morally instructive. Edgeworth and Sedgwick, of course, fit readily into the category, but she described a course of reading—one that she never followed for more than a few days—that in fact placed the novel in a decidedly secondary role. While at Waltham for several weeks, she outlined the following schedule for herself: "Today I have read in Paley Mrs Hamilton's letters and [Hume's] History this is what I want to do every day I am here. In the afternoon we worked and began to read Tales of my Grandfather by Scott which I think I shall like" (15 July 1828). The morning's reading was given over to instruction. Paley served the religious needs with his *Natural Theology* and Hume the historical ones with his *History of England.* The letters written by Elizabeth Hamilton directly engaged the issue of moral instruction. Designed for the benefit of young women, they offered a course in domestic employment, with special attention to the care of young children backed by a firm plea for the education of young mothers. The caretakers Hamilton described were well-read individuals.[13]

In this scenario, Tilden reserved fiction for the afternoon and designated its reading as communal. As the women sewed, someone would read.[14] She apparently separated communal from solitary reading, thinking of the former as entertainment, the latter as instruction. Fiction, however, did not always fall into the category of communal reading. While certain novels were mentioned only in connection with the sewing circle, others merited both individual and group reading. Commenting on the popular *De Vere*, she admits that it had not merited the time she had spent on it. It would have been more appropriate for the relaxed concentration of afternoon listening.[15] Edgeworth and Sedgwick, on the other hand, belonged to both categories of reading, and her preference seems to have been for the individual and private reading of these, her favorite authors. Roche's *Children of the Abbey* was most decidedly a work to be read alone, but in this case the issue seems not to have been instruction but rather identification. The privacy of individual reading allowed the reader the closest identification with the heroine. The protagonist in Roche's novel faced her difficulties alone; likewise, her reader preferred to read of those difficulties in the solitude of her own thoughts. In contrast, Tilden rarely read Scott's fiction to herself. Whenever she mentions one of his novels, the comment appears in the context of communal reading with her sisters.

Her categories of reading did not end with the distinction between individual and group, for she also devised different methods for responding to what she read. Borrowing the suggestion of her former teacher, she wrote abstracts from memory of the British monarchs' reigns.[16] Scott's poetry warranted another approach. She committed several passages from *Marmion* and *The Lay of the Last Minstrel* to memory. This memory work was accomplished in the afternoon while she performed other tasks. Memorizing poetry and sewing chemises turned out to be compatible activities.[17] Other poems, however, did not yield so readily to divided attention. While Milton's *Paradise Lost* was read aloud in the afternoons, Tilden returned to the poem in the mornings, to read to herself what she had heard the previous day. She also drew on another resource, turning to her aunt's encyclopedia for information on Milton's life.

While biography seemed helpful in some cases, summary worked well in others. After finishing Thomas Moore's *The Epicurean,* she provided a sermon illustration by way of a brief synopsis: "Alciphon the hero is disturbed at the idea that there is no immortal state and that every bright and beautiful being must perish forever. At last he is converted to Christianity by a young Egyptian girl and an old man who were Christians" (18 October 1827). She remembered the book for its "proof" of immortality. That the instrument of the hero's conversion was a young girl was also well worth remembering. Concluding her comments on the book, she writes, "I think the book is interesting and certainly displays imagination."

Fiction's display of imagination was what both attracted Tilden to novels and sanctioned her reading of them. Closely identified with her ideal of the "well-cultivated mind," imagination was an indispensable part of Tilden's model character. An "improved mind" was an imaginative one, and by Tilden's estimation, imagination was most immediately cultivated through reading. Reflecting on the activities of a woman's day, Tilden contrasted the "amusement and pleasure" of sewing with the "amusement and interest" associated with the written word. Comparing the life of city and country, she maintained that women were better able to live happily in the country because they did not require a constantly changing set of circumstances. Where men needed external stimulation, women drew on the self-contained powers of the imagination:

> Our days here [in Waltham] have lately passed pretty much alike. I think it must be better for ladies in the country than gentlemen, for let them be ever so fond of reading &c this will not last a great length of time, while ladies have great amusement and pleasure in sewing, yet I do not like that ladies should be wholly devoted to sewing, they ought to read and improve their minds, for though a lady is not called upon to exert her talents so publicy [sic] as a gentleman, yet by cultivating them she has a source of amusement and interest very great to herself and also useful to others. (23 October 1827)

In this entry, she quickly qualifies her comments on sewing, carefully bracketing them with the other activity of her day. Sewing, by her estimation, did nothing to "improve" the mind, whereas reading offered the opportunity for further intellectual development. Reading *both* delighted and instructed. She gave it precedence over other daily tasks, a step that likewise gave precedence to the self over others. Her phrasing marks this distinction. The benefit to the self is described as "very great." No such emphasis accompanies the term "useful," and the phrase at the end of the sentence functions like an afterthought. First and foremost, reading creates a world in which the individual's own talents can be developed. That such study is "useful to others" is all to the good, but it does not merit pride of place in her scheme of improvement.

Defining a course of "instructive" reading for herself yet letting fiction regularly interrupt her plan, Tilden reflects the flux in which novel reading remained. Although reading in itself was accorded a certain respect, un-easiness lingered when it came to assessing the effect of the novel on the reader. As Nina Baym pointed out in her study of the antebellum reviewing audience, reviewers well into the 1840s worried about the problematic ex-pectations raised by the worlds delineated in many novels. One reviewer from the conservative *Ladies' Repository* (April 1843) cataloged the danger-ous techniques by which novels succeeded so well: "rare adventures by land and sea, hair-breadth escapes, sudden reverses of fortune, heart-rending separations, and miraculous meetings, in connection with high wrought portraitures of peerless beauty, and extravagant delineations of character, all have a tendency to gratify by excitement. . . . The mind becomes un-governable" (in Baym, *Novels, Readers, and Reviewers,* 39). The reviewers feared the consequence of what they saw as unnatural stimulation. If the reader's mind grew accustomed to the "extravagance" of fiction, then it would not only lose its governing principle but would in fact become "un-governable."[18] Sedgwick was praised because she, in one reviewer's words, "never appealed for the interest of her works to the morbid love of excite-ment" (in Baym, *Novels, Readers, and Reviewers,* 56). The same could be said, and in fact was, of Edgeworth.

Sedgwick's and Edgeworth's novels were closely connected by their shared interest in the instructional value of fiction. Both writers allied themselves with a moral agenda: they saw their work as part of a larger task. Through their creation of fictional character, they sought to improve the reader's. Given their attention to moral improvement, their fiction was applauded. In contrast to the more chaotic moral world of the gothic novel, the do-mestic order established in Sedgwick's and Edgeworth's novels easily laid to rest any lingering worries that readers would be led astray in the very act of reading fiction.

This was most pointedly the case with Edgeworth's first novels. Written and published at a time when fiction still met with distrust, Edgeworth's work was consistently praised for being everything a novel was not. Her characters insistently referred to themselves as living lives that did not be-long in novels, and the female characters specifically prided themselves on their difference from the heroines of romance.[19] Even characters like Rosamond Percy in *Patronage,* who readily compared her "reality" to the novels she read, are blessed with a healthy dose of prudence and a clear abil-ity to distinguish between "fiction" and "real life." Contrasting her sister's character with the romance heroine, she clearly establishes the attributes that belong only to fiction: "I have the greatest sympathy and admiration for your true heroine in a book; but I grant you, that in real life, in a private room, the tragedy queen would be too much for me; and the novel heroine would be the most useless, troublesome, affected, haranguing, egoistical, insufferable being imaginable.—So, my dear Caroline, I am content, that you are my sister and my friend, though I give you up as a heroine" (81).[20] Such rational commentary from the characters guaranteed their respectability. Edgeworth's heroines were distinguished by their passion for reason. In her fiction, readers need never worry about dimming their moral sense or losing sight of their duty.[21]

By the time Sedgwick began writing in the early 1820s, the criticism of novels had once again shifted. At this point, it was assumed that fiction would be part of an individual's reading. The concern now lay in how to balance fiction against nonfiction. A clear hierarchy existed: as Tilden's daily schedule suggests, the study of history, biography, and religious works took precedence over the leisure activity of reading novels. Although associated with leisure, novel reading was nonetheless perceived as an *activity*. As such, it was preferable to idleness and privileged over certain other, less edifying entertainments. In Sedgwick's words, novels provided a respectable activity for individuals who would "otherwise be less profitably employed" (*Redwood*, ix).

Profit extended beyond the activity of reading. Novels offered their readers a promising character, both through identification with the protagonist and in their role as reader. Predicated on a sympathetic interpretation of apparently compromising circumstances, the novels cast their readers as careful and knowledgeable interpreters. The readers stood in a distinctly privileged position. They alone understood the protagonist's story. In contrast to the ready and frequent misinterpretation of character practiced by the characters within these fictions, the reader saw the complexity behind an apparently simple appearance. Allied with the knowing narrator, the reader gained a highly desirable character for herself. With her wise acceptance and careful interpretation, she was generous and farsighted. Her virtue lay in discernment. She alone knew the value of the characters who labored under misinterpretation. The consequences for the reader were as desirable as the character she had been given. Encouraged by the novels' narrators to sanction the female figures, she legitimized their qualities in herself. Where the heroines were distinguished by individual action, the reader was encouraged to engage in such activity herself. Where the characters triumphed because they trusted to their own knowledge of right, the reader learned to adopt an authority she could also call her own.

For Tilden, reading offered a means of self-definition that connected past and present. Increasingly distanced from her identity as the *school*girl, she held tightly to her routine of reading. The variety of her reading attested to her ongoing study; the specificity of her interest in domestic fiction illustrated the particular concerns of her present moment. In fiction, she found the experiences that most closely paralleled her own, especially in those novels she read by herself, apart from the communal setting of the household. In these fictions, the character's importance was never in doubt. Significance had virtually been written into the protagonist's very existence, for the novel was created as her story. Tilden looked to these fictional characters, struggling to acquire their "importance" through her "usefulness."

As Tilden gradually moved away from a collective identity, a member in a particular "set of girls" defined by their shared experience in school, she began to see herself in terms of a separate and isolated individuality. No longer part of a group beyond the family, she sought an identity within a household of daughters. She longed for useful work and was initially pleased with her job of "underhousekeeper," rotated monthly among the sisters. When her mother designated her as "little mother" to her youngest sister, she embraced the possibility of finally contributing in some significant way to her family's life. She praised her sister Catherine's work in the Sunday school and was all too eager to substitute for her when circumstances favored her with this work. She outlined her day in terms of how many pages of history she would read and how much progress she would make on the sewing tasks that were clearly the work that was never done.

And yet, behind this appearance of meaningful activity lay Tilden's continuing questions about how to interpret her actions and place her character. At times, particularly in the opening months of 1827, she herself readily called appearance into question, noting that the conventional interpretation might well not be accurate. Sounding like the Daisy Miller of an earlier generation, Tilden summarily dismissed a rule of etiquette as "ridiculous." Walking on the slippery Boston streets of early February, she records a mishap and its possible misinterpretation:

Soon after I had turned the corner of Otis place Sarah called out to me to stop, and I just then *slipping*, but not *falling*, H[enry] Sturgis asked me if I would not take his other arm. (Sarah having one) So I accepted it. I believe that it is not generally thought proper for young ladies to walk *arm in arm* with young gentlemen, however proper or not I did,

and I do not [know] but what I shall again, it is *only etiquette* which
prevents, and which I think is *very ridiculous*. It is sometimes even said
that you are engaged if you walk in that way with a gentleman. (2 February 1827)

When it came to being proper, Tilden preferred to remain on her feet.
Defining herself against the rules, she refused to let conventional interpretations dictate her appearance. Rather than falling down for propriety's
sake, she chose an action that might well be misinterpreted. When viewed
through the lens of socially coded behavior, the appearance of Anna Tilden
and Henry Sturgis walking arm in arm announced their engagement. When
seen through the lens of Tilden's experience, such an interpretation could
hardly be taken seriously. What etiquette failed to see were the slippery
streets, the very reality that made the questionable appearance possible.
This could well be seen as defiance of the safest sort, since etiquette's eyes
might easily be opened and an exception to the rule granted in the event of
winter walking. Tilden, however, leaves the safety of reasonable exception
with her comment that her aberrant behavior will not be dependent on
circumstance. She will, in all likelihood, walk "that way" again, and not
simply because the weather dictates. Walking arm in arm holds year-round
possibilities.

A week earlier, Tilden had recorded another breach of etiquette with disarming nonchalance. Standing at the door of her house with a friend from
school, Tilden included her cousin George Tilden in the conversation when
he spotted them standing in the doorway. After the conversation, Tilden's
mother firmly let her daughter know that such behavior was not acceptable. Tilden's phrasing, however, suggests that the reprimand might not
have been taken as seriously as its author intended. Tilden dutifully records
her mother's comment yet calls its authority into question. She writes,
"Mother says that us girls *must not* stand at the door and talk, especially
with young gentlemen it is a bad practice, she says and besides it does not
look well" (29 January 1827). Tilden distances herself from her mother's
rule. She involves herself only by the vaguely inclusive "us girls" and then
qualifies the importance of obedience. The rule of behavior is limited to a
particular speaker ("it is a bad practice, *she* says," emphasis added) and its
rationale weakened. What was a "bad practice," with all its attendant con-
notations of morally questionable action, becomes in the end a matter of
appearance: "and besides it does not look well."

A week later Tilden's journal entry about Boston's icy streets indicates how readily she would work around suspect appearances when their conventional interpretation was so far from her own. In such cases, Tilden found it relatively easy to separate appearance from interpretation and substitute her own interpretation as the more sensible one. This appeal to common sense, however, did not govern all circumstances. In Tilden's experience, rules for public behavior were one thing, rules for the private expression of character quite another. Her appearance of "temper" met with no such sympathetic interpretation. No matter how she configured it—whether through the lens of common sense, or of religion, or of fiction—it remained the one attribute that seemed to have a permanent, conventionally coded interpretation. The appearance of "temper" meant the insufficient cultivation of self-control, a failure of discipline and hence of character. The exemplary ideals in the ministers' sermons never displayed temper; neither, for that matter, did the heroines in domestic fiction. Jo March was a generation away, and while there were Hope Leslies to prepare the way, Sedgwick's character was defined by a good-natured impetuosity that resembled Tilden's "temper" only by its impulsiveness. And yet the impulse may finally have mattered more than the presence or absence of a controlled temper. In the novels Tilden read, appearances unfailingly worked against the fictional daughters, and yet their actions were always acquitted. Accustomed to reading about heroines who were frequently misinterpreted, Tilden learned to see how she as well might not be judged so critically, might indeed be interpreted sympathetically, if the incidents of her life could only be framed within the right narrative for the right reader.

JUDGING APPEARANCES: THE ROLE OF THE SYMPATHETIC READER

The reciprocal relation between character and reader is central to every novel Tilden noted in her journal. Whether the creation of Edgeworth, Sedgwick, or Roche, the main female character was guaranteed a sympathetic reader. Differences arose over how this sympathy was elicited, but in each case, the narrative directed the reader to interpret with care what the novels' characters had mistakenly judged. Every female protagonist struggled against misleading appearances; the duration and extremity of the struggle might well be said to define the difference between the gothic and the domestic novel. But in the end, female character was vindicated. Each author played her own distinct variation on this theme. Edgeworth's young women deliberately isolated themselves, choosing a self-determined solitude in which they alone knew their truth. Roche concentrated on the reader herself, using the narrator's voice to speak a privileged insight to the reader. And Sedgwick combined techniques used by both the gothic and the domestic writers. She added action to the central character's isolation and supplemented the sympathetic narrator with a sympathetic character within the narrative itself.

Sedgwick guaranteed the operation of a reassuring moral law within the universe of her novels. While appearances acted against her heroines, Sedgwick never let misinterpretation take effect. She pointedly refused to let the heroine's character suffer in the eyes of those around her but cleared her character almost immediately. At the same time, the characters never faced the self-defeating role of having to defend themselves. When their actions could not speak for them, another character stepped in as interpreter. For example, the narrator of *Redwood* lets us see Ellen Bruce in action, and although certain of her benevolent deeds are hidden from our sight, other characters willingly tell her story.[22] This is particularly the case with Deborah Lenox, the most clearly defined physical presence of the novel. When Debby appears, Sedgwick signals her entrance with a highly visual description. Her gestures are notable, her voice strong. Tall and lanky, she takes up a good amount of space and never fails to claim such space as her own. Her presence literally calls attention to itself, and she extends this power to others. Through her unselfconscious remarks, she directs all eyes toward Ellen's goodness and overrules any protest from her subject of conversation. Despite Ellen's discomfort, Debby unfalteringly maintains that in describing her virtues, she benefits the listener. She uses the moral of her story to countenance her praise of Ellen. Couching the following comments as an illustration of "the secret of happiness," she adopts the sanctioned way of publicizing Ellen's character: "The truth is, Ellen has been so busy about making other people happy, that she has no time to think of herself; instead of grieving about her own troubles, she has tried to lessen other people's; instead of talking about her own feelings and thinking about them, you would not know she had any, if you did not see she always knew just how other people felt" (368). Ellen clearly embodies the "true Christian character" so highly praised by the ministers, yet as a character in a novel rather than an illustration in a sermon, she is granted a life of her own. Ellen, who is a party to this conversation, attempts to interrupt Debby's comments and laughingly dismisses the words as flattery. At the same time, Debby is allowed to say for Ellen what Ellen cannot say for herself. She acts as Ellen's representative, the individual who makes public the actions by which Ellen's character can best be known. She concentrates on Ellen herself, paying no attention to the uncertainty surrounding Ellen's background. For Debby, the only past that matters is the individual past: what the person herself has thought and done.

Debby Lenox interprets the main character's actions. Should any appearance seem suspect, she points to its effect as the best evidence of the action's worth. Sedgwick places a truth teller within the story itself. In *Children of the Abbey,* Roche provides no such champion for her central character. She restricts truth telling to the narrator alone. The emphasis shifts to the reader. In the absence of an internal representative, the narrator rallies the individual outside the narrative to play that part. Alone among the characters, the reader knows the truth behind the protagonist's situation. She shares the narrator's omniscience. *Children of the Abbey* sharply divides the reader's from the characters' knowledge. The characters live in a chaos of suspicious appearances; the reader occupies a far different place. Given access to Amanda Fitzalan's thoughts, she knows exactly how misleading appearances can be.

Amanda is caught in every imaginable compromising situation. Her credibility is forcefully shaken in the eyes of the other characters, for appearances are always against her. She is seen reclining in the arms of a notorious scoundrel: the character who observes this does not know she is virtually captive and has taken refuge in one of her many episodes of fainting. Traveling alone to London, Amanda gives a simple reason for transacting her business in person. This reason is deemed insufficient to countenance the impropriety of her action, and those who judge her assume that her real business is to meet a clandestine lover. Unlike Ellen Bruce, Amanda is not given the benefit of an immediate explanation but instead suffers the judgment conventionally associated with suspect appearances. She is condemned by her suitor, ostracized by society, and forced into exile.

While the novel's characters unfailingly assume the worst about Amanda and act on their assumptions, Roche's reader never shares their perspective. The narrator guarantees the reader's sympathy *and* the reader's power. Only the reader can correctly interpret character because the reader alone is given a full and lavish description of Amanda's thoughts.[23] In the company of the other characters, Amanda is silenced, rarely allowed to say what

she means. Interruption characterizes her conversation. The narrative passages, however, foreground Amanda's thought. Roche presents this activity
of Amanda's mind both directly and indirectly. Lengthy sections are devoted
to Amanda's "reveries." Where her thoughts are not displayed directly
through her words, the narrator carefully shows the reader the "nature" of
Amanda's mind. We learn both what she thinks and what prompts her
thoughts:

> Solitude to Amanda was a luxury, as it afforded her opportunities of
> indulging the ideas on which her heart delighted to dwell. . . . From
> soothing [her father's] passing hours, beguiling her own with the ac
> complishments she possessed, and indulging the tender suggestions of
> hope, a pleasure arose she thought ill exchanged for the trifling gayety
> of the parties she was frequently invited to; she was never at a loss for
> amusement within Castle Carberry, or about its domain; the garden
> became the object of her peculiar care; its situation was romantic, and
> long neglect had added to its natural wildness. Amanda in many places
> discovered vestiges of taste, and wished to restore all to primeval
> beauty. (155) [24]

Amanda is here displayed solely for the reader's approval. Her solitude is
emphasized; she is alone in her thoughts. Her father, the one person with
her, is identified only as a passage of time. Her activities come under no observation except the reader's, who watches her choose "true" over "false"
luxury. Amanda admirably prefers a solitude of thought to a society of brilliant appearance; yet her luxury is no indulgence. She spends her days comforting her embittered father, continuing her intellectual development, and
pursuing her art in her careful nurture of nature.

Such a figure could only evoke sympathy from a reader named Anna
Tilden. The stark difference of circumstance faded behind more notable
similarities. Both revered fathers whose lives had been destroyed by a world
over which they had no control. Both preferred a luxury of solitude devoted to intellectual and artistic pursuits.[25] Both experienced persistent
hardship; both struggled against their misunderstood appearances. Fictional character met the lived reality of this particular reader. It would seem
that Tilden even borrowed Amanda's reasoning for her own position. As
with Amanda, the pleasure of solitary imagination far exceeded the "trifling
gayety of the parties she was frequently invited to." In Tilden's words,
"There is a party at S[arah] Blake's to night which we have declined. I do

not feel much if hardly any regret in not going to these parties" (17 December 1827).

Tilden's fascination with Roche's novel speaks directly to the role it provided for its reader. As reader, she was the individual who rightly understood the misunderstood character of Amanda. And in the process, her own circumstances were sympathetically highlighted. The process was not solely the province of gothic fiction; it identified the domestic version as well. In each, the young female reader was readily invited to identify with the main character. This identification extended beyond a vaguely imagined similarity. The connection between character and reader was drawn on the level of daily life. Whatever the extremities of the heroine's situation, her experiences were nonetheless punctuated by the particular dilemmas faced in the ordinary stretches of day-to-day existence.

From Tilden's perspective, for example, Edgeworth's treatment of physical beauty would have been highly attractive. Edgeworth rarely described what her heroines looked like; little visual detail is given. Female protagonists were defined by their responses, by their actions, by their words, but never by their physical appearance: no mention of gracefully curved lips or neatly diminutive feet; no trim outfits or angelic halo of hair. For a reader like Tilden, Edgeworth's omission offered a desirable alternative. Tilden consistently sought to free herself from the limitations of her physical appearance. Her journal records how difficult the process could be. Efforts to make appearance carry a certain significance met with ridicule. Her attempt, for example, to display the intellect of a high forehead resulted in the remark that she looked like a shorn sheep. When she stepped aside from fashion, she was told she looked "plain as a Quakeress." Her efforts to represent herself through her physical appearance ended in trivializing misinterpretations. No wonder then that Edgeworth's female characters proved attractive.

Edgeworth makes her virtuous young women meticulously careful when it comes to their appearance. Not only do they avoid calling attention to their physical characteristics, but they often refuse, literally, to appear. They would rather be absent, if their presence is likely to be read as a play for power. When Belinda Portman realizes how her appearance at social events is represented, she quickly curtails her public appearances and at one point leaves the city to avoid the interpretations that haunt her. Disappearing from the public eye, she hopes to avoid its speculations. In *Patronage*, Caroline Percy makes a similar choice when she refuses to take part in a fashionable evening of playacting, deciding to remain in the audience rather than display herself to potential suitors.

Unlike the daughters of more fashionably ambitious parents, Caroline prefers absence to a misleading appearance. Careful of both her manner of dress and her manner of expression, she refuses to call attention to herself. The reader, in fact, is given very little sense of Caroline's physical appearance. We are told she is "beautiful," but as the description makes clear, this beauty is not to be confused with particular physical attributes: "She was beautiful, and of an uncommon style of beauty. Ingenuous, unaffected, and with all the simplicity of youth, there was a certain dignity and graceful self-possession in her manner, which gave the idea of a superior character" (10). Her beauty is defined as quintessentially moral. It exists in terms of the admirable qualities she possesses. No physical specificity is given to this "idea of a superior character." The attributes remain abstractions, detached from a particular form; they are, in effect, their own appearance, requiring no further description.

The reader is provided with only one distinctly physical description of Caroline, and in this literal portrait, the moral character once again takes precedence, leaving the physical person undefined. After a fire at the family residence, Percy Hall, a new window is installed in the hallway, a window that portrays Caroline's heroic act of saving her nurse Martha from her burning bedroom. A work of gratitude undertaken by the nurse's son, the glass portrait shows Caroline "assisting [the son's] decrepit mother down the dangerous staircase" (70). The only other piece of information we are given is that the work was completed and set in place on Caroline's eighteenth birthday. An act of benevolence celebrates her majority. Nothing else is said about the window until long after the Percys have been forced to leave Percy Hall. Touring the estate with the insistently ambitious Falconers, Count Altenberg, whom Caroline will eventually marry, is immediately struck by the portrait window. His companions are equally as interested, and they begin to define Caroline's beauty in terms of the society beauties of the day. One person thinks it is "something like Lady Anne Cope," while another terms it "a great deal handsomer than any of the Copes ever were, or ever will be." Three other well-connected families are mentioned, and in this comedy of self-referential definition, we learn that one character thinks the portrait has "the Arlington nose," another that it has Lady Coningsby's eyes, another that it has simply the "look of Lady Mary Nesbitt." In this game of naming family resemblance, we in fact see nothing of Caroline, since the similarities the characters see are purely imaginary, and we are not privy to the originals in the first place. The scene ends with Count Altenberg claiming, "It is the most beautiful face, I ever beheld," only to be assured by the artist who happens to be on hand that it is "not nearly so beautiful as the original" (315). We are left with an undefined image of physical beauty, asserted, confirmed, but not visually described.

Edgeworth uses Caroline's physical invisibility to display her moral attributes. Distinguished by her "ingenuous sensibility" (569), Caroline refuses to adopt the fashionable persona of the inscrutable, marriageable young woman whose quickly shifting moods conceal her real feelings. Instead, she adamantly stands by her belief that anything other than absolute frankness is misleading. Arguing with her aunt over the proper behavior toward a potential suitor, Caroline maintains that she cannot in good conscience remain silent if she knows his interest will not be reciprocated by hers. Lady Jane, representing the society position, charges her niece with "indelicacy." For a woman to speak first is the grossest breach of decorum. Caroline responds that silence on the woman's part would in fact be "more disingenuous, more cruel," than simply assessing the situation and ending a dead-end prospect before the wrong turn was taken. While Lady Jane's charges of "indelicacy and impertinence" are troubling to the scrupulous Caroline, she prefers them to her own verdict. She would rather be criticized for "unwomanly" behavior than experience "self-reproaches for the want of candor and truth" (480–81).

Caroline's consistent adherence to "truth" does, however, involve her in a singular—and familiar—form of silence. When Caroline fears that her feelings reveal flaws of character, she carefully conceals them. Candor countenances silence as long as silence reflects self-control. This alone is the secrecy Caroline will practice. Speaking to her mother she says, "The best, the noblest, the most delightful feelings of the heart, may lead to the meanest, the most odious.—I have, within a few hours, felt enough to be aware of this.—I will leave nothing to chance.—A woman should never expose herself to any hazard.—I will preserve my peace of mind, my own esteem" (397). What those "meanest . . . most odious" feelings are she will not say. She keeps her own counsel. "Leav[ing] nothing to chance," she charts her course of action by her own standard. She will maintain self-esteem at all costs, and in the world of Edgeworth's novel, the cost is simply withdrawal. Caroline separates herself from the social functions that would require her to assume a prescribed persona. As one character comments, "Caroline

Percy never exhibits in public" (37). She avoids exposing herself to the hazard of appearance. Better to disappear than to run the risk of mis-interpretation.

Caroline stakes her action on an inner authority. It demands her full at-tention, and she will not disobey its sanctions. Her world is distinctly inte-rior; her actions appear only indirectly in a later representation (as with the portrait window). The reader fills the role of admiring observer. Revising Edgeworth's emphasis on the isolated, virtuous woman, Sedgwick high-lights her characters' authority by allowing them a far greater range of activity. Where Caroline Percy's greatest act is one of absenting herself, Sedgwick's characters use the authority of their own esteem to act directly on the world around them. Their representation also acts on the reader. In sanctioning the character's authority, the reader licenses her own.

In Sedgwick's novels, character emerges through a principled disobedi-ence. Established authority rarely merits acceptance. Sedgwick consistently shows it to be flawed, corrupting individual character rather than support-ing it.[26] To escape its mistakenness, the character adopts a new model of authority altogether. Hope Leslie is Sedgwick's exemplary figure in this challenge to an established order. In place of the patriarchal structure of the Puritan community, Hope substitutes her own sense of right action. She does not so much defy authority as dismiss it. When her attempts to work through society's channels fail, she readily breaks the law. Regardless of what the governor says, she will take her own way and act on her own convictions.

Sedgwick structures her novel as a debate between "liberty" and "author-ity." Replaying the question that plagued the historical John Winthrop, she uses her fictionalized version of his character to show the limitations in the patriarchal authority of the Puritan past.[27] Sedgwick's Winthrop is intro-duced as a model of disinterested benevolence. He seemingly weighs all de-cisions with admirable deliberation, seeing with an eye that might be called "objective." He acts the part of the wise counselor who readily keeps in mind the good of his community. This, at least, is the appearance Sedgwick gives him. His actions, however, suggest something different, for when it comes to judging character, he is dangerously deceived by appearances. Taken in by Sir Philip Gardiner's performance of piety, Winthrop believes him to be a committed Puritan, an ideal member for his community. Sir Philip plays his appearances well. He has studied exactly the right phrases, the proper mannerisms, that signal to those in power that he is indeed one of them. Fooled by his mimicry, Winthrop fails to see the unreformed rake beneath the Puritan garb.

Sedgwick's Winthrop is very much the voice of an unchanging order. His work is designed to maintain the particular status quo he has created. He seeks to overcome any threat to this order, whether it means splintering the Indian tribes to prevent them from forming an alliance that could challenge the Puritan community, or "taming" the wildness he sees in Hope Leslie. He refers to Hope as a "lawless girl" in need of a more rigid surveillance. Since she has, in freeing the imprisoned Pequot woman Nelema, literally broken the law, Winthrop's designation is not without meaning. Considering the future that may follow from her past, he seeks to control the direction her life will take. He proposes marriage as the means by which to bring Hope back under the arm of the law. In his world, marriage becomes a matter of state policy.[28] The person he has in mind as husband for Hope Leslie is a historian, a person whose life is regulated by the past.[29] Winthrop imagines that the historian, with his "modest authority," will frame his wife within the same regulations. When William Fletcher, Hope's guardian, disputes this choice, Winthrop's response suggests just how eager he is to confine Hope Leslie to the safe grounds of marriage. He proposes Sir Philip Gardiner as a ready alternative, even though Gardiner is a man whom he has only just met. Fletcher questions him on this seemingly hasty coupling, and Winthrop admits that his main concern is to marry Hope to someone with apparent authority. His language is revealing. He tells Fletcher, "I am impatient to put jesses on this wild bird of yours, while she is on our perch" (154–55).[30]

Hope is not so easily caught. Described by the narrator as "open" and "fearless" (122), she is compared to the uncontained beauty of nature. Distinguishing Hope from her readers, Sedgwick asserts that the seventeenth-century young woman was in fact more at liberty than her nineteenth-century counterpart. While such comparisons may well be more fiction than fact, Sedgwick's point is clear. In comparison with individuals "formed by art, restrained within prescribed and formal limits, and devoted to utility," Hope is free, and she acts accordingly. Convinced of Nelema's innocence, she does not hesitate to orchestrate her escape. This first experience of lawbreaking stands her in good stead, for when her cousin Everell Fletcher fails to free Magawisca, she readily puts another plan into action. Once again successful, she liberates an individual who, like herself, is defined by her freedom.

In the interest of this freedom, Hope chooses silence when it suits her needs, adopting secrecy as a mode of operation. She not only keeps secrets but willingly manipulates appearances to create them. For example, to cover her part in Nelema's escape, she first shapes her facial expression to meet the occasion and then weaves a narrative that establishes her participation in only the most metaphoric of ways. Writing to her cousin Everell, she relays the events that elapsed from the time of Nelema's trial to her "mysterious" disappearance. Reporting on the court scene, she gives the details of her testimony, re-creating the dialogue with apparent accuracy: "My testimony was extorted from me, for I could not disguise my reluctance to communicate any thing that could be made unfavourable to her.... I said, 'It was better to mistake in blessing than in cursing, and that I was sure Nelema was as innocent as myself'" (109). Her words, she tells him, carried little weight with the magistrates. They rebuke her for being "too forward" and then assure her that they consider her comments as no more than "the whistle of a bird" (109). Outside the courtroom, Hope no longer feels compelled to tell the truth. Claiming no direct knowledge of Nelema's escape, she reports only the conjectures of the community. She disguises her own role by blurring her response. She tells Everell that she was "awakened from a deep sleep," and on hearing the news that Nelema had escaped, she "trembled with surprise, pleasure, or whatever emotion you may please to ascribe to me" (110). Leaving him to interpret her response, she goes on to report a dream she purportedly had at the very time of Nelema's escape. She describes this "dream," complete with a conversation with Nelema, and asks Everell to expound its meaning. She then reports the servant Digby's remark that "an angel had wrought for the innocent old woman" (113).

In the event the clues are not clear enough, the narrator solves the riddle in the next chapter. Since the western Massachusetts community in which Hope was then living possessed no jail, Nelema was imprisoned in the magistrate's cellar. Hope, who was staying with the family, easily determined which key opened the cellar door and did not hesitate to use it when the time came. The dream she reports to Everell is in fact reality, and Digby's "angel" is none other than Hope herself. The narrator calls Hope's actions "bold, dangerous, and unlawful" but presents them as the natural consequence of Hope's character. Unaffected by the power of any external authority, she considers, not the law, but the spirit of her action. The narrator comments, "Hope Leslie took counsel only from her own heart, and that told her that the rights of innocence were paramount to all other rights, and as to danger to herself, she did not weigh it—she did not think of it" (120). Like Edgeworth's Caroline, Hope stands firmly by the decisions that respect her own sense of right. She refuses to follow society's rules when they stand in the way of "principle." But unlike her British counterpart, the counsel of her heart demands an active engagement in the world. Caroline keeps herself out of the public eye. She painstakingly scrutinizes every thought, refusing to act unless certain of the consequences. In contrast, Hope does not hesitate to enter and speak within any space, public or private, whether prison, governor's parlor, or courtroom.

In this war between liberty and authority, Hope clearly wins the battles as well as the sympathy of the readers. In a novel punctuated by "pattern women," Hope persuasively breaks the mold. She is self-determining without forfeiting her compassion for others. She is characterized by "habitual frankness" but harms no one with her direct speech. Refusing the model of passivity set before her, she does not defy or even criticize it but simply admires what she cannot herself be. She carefully shapes appearances to achieve her goals; yet the stories she creates are never credited as lies. Even when the magistrates discern the reality behind the appearance, they make allowances for her behavior. Not only is Hope graced with a sympathetic narrator and certain allies within the story, but she acts with impunity and her actions, in the world of this novel, take effect.

While Hope may well be the character who enjoys the greatest liberty, the conclusion of her story once again raises the duplicity of appearances. In the last chapter, Sedgwick provides the conventional ending but will not put it on display. Hope's story ends with marriage but receives little attention; it is one event among many. Its description, such as it is, lies buried within the narrator's final comments on the entire cast of characters. In fact, Sedgwick pointedly refuses to describe the wedding itself. She leaves that task to the female adolescents in her audience, whom she identifies in terms that both criticize and praise. They are "the misses in their teens," "the most indulgent class of our readers." "Indulgence" is a double-edged word; more frequently deemed vice than virtue, it nonetheless connotes sympathy. The "indulgent" reader is the least judgmental and the one most suited to understanding the interpretation of appearance. Sedgwick grants an opening to her indulgent readers' imagination. They are invited to "adjust, according to their own fancy the ceremonial of our heroine's wedding" (348). The choices are several: the reader can break the boundaries of time, imagining a nineteenth-century wedding for the seventeenth-century

character. She can revel in the conventional thoughts of wedding break-
fasts, bridal gowns, and wedding journeys. Or she can choose, as the narrative suggests she do, not to imagine the wedding at all, but simply to move
on to the next paragraph.

In Sedgwick's representation, Hope virtually disappears into marriage.
The single paragraph on the wedding makes no mention of Hope's name.
She is simply "our heroine." While her husband is not the safe choice of the
historian William Hubbard but the more mercurial Everell Fletcher, the
couple's immediate acceptance into the community suggests that, just as
Winthrop predicted, marriage would indeed put the "jesses on this wild
bird." Marriage ends Hope's story. The narrator would just as soon keep
this ending out of sight and quickly moves beyond that event to where a
story continues. Sedgwick concludes with the image of the young unmarried woman, but the image, of course, can no longer be embodied by Hope.
In her place stands the exemplary Esther Downing, a singularly interesting
character to bring the story of authority to its close. Leaving her story
where most of her readers lived, Sedgwick ends the novel by celebrating the
life lived independently of marriage.

The celebration renders an appearance ripe for the reader's interpretation. Focusing on character, the reader draws one conclusion; focusing on
circumstance, the reader finds a very different story beneath the appearance of Sedgwick's words. If character rules, then traditional authority is
reinscribed. Esther is everything that Hope is not: she embodies the lawful-
ness so highly prized by patriarchal authority. She is obedient to a fault.
When Magawisca is imprisoned, Esther refuses to help free her but instead
works to convert the prisoner to Christianity. The only freedom Esther en-
visions is one defined by obedience. The woman who remains unmarried
in this novel, thus, poses no threat to the established order, and in fact, her
actions in the narrative uphold it with unwavering devotion. The story of
circumstances, however, leads the reader to another conclusion. Sedgwick
ends with a moral, presented in no uncertain terms. Praising Esther's life
because it was not focused on one individual alone, Sedgwick tells her
reader "marriage is not *essential* to the contentment, the dignity, or the
happiness of woman" (350). Esther's world extends beyond the limited
realm of the married woman. Freed from the obligations of a single "home,"
she escapes the self-enclosed concentration on husband and children.
Sedgwick champions this life; marriage by contrast shows a flawed character. The woman, as wife, mistakenly "give[s] to a party what was meant for

mankind." The quotation closes the novel, and the reader is left to contemplate the implications. Esther takes the better part because her life of devotion benefits the greatest number of individuals. In this calculus of good, however, questions remain unanswered. Does the single life free her to live by her own authority, or is freedom bounded by the conventional province of Esther's "Christian graces" and "disinterested devotion"? Can the reader claim a freedom the exemplar cannot?

For Tilden, the question would press with increasing force as days of adolescent reading became days of adult employment. The story of the beneficent single woman, with or without the constraints of exemplary virtue, offered a luxury only the imagination could afford. But in 1827 when Tilden first read *Hope Leslie,* such luxury was still evocatively possible. Tilden was sixteen with two older unmarried sisters. Distanced from the prospect of her own adult life, she could turn to her sisters Sarah and Catherine. Like the characters Hope and Esther, they were just imaginably older. Esther's "disinterested devotion" might well seem akin to her sisters' participation in the Federal Street Church's Sunday school. The virtue of Sedgwick's character was found close to home, her agency apparent in the sisters' work of benevolence. Tilden herself, however, would appropriate this model only by a secondhand association. Her self-representation was far different from Sedgwick's character. Esther's calm acceptance of circumstance and unwavering faith in Christianity and its ministers would become increasingly untenable in Tilden's daily experience. As the adolescent became the adult, the definitions of freedom became fewer, dwindling to the strange and strained liberty of imaginative self-disguise.

Freedom is a markedly circumscribed commodity in Edgeworth's early novel *Belinda.* Like the other novels Tilden read, it foregrounds the interpretation of appearance and invites the reader to praise the character's principled action. Praise, in this case, may not mean sympathy. Belinda's course of action reveals a character in the process of perfecting itself; yet Belinda achieves perfection at the expense of understanding. The process conceals the character. The reader remains on the outside, increasingly distanced from Belinda's thought. She is an emblem of individual authority and right action, a highly desirable, and finally inaccessible, character. The reader is given a model in Belinda, one that Tilden found eminently useful. She represents a life the reader could imagine for herself—but only as a last resort.

The novel offers a most complex discussion of appearances. As with the later *Patronage,* this work champions the "reasonable woman," but unlike Caroline Percy, Belinda Portman develops her character out of her own experiences. Where Caroline is confirmed in her beliefs and lives only to enact them, Belinda is introduced as a character not yet fully formed. Her upbringing in the country (as opposed to the city) has given her a taste for books and "domestic pleasures." She is "disposed to conduct herself with prudence and integrity" (1); yet this disposition is seen as simply that, a possibility, an inclination. As Edgeworth's narrator tells us, "her character . . . was yet to be developed by circumstances" (1).[31]

While Belinda experiences her fair share of trying circumstances, the pivotal incident occurs early in the novel and effectively turns her disposition into an immutable part of her character. Her formation of character is precipitated by a masquerade, an evening of disguise. Planning to attend a masked ball with Lady Delacour, Belinda is first cast as the muse of comedy, while Lady Delacour assumes the figure of tragedy. Lady Delacour readily lets this decision become common knowledge among her society acquaintances. Their costumes thus provide a transparent mask. The other partygoers know the character of the individual whose face does not appear. However, Lady Delacour decides at the last minute to switch costumes with Belinda, and they arrive at the ball with their expected personae reversed. The partygoers, of course, have no knowledge of the change and assume that the appearance of each muse announces the presence of a particular person. Under cover of her unanticipated mask, Belinda hears words not intended for her ears. Made part of a conversation that takes her as its topic, she is characterized as yet another of the "catch-match maker" Mrs. Stanhope's nieces, schooled to be manipulated into a "good" (read "lucrative") marriage by an elaborately constructed artifice that lasts only until the wedding is safely over. Belinda is compared to goods that have been advertised widely and have become as cheap as they are common. She is likened to a gun that will not fire and to a house that will not sell. Caught in the middle of this conversation, Belinda keeps up her mask, disguising her voice to make certain her actual character is not revealed.

She can maintain the appearance for only so long, however, and when the muse of comedy joins her group, she pulls Lady Delacour aside and asks that they leave. Belinda protests that she only needs "air," but when Lady Delacour suggests the logical act of taking off her mask, Belinda refuses, not wanting to reveal her identity to those who had been talking about her. Lady Delacour, however, insists that the "mask must come off" (19). When Belinda finally agrees, her face becomes yet another mask as she quickly turns from deathly pale to a humiliated blush. Yet what truth does this blush reveal? It could mean either acknowledgment or repudiation of the role in which she has been cast. Clarence Hervey, the one individual whose opinion Belinda values, is also the one character to witness the unmasking. Seeing her response to the accusation against her, his response parallels hers. Effectively stunned by the recognition, he too is rendered immobile. Only Lady Delacour remains active, ordering her carriage, dispensing farewells, and making the necessary arrangements for their departure.

Once in the carriage, Lady Delacour advises Belinda to put on her mask once again. When Belinda begs that she be taken home rather than be forced to endure another masked ball, Lady Delacour encourages her to take a different course: "You have nothing to fear from me, and every thing to hope from yourself, if you will only dry up your tears, *keep on your mask,* and take my advice; you'll find it as good as your aunt Stanhope's" (21). From Lady Delacour's vantage point, masks are useful items and advice is itself an interesting mask. Belinda takes Lady Delacour's advice, though not exactly in the way it had been intended. After the scene of the masquerade, Belinda dons a mask of self-control behind which even the reader cannot see. For the rest of the novel she rules herself by principle. Acting on her deep distrust of appearance, she eventually merges with the abstractions she emulates. Her careful self-control serves well to mask any underlying turmoil. The reader is not privy to Belinda's struggles, and only rarely to her thoughts. We see the outcome in her always virtuous decisions, but we are given few chances to see behind her mask of self-control. The reader might well question whether she wears a mask at all, for her integrity should guarantee an appearance that needs no disguise.

Like Caroline Percy, Belinda refuses to "exhibit in public," and in the world she inhabits, the public is increasingly private. Her world grows smaller. She retreats from the fashionable world, retreats first within the Percivals' estate and then within Lady Delacour's house, and finally retreats within a self that offers few clues to its interior. As the novel unfolds, Belinda becomes more and more like a minister's example, her exemplary appearance created at the expense of the inner life. Whatever lies within cannot be expressed unless it perfectly matches the virtue being represented. In this way, Edgeworth plays her own game with appearances, essentially turning them into a mask that the character must never drop. In the end,

Edgeworth's lesson about appearance sounds a cautionary note. The safest way to avoid misinterpretation is to construct a singly dimensioned appearance that will tempt no one to look beyond it.

Whether by Caroline Percy's transparent absence or Amanda Fitzalan's misinterpreted presence, these novels call attention to the fact that appearances do not simply interpret themselves. They break apart the unthinking connection between appearance and interpretation, revealing any number of situations in which the conventional explanation of behavior is simply inadequate. An action may well not reveal the whole truth behind it, but the lie belongs to a codified interpretation and not to the event itself. These novels pose a radical challenge to the world in which their readers resided. If appearance carried with it no intrinsic meaning, if the assumed interpretation was more often wrong than right, then the individual might well assume the position of definitive interpreter and pursue actions that others would call into question. What these novels offered was a promise, risky but exhilarating, that the reader could study her own course and pursue her own action. Misinterpretations would occur as inevitably as they did for the characters she read about, but she trusted that sympathetic understanding would follow as it had for her fictional counterparts. In the end, what characterized the heroine was the fact that she was fully understood, a characteristic that said as much about the reader as it did about the heroine.

READER TURNS WRITER: THE FICTIONS OF THE JOURNAL

In her journal, Tilden's representation of misunderstood character echoed with the novels she had read. Whether writing her own questioned action or overturning a verdict rendered summarily against a friend, she borrowed her framework from fiction. While the ministers' sermon illustrations worked best for descriptions of sainted mothers and suffering invalids, the novelist's dramatization of anecdote was more appropriate for incidents of questionable behavior. Where individual action required explanation, Tilden found that sermons furnished only judgment. A story, on the other hand, provided the reader with a chance to think through the events as they unfolded and to discern the reasons behind the action. Fiction offered an understanding evaluation of events.

The "heroine" she sought to explain was not always, or even often, herself. She most readily turned "narrator" to another's "character," as is illustrated in the story she tells about her friend Ellen Sturgis.[32] A former classmate at the Emersons' school, Ellen came under sharp criticism within the Tilden household shortly after her brother's death. William Sturgis's sudden death had shaken the members of the Federal Street Church. The event had been entirely unexpected. No long-suffering patient enduring ill health, Sturgis was a promising young Harvard student who was killed in a freak boating accident. The situation was one to try the "true Christian character," and by the minister's assessment, Ellen Sturgis failed the test. After observing Ellen at tea with her family, a gathering at which Anna herself was present, Gannett concluded that Ellen's behavior suggested a highly inappropriate frivolity. He was not alone in his conclusion, as Tilden's comments indicate: "This morning at [the] breakfast table Mr Gannett was speaking of Ellen Sturgis, he seemed to think as some others do that she did not seem to think much of her brothers death, he said the evening before at tea table she did [not] behave as if she thought of it" (2 September 1827). Ellen's behavior had raised questions in other individuals' minds. Voicing his opinion, Gannett joined the company of observing critics. Tilden herself deemed her friend's actions "wrong" and had in fact spoken directly to Ellen about the very issue. In her entry for the previous day, Tilden described the conversation she had with Ellen, after Gannett left: "I had a good deal of conversation with Ellen, I think she wants more thought before speaking and acting, I talked to her pretty plainly which she seemed to receive very well, I think that friends ought to tell each other of their faults if they think they can be corrected. I meant to be a friend to Ellen" (1 September 1827). Troubled by Ellen's apparent thoughtlessness, she offered her friend frank criticism and counsel. Exactly what Tilden urged remains unrecorded, but her assessment of Ellen's situation suggests the content of the conversation. "She wants more thought before speaking and acting": Tilden's comments cover familiar ground, for within her own experience, her sister Catherine had often spoken to her about her unrevised remarks. Spontaneous expression was deemed problematic, and Tilden urged her friend to temper spontaneity with thought.

By Tilden's account, Ellen responded favorably to this criticism. Framed within the context of friendship, the remarks were intended for the friends alone. Their conversation was private; criticism was offered directly and with the single purpose of enabling "improvement." In this context, criticism was clearly distanced from judgment. Tilden would bring Ellen's "faults" to her attention, but she would not judge her by these faults, nor would she take her private criticism and turn it into a kind of public verdict. When others judged Ellen by her behavior, Tilden would come to her defense even when it ran the risk of including her in this judgment.

After Gannett made his comments at breakfast, Tilden reported that she promptly spoke on her friend's behalf. In response to his remark that Ellen "did [not] behave as if she thought" about her brother's death, Tilden records the following: "I said she did [think of it], then Mr G says 'she did' I replied yes sir." The terseness of Tilden's remarks conveys both the rhythm and inflection of the exchanged words. In contrast to the opening of the entry where Tilden writes that Gannett "was speaking" about Ellen, the ongoing commentary is here interrupted by the two-word exchanges: "she did," spoken by Tilden, then repeated by Gannett as a question, "she did[?]," and followed by Tilden's "yes sir." The final two words and her reflection on them suggest a distinct tone of voice. They are spoken hastily, as a retort, in the face of evidence that supports Gannett's, and not Tilden's, conclusion. The entry continues, "I replied yes sir for which I am sorry as Ellen did not say that she did, so I could not be certain. Mr G —— asked me if she acted as if she did and I said no, I could command my feelings no longer but left the table and went up stairs" (2 September 1827). Like a character in a novel, Ellen was liable to be judged negatively by those who simply observed her actions. Gannett's question is precisely to the point. When he calls attention to Ellen's appearance, Tilden can offer no argument against how those actions appear. What she knows, however, is based on more than observation. Her defense of her friend depends on information to which only she had access. Her conversations with Ellen, both from the previous night and a few days earlier, offered a different way of understanding Ellen's behavior. The conversation after tea had clearly led Tilden to believe that her friend was unaware of how others were interpreting her. Ellen's response also assured Tilden that this apparently thoughtless behavior was not as culpable as it seemed. When Ellen received Tilden's criticism "very well," Tilden saw evidence of a different character than the one attributed to her by critics like Gannett.

While this conversation offered an alternate reading to Ellen's character, an earlier exchange provided evidence that the sister had indeed thought about the brother's death. Tilden's first conversation with Ellen after William's funeral told a very different story than the one Gannett observed a week later. What Tilden records in her journal illustrates an individual who had not only thought seriously about her brother's death but who demonstrated her character in her remarks. Tilden writes, "Ellen spoke more of William today she says his death was so sudden, that it seemed more like a translation, she would not call him back, he is saved from the many troubles of this world" (23 August 1827). Tilden's remarks make clear that this was not an isolated thought on Ellen's part. She "spoke more of William today" continuing a conversation that had begun earlier. Her comments were none other than exemplary. Not only did she demonstrate a praiseworthy acceptance of death, but she added her own signature to the desired response. Giving William a sacred character, she described his death as "translation," presumably to heaven, in the biblically honored tradition of Elijah.

A week later when Tilden maintained that Ellen did indeed take her brother's death seriously, this conversation was most likely the evidence on which she drew. What Gannett witnessed was not the whole story. Extrapolating from other occasions, Tilden staked a claim on what Ellen had thought rather than on how her actions then appeared. She realized the danger in such a position. Prior thought did not guarantee its continuation in the present. She expressed her discomfort directly in her entry. Ellen had not that evening told her that she had been thinking about her brother's death. Tilden relied instead on comments that were a week old. As she wrote, "I could not be certain" of what Ellen thought, but a week later her assumption seemed borne out by Ellen's action. Staying in the Tilden household for a few days, Ellen appeared quite different than she had at the much contested tea. In contrast to that conversation, she was silent, a silence that Tilden felt she could clearly read. "In the evening we sat in the front parlour for some time. Ellen held my hand nearly all the time, she seemed rather sad upon the whole" (8 September 1827). There is no mention of conversation. The evening is described as a silent scene in which Ellen's gesture of affection is read both as the true indication of her feelings and as the tacit acknowledgment of her friend's sympathetic understanding.

Tilden served as both narrator and reader for Ellen's character. When the case was her own, however, it became exceedingly difficult to play all the parts. She clearly felt herself in the position of the misunderstood character, longing for the individual who would "rightly underst[and]" her, and fearing that her family members did not perceive the reality beneath her "ill-tempered" appearance. Even in the situation of Ellen's defense, Tilden found herself interpreted by others in a way that was not strictly her own. Recording what happened after she left the breakfast table, she reports that her sister Catherine followed her upstairs. Cast as a peacemaker, Catherine played a curious part. Hers was a familiar role from fiction: she was the individual who negated misunderstanding by correcting misinterpretation. She comes to report that Gannett did not realize the importance of the friendship between Anna and Ellen, and implies that he would not have ventured his comments had he known this. At the same time, Tilden's representation of the conversation with her sister suggests a certain discomfort with having become a character in her sister's narrative. Tilden first claims certain conciliatory words as her own—"I told her that I begged him to think no more of it"—but immediately revises this to reveal the source of "her" comments. She writes, "or rather she [Catherine] asked me if she should not say so and I told her yes." Catherine constructs a pleasing appearance to take back to the minister, providing her sister with the words by which to close the particular scene. Tilden acquiesces, but the terms were troubling. "To think no more about it" only perpetuated the problem of misinterpretation. What was required was further thought.

Tilden increasingly records the need for "further thought" in relation to her own situation. Longing for someone who would read her character as she had read Ellen's, she did not want to function either as the character in someone else's narrative or as the failed example in her minister's sermons. What she sought was a sympathetic reader; what she struggled with was a way in which to tell her own story. To become her own narrator was decidedly problematic. Authors spared their female protagonists the compromising situation of defending themselves. The narrator or a character within the story said for the character what she could not say on her own behalf. Unable to call attention to their own virtue without falsifying it in the eyes of the reader, these characters were gifted with the explanations from either the omniscient narrator or their fellow characters. For Ellen Bruce there was Debby Lenox; Lady Delacour spoke on Belinda's behalf. Even the outspoken Hope Leslie benefited from her narrator's comments.

In Tilden's case, such narrative intervention was problematic at best. As in the example with Catherine, when others told her story, it was no longer her own. Writing in late March 1828, she acknowledged her dis-ease: "Oh dear me I have felt pretty bad this day & dont think my feelings have been understood" (22 March 1828). She omits any explanation from this entry; she records neither what prompted her "feelings" nor who failed to understand them. A few sentences later she notes that she left the parlor earlier than usual in the evening. Her phrasing suggests varying interpretations of her action. She wrote, "I went to bed or rather up stairs early." To those who read appearance as an uncomplicated representation of reality, Tilden left the parlor to go to bed. For others, an early departure from the family gathering could well indicate a different meaning. She went up stairs because she had been misunderstood. The perceptive reader would see in her action something more than met the eye.

At the same time that Tilden longed for the right reader, she also felt another aspect missing from her daily narrative. Reflected in her many comments about "usefulness," the difficulty centered on the problem of "plotting" a life in which there were no precipitating events. What Tilden faced was an ongoing and seemingly endless routine of struggle. The family's financial situation remained unstable, as it had for several years. Her activities within the family offered little variation. There was seemingly no crisis on which a plot could turn and a narrative be structured. While the death of William Sturgis transformed Ellen into a potential heroine, Tilden's days offered no such possibility—at least not until 1829, and even then only slowly and largely in the retrospect introduced several years later.

From the vantage point of the early 1830s, 1829 was a year of signal importance in Tilden's life. According to a letter written to her minister in 1832, Tilden began doubting the existence of God and the likelihood of immortality during this year. The letter remarks that she had kept these doubts to herself for three years. At the moment in which she broke her silence and revealed this long-kept secret, she began to plot a narrative that would indeed turn on the interpretation of appearance. She initially tried out the role of virtuous silence, a role she had learned from both ministers and novelists. Like Caroline Percy, she drew on the secrecy of self-control in an attempt to regulate the feelings she would not let herself express. Reminiscent of the fictional character, she sought to preserve self-esteem through silence. Having faced the fact that, in Caroline Percy's words, "the best, the noblest, the most delightful feelings of the heart, may lead to the meanest, the most odious," Tilden sought to keep her wavering faith to herself. But unlike her fictional counterpart, there was no one to tell her story, no one to make her silence audible.

CHAPTER FOUR

Losing Faith and Finding Fiction: Tilden's Spiritual Crisis and Its Unorthodox Solution

From a world peopled by exemplary figures, one story had been missing. While Tilden heard the minister preach on heroically endured suffering and read the fictional lives of women defined by noble action, few words were spent on the individual who questioned God's existence, doubted immortality, and acknowledged how much she disliked her duty. If such a character were present, it would invariably be the "bad" example, the figure toward which Tilden clearly could not aspire. Her experience did not fit neatly into the narratives available to her.

The story of an extended crisis with no prospect of a satisfactory resolution was not the story told by ministers or novelists. To write it required invention. What Tilden could not draw directly from sermons and novels she had to create for herself. Writing her way out of a six-year period of spiritual crisis, Tilden borrowed the ministers' conventions and set them in the novelists' framework. Crafting a narrative out of her life, she constructed a fiction that wrote her into the "consistency of character" valued by novelists and ministers alike. Tilden's own experience was a world apart from the female protagonists she admired. While they triumphed over crises of relatively short duration, she faced years of uncertainty. In her experience, "crisis" was ongoing, woven so tightly into the events of her days that it had become inseparable from life itself. By the early 1830s, the Tildens' financial difficulties had settled into a permanent condition. Bryant Tilden continued to struggle in the unfavorable economic climate of the period. In 1830 he was listed in the Boston directory as "merchant" with a business address at India Wharf. Two years later he was still listed but with no street address. Two years later he left on what would be his last trading voyage.

By this time the Tildens had long ceased to rely on him for their sole economic support. Like so many other young women, the Tilden daughters

went to work with the skills they had. In 1830, Catherine, the oldest unmarried daughter, opened a school for young ladies in the Tilden home. Her
sisters Sarah and Anna, and eventually Zibby, taught with her. The more
teachers, the more students, and initially, a larger number of pupils was
preferable. Every additional student meant additional income, and the
family needed every penny.

There were not only the household expenses to consider but additional
financial burdens to shoulder as well. It was the familiar story of sisters
financing their brother's education. The only son, Bryant, was thirteen years
old in 1830, rapidly approaching the age in which his education would determine his future. In a letter Catherine received from Gannett in late January 1830, advising her to open a school, the connection between her work
and her brother's education was all too apparent. Gannett had offered to
oversee Bryant's education himself but had grown uneasy about his success. Looking at the prospect, he wrote to Catherine, "The observation of
the last week inclines me to the opinion that he had better go to school,
even at an expense of $50 a year." The sum was by no means inconsequen-
tial, as Gannett's phrasing suggests. The "expense of $50 a year" in real
terms meant at least three more students, since the Tildens charged $20 for
tuition.[1] It would mean additional work, additional constraints on their
time, but for the sake of their brother's "intellectual and moral improvement," they would take in as many students as they possibly could.

"YOU ONLY NEED TO REPRESS YOUR SENSIBILITY": THE TILDENS' SCHOOL FOR YOUNG LADIES

In a city where public education was celebrated often more in theory
than practice, private schools opened—and closed—with remarkable frequency. The Tildens' school fared better than many. Lasting for seven years,
it closed only because two of the sisters married and the other two were too
unwell to teach.[2] The school's success, however, brought little satisfaction
to its teachers. Burdened by both the amount and the type of work, they
suffered while the school prospered. When Anna Tilden again began keeping a journal in 1834, her first comments about her sisters suggest just how
costly teaching could be. Sarah, Catherine, and Zibby were all sick, and the
prospects of recovery for the latter two were uncertain. Catherine would be
an "invalid for some time," Zibby for "a long time" (21 April 1834). Tilden
herself wondered if she would be able to remain in reasonable health given
the physical exhaustion she experienced each day.

Their illnesses were worrisome on several counts, and not the least for the effect on the school. "I hope our schools will not suffer for this sickness in our family," she wrote, "it seems so unfortunate for us, but we must hope for the best." Such hope was hard to generate, however, given her "weariness" and her increased and undesired responsibilities. With her older sisters sick, the management of the school fell to her. By her account, it was interminable work, and by the time the day's duties were finished, she had little energy and less inclination to engage in any "leisure" activities. She longed for some other alternative and feared the consequences of their ongoing venture, but she could see no real possibility other than teaching school: "I trust that such weariness as I now daily undergo will not eventually make me sick also, for there is more than enough to be taken care of now. If we could devise any plan by which we might be supported without so much labour I should be very glad, for I dread our being confirmed invalids in consequence. I am daily so tired that I seldom feel willing to make the exertion to see my friends or talk with them" (21 April 1834). In the space of three sentences, she twice mentions how tired she felt. Wearied by her daily routine, the only alternative she could directly imagine was one of related monotony. From overworked teachers, she and her sisters would become "confirmed invalids."

While the sheer amount of work may well have been burdensome in itself, Tilden's weariness did not stem simply from her duties in the classroom. Bound to the work of teaching was another burden, a model of identity that for Tilden was anything but desirable. The "teacher" was yet another exemplary figure whose virtues were the very characteristics Tilden found most difficult to acquire. In his letter to her sister Catherine, Gannett envisioned an extensive course in self-denial:

You have the desire and have formed the habit of self discipline[.] You are willing to make exertions and sacrifices. Your nature is a concentration of warm disinterested affections. You only need to repress your sensibility. It must not only be regulated but be partially extinguished. I should say to you, as we say sometimes when there is more fuel, or more kindling stuff (excuse my homely language) in the fireplace than is pleasant—"There is too much fire—*put out some of it.*" You sympathize too strongly, if not too readily with others. You are too sensitive to mortification or disappointment. I mention these traits because they might be called forth by the circumstances of a school— (25 January 1830).

Judging Catherine eminently well qualified as a teacher, he reminded her that only one thing was lacking. Or rather, it was all too observably present. For her school to succeed, she must subject herself to a radical change, "disciplining" part of herself out of existence. Gannett told her to "repress" her "sensibility" and "partially extinguish" it.

Not simply a minor revision of character, this work meant denying a central part of herself. Her ability to feel with and for others was too prominent, Gannett suggested. She involved herself too fully in their lives. An overactive sensibility was her failing. On this point, Catherine could easily count herself in the company of numerous heroines from late-eighteenth- and early-nineteenth-century novels, though as Maria Edgeworth made clear in her characterizations, sensibility was to be kept within well-defined bounds. The ministers' sermons illustrated just how carefully those bounds were to be honored. Among the Unitarians, "sense" held greater sway than "sensibility," and while they argued that their version of character did not exclude the realm of sympathy, their alternative made clear that regulating sensibility meant repressing it. In the place of Catherine's too ready "sympathy," Gannett counseled a greater reliance on "disinterested affections."[3]

The two were anything but synonymous. "Disinterested affections" demanded a certain separation of self from circumstance. The individual remained at a distance, observing, helping, counseling, but not part of the experience as it was actually lived. "Sympathy," on the other hand, worked from a markedly different premise. The individual felt him- or herself in the situation with the other person. Self and circumstance were inseparable, and the individual's power came from the ability to identify closely with another individual's thoughts and feelings.[4] From Gannett's point of view, Catherine's sympathy was a far too powerful part of her identity. To succeed as a teacher, she would have to change her character.

Gannett's advice included all of the sisters, and it was no easier for Anna to follow than for Catherine. In her 1827–28 journal Tilden had written, "I love sympathy dearly and like to feel it for others" (16 July 1828). Three years later, the characteristic she praised would become, like her frankness, another trait to eliminate painstakingly from her self. The difficulty may well have been heightened by the very nature of what Tilden was required to teach. While no specific documentation of the school's curriculum remains, Gannett's 1830 letter provides a clue. Reassuring Catherine of her qualifications as a teacher, he lists the subjects she would be required to cover: writing, grammar, geography, arithmetic, French, and Latin. In each case, he reminded her that more study on her part would be necessary, but he assured her that an hour's study each night would happily keep her ahead of her pupils. He dispensed with any need to teach the "accomplishments": music, drawing, dancing, painting, embroidery, what had often been considered the staple of female education.[5] He divided this group of subjects into two categories. Music and dancing, he argued, should be taught by professionals. Painting and embroidery were, in his words, "seldom of any use" and could easily be omitted from further consideration.

What Gannett did include for further consideration was yet another aspect of the traditionally defined education for young women. Dismissing the art of embroidery, Gannett turned to the task he found decidedly more useful: sewing. He termed it a "knowledge . . . so important to a lady's comfort and usefulness" and assumed it could not be omitted from any successful school for "young ladies." The distinction he drew between sewing and embroidery is telling. Embroidery held no importance in Gannett's eyes. He neither saw it as art nor valued the creativity of design and skill of execution that stood behind a well-worked piece. From his perspective, time spent in fancy needlework was time wasted. The elaborately worked pieces that appeared on footstools, cushions, and wall hangings fell short of the shirts, chemises, and dresses that were assumed to mark the value of a woman's days.

In his description of the curriculum for the proposed school, Gannett placed sewing in a category by itself. It was given a special position, not the professional status accorded to music but a place of importance that divided the roles of male and female teachers as well as of their pupils. Separating it from the other subjects that the Tildens would be expected to teach, he clearly felt that its centrality to female education was unquestionable. It was the one area that he designated by the word "important."

Gannett, however, perceived one potential difficulty. Citing Catherine's "distaste to the needle," he questioned whether she would be able to teach sewing to her students. Although he assumed that a "daughter of Mrs Tilden" could not be "ignorant" of such important knowledge, he nonetheless hesitated to cast her as the instructor. He suggested she use her sisters instead. He commented, "some of you must know how to teach sewing." What he could not guarantee, and apparently did not consider, was whether Sarah or Anna or Zibby felt any less distaste for the work than did Catherine. Anna's comments on sewing in her 1827–28 journal suggest that, like Catherine, she begrudged the time she gave to this task. Given the choice between sewing and reading, there was, to her mind, clearly no choice. The book always came first, though "duty" rarely countenanced such a preference. That she could sew was clear; that she liked to sew was questionable. If indeed Catherine took Gannett's advice and assigned Anna the task of teaching the students to sew, it comes as no surprise that Anna grew to dislike the school with such intensity.

By the fall of 1834, she was no longer trying to make the best of their bad situation. Writing in her journal on the Sunday after Thanksgiving, she found little reason for gratitude: "My school I do so much dislike, its cares, its responsibleness, its duties, its many nameless disagreeable attendants" (30 November 1834). Her representation of her students is curious. In her list of "dislikes," they are simply one more item. Equivalent with "duties" and "cares," they are things, not persons. Drained of any individuality, they lack the most fundamental element of identity. They are "nameless." Tilden identifies them only as being "disagreeable."

By her description, it would seem that she had not only "extinguished" her sensibility but done the same to her "disinterested affections." Gannett's advice about the proper identity of the teacher echoes uneasily in Tilden's words. Her own distaste for teaching reveals just how problematic Gannett's assumptions were. His comments on what qualified a woman to teach strikingly illustrate what his particular society took for granted just as strikingly as Tilden's journal articulates the cost of these assumptions. From Gannett's point of view, teaching young women required no specialized training. Individuals, like Catherine or her sisters, who had spent some time studying a variety of subjects could readily take this learning and replicate it for their students. The few years of Latin or French sufficed to occupy the short amount of time that the next generation of female students would be allowed for their own study. In his letter to Catherine, Gannett repeatedly assured her that her own fragmented years of education were more than enough to qualify her for her position. An hour's study of French a night, an hour's review of Latin a day would, he maintained, make it perfectly possible for her to teach these subjects that, in his words, she had studied "a little." As far as the "elementary branches, writing, grammar, geography and arithmetic," he felt even less concern. "You could easily make yourself familiar with them," he told her.

Gannett's words reveal the opinion, still commonly held in the 1830s, that schoolteaching, and in particular the teaching of young women, was a task any literate woman could do. At a time when the concept of "professionalism" was beginning to emerge in law, medicine, and even Gannett's field of religion, certain occupations were marginalized, if not excluded.[6] Gannett took for granted that Catherine would require no special training in order to teach the subjects common to women's education. Where he felt special training was required, he simply removed those subjects from consideration. Music and dancing were to be taught by "professional masters." The Tilden sisters should clearly leave such work alone. In the case of the other "accomplishments," he dismissed them out of hand. Sewing, he maintained, would more than amply fill the void.

Looking back to the school Catherine herself had attended, the difference is striking. Instruction in sewing was markedly absent from the Emersons' school. Given their Harvard and Latin School backgrounds, their emphasis lay elsewhere. Although William and Waldo Emerson had as little specific teacher training as did Catherine, they taught from the base of a decidedly more systematic education than any of the Tilden daughters had experienced. The Emersons could look to their years at Harvard as well as their earlier experience at Boston's Latin School. The Tildens could look to intermittent years of schooling, in a variety of places from a variety of teachers for sporadic lengths of time. Unlike that of the Tildens, the Emersons' formal education was continuous. It had never been interrupted because of household duties or economic considerations, even though the Emerson household was no better off financially than the Tildens. And while William opened his school as a way of financing his younger brothers' educations, their education had never been purchased at the expense of his. Even in an age in which education was far less systematic than our understanding of the curriculum today, the Emersons' education was unquestionably more coherent, directed by a well-defined goal and sanctioned as an endeavor of critical importance to its society.

Boston prided itself on its interest in and the availability of education, but the early decades of the nineteenth century revealed sharp distinctions drawn by lines of gender and class.[7] Education was an undeniably expensive project. While there were numerous free public primary and grammar schools, the situation for children over the age of eleven changed dramatically. For boys, both the Latin School and the English High School provided "free" education, but the schools were not equally available to all. Admission was highly competitive, and the boys who had been educated privately generally edged out the students who had attended the public, and more crowded, grammar schools.[8] For girls, private education was virtually all that was available after grammar school. For a few brief years, the city operated a public high school for girls, but it was closed in 1829 as a measure of economy. Arguing that its pupils came largely from families who could afford to pay private tuition, Mayor Josiah Quincy cut short Boston's early attempt at providing a high school education for young women.[9]

For those who could afford private schooling, the choices were many. This proliferation of choice, however, says more about instability than variety. In an age when increasing numbers of young unmarried women needed to provide economic support for their families, teaching became one of the few jobs readily open to women. Here again the issue splits along class lines. While the very necessity of working inevitably lowered a woman's class standing, where women worked was largely determined by the class into which they had been born. For example, domestic service as well as factory work would have been unthinkable for the Tildens. In 1830, still on the borders of the merchant class, they would work in their own home and in an occupation that kept them within the pale of "respectability." Teaching announced the family's former standing; they had once been able to send their daughters to the schools their daughters now ran.

Although "respectable," teaching remained an emblem of economic distress. It was not a "profession" but an expedient. Not expected to work for money once they married, middle-class women taught school in the years between being daughter and becoming wife. It was an interim activity, defined as a short-term occupation in which young women practiced a new form of usefulness. This "interim," however, might well endure a long time, if not a lifetime.

For Tilden, every year in the classroom brought yet more reason for discouragement. As the school became a permanent fact in her life, so too did her spiritual crisis. By her account, her first doubts dated from the year before the school opened, but by the fourth year of the school's existence, the two were inseparably connected in her mind. Were her faith stronger, she told herself, her dislike for the school would be weaker. Evaluating her undutiful response to her daily activities, she read her reaction as a verdict on her spiritual estate. It reflected another verdict as well, the state of the family finances. The following passage, quoted at length from an entry written in late June 1834, makes clear just how much matters of faith entered into matters of identity and how both were framed by questions of economy:

Is it wrong for me to feel as I do about school, my pride I know is a good deal touched, and yet why should it be? what matter if others don't think as well of us for keeping school—in truth not any matter, but I have not as yet found out [how] to get rid of all my disagreeable feelings. I feel *now* more discouraged than ever, and more inadequate to the task. I do not take hold of it with a good and free spirit, and I am not happy in it. I think if I felt *well* in health my mind would be in a better state about it, but I am so utterly weary, that I know I am not agreeable and good tempered, but this is not sufficient excuse. Then why don't I do differently? There are many circumstances about the family and my friends which do disturb me exceedingly. I must try for a more firm reliance on Heaven, and as Mr G[annett] said this afternoon, I must neither despair or despond. (29 June 1834)

Reminiscent of the earlier journal, this passage cites "temper" as one of her major faults. She offers an explanation for its occurrence by citing her "weariness," the word that rings like a refrain throughout the 1834–35 journal. Were she in better health, she asserted, her mind "would be in a better state." Looking to her physical distress to explain her mental malaise, she attempted to vindicate herself from criticism. The attempt failed, however, for while it might explain her behavior, it could not excuse it.

Explanation itself failed in this passage. Each attempt led to the same conclusion. No matter how sympathetically she presented the situation, every interpretation fell short, turning into an excuse that by definition would be insufficient. Acknowledging that her "pride is a good deal touched," she revised this comment into a statement of self-blame by asking the rhetorical question, "and yet, why should it be." She followed this up with another question, also meant to be rhetorical, also revealing the powerful reality she could not reshape with her words. "What matter," she asked, "if others don't think as well of us for keeping school." To Tilden, it obviously mattered a great deal, but she would not let herself entertain this viewpoint as an acceptable one. She concluded the question with an effectively silencing response. "In truth," she told herself, "it is not any matter."

By her assessment, this "truth" was riddled by uncertainty. She had not yet "found out" a way of ridding herself of her "disagreeable feelings." While she could explain them, she could not change them. She also found it impossible to alter her behavior. "Why don't I do differently," she asked herself and began her answer with a cryptic explanation. She mentioned unspecified "circumstances" that "disturb[ed]" her "exceedingly." Such a comment, however, could provide no adequate explanation. By the logic of her ministers, difficult situations were designed to strengthen character, not paralyze it. In the next sentence she turned to what she must "do differently." Her mandate came from religion. It spoke the final word in this entry, providing answers that neither explained the situation nor excused the individual. What she lacked was faith, here defined as the ability to separate herself from her circumstances. She told herself to "try for a more firm reliance upon Heaven." And when all else failed, she could turn to her minister's words.

Those too would fail, for three months later "despair" is the tone that permeates the journal. By late September, her ever present "weariness" had become weariness of life itself. Surveying her life, she concludes that she lived only because she feared death:

> It seems to me that if I could only conquer the "*fear* of death, of all most base," I should be glad, certainly willing to lie down and die! What have I to live for? My parents have children enough, better than I am who will love and take care of them. I have no other, and never shall have any ties more binding than now, and I am unhappy and discontented nearly all the time. Is this right, need it be? But I can't feel a permanent interest in anything. I am not an equal in character or intellect, with those whom I would be, and I really feel alone in myself. (28 September 1834)

Tilden's self-characterization hinged on isolation. She felt "alone" in herself. Her only connection to others no longer seemed fundamental but had become hauntingly inconsequential. Her parents, she commented, had "children enough." The one "binding tie" of daughter to parents and sister to sister no longer held, and in its dissolution, she questioned the value of her existence.

REVISING FAITH: TILDEN'S QUESTIONS AND UNITARIANISM'S ANSWERS

Tilden's response reflects the distinctly Unitarian framework in which she could articulate her spiritual crisis. Her ministers preached a reason-based faith. Intellect presided, rigorously governing what could be accepted as "true religion." Responding to the evangelical concept of conversion, for example, Unitarian ministers leveled their favorite charge of "irrationality" against its defining element. They argued that a sudden and complete change could not be trusted. Any substantial difference in an individual's life occurred only through the deliberate and painstaking process of revision known as the "formation of character" and preached under the "doctrine of probation." Human life was a relentless struggle. The individual used each difficulty as one more occasion to form and re-form character, and the process never ended. As Henry Ware Jr., one of the strongest voices of probation, told his congregation, "Not an hour can pass, nor a plan be devised, nor a deed done, nor a word be spoken, which ought not to be affected, determined, by the consideration that it bears on our probation. For, whether slight or momentous, it affects our character; and character is the one thing essential" (*Works*, 3:416–17).

The prospect offered Tilden little comfort and less hope. Framing a "rational" response to her mounting despair, Tilden discovered the inadequacy of explanation. Fiction functioned better than sermon; yet her age— a young woman in her twenties, no longer the novel-reading girl of late adolescence—demanded that she shift her energy to replicating the minister's narrative. Unlike her counterparts in the evangelical tradition, she could not hope for a conversion experience. What centered their lives would not hold hers together. Looking to the future, she saw a continuous fragmentation of experience, an unbroken repetition of the present.

Tilden longed for the certainty provided by conversion yet could practice only the uncertainty guaranteed by probation. She worked diligently with the Unitarian guidelines for facing a spiritual crisis, but her efforts yielded troubling results. She could imagine no particular end to her crisis, only multiple techniques to be repeatedly reworked. In 1829, as she began to question her faith, her sermon notes grew longer. She turned first to the minister's words, imagining that her faithful record of them would provide the best answer to her questions. When sermons failed, she turned to conversation, seeking in the minister's study what she could not gain from the pulpit. To effect the change in character she felt she so desperately needed, she systematically continued her work of putting the ministers' words into practice. Every effort was carefully framed by her understanding of how the individual was supposed to answer questions of faith.

Even her earlier decision to keep these doubts to herself for three years reflected a common Unitarian guideline. Whether she had read it in Ware's *Formation of the Christian Character* or heard it from Gannett's or Channing's sermons, secrecy was one strategy essential to the individual's probation. In Ware's devotional manual, he instructed his readers to keep their doubts to themselves: "Say nothing of your thoughts and feelings to any, but one or two confidential friends" (*FCC* 42).[10] And even these friends were expendable. In his delineation of the ideal spiritual struggle, the individual worked solely with God. "The best religious character [was] formed in retirement, by much silent reflection, and private reading and prayer" (*FCC* 42). Tilden took precisely this approach, and when she felt no closer to a solution in 1832 than she had in 1829, she turned to her minister. This too was countenanced, and in fact recommended, by Ware. After advising the reader to stay away from conversation, he provided a certain framework in which some discussion could occur: "Shun . . . rather than seek, much communication with many persons. But some counsel and encouragement you may need. Apply, therefore, to your minister. He is your legitimate and true counsellor" (*FCC* 43). In her first letter to Gannett, Tilden included just such a justification. Telling him that she had studied William Paley's *Evidences of Christianity,* that she had been "anxious" to attend all church services, and that she had bided her time hoping her uncertainty would gradually dissipate, she concluded that her silence had lasted long enough. And thus she made her "confession," asking for his guidance on the problem she could state but not solve.

She identified her problem as precisely a matter of perception. She wrote to Gannett, "It seems to me that my difficulty lies not in the *want of proofs,* but in not being able to fasten these proofs with the conviction of *realities* upon my own mind" (September 1832). Earlier in the letter she had pointed to two issues of concern: they were none other than the cornerstones of Unitarian faith. She could no longer take its major premises for granted. She doubted God's existence and questioned whether immortality was not finally a play on words. On the first count, she told Gannett that when she put the question plainly, she could not produce the "right" answer. "But no," she wrote, "when I again asked the plain question, do I feel satisfied about Christianity (and shall I tell the truth) the existence of a——oh I can't write it! I cannot give an honest assent."

Unwilling to write out her doubt in full, she nonetheless revealed its full extent. Nor could she hide her serious reservations about immortality. Sending Gannett's words back against him, she questioned a troubling inconsistency in his preaching. She reminded him of one of his vestry lectures in which he told his listeners that the Greek word used in the New Testament to describe "everlasting punishment" meant simply "of long duration." Her next question was fatal to his argument. "Is not," she asked, "the same word used when *eternal life* is mentioned? if so why then would you say that *eternal* life is sure?" [11]

With immortality uncertain and God's existence questionable, there was little hope that she could find answers in the doctrine of probation. The difficulty was further compounded by the uneasy split between faith and intellect expected of the believer. Tilden herself felt this keenly. In her first letter to Gannett, she acknowledged that she did indeed see a solution to her problems. Were she to "become calm and quiet," she wrote, "I should then find that I had needless anxiety." But this was precisely the identity she could not create for herself, for to do so she would have to, by her own admission, "give up thinking." Calmness, the "quiet self possession" of which Ware spoke, was purchased at the price of thought, and in 1832, Tilden would not make the trade. Identifying herself as an individual who had always required a "mathematical demonstration" before committing herself to any belief, she faced a crisis of faith that invariably called her own identity into question. What Unitarianism asked of her she could not give, but without its sanction she felt herself cut off from others. As she wrote to Gannett in 1833, what her spiritual crisis had taught her was how to conceal her feelings. This was, she admitted, the "one thing" she had learned in the four-year span. While she had not discovered how to change her character, she had learned how to conceal her identity. She split her life not only between faith and intellect but between what she revealed and what she concealed.

She herself was not always certain where to draw the line. In her 1834–35 journal, she explored a number of ways of accounting for her feelings of crisis. Each remained inadequate, and some she would only admit tangentially. Her most common explanation was health. Were she not so "weary," she could meet the daily dilemmas without despair. What she says less about as cause for her difficulties and what she finally would not admit as the largest part of her problems was the economic disarray in which her family lived. With apparent good humor she would comment that she wished she did not have "to look at both sides of a sixpence before spending it." She did not, however, go further and make the troubling connection between the specific issues of her spiritual crisis, the particular realities of the family's situation, and the unsettling doctrine of probation. That Tilden's doubt centers on the key elements of probation comes as little surprise given the promises made by this particular doctrine. The other half of probation was compensation, and the ministers did not scruple to suggest that life in heaven would more than offset any material hardships on earth. While they were careful not to pave the streets of their heaven with literal gold, they nonetheless implied that the "final good" waiting for the obedient individual was distinctly substantial.[12]

That such a promise would prove attractive to Tilden is readily apparent. A life without financial worry might well serve as her most concrete definition of heaven. But problems arose with such prospects. An emphasis on money was always a problem for Christianity, and it was no less a part of Tilden's own uneasiness about connecting her crisis of faith with her family's crisis of finance. And even had she learned to rationalize the integral place money occupied in her probationary state, one haunting possibility remained. The doctrine of probation itself might simply be one more rationalization among many. Could the ministers deliver on their promises, or would they simply turn bankrupts like her father?

Despite her efforts, she could not make faith, intellect, and experience merge. While she could follow the Unitarian arguments for the proof of God's existence and admire their internal consistency, she remained outside the system. It made sense in its own way but not in the lived reality of her experience. The case of immortality was even more problematic. The conclusions drawn by the ministers obeyed a logic that was not her own. She questioned the concept on the basis of mistranslation: did the Greek word really mean "forever"? She was disconcerted by the seeming circularity of the ministers' argument when they grounded immortality on the human desire for it. From her own perspective it was all too evident that desire had little to do with what did or did not exist. Simply wanting an alternative to teaching by no means guaranteed that such an alternative could be found. There was no reason to expect that the case with immortality was any different. What Tilden all too often discovered was that the ministers' words finally did not speak to her situation. As she wrote to Gannett, politely thanking him for loaning her some of his sermons, "I have just finished reading your sermons, for which I sincerely thank you, at present they are not the comfort to me which I had hoped" (15 March 1834).

Tilden's spiritual crisis may well have been compounded by yet another dimension of certain Unitarian assumptions about the spiritual life. In the world they presented in their writings, the ministers created their own versions of spiritual crises and neatly divided them across gender lines, a particular crisis experienced by men, another by women. This division was particularly evident in the religious fiction of the period. Henry Ware Jr. once again provides one of the best examples. In his pamphlet *The recollections of Jotham Anderson*, first published in 1824, Ware detailed the religious experience of two individuals. In the case of Jotham Anderson, whose memoir the work ostensibly is, the story provides a pointed moral against the dangers of evangelical Christianity. Taking his character, the young Anderson, to his first job as a village schoolteacher, Ware immerses him in a community whose life centers around revivals. Anderson himself, we are told, comes from a family in which faith assumed a "calm and subdued tone" (*Works*, 1:15). In contrast, Anderson's new environment presents him with a fervor he had never before witnessed. Noting the vast difference between his version of faith and the community's, he begins to question which was the "true religion." His uncertainty leads to a spiritual crisis, which the revivalists in the story clearly assume will end in conversion but which Ware neatly resolves by having Anderson turn to the study of Scripture. Anderson is saved by this solitary study of the word and immediately decides to leave school teaching and become a minister, unquestionably of the Unitarian variety.

For Ware's audience, the story was a familiar one. Ministers often started off teaching in village schools, and Unitarians were often created by an earlier negative experience with the Calvinism resurgent in the revivalists.[13] The young man's path was clearly delineated and firmly grounded in particular action. He resolved his crisis by stepping into the pulpit. This, however, was not the only story of spiritual crisis in Anderson's "recollections." Taking him into his ministry, Ware introduces the teacher-turned-minister to a woman whose life played out a distinctly different crisis of faith. Anderson meets Mrs. Holden when she is near death. Her life has been defined by suffering. Unlike Anderson, she had no "childhood faith." She was not "properly impressed with religion," we are told, largely because her stepmother failed in her maternal duties. The situation goes from bad to worse: she marries an abusive husband, gives birth to four children, and watches all but one of them die slow, painful deaths. Her first glimmerings of faith occur thereafter. When her minister prays, she experiences a gentle "awakening" that sends her back into her unhappy home to suffer patiently but hopefully. When her husband finally abandons her and their single living child, she moves to the village in which Anderson preaches. By this time, she is close to death, but Ware assures his reader that her life has been full. Her greatest happiness consists in her conversations with her minister about "the light, the comfort, the promises, the peace of the blessed Gospel."

Mrs. Holden dies in peace, with no doubt that the promises of the gospel would be fulfilled. She is the epitome of the patient sufferer and could well be said to enact Ware's vision of the "docile disposition." Her crisis, unlike Anderson's, is defined by the issue of obedience. In youth, she failed to learn that essential lesson. The consequences of her neglected childhood weigh heavily on her character, and through no fault of her own, she bears the burden of the untaught lessons in "womanly duty." Her faith emerges only through experience *and* the minister's guidance: her children die and her minister counsels. For her, the inconsistency of certain doctrines is not significant. What she needs is consolation; her religion is based solely on the faith that could readily separate itself from intellect.

Tilden's difficulty in making this separation reflected both her experience and its difference from the normative story of the woman's spiritual crisis. If anything, her doubts were closer to Jotham Anderson's. Like him she questioned the faith that had been taught to her; like him she turned to the study of Scripture. But unlike him, she was barred from the pulpit. Where he could turn his study of the problem into his vocation, Tilden had no such alternative. The choices available to her were in fact much closer to Mrs. Holden's. She could become the patient sufferer. She could set aside the hard work of articulating faith, delegating that task to her minister. She could regulate her conversations so that they that emphasized the consolatory power of religion over its arguments. These were clearly the choices she was expected to make, and she worked relentlessly to find a way of making them her own. While she could not accept them without alteration, she hoped to find a way of reconciling her words with her ministers'.

TILDEN'S 1834–1835 JOURNAL: STYLING FAITH THROUGH FICTION

Tilden's ongoing and complicated work of revision suggests the double-edged power of the governing conventions. Although the ministers' models imposed an identity she could not assume, they also offered material with which she could work. Designed for their readers' use, these models were certainly prescriptive but not necessarily proscriptive. Twentieth-century readers have mistakenly attributed a rigid inflexibility to the minister or novelist of "sentimental" fictions. Their readers in fact proceeded in piecemeal fashion, borrowing the elements that best fit their circumstances. The imagined possibilities, whether in sermon or novel, were readily shaped and reshaped by their readers. At its best, such revisionary work yielded creatively complex ends; the highly skilled and experienced reader crafting her own interpretations out of the words she read and heard. Words authored by one individual could be appropriated by the reader for her own authority. Even in the midst of a narrative that ostensibly bound the self, the reader could write her way into a different place. If the master's tools could not dismantle the master's house, they might, and indeed could, radically redesign its interior.

Tilden's 1834–35 journal largely reflects this attempt. Working with the pattern set out by her ministers, she undertook what she called the "work of reformation" (30 November 1834). Initially turning to the power of the good example, she filled her entries with exemplary characters. In all cases, these individuals were noted by Tilden for their ability to suffer without complaint. Whether facing their own death or the death of loved ones, they quietly accepted their situation and looked resolutely, as Tilden herself could not, to the "hope of Heaven." She praised them for their singleness of purpose; she used their lives to remind herself of the "correct" response to hardship. Recording the death of Catherine Gannett, her minister's niece and a close family friend, she turned to a conversation between Gannett and herself in which he described Catherine's death. In the best nineteenth-century fashion, it was remembered as a "beautiful" death in which the dying individual embodied unwavering faith. In Gannett's description of the death, Tilden found a particular clue to her friendship with Catherine. She writes, "I never loved her more than now, for I feel that I never understood her so well before." What she understood was, in her words, Catherine's "remarkably consistent and natural character." Her language echoed the minister's. Consistency of character was highly prized, and given Tilden's next comments, it is clear that Catherine Gannett's consistency was precisely what the ministers praised. Tilden writes, "She sought her Heavenly Father with real earnestness and, she found the object of her wishes. *He* was her stay and support in her severest moments" (20 April 1834). Tilden singled out the characteristic with which she herself struggled most. While she too might be said to have "sought her Heavenly Father" with real earnestness, unlike Catherine Gannett, she had not found the "object of her wishes." What Tilden hoped to experience, but what remained problematically elusive, was the certainty provided by an unquestioning trust in God. She might look to God as her "stay and support," but she continued to see only the prospect of unrelieved suffering.

She hoped to reap the benefit of the "excellent lesson" provided by Catherine's death. "It seems," she said, "to have given me a more determined

purpose for doing than I have had before." This seeming possibility, however, was not borne out in the months to follow. Although she continued
to read the right lessons out of her daily events, these correctly phrased interpretations remain pointedly separate from the descriptions of her own
feelings. In the first several pages, in fact, she does not mention her feelings
at all. The absence is significant, for her opening sentence of the journal
had stated its purpose as precisely such expression of feeling. She had written, "There are times when I think it may do me good to see my own
thoughts and feelings expressed, I may then have a clearer idea of what
I am" (20 April 1834). Writing for the sake of understanding herself, she
firmly established the connection between expression and identity. Even as
the journal moved toward describing exemplary figures and away from an
articulation of her own feelings, she nonetheless pointed to the importance
words played in comprehending character. She claimed that her conversation with Gannett had given her a greater understanding of his niece. In
turn, she envisioned a further consequence of their discussion: his words
about Catherine's character would help her to reshape her own.

In the process, however, it became exceedingly difficult to maintain an
open expression of her "thoughts and feelings." Her initial declaration of
intent glaringly conflicted with the Unitarian model she was attempting to
follow. In contrast to the open-ended course she set for herself, it counseled a much more structured path. Where she initially thought to use writing as a way of discovering her identity—of finding out through words
"what *I am*"—the Unitarian model of self-examination demanded a very
different process. "Identity" was not so much to be discovered as revised.
Certain "thoughts" were to be studiously avoided, others to be as carefully
cultivated. Rather than expressing feelings, the individual was expected to
"conquer" them. The language is the ministers'. It was what Gannett had
told Tilden's sister Catherine when he advised her to open a school. It was
what Ware told his audience in *Formation of the Christian Character*. The
self-discipline they advocated was designed to silence particular aspects of
an individual's identity. To achieve "consistency of character" meant sup-
pressing a wide range of particular thoughts and feelings.

In the first months recorded by the journal, Tilden's attempt to foster
such consistency resulted in a clear division between the answers she knew
were "correct" and her own unresolved questions. She was quick to read
the moral out of any occasion. She would write a hymn of praise to home
or carefully note that her family's difficulties were the "best trial" for them.
In such cases, her language plainly echoed the words from the pulpit:

"amidst all our troubles we have great comfort in the happy home which we possess"; "I am sure we ought not to complain, and is not this the best trial for us" (21 April and 15 June 1834). She struck the right note, but in each case, the words bred discord with the sentences around them. One passage celebrated home, calling attention to how "united" her family was and how firm was their respect for each other; another pointed to the clear unhappiness facing individual family members and the real reasons for calling respect into question. Describing her father, Tilden writes, "Oh may our Heavenly Father, *guide* and *guard* him, may he see things as he ought, and may he be the noble creature, he was made to be" (30 November 1834). While the specific questions surrounding Bryant Tilden's morality remain unknown, his daughter's concern spoke plainly against the myth of "unity" she had earlier created.

Throughout the first half of the journal, Tilden worked relentlessly to merge her daily events with the ministers' mythic world of Christian heroism. Every effort only furthered the division between her world and theirs. The celebration of Christian character was transformed into a condemnation of herself. The words of Christian consolation brought nothing but a greater feeling of alienation. Writing in June, two months after she began the journal, she admitted that she felt "more discouraged than ever." Discouragement in this case was closely tied to her increased sense of disparity between her own identity and the character she praised. Defining herself as "inadequate," she once again tried to fit herself into the Unitarian model. "I must try," she told herself, "for a more firm reliance on Heaven" (29 June 1834).

A month later, such issues of effort were out of the question. Her fears about illness had been realized. She breaks off one of the shortest entries in her journal with the words, "I do not feel well enough to write any more" (27 July 1834). Perpetually failing to find the Christian consolation that her religion promised, she took up the identity that would perhaps provide reassurance at last. As with her friend Catherine Gannett, physical suffering might well create the situation in which reliance on God finally became a possibility she could realize. For the month of August her family scraped together the one hundred dollars it would take to send her to the most picturesque places in New York State. With aunt, cousin, and minister, she embarked on a month-long journey designed to restore her to health. Journal entries end. The only piece of writing surviving from this period is a letter to her mother written at sunrise on Lake George. Her exclamations over

the beauty and her protestations of cheerfulness speak directly to the setting but could not readily be carried back to Boston. When she resumed
writing in her journal in late September, she expressed only greater despair.
She questioned her importance in the family and recorded her feeling of
utter isolation. At this point, the question of whether God existed receded
into the background, replaced by her own increasing self-blame. Where
she had earlier drawn on her own experience to explain why the basic
tenets of Unitarianism no longer held the "conviction of realities" for her,
she by now had exhausted all possibility of making her reality match her
ministers' conviction. She instead accepted a "conviction" of a different
magnitude. Turning the verdict against herself, she judged her dissatisfaction to be the clearest evidence of her own inadequacies of character.

Behind the self-blame lay a variety of reasons played out on a single
theme. It finally was more desirable to turn the judgment against herself
than to accept once and for all the possibility that the Unitarians' carefully
constructed system of meaning was simply that—a construct. As long as
she found some way of accepting the Unitarian schema, she could assign
significance to her family's suffering. She knew where to place herself, even
if that meant in the company of bad examples. On the other hand, if her
worst fears were realized and the relentless and unrewarded struggle of this
life brought no compensation in the next, then life was indeed a chaos in
which individuals endured existence for no reason. And thus, Tilden turned
from questioning the system to questioning herself. It required her to
sacrifice her earlier identity, but the sacrifice itself became one more proof
of how ubiquitous the doctrine of probation was. She had failed her various trials and was now living out the consequences.

Throughout the fall of 1834, the journal entries worked from this premise. She no longer attempted to explain her feelings but simply noted them,
acknowledging them as a permanent part of herself. Her acknowledgment
turned to fear and her fear to silence. She worried that there were circumstances she would not be able to "overcome" and feelings she did not know
how to "conquer." While she continued to articulate her feelings, she became increasingly circumspect about specifying the circumstances from
which they arose. Refusing to speak of herself without the cover of abstractions, she concealed the particular causes of her unhappy effects. She would
not identify her father's indiscretion. She would not name the individual
whom she found so "interesting" but whose life, she was convinced, could
be no "concern of [hers]."

She instead turned to the prescribed language of faith. Struggling with the "circumstances of life" she could mention but not name, she wrote: "One thing I am sure would make me happier and better, if I had more religious trust and confidence in my Heavenly Father, more independence of mind, more singleness of heart and of purpose" (30 November 1834). She resolved to "find out and to perform the *right*," but every statement of resolution concluded with a lament over how impossible such resolutions were. The following passage speaks forcefully for her hesitation: "and oh how hard the right is! would that I could make it easier. I feel that I do not try resolutely. I ought to try independently of people and circumstances. I will try this next week to do differently, yes to do better, perhaps I may find a relief in it. *But* the work of reformation with me is so immense that it perfectly makes me shrink within myself" (30 November 1834). She apparently intended to end the entry there, drawing a line to the side of the page after the period. But she could not let this qualification have the last word and thus wrote above the line, "I will try." She then went on to remind herself of the promise held out by even one action performed well. "Oh," she exclaimed, "if I could but succeed in one thing then I am sure I should be happier and better." Thoughts of success quickly faded, however, and the phrase "happier and better" reminded her of her own unhappiness. "Should I not have been happier and better if I had never known ———," she writes, "I am afraid I should." Pulling herself away from these thoughts, she attempted to revise her comments into a cautionary tale. They could serve as "warning" to her. She followed her own advice, reminding herself that her best hope lay in cultivating a belief in immortality. What she needed, she told herself, was "such a feeling of right doing such trust and belief in Heaven that the Hope of hereafter may sustain me." Returning yet again to Unitarianism's answer, she found precisely the right phrasing to articulate the right identity.

What she expressed, however, she did not feel. She concluded the entry with another lament, one that spoke pointedly of the effect of silence on her sense of self. The sentence opened with a phrase that could at first be mistaken for the preface to a happy resolution: "I feel now that I have written this. . . ." The sentence might well end with a statement of reassurance. Once she had clearly written out what needed to be done, she could undertake the task of doing it. Tilden's sentence, however, tells another story. In place of the triumphant ending, there is yet another admission of defeat. She wrote, "I feel now that I have written this I still have a leaden weight upon my heart and soul, I have so much *to do!* oh that I dared to talk of these feelings!" The problem turned curiously upon a point of expression. Repeating the right formulas could not remove the "leaden weight" under which she labored; her only hope for its removal continued to lie, not in the repetition of doctrine, but in conversation. She wanted to discuss her own particular reactions to her own problematic situation. In the concluding exclamation, she implied the solution that alone might work. Could she "talk of these feelings," she might well find the ability to move beyond the certainty of failure.

At this point, such conversations were an impossibility. She felt no more inclined to speak with her sisters than she had a year earlier. The amount of time demanded by the school and her own uneasiness in social gatherings enclosed her within a circle by herself. Where in 1827 she had longed for a friend who would "rightly understand" her, in 1834 with the death of Catherine Gannett, she found no one she could comfortably call "friend." Even Gannett, to whom she had turned for spiritual guidance and indeed friendship, was no longer a possibility, for he was at the center of the circumstances she would not describe.

Her journal comments about the troubling relationship are indeed cryptic, substituting a double line for the individual's name and removing any mention of gender by consistently replacing the singular with the plural pronoun. What can be pieced together suggests that her trip to the picturesque sites of New York State presented her with a terror quite different from the occasional exposure to the sublime. Her travels brought nothing but confusion into her relationship with her minister. The man who had been brought into the family as "brother" was acting as something else. His behavior was oddly puzzling, for he turned to Tilden as a confidante, but not necessarily as his future wife. She listened to his self-criticism, to his vows never to marry, and to his uncertainty over his feelings toward the widowed Mrs. Bliss. His own references to her were apparently extremely difficult to untangle.

Few records of their conversations remain, and even fewer of his early letters to her. The earliest dates from three years after their correspondence on her spiritual crisis had begun. Writing in January 1835, he sent her just the sort of letter she might expect from a minister—or a lover. The difference is blurred. In her journal she accepted only the former possibility and duly noted that she had received a "kind letter" of "reproof" from Gannett. In the letter itself, the tone was ambiguous. Gannett began by apologizing for his criticism of her the night before. He told her that what her feelings demanded were "tenderness and sympathy," and he assured her that such were the feelings of his "soul." He wrote in "kindness and affection," because he wanted to see her "giving and receiving delight." He signed himself "yours affectionately" and assured her that she would "give true pleasure" to him if she called on his aid.

His language was certainly filled with affection and written with little restraint. And yet it was not exactly the phrasing of a prospective suitor, for he clearly displayed his ministerial vocabulary throughout his words of affection. He used his concern over her unhappiness as an occasion to remind her of her duty. "Do not let your sad or wearied feelings gain the mastery over you. You *can* conquer just that temper—of self-discontent. . . . Do not give yourself up to the influences which your own heart creates. . . . Take your discipline—every part of it—the most secret and personal— cheerfully." The letter balances interdiction against injunction. Gannett instructs Tilden in both sides of the "ought": what she must, and must not, do. In every case, his comments echo emptily against the lived reality of her daily experience. Her feelings had already gained mastery: she felt increasingly discontented; she could not take her discipline "cheerfully." The last two imperatives on Gannett's part may indeed have been the most keenly felt by Tilden. She was uncertain how much he understood of her own feelings for him. If he knew she loved him, then his counsel to guard against the "influences" of her heart and to submit cheerfully to the "most secret and personal" discipline was a pointedly indirect way of reminding her that he was decidedly her minister and only her minister. No other relationship was to be imagined between them.

In the journal entry in which she noted receiving Gannett's letter, she wrote with resignation. Discouraged by her "broken resolutions," "disheartened and wearied," she unequivocally leveled an unfavorable judgment against herself. Citing her "wrong conduct," she mentioned Gannett's words of criticism and exclaimed, "Richly do I deserve every body's reproof." She repeated the phrase "wrong conduct" twice, saying that she felt no need to detail exactly what this involved because she was so thoroughly acquainted with every aspect of her behavior. The depth of her knowledge only provided another opportunity for self-blame. "Then why don't I try more than I do[?]" she asked. She gave no answer to this question, only a veiled reference to her difficulties with Gannett. Calling it a subject that kept her "unhappy continuously," she again turned to the Unitarian paradigm. If she could only "make up her mind resolutely to live for Heaven and not for earth," she felt that she would not "mind these other affairs so much." Her next thought took her to the prospect of death and how imminent her own death might be. At the end of the entry she returned to her "broken resolutions," giving herself another set of specific actions to monitor. A single thread runs through them all. In each case, success depended on her ability to silence herself. She must remain "quiet" however "horrid" she found the task of keeping school; she must "not disturb the peace of others by [her] complaining" nor voice her criticism of her sister Mary. And she must "avoid as much as possible the subject of ————." The only possibility for breaking these various silences was one she did not keep. She advised herself to monitor her improvement by writing in her journal the following week, but she wrote nothing in her journal for a month.

When she returned to her journal in mid-February, the issues were familiar, but the voice was new. Declaring her spiritual crisis to be nearing its end, she wrote with an uncharacteristic assurance yet envisioned a future hauntingly similar to the past. As with earlier entries, there were numerous comments about the difficulty of her task and the effort required. She advised herself to practice "strict self discipline" and stated her desire for "perfect purity and singleness of heart." She referred to her many "broken resolutions" and created new ones to take their place. These "new" resolutions were familiar enough; they restated her list from the previous month.

While much remained the same between the two entries, there was a fundamental difference. Where the January entry formulaically repeated its comments on self-discipline, the February entry spoke with a conviction unheard in previous passages.

It is rather more than one month since I have written in this book, and oh what an *eventful* month it has proved to me! Little did I dream that all which has been *uttered* by me would ever have been done, but the *truth is told!* and shall I regret it? I have broken many resolutions, I have been fearfully tossed & agitated in my own mind, I have suffered, oh! more than words can ever tell! And now shall my suffering my experience, be of no avail, God forbid that it should be so. Oh may I learn, and be willing to take instruction from the past, and may all

that has happened make me better, make me a Christian. I hope and
trust and pray to Heaven that from this day I may *repent,* that I may
see the error of my ways, that I may endeavour *earnestly* and constantly to correct them. May I be so firmly convinced of the truths of
Ch[ristiani]ty that certainly by the first Sunday in May if not sooner
I may be proposed for admission to the Church. (15 February 1835)

In this passage she spoke with the voice of retrospect. Writing after the
month was over, she knew what had happened but would not reveal it in
her writing. Her emphasis shifted from the "untold truth" to the truth she
would tell, the story she would construct about her own life. Creating a pivotal moment of action through the medium of her words, she provided a
single, time-bound event around which she could structure a new, firmly
bounded identity. In her journal she declared her desire to join the church
and become an "acknowledged Christian."

    She had seemingly reworked the evangelical conversion experience into
an acceptable Unitarian counterpart. Similar to the evangelicals, she emphasized a particular moment distinct from all others. But the framework
was clearly Unitarian. Hers was a self-willed conversion. In good Unitarian
fashion, it was progressive and prospective. It began from that day and
would continue for the rest of her life. Yet unlike the Unitarian interpretation, she clearly planned for this particular day to carry a meaning attached
to no other moment in time.

    If the journal entry seems a puzzling mix of Unitarian and evangelical
constructs, the confusion is largely cleared up by turning to yet another
rhetorical tradition. In the novelists' conventions of representation, Tilden
found the structure she needed to tell the story of her spiritual crisis. The
evangelical conversion narrative was a genre of which she would have had
only minimal knowledge. The Unitarian sermon offered an unsatisfactory
blend of experience and doctrine. When left solely to the sermonic conventions, she found no hope in the promises of its language. But when crafted
into the structure of the fictional narrative, the otherwise empty phrases
took on real meaning.

    In the opening sentences of the 15 February journal entry, Tilden set her
experience within the exclamatory suspense of the gothic novel. The repeated exclamations, the heightened language, the concealment of particular events: Tilden drew together the most familiar elements of the gothic

narrative. Like her fictional model, her exclamations hid the events they ostensibly declared. Couched as abstractions, they conferred immediate significance without risking specificity. Using the language of crisis, she called
attention to the experience of the crisis itself rather than the particular elements of her difficulties. Freeing her experience from its all too ordinary
limitations, Tilden invested it with the importance characteristic of the actions in a gothic novel, where every action was defined as significant.

This rhetoric of crisis with its power to transform the ordinary into the
phenomenal was not the only technique Tilden borrowed from the fiction
she read. In addition to using the exclamatory suspense of the gothic novel,
Tilden practiced a manipulation of audience commonly used in the domestic fiction of her favorite author, Maria Edgeworth. As Edgeworth's treatment of character in *Belinda* suggests, the author carefully controlled the
reader's access to her characters' minds. Granting the reader more knowledge than any of the characters, she nonetheless kept certain characters out
of reach. They were typically the young unmarried women who in the
course of the novel became virtue incarnate. As the character progressed in
virtue, she characteristically became less available to the reader. Belinda,
for example, is literally absent for several chapters, and when she reappears,
she defines herself by her dutiful actions and keeps herself safely apart from
any conversation that might reveal more than she chose.

By keeping Belinda's mind out of sight, Edgeworth turned her character
into an exemplar defined by singleness of purpose. She was perceived as a
"consistent character" precisely because Edgeworth restricted the reader's
access to Belinda's thoughts. Reclaiming an image used earlier in the story,
Edgeworth figuratively masked Belinda's character. Her thoughts remained
veiled. We see little beyond her appearance. The reader's role lies in interpretation. What do we see behind the mask of considered calm Edgeworth
presents to her audience? Does the surface reflect harmonious resolution,
or does it conceal the battles by which such conflict was resolved?

In her letter of 26 February 1835, Tilden borrowed the novelist's technique. She wrote Gannett into the role of reader while she controlled his
knowledge of her character. Telling him that she would, after this letter,
don the mask of a desirable character, she had finally blended the minister's
and the novelist's paradigms. The "new" identity that she constructed for
herself depended on a fiction with firm religious endorsement. She would
appear "cheerful" before her family, even though her feelings were quite

different. The discrepancy, however, would be unknown to them, for she remarked, "As *they* will not know it is a mask I am wearing, they will be satisfied."

Tilden's underlined pronoun clearly points the difference between her family members and Gannett. While they were simply characters in her narrative, Gannett had been in the position of reader. She had told him her thoughts and feelings; he had known her mind, but at this point in the story, she informed him that his knowledge would soon change dramatically. She offered him one last glimpse into the character of her mind, enclosing part of the 15 February journal entry with her letter. In addition, she returned a sermon she had borrowed together with her commentary on it. Earlier she had responded to his words with questions. Now she used another strategy, building answers out of his words, using his words to mask her own.

The contrast in tone between her journal and her response to his sermon is striking. She took his sermon, a sermon on resolving religious doubt, and point by point addressed the major issues he raised. She defined the extent of her religious doubt, acknowledged the root of her problem, and asserted that she had seen the earlier error of her ways. She maintained that her "disposition" was never the problem but that the difficulty resided in her intellect. She then made the concession she had once refused to make: "I have wanted to *see,* to *know* too much." The split between faith and intellect that had initially formed the center of her doubt was now dismissed in one sentence. She briefly mentioned the "agonizing wants of [her] soul" but spent no time describing them. The rest of her response reads with the third-person polish of a sermon.

Given its placement in the letter to Gannett, this exercise of intellect looks strikingly like a mask. Placed as the last enclosure, it is prefaced by the journal passage in which the tone is decidedly *not* that of argued discourse. The journal entry speaks with the heightened emotion of gothic suspense. Proclaiming that the truth had been told, she would nonetheless conceal its identity in this passage. The words that had become manifest in action, as well as the actions themselves, are unknown: "Little did I dream that all which has been *uttered* by me would ever have been done, but the *truth is told!*" She readily emphasized the turmoil she had experienced, but she as readily kept its substance to herself. Rather than resolving the suspense of the entry, she chose to sustain it. Expanding the initial exclamations into a series of assertions, she wrote with the certainty of the novelist who knew more than the reader. What knowledge she provided for Gannett came in the form of her carefully guarded response to his sermons, her carefully chosen journal passage, and her pointed reminder that this communication from her would be the last. Declaring her new identity as a repentant Christian who would soon be acknowledged as a church member, she borrowed the novelist's language to create a narrative she alone could control.

It was an identity predicated on a dramatic isolation from others. As her letter to Gannett made eminently clear, this new identity depended on separation. She would be seen, but not understood, a figure made exemplary by her silence. The moral read out of her life would say little about her "thoughts and feelings." In this particular moment of the journal, Tilden wrote a narrative in which her life as a character was distinctly different from her role as the author. Casting herself as the individual no other character would be able to know, she carefully used her character's isolation to control her audience's knowledge.

At a point of despair, Tilden had broken her silence in order to act as her own narrator within her own narrative. Protecting herself from a charge of self- (invariably defined as self-righteous) defense, she chose both an exemplary form and an exemplary reader. Making use of the letter's respected status, she framed her narrative within the context of advice. The form of the letter was readily associated with instruction; it was the genre of choice for conduct manuals of the day. Yet the letter written for advice could easily merge with the personal letter of friendship. The writer sought both counsel and understanding and in this dual search was licensed to write directly, openly, about her life. Correspondence thus allowed the individual to tell her own story without incurring judgment for this act. It also guaranteed the writer a reader. Turning to her minister, Tilden invited Gannett to take this role. It was admittedly an act of faith on her part, for she did not know whether he would prove to be the sympathetic reader she imagined. Assuming the role, would he learn to interpret appearance rather than judge it?

His response yielded a problematic answer, for his interpretation of her words evoked images of judgment. When he finished the collection of writings she had sent him, he told her of a singular experience. He wrote, "By an almost instantaneous revelation I saw the folly & guilt of my past life." Her words were indeed powerful. Through them, he told her, he had been "led to see [his] salvation" (25 February 1835). The result of this religious experience was like a moment borrowed from a novel. Where she proposed church membership, he proposed marriage. In her letter she had anticipated the life story of a benevolent solitary. She would exchange the outspoken Hope Leslie for the silent Esther Downing. He countered by offering a different conclusion, one whose meaning would be as ambiguous for Tilden as it had been for the fictional Hope. With his proposal of marriage, she confronted the story that she thought both their lives could never tell.

CHAPTER FIVE

Assuming Authority: Letters, Persuasion, and Miracles

In proposing marriage, Gannett offered Tilden the novel's common end. Characters' lives closed on the threshold of union, and as far as our conventions have taught us, the novel's closure promised unambiguous identities to its heroines. Through marriage, the dutiful daughter escaped the trap of misunderstood appearances. Becoming "wife" meant dropping masks, abandoning secrecy. In a word, it meant leaving the world of fiction and entering the minister's world, where appearance was its own interpretation. But for every character whose story ended in marriage, there was a character whose fictional life concluded if not with freedom then with its close relation.[1] The life that the nineteenth century had learned to designate by the phrase "single blessedness" appeared in the fiction of the times. Her figure was a familiar one to readers—Esther Downing, for example, in *Hope Leslie*. In the words of her creator, she "illustrated a truth, which, if generally received by her sex might save a vast deal of misery: that marriage is not *essential* to the contentment, the dignity, or the happiness of woman" (*Hope Leslie*, 350).[2]

Tilden might well have had such characters in mind when she wrote to Gannett in February. While her self-styled masking sounds more like the continuation than the conclusion of a fiction, her self-characterization left her ambiguously poised between a character like Esther Downing and one like Ellen Redwood. To remain "masked" was to remain marriageable, yet in her letter to Gannett, Tilden clearly defined herself as the unmarried church member devoting her life to the work of benevolence. In his proposal, Gannett essentially combined the plots and revised Tilden's narratives. Offering her marriage, he offered her a life's work and a character as vividly drawn as any in fiction. Marrying a clergyman, she took on the role of the minister's wife, an arduous identity, fully scripted in a well-known narrative.

The minister's wife was the epitome of the exemplar. Her life was virtually defined as "example." Every word mattered; every action counted in the work of her husband's ministry. If he was, figuratively, always in the pulpit, she was always in the parish. Extensive rounds of visiting, careful attention to the sick in the congregation, predominant positions in the benevolent organizations: her presence was required daily in many places. Above all, her character was to speak as powerfully as her activities. She preached a silent sermon through her unfailingly serene appearance. Hers was a "calm and quiet" mind. Her identity, Tilden felt, was one she could never assume.[3]

Even after accepting Gannett's proposal, Tilden registered profound uncertainty over her (earthly) future life. Given the characteristics most distinctly associated with the minister's wife, Tilden's uneasiness was hardly surprising. An individual who preferred solitude to society, who defined herself by the chaos in her mind and chafed under the control of others, she looked to the future and saw only an unending battle in the work of self-reformation. Once again the major project was formation of character; once again the individual fell impossibly short of the mark. Her letters from the spring of 1835 and well into the summer are defined by apology for the poor appearance she made. Writing to her minister, soon to be husband, a month before their engagement was announced, she asked him to forgive her "almost unkind manners" and assured him that she would increase her endeavor to "do right." What stood in her way was the increasingly public nature of her work. The eyes of the congregation were upon her. While she acknowledged the inescapable reality of her situation, she met it with fear. She comments, "I think as you do, that it is better for me to remain at home, for much of future usefulness will depend on impressions now received, but when I think of that, then arises Care and Responsibleness from which I shrink" (4 May 1835). The description is telling. She used the same phrase to describe her anxiety with the role of minister's wife as she had used for her utter dislike of her duties as teacher. In this case, she trusted to time, to better health, and to love to provide a remedy to her fears, but throughout the summer her letters record remarks about conduct she calls "incurable." The dutiful daughter and the dutiful wife shared much in common.

Shortly before their wedding, Tilden again wrote in apology to Gannett, repeating her request for forgiveness. Bound into this ritual of regret, however, was an unwavering emphasis on explanation. She would not excuse her behavior, but neither would she condemn it. What she wanted above all was to create the context in which her feelings and actions could be understood. In this last letter before the wedding, she describes the cost of marriage:

> It has never seemed to me so like reality that we were to be married as now, and how can I help having many strange and painful feelings, mixed up with an *entire* persuasion of future happiness with you. Only think, I shall leave the best and dearest of Mothers, and all my family to whom I am so strongly attached. I must enter upon new duties to which I do not feel myself equal. I shall never again have that right and place in my home which I now have. There is much, much that is painful to dwell upon that I must feel, and that you can't feel, We are so very differently situated we cannot feel alike in this instance, but you may & I trust will perfectly understand me. (undated, autumn, 1835)

Looking to the future, she vividly saw what she left behind. Separated from her mother, she lost her place in the family. While she had at times doubted that place and questioned the rights she could claim, the familial setting was by definition familiar. In the new world of marriage, however, she had as yet no home. Her place was determined by duties she feared she could not fulfill.

Her portrait of marriage was punctuated by loss and fear. She traded the well-defined past for an uncertain "future happiness." At the same time, she asserted that such sacrifice would be rewarded. Tilden termed herself "unequal" to her duties, was willing "to give up all and every thing," yet thanked God for allowing her "so much of Heaven here." With her earlier uncertainty about immortality, this "Heaven" on earth seems a curiously unimaginable place, as does the figure to which she gives thanks. During her spiritual crisis, she had doubted the existence of God and questioned the likelihood of immortality. She virtually could not put "heavenly" and "father" together.

That she was willing to exchange the particulars of her familial present for an unknown future is the theme of her letter, but it is a theme with a number of variations. Describing her response to the imminent change in her life, she calls her feelings "strange," "painful," and particular to herself. She maintains that Gannett cannot experience anything comparable to her experience but trusts that he can nonetheless understand this world even though he cannot enter it. Hers is far from a passive trust. She does not leave his understanding to its own devices but provides a way to mediate it. The vehicle is the imagination, and the method is reminiscent of the reader with a book. She writes, "If I could only change our natures for an hour, you be Anna and I be Stiles, you would not blame me for sometimes being sad at the thought of really being married, however full may be the fount of love." She posits an empathic identification. He assumes her character while she assumes his. Exchange effectively creates the understanding she desires. Could he take on her identity for a single hour, he would inevitably see marriage from her perspective. She herself, however, ventures no speculation on what she would find were she suddenly the minister rather than the wife.

This imagined shift in identity soon proved to be more than a fiction. Fearing her inadequacy as "minister's wife," Tilden was not required to meet the circumstances that prompted those fears. In the first years of her marriage, she was, in effect, given a reprieve and the opportunity for re-forming her role in her own image. As her husband's health steadily worsened, Tilden was gradually freed from the activities originally expected of her. The exemplar designed for the parish played an increasingly marginal role, since the "help-mate" who took part in her husband's ministry was hardly a viable figure in the absence of that ministry. As Gannett was forced, over the course of several months, to set aside his various parish duties, Tilden reclaimed and reworked attributes she had once discarded. In contrast to the set pattern that had regulated her images of self in the months before their wedding, the months that followed offered no predictable order. Never certain what the next week would bring, Tilden shaped the virtues she had admired in the past into an identity that closely resembled her present.

Emerging from her earlier role of failed exemplar, Tilden created an exemplary character she herself could embody. Her letters from 1836 speak with an authority absent from any of her earlier journals. In contrast to the self-questioning voice of the late 1820s and early 1830s, these letters are distinguished by confident assertion. Written during Gannett's absence from Boston, they exist precisely because the conventional models of authority could no longer function. Gannett's physical and mental collapse virtually paralyzed his ability to make decisions. Sent first to rural Massachusetts and then to Europe, Gannett was separated from the literal center of Tilden's world. His absence meant her opportunity. Remaining in Boston, the center of the authority they both trusted, she became the voice who spoke for the wisdom of Unitarianism. In late spring of 1836, she faced the difficult task of convincing Gannett to accept his congregation's offer of a year's leave with full pay. Letters became her tools in a complicated process of persuasion. After nearly six weeks of correspondence, Tilden's letters yielded the result toward which she had written. Gannett accepted his congregation's offer. Four months later, letter writing resumed when Gannett left for the "therapeutic tour" of England and Europe.[4] With Gannett's departure, Tilden took up a new role; she served as Gannett's link to Boston, his source of information. She promised both reliability and consistency. She would write regularly and frequently, adopting the tone she felt best suited her role as informant. Returning to her old model of "frankness," she declared that "plain speaking" was the only way she could express herself.

THE READER'S AUTHORITY: TILDEN'S 1836 LETTERS TO GANNETT

The letter provided her with the exact form for this expression, allowing her an authority she could not exercise elsewhere. Fiction writing was beyond the prospect she imagined for herself. Sermons were even further removed from her possibility, requiring as they did the imprimatur of profession. Publishable forms fell outside the world of her writing experience, and the private forms were few. By the mid-1830s, Tilden clearly connected journal writing with a process of self-examination that invariably yielded swift and damning criticism. Her daily or weekly entries not only called her self into question but censured and censored it.

Letters operated on a different set of expectations. Like the journal, the letter was a readily accessible form, but it carried a different weight. In Tilden's experience, letters were the genre of advice. Her adolescent reading had given her several opportunities to examine the nonfiction form so frequently practiced and published by women. Here was a form that required an active mind but not the novelist's genius for imagination, that made morality central but did not dictate a clergyman author. Where the late adolescent's enthusiasm for novels was deemed inappropriate in the young woman of twenty, the letter was a happily sanctioned alternative. It offered both the pleasure of reading and the power of writing. Between salutation and closing, the writer's voice went unchallenged.

Within the letter, Tilden could define her position without immediate opposition. Whatever the response, her words remained intact; the voice

that spoke in the letters was decidedly her own.[5] Letters also offered her a
way of appropriating recognized authority without sacrificing her voice to
it. She could ally herself with others while maintaining her distinct representation of self. This alliance appeared in two distinctly different situations, first when Gannett was in Leicester, Massachusetts, and later when
he traveled to Europe. Gannett's proximity to Boston and the certainty (or
uncertainty) of his future plans shaped the ways in which Tilden defined
her authority. In the letters exchanged between Gannett and Tilden before
he left for England, this representation revolved around the question of
"right." Gannett claimed a singular vision; Tilden alternately allied herself
with her husband and with William Ellery Channing and the Federal Street
Church.

After Gannett's departure for Europe, Tilden's letters played ever more
heavily on her alliance with Boston Unitarianism. Now acting as his source
of information, Tilden involved herself in the issues then vexing the Unitarian establishment. As the controversy over the interpretation of Christ's
miracles grew, Tilden shaped her letters around the latest commentary, giving her own position equal weight with that of Gannett's colleagues. Using
the issue of miracles, she joined the Unitarians in their most extended discussion of authority. In her letters, she placed herself in the midst of these
discussions, borrowing the attributes that would identify their authority as
her own.

Recuperating a quality she had once tried so diligently to silence, Tilden
reclaimed frankness, turning it into an essential virtue. The direct manner
of speaking for which she had once been criticized now became her
strongest resource. She identified it as the distinguishing mark of her character just as the declarative statement became the signature of her prose.
Writing to Gannett in late May, she refused to hedge her perception with a
morass of qualifications. Assertion suited her purposes better. "Your conscience is *sick*," she told Gannett, and she then added, "I know I have been
very plain but this is my way" (30 May 1836).

Her letters from late spring are styled on an aesthetic of "plain statement." Her prose, characterized by short declarative phrases alternating
with varying uses of the imperative, was crafted as part of an open, ongoing
discussion. In part protected by the time that elapsed between when she
wrote and when she received a response, this frankness increased markedly
after Gannett's departure for England. Writing to Gannett in mid-December,
having heard nothing from him since his boat sailed in October, she

instructed him on how he should read her tone: "You must not call me *too* frank in writing to you of my thoughts and feelings. . . . I must be honest with you or write nothing" (16 December 1836).

What licensed this frankness now where it had been censured before was the context in which she wrote. As daughter, she had been expected to be dutiful. In her journal, she had increasingly held herself to a model of self-examination that demanded self-censoring. Letters, however, brought different expectations with them. Even in the earliest letters to Gannett, when she first broke the silence about her religious doubts, the form provided her with a chance to use the direct expression she had long admired. In that case, the letter served as buffer between herself and the person she addressed. To voice her doubts, she required the protection of indirect response. Associating her doubt with shame, she preferred the written over the spoken word. In conversation, she could be confronted immediately; judgment was instantaneous, rendered in a glance or in a few sentences of criticism. Through the mediating presence of the letter, judgment was postponed. Not only did it delay the time for response, but it replaced the person with paper. A letter could be read in the extreme privacy of solitude. A conversation, no matter how private, was always a matter of one self with another.

As Tilden's circumstances changed, so too did her use of the letter. Where the letter in 1832 had been designed to create distance between two individuals, in 1836, with Gannett's literal absence, letters created the illusion of presence. Tilden frequently cast her letters as conversation. Her written words stood for their spoken counterparts and may well have "spoken" where a literal conversation would have yielded silence. What made a frank expression of ideas possible was a written, rather than a spoken, exchange. Following one of her comments on the frank tone of her letters, she gives a clue as to how the two were connected. "I love to *talk* to you in this way since I cannot see you," she writes. His absence may well have been responsible for her mode of expression. She could "talk in this way" precisely because he was not present. The style she associated with the letters was a function of the distance between them.

Her opportunities for frankness reflected the very premises on which the letter was constructed. Most frequently used to communicate across distance, it sought to collapse that distance in the allusions created within it. Evoking a world of which each correspondent was a part, it privileged the shared world of evocation over the separate locations from which each correspondent wrote.[6] Concurrent with this collapse of space was an analogous collapse of time. Writing the letter, the individual conjured up the correspondent's presence. Reading the letter, the correspondent was drawn into the present, now past, in which the words had been written. And behind this illusion of contemporaneity was the expectation of communication. Response was forthcoming. When the letter was read, it would once again suspend the writer's and reader's lived time and place them in a fictive verbal present.

The illusion was fragile. While creating the fiction of a shared present, the letter also disrupted it. The evidence of the physical object ran counter to the power of the words. Pieces of paper lay where the writer could not stand.[7] The very act of reading or writing a letter was a perpetual reminder of the distance and time separating correspondents. To receive a letter was to be confronted by the writer's physical absence; to write one was to be reminded of the time that would elapse before a response could be returned. Tilden used this suspended time to her advantage, but it was an advantage singularly dependent on the expectation of a response. Her work was persuasion; to that end, she sought to establish herself as a trusted and compelling source of information. She also sought acceptance within the Unitarian establishment, an acceptance earned by her reliable representation of its central debates. If her words fell on deaf ears or met with a dismissive eye, her work simply failed. Without words sent in return, Tilden's "plain speaking" could not be distinguished from silence. Her authority rested on response.

Then, as now, *authority* is a word whose definitions mirror the unsettled debates within a given society. In Tilden's Boston, such debates reflected the continued uncertainty over what *authority* meant in the decade following Andrew Jackson's administration. The era of Federal Boston was fast becoming an irreclaimable part of the past, and as economic conditions worsened, uncertainty increased. The Unitarian Church, defined as it had been by the upholders of Federalism, experienced its own crisis of uncertainty. Given the continued rise of revivalism, liberal Christianity could no longer comment critically from the center of the religious world, for the old center was ebbing toward the margin.[8] Faced with dwindling church attendance and membership, liberal Christianity struggled to redefine itself. In some cases the battles reinforced the status quo. A young Waldo Emerson attempted to convince his congregation to drop the sacrament of the Lord's Supper because he could see no authority for its continued observance. His congregation declined this possibility for change.[9] The topic of "probation" was taken up in full force in the Unitarian pulpit and by the periodicals in an attempt to create a compelling alternative to evangelical conversion. But the controversy that raged hottest and longest in the 1830s surrounded the interpretation of miracles. Could a religion that prided itself on reason and reliance on natural law subscribe to a fundamental suspension of nature's law? And yet, if the miracles were naturalized, would religion remain? Having already downplayed Christ's divinity, could a system of religious belief survive the loss of the miracles? In their absence, on what authority could Unitarianism lay claim to Christianity?

Consideration of the miracles was never far from Unitarian discussion. The conversations often turned contentious; the call for "free and frank" discussion was frequently treated as a challenge to a battling debate.[10] Whether pursued in the pages of the *Christian Examiner* or in the city newspapers, the question was delineated for a wide-ranging audience. All were invited to enter the discussion, the laity as well as the clergy, the reader/listener as well as the writer/preacher. But whose position would carry the greatest weight? What was the reader's authority?

For Tilden, writing in the 1830s, the question was a very real one. She could define herself only as reader and respondent. Unlike her husband and his colleagues, she could claim no public pulpit voice. In contrast to the novelists she admired, recognized authorship was closed to her. The moral imperative lodged in sermon or fiction could not be claimed by her in its generic equivalent. She would never preach sermons, nor would she write novels. Authority, if it came at all, would have to come in a different form and be shaped in a different way. Immersed in a world that defined her by her duties, there was small opportunity to privilege a self identified by its distinctness. Hers would not be an authority grounded in origination and its myths. Her role was responsive, her days filled with activities that emphasized the intricate involvement of one life with many others. Whether reading scriptural commentary as an aid to understanding the Bible or consulting her future husband about the advisability of a few weeks away from Boston, she worked within a framework of response. To originate ideas would have seemed a myth indeed and a useless one at that. For Tilden, authority was possible only in the context of response.

What she could credibly lay claim to was her experience in the audience, either as reader or listener. Her adolescence and early adulthood might well be characterized by her reception of words, written and spoken. Between the Sunday sermons, the weekday lectures, and the reading of novels, histories, religious commentaries, and journals, Tilden's time was virtually punctuated by words delivered to her in a variety of forms. She read and reread the novels by the most eminent writers of "moral fiction" and participated in the conversation groups created by reading societies.[11] In her study of Scripture, she applied the techniques of biblical higher criticism and continued her activity of taking notes on the sermons she heard. By the time of her marriage, Tilden was a reader and listener who had long been involved in the practice of interpretation.

Tilden's work sharply delineates the complex ways in which nineteenth-century middle-class women used their reading. Before turning to Tilden's particular craft, it may well be useful for late-twentieth-century readers to once again assess their own uneasiness as readers of the past. Under a model that assumes that a flawed convention can never yield a tenable result, Tilden's work might well seem a lost cause. In fact, under the position represented by Douglas's *Feminization,* Tilden would be doubly doomed. To craft authority within a system that only allowed influence was problematic enough; but to ally oneself with the ebbing authority of the ministry would be, in Douglas's assessment, effectively to write oneself into a position of impotence. Yet such was clearly not the case with Tilden. She crafted a theory of authority that she could in fact practice. Borrowing the minister's models did not mean accepting them wholesale. In these appropriations lay a world of difference. The reading listener engaged in the work of practical reform: the issue was what could be changed in the actually foreseeable future.

Central to this work was the representation of the interpreter herself. Following closely from the Unitarian trust in "character," Tilden worked to create a persona for herself as the consistent and credible reader. For her words to be persuasive, the speaker would need to be clearly and carefully defined. Where she had failed in other forms, she succeeded here, largely because the characteristics out of which she could shape this figure were characteristics that had long been her first choice among virtues. With a minister as her audience, she would rely most fully on a persona who drew on the tone of his colleagues' debates. Her voice would speak in the spirit of "free and frank" discussion. As his wife, her authority was marginal; as an individual associated with William Ellery Channing, she wrote words he could more readily accept. In the letters from late spring 1836, she balanced her position between Gannett and his church. To establish authority, she first borrowed it, allying herself clearly with those in prominent positions of recognized power.

Tilden initially placed herself with her husband. In her first representation, they stood in the same relation to the congregation. Both minister and minister's wife needed their parishioners' wisdom, and for both, duty was fulfilled by following the guidance of others. Writing on 25 April 1836, Tilden emphasized the resemblance between her circumstances and his. Counseling Gannett to follow her example, she told him, "I have not stopped to say one word about my own *feelings* in all this, we must both of us feel a great deal, but at this time it is our duty to be guided by the advice and kindness of those who are so interested for us." She asserted the shared aspect of their experience. Despite her presence in Boston and his in Leicester, or his role as minister and hers as minister's wife, they figuratively stood in the same place and in the same relation: "it is our duty." Writing again the next day, she began to alter the terms and introduced a distinct difference between them. She returned to the theme of duty, but in this case, the duty was his alone. In this small space after sending her previous letter and before receiving his reply, she shifted the nature of her connection with him. Claiming her own agency, she adopted the imperative to frame her request and script his response:

> Do give me your consent to go on with the plans I proposed to you yesterday. You must now be convinced that *people* think you right in giving up for one year, in consideration for them you *ought* to say nothing about leaving them, they would not consent to it, never was being more beloved than you are. You now have *time* and *means* for restoration and it is your *solemn duty* to abide by Dr B[igelow]'s advice, and use every means to regain a sound mind and body. Rest, Regularity and Recreation in strict attention to diet etc will yet bring all right. If woman's love and anxiety could restore you, it would be done, but God's will be done. He will help us, He will not give us more to bear than we are able. He has ever been, He will be merciful to us and we must trust in Him. (26 April 1836)

To make acceptance of her plans his only viable response, she exercised a power of assumption unique to the form of the letter. In the days between a letter sent and a reply received, the letter writer can use this time to continue the correspondence along her own lines. With a response forthcoming but not arrived, Tilden could imagine Gannett's response as she pleased and in so doing continue her attempt to guarantee that his response would be hers. His responding letter and her newly written one would, she imagined, cross in the mail. She would receive his response to her first letter about the same time he received her second letter. Thus, the second letter would act as a curious echo of the first. Had he replied as she desired, her words simply confirmed his action. If his reply did not match what she had projected, a more complex possibility arose. Her letter, arriving with the announced certainty that he would have acted just as she had assumed, offered him the ready opportunity for revising what would then be seen as a hasty reply.

Her own position was strategically mixed. She presented herself as distinctly separated from him. The plans are hers; the duty is his. Assuming that her previous letter had acted on him as she desired, she concluded that he "must now be convinced" of his congregation's firm support. She defines her sentences by "musts" and "oughts." She advises him by repeating his doctor's advice. She offers encouragement, repeating his parish's deepest hope for his recovery. And she concludes her counsel with a phrase that may have been the doctor's and, whether quoted or not, speaks with the power of the proverb: "Rest, Regularity and Recreation." She capitalizes on words she believes will carry weight with her reader.

Separating herself from her correspondent, she nonetheless returns to a point of identification in the literal closing of the letter and in the two sentences that precede it. In these last sentences she reminds him of her own limits. "If woman's love and anxiety could restore you . . .": she writes with the clear acknowledgment that this aspect of her particular identity had not, in fact, been able to effect the work she wished done. His health continued to decline despite her "woman's love." In this moment, she draws on the conventional relation of authority between husband and wife and the particular aspects of their own difficulties. In society's eyes, "woman's love" was the most powerful force she could wield, but her own strength had failed. Like Gannett in his collapse, she was disempowered. Stating her own weakness, she reestablishes her identification with Gannett and from there returns to what marks their connection. In the end, it is no longer Tilden as "I" and Gannett as "you"; she concludes by designating them as "us," involved in the same work of endurance and trust. "He will not give us more to bear than we are able. . . . We must trust in Him." The commands now include them both. In closing, she signs herself "Your own Anna." And as if to reinforce that connection between them, she inserts on the same line as the closing a sentence apparently added after the closing was written. "I cannot say how much I long to return to you." The letter concludes with the reassurance that his will is her own, that he remains at the center despite the geographic fiction this creates. Gannett, staying in Leicester,

Massachusetts, is outside the real center of authority located so clearly in his church in Boston. He is the one who eventually will return, but Tilden reverses the logic, ending this letter with an appeal to his authority and a bracketing of hers.

Written as if to intercept Gannett's response, this letter could exercise little of its desired effect because her first letter did not arrive as soon as she had expected. Gannett did not receive the letter for a number of days. In the meantime, her second letter arrived, complicating her already difficult task of persuasion. The second letter was designed as an extension of the first and depended on it for its intended interpretation, but the first words Gannett received from Tilden were second in her line of strategy. Missing was the letter in which she had so carefully identified their duties as one. In its place, was a letter that suggested that she had indeed acted on her own authority, independently of his consideration. His response was open criticism, telling her that she had "sadly erred," asking her how she could imagine she was "doing 'right,'" and finally setting her on the threshold of his ruin. He drew on certain imperatives of his own. "Do not," he told her, "let me feel that you are instrumental in my entire overthrow" (26 April 1836). Blaming her for his doctor's advice, he suggested that her words had unduly influenced Bigelow's perspective. "Just what have you been telling him?" he asked. His next sentence suggests the answer he imagined. "If I am crazy," he wrote, "send me to Charlestown [site of the most prominent asylum of the day]; if I am not, then let me at least have a voice in the arrangement of my own affairs." What she had initially addressed in her letter, that their "voices" must equally give way to the guidance of others, had not had a chance to be heard.

At this point, Gannett adamantly rejected her plans as well as the advice of either his congregation or his doctor. For the next month, Tilden would work both to regain his confidence and to persuade him that the only voice he could claim in the decision was the voice of consent. It was difficult work accomplished almost entirely through her letters. She made one brief trip to Leicester in early May to straighten out the confusion created by the delayed arrival of her miscarried 25 April letter. But the real work was reserved for the letters themselves. Drawing on every strategy she could imagine, she sought to convince Gannett not only to accept the church's offer but to see this acceptance as his "duty." She termed it a matter of "conscience" in which obedience to others' advice was synonymous with "right" action.

To accomplish this task of persuasion, Tilden ranged from simple assertion to despairing pleas. Her initial hope of an easy resolution quickly gave way, and she undertook a sustained discussion of why the best possibility lay precisely in what he rejected. Throughout the month, she continued to rely on the power of the clearly acknowledged authorities. She readily added herself to the list, stating as early as 27 April just where she stood. Having reassured him that she had never intended to act without his "concurrence," a word she borrowed from his letter and returned to him in her response, she nonetheless separated herself from his view of her. She wrote, "I am not, ought not to be censured for the kindly intended measures of your friends. That I thank them, and think they are right I must acknowledge." She balanced her identity between Gannett and his friends. She was free from any blame he might attach to the plans he rejected, but she was also allied with those friends. What they proposed, she judged to be "right."

Increasingly during this month and well into the fall, Tilden appealed to what she represented as an independent sense of the "right." The word acted as a guarantor of her action, and the consensus of friends provided a guarantor of the word. In early May she assured Gannett that she had "acted in the sight of Heaven." Citing a central arbiter of "right," she adds, "My judgment tells me I have done right[.] So many good friends can't be mistaken." Her "judgment" coincided with "their" view, and in that combination, she claimed the authority for her action. She was backed by the agreement of a particular, respected group.

By the end of the month, she had taken her right to the edge of autonomy. Instead of allying herself with them, she assumed the more powerful position of the individual who created alliances rather than the individual who joined them. "Dearest Stiles," she wrote, "I do not mean to be unkind in any expression which I have used, but I cannot think I am wrong when every one agrees with *me* and no one with you" (31 May 1836).

Backed by his congregation, she singled herself out as right and then consolidated this position by articulating what she called "the truest religion and philosophy." In a statement of faith that revised her husband's precepts, she instructed him about the uses of the past and the definition of the Deity. Where Gannett counseled himself and others to study the personal past rigorously, searching out errors and marking their failures, she advocated selective memory. "The truest religion and philosophy," she wrote, "is only to make such use of the past as will secure our future usefulness and improvement" (31 May 1836). As she made clear, remorse impeded usefulness, and thus its causes were best forgotten. Knowing that he would respond to this position by criticizing her leniency, she countered with an image of God familiar from William Ellery Channing's sermons. Imagining his response, she writes, "Now don't say 'Anna places her standard of right too low'[;] it is not so," and answers his imagined comment with her own statement of faith: "I believe simply this, that Our Heavenly Father has much more mercy for us than we have for one another. He alone knows the trial of the spirit. I think He means the end of all retribution to be productive of the greatest amount of happiness and virtue. He desires the utmost purity and rectitude in all of us, at the same time He remembers our temptations and liabilities to wrong doing." Emphasizing God's mercy, she revised the standard of judgment that had once been so difficult an obstacle to her own faith. Acknowledging that humans judge without mercy, she turned to a merciful God who substituted understanding for judgment. Able to explain the individual's actions, especially when those actions fell short of an ideal "purity," this Heavenly Father saw no need for mixing judgment with blame.

Tilden's God of mercy united happiness with virtue but gave pride of place to the former. It was happiness that made virtue possible, a point with which Tilden concludes this passage. Returning to her husband's stand, she criticizes it precisely because it prevented the individual from putting virtue into action. She writes, "It is very plain to me dear Stiles, that your system of suffering and remorse is not right—and why? because it does not, it never can make a better Christian of you. You are not so good or so useful when you are suffering from depression dwelling on the past and full of dread for the future, as when you cheerfully give yourself up to the influences about you." Tilden counseled a pragmatic cheerfulness. True religion depended on a careful editing of the past. In looking back, the individual set aside the actions that went by the name of sin. When remorse over the past impeded action in the present, a revision of perspective was required. To be useful one needed to be "of good cheer."

Preaching "future usefulness," Tilden established her position with a clear and authoritative precedent. Citing Christ, she reminded her husband that he did not preach a gospel of remorse. "Jesus I am sure no where tells us that it is doing right to be full of regret[.] He says 'go and sin no more.'" Her choice of biblical quotation is telling. Evoking Christ's refusal to judge the woman caught in adultery, Tilden separates Gannett from judgment, whether by the group or by the self. She then cites herself as example. "I am convinced," she tells him, "that *I* cannot do as well and am not as good when I am constantly full of remorse." Alluding to the period of 1834 when despair defined her days, she used herself as an example. She had then believed remorse was the only appropriate response to the past; she now saw a different prospect. To confirm the success of both her revised ideas and of herself as their embodiment, she privileged her definition of Christianity and backed it by Christ's example. She comments, "Christianity I am sure is cheerful, and full of brightness and hope." She concludes by offering him the image of a cheerful Jesus: "We do not find any records that Jesus was desponding, oh do let us catch more of his cheerfulness and we shall be much better Christians—."

Although Gannett could not fully adopt her version of Christianity, he did finally accept her advice.[12] Early in June, he sent a letter to the church in which he agreed to take its offer of a year's leave at full salary. Telling his wife that he was planning to write the letter the following day, he told her that his decision was the result of her "arguments & entreaties" (2 June 1836). He offered no hope beyond this decision. He was, he said, "almost in despair about [his] character." Defining himself by "stubbornness" and "insensibility," he felt that God himself was ready to abandon all hope that any reformation of character was possible. The thought was a familiar one to Tilden, reminiscent of her own despair two years earlier. Again drawing on herself as example, Tilden revised the "hope of heaven" she had not been able to experience in 1834 into an "energetic Hope" for a more immediate future. Consistently responding to Gannett's despair with her own faith, she made clear that such hope did not come naturally. It required an effort of will both to create and to sustain it. And guiding its creation was an open acknowledgment of how difficult such work was.

Tilden worked relentlessly and finally with success to provide Gannett with a convincing revision of his religious duties. With the question of salary answered, she settled the final details of leasing their house on Hayward Place and then met her husband in Leicester. A few days later, Tilden's mother joined them. The spring had been no easier for mother than for daughter. Bryant Tilden's most recent voyage had failed. His business practices were called into question, not simply in respect to poor management but also in regard to ethical questions. Although Tilden never mentioned exactly what the suspicions were, her letters make clear that her father's shortcomings were deadly serious.[13] Where Bryant Tilden erred, Zebiah Tilden suffered, and thus she joined her daughter and invalid son-in-law/minister for a prescribed trip to Saratoga Springs.[14]

While the scenery delighted, the "cure" fell far short of their expectations. Gannett returned to Boston with no visible improvement in his health, and Dr. Bigelow then prescribed the more extensive regimen of the Continental Tour. Counseling Gannett to travel to England and Europe, he hoped that a combination of Old World art, literary conversation, landscape, and the ubiquitous waters would succeed where the New World offerings had failed. Bigelow imposed one condition. Gannett would travel without his wife, for Bigelow firmly believed that her presence would make it impossible for his patient to escape his past. And thus Gannett sailed for Europe on 11 October 1836 for a journey of at least ten months.

In her husband's absence, Tilden cast herself as his primary source of information. She reported not only her visits within the parish but the particulars of various families—whose businesses had succumbed to the economic crisis, whose health was failing, who was born, and who died. She described the ministers who filled his pulpit, commenting on their pulpit manner as well as on the topics of the sermons themselves. Surveying the field, she heralded the promising new ministers of the day. She also criticized the system for bringing inexperienced preachers too quickly into the pulpit. She carefully noted when Channing himself preached, indicated the state of his health, and celebrated the power of his discourse.

Although she concentrated on the world within the parish, her information was not confined to it. She reported the birth of her former teacher's first son: "Mrs Waldo Emerson has a son. Some ask the question was he born with *wings?*" (5 November 1836).[15] She described the burial in Mount Auburn of a young father and the religious instruction such a burial would provide. She recorded her own reading and commented on the most recently published books and how they were received. She told him the rumor that Harriet Martineau could find no American publisher for her book *Society in America,* the work that would indeed, when published, win her no new friends in the United States and lose her several old ones.[16] Tilden praised the newly published books by Eliza Farrar and Catharine Sedgwick. She defended Farrar's *The Young Lady's Friend* against critics who called its propriety into question. Having read this advice book written to and for young women, she took no offense at the discussions of body odor or the detailed description of digestion. She maintained that the author had committed no indelicacy and in fact had written a work that would provide young women with much "they ought to know." She was by no means bothered by what other readers found as a blamable lack of decorum. For herself, she found "very little objectionable matter" in the work and much that was indispensable. She maintained that the guiding premise of the book was beyond reproach. "She refers each action to strict principles": a good Unitarian could ask no more (11 November 1836).[17]

Tilden reserved similar praise for Sedgwick's short fiction *The Rich Poor Man and the Poor Rich Man*. A publication sponsored by the Unitarian Association, it received a laudatory review in the November issue of the *Christian Examiner*.[18] Whether Tilden read the book or the review first is unclear, but her praise for the work was unqualified. She not only gave copies of the book to her friends but took one of the character's lines as guiding words for herself. Calling them a "sermon in themselves" and quoting them in subsequent letters, she took Sedgwick's phrase as her own: "God gives the opportunities."

The words were decidedly appropriate to Tilden's situation. Gannett's illness, defined as a trial sent by God, provided Tilden with opportunities for self-expression that would otherwise have been unavailable. With two months standing between the correspondents' letters, Tilden felt free to voice her opinions. She exercised this freedom on a variety of topics, ranging from her work in the parish to the state of his health. She continued to assert her conviction of "right." As if in response to the doubts she imagined he would still be harboring, each letter included its own version of how certain she was that they had made no mistakes in their course of action. She reworked the identification she had earlier adopted, using herself as an exemplary alternative to his self-denigration. In her first letter after his departure, she vowed to make the winter a "season of improvement." She carefully acknowledged the existence of troubling feelings surrounding their separation but neatly contained their expression to a simple and direct report. She recorded the extensive visiting she undertook among members of the congregation, referring to these individuals as "our people." A letter did not leave Boston without its description of her round of visits and its accompanying comment about how she now looked forward to their work together in a joint parish ministry. With a confidence far different from the fears of the previous year, she now relished the chance to be the "good minister's good wife." For the present, however, it was clear that she enjoyed working with the congregation alone.

THE MIRACLES CONTROVERSY
AND THE PROBLEM OF UNITARIAN AUTHORITY

Providing running commentary throughout these letters, Tilden delivered both the news and her evaluation of it. In short, she became Gannett's authority on the concerns of his congregation and on the affairs of Boston. Nowhere did this newly acquired authority come more strongly into play than in her reports on current events within Unitarianism itself. The months immediately following Gannett's departure gave Tilden volatile material with which to work, for the autumn of 1836 saw one of Unitarianism's pivotal issues foregrounded in an increasingly conflicted debate. The topic was the interpretation of miracles; the question was whether belief in Christ's miracles was necessary to "Christian faith." The discussion ranged beyond religious journals, entering the pulpit as ministers discussed what the miracles meant. And the debate was not limited to a Unitarian audience alone. Andrews Norton published an outraged protest in the *Boston Daily Advertiser,* the city's leading newspaper. What has become known as the "miracles controversy" raged with revived fervor in the closing months of 1836, and Tilden, chronicling the events for one of the American Unitarian Association's founders, assumed a place within the discussion.

The debate was sparked by George Ripley's review in the *Christian Examiner* of James Martineau's recently published *Rationale of Religious Enquiry.*[19] Although Martineau's book itself would have drawn the American Unitarians' interest, it was Ripley's review that turned interest into debate. Appearing in the November issue of the *Christian Examiner,* the review praised Martineau's work for calling attention to the necessity of reform. Using Martineau's preface as a point of departure, Ripley began his review by criticizing the present. Evaluating the state of theology, he found it trapped in the sixteenth century, "cold," "lifeless," and "petrified."[20] "We are not aware," he wrote, "of a single effective endeavour to advance theology to the rank of a free, intellectual pursuit" (226). Ripley saw Martineau's work as a preliminary step in changing the character of religious discussion. He applauded the British writer for "the singular freedom and frankness with which he advances his opinions and pursues them to their legitimate consequences" (240). In Ripley's eyes, Martineau had successfully made "free inquiry" the guiding force behind his theological pursuit.

Appropriating this "spirit of frank discussion" (228), Ripley made it clear that Martineau's work had not gone far enough. Certain topics, he maintained, "demand[ed] a more complete and scientific discussion." These topics were none other than the most controversial sticking points within Unitarian debate. Ripley took issue with Martineau on the meaning of inspiration and the nature of miracles. Martineau had argued that, given the discrepancies between the gospel accounts, the writers of the New Testament could not have been writing under the power of divine inspiration.

For Martineau, inspiration signaled infallibility; the Holy Spirit made no mistakes. To read the New Testament, however, was to read a different story. If it was read as the work of divine inspiration, one confronted the image of a divinity that could not keep its stories straight.[21] Martineau maintained that the Scriptures were a distinctly human work. In the absence of inspiration, he argued strenuously for the importance of the miracles. In his view, Christianity depended on a full acceptance of Christ's miracles as miracle, an actual divine suspension by God of natural law.

Ripley found Martineau's position problematic. To reject inspiration and accept miracles presented a troubling inconsistency. From Ripley's perspective, once the Scriptures were seen as the sole product of humanity, the miracles were, by implication, a construct of an all too human interpretation. Ripley commented, "It is rather a singular combination of opinions, to deny the inspiration of the sacred writers, and to defend the miracles which they record as the essential foundation of the Christian faith" (248). A fallible human document might well have mistakenly attributed natural events to a supernatural source.

Ripley attributed Martineau's inconsistency to a mistaken understanding of both inspiration and the miracles. Arguing that "inspiration" need not mean "infallibility," Ripley claimed that inspiration appeared in many forms. Asserting that human nature was in part defined by its capacity for receiving "truth," he maintained that in certain individuals, this capacity was closer to perfection than in others. Those individuals were said to be "inspired," and Ripley felt no hesitation in attaching the word "supernatural" to such an occasion. "We say of the mind, in which the essential ideas of religious truth exist in signal perfection, independent of human agency, that it is supernaturally inspired" (246). Christ, of course, was the mind Ripley had in mind, but he did not associate this perfection with a substantial difference between Christ and other individuals. The New Testament writers were "favored with an inspiration, similar in kind, though less in degree" (246). Inspiration, in Ripley's refiguring, became potentially available to all, though realized only by some. Based on the "common endowment of human nature" (243), inspiration was grounded in the divinely given ability to perceive truth directly.

While Ripley reclaimed inspiration by separating it from its connection with infallibility, he made no such effort to establish the miracles on equally firm ground. Viewing miracles as an expedient, he firmly opposed Martineau's argument that they were indispensable to Christianity. Citing the other occasions of miracles in the Bible, Ripley argued that they were simply a means to a particular end, "the agent for accomplishing a practical effect" (251). Distinguishing the "revelation of spiritual truth" from a proof of its authority, he separated the "evidences of Christianity" into two categories. On the one hand, there were demonstrations addressed to the senses and designed to effect a particular action. On the other hand, there was the agreement between human perception and spiritual truth. In Ripley's system, the latter was clearly the most important and firmly independent of miraculous proof. The proof of Christianity lay elsewhere, in its correspondence with the human mind. The divine nature of Christianity became apparent through its distinctive internal consistency. It revealed the divine elements within human nature that the human mind in turn recognized as its own.[22] Miracles in Ripley's schema did not have the power to "confirm" the truth: only the mind could do that. They could, however, attest to its authority (252).

Ripley presented his work in the context of a "free and frank" discussion. Response, however, did not always follow in that "spirit of frankness." Andrews Norton, publishing his criticism of Ripley's review in the *Boston Daily Advertiser*, attacked Ripley for his position on the miracles. Agreeing with Martineau, Norton maintained their centrality.[23] His tone was far from cordial. Never known for his diplomacy, Norton made no attempt to couch his disagreement in polite terms. Where Ripley had cast his criticism of Martineau in the form of "suggestions," not "controversy," Norton unabashedly framed his response to Ripley as nothing other than dispute.

Norton's contentiousness illustrates how deeply the question of miracles cut into the fabric of Unitarianism. His nervousness, as much as Ripley's commentary, reflected the ongoing difficulty faced by a faith that defined itself by reason and prided itself on its use of the most sophisticated methods of scriptural interpretation. Ripley wrote that "miracles do not compose the essence of Christian revelation, but were intended to facilitate its reception and establish its authority" (248). In so doing, he maintained that he stated an idea no Unitarian would reject. What he did not say, however, was how troubling the question of authority was for Unitarianism, both with and without the miracles.

By the 1830s, the discussion of authority had ranged over numerous topics. The sacraments came under question, as did the worship service itself. Even the Sabbath was not untouched, as the many sermons defending its observance suggest. Virtually no area of religious belief was excluded. Not only were the miracles involved, but so were the biblical writings themselves. It is no coincidence that Ripley's focal points were exactly the issues that brought authority to the fore and invariably raised questions about the authority of Jesus as well. The Unitarian dilemma in the first part of the nineteenth century might well be styled as a crisis, if not of authority then over authority. What the ministers sought was a fail-safe method for establishing Christianity's authority even when it was separated from all that had earlier characterized it.

The process had started long before Boston Unitarianism could be said to exist. With the development of the German higher criticism in the eighteenth century, biblical interpretation had been radically revised. Growing out of the study of ancient civilizations, it treated Jesus' Jerusalem as it treated Homer's Greece. Arguing that biblical writings could be analyzed using the same methods devised for secular works, higher criticism called into question the privileged position of sacred texts. The authority of the Bible had once been seemingly unassailable, protected by its very definition as Scripture. With the contextualizing practiced by the higher critics, such authority could no longer be taken for granted. If the Scriptures not only reflected the particular period in which they were produced but depended on it for their meaning, then the writings were something other than a divine word spoken for all time.

For the Boston Unitarians writing in the early nineteenth century, higher criticism was all to the good. In a faith that grounded itself firmly in reason and worked diligently to rid Christianity of any apparent inconsistencies, biblical interpretation as practiced by the higher critics proved to be a useful tool. Given the discrepancies within Scripture—whether in the stories about Jesus' life or in the uneasy clashes between a God of love and a God of wrath—higher criticism became a way of explaining away certain troubling contradictions. Contextualizing never failed the Unitarian ministers in their attempt to separate the chaff of local references from the wheat of spiritual truth.

The ministers were by no means inclined to set aside scriptural authority altogether, but the contextualizing so successful in one context produced difficulties in another. If the Bible could be read as any other text, then where did its authority reside? Martineau dismissed divine inspiration; Ripley attempted to reclaim it. Both men implied that for Christianity to retain its authority, it had to stand on some distinguishing power unique to itself. Martineau found it in the miracles, Ripley in its accord with human nature, but in each case, authority was placed on shifting ground. To rely on the miracles as fastidiously as Martineau did meant making exceptions to a reason-based religion. Emphasizing the correspondence between divine and human nature ran the risk of turning Divinity into humanity's creation.

To avoid either extreme, the proponents of liberal Christianity turned to Jesus. Yet he was the answer who raised further questions. Firmly situated within the debates over Christ's double nature, the figure of Jesus moved uneasily between natural and supernatural worlds. If Christianity meant a belief in Christ, could Unitarians claim the term? They argued strenuously for themselves as Christians, hence their preference in Boston for the phrase "liberal Christianity." But behind their claim to a name lay the riddle of Christ's distinct being. Was his special nature proved by the miracles: he could do what others could not. But then, as Ripley pointed out, there were many other individuals in the Bible who performed miracles. If, in fact, as Ripley argued, Jesus used miracles only as a visible manifestation of authority, where did the "real" authority reside? The vast majority of Unitarian ministers said "character." Jesus' words were believed because no flaw could be found in the speaker himself.

Ripley's comments prefaced an anarchic anthology of discussion. The publication of William Henry Furness's *Remarks on the Four Gospels* was announced in the same edition of the *Examiner* as Ripley's review. Furness was at that point settling into his relatively new ministry in Philadelphia.[24] He was well known in Boston, but what he published in 1836 would make Boston think twice about its up-and-coming ministers. Stepping boldly beyond Ripley's sidestepping, Furness naturalized miracles, turning them into a proof of character. The "pure in heart" might not only see God but be God. Two years later, the most promising Unitarian minister of the early 1830s would enter the debate during his commencement address at the Harvard Divinity School. When Emerson pronounced as monstrous the conventional interpretation of miracles, he was one voice the more in a debate in which he would have neither the first word nor the last.

THE SPIRIT OF FRANK DISCUSSION:
TILDEN'S RESPONSE TO THE MIRACLES CONTROVERSY

The Unitarian debate over authority produced more controversy than it ever yielded resolution, but during its periods of conflict, the laity often came out the winners. Tilden is a case in point, for she used the miracles controversy of 1836 to prove her powers of interpretation. Reporting the events to Gannett, she identified herself as an active party in the ongoing discussion. Here in short is the chronology of events. When she wrote to Gannett on 11 November, she had already given Ripley's review a preliminary reading. She had read Norton's piece in the *Advertiser* and was planning to read Ripley's essay again before registering her own position on Ripley. At the same time, she also stated that she wanted to get a copy of Martineau's *Rationale* so that she could read the work as a whole rather than simply in the extracts Ripley had included.[25]

Three weeks later, she reported that she had reread Ripley's article. She found little with which she disagreed. Stating her own view on the miracles, she added that her next project was to read Furness's book. Waiting to obtain a copy of it, she commented, "I am impatient to see what Mr Furness has to say about [the miracles]" (4 December 1836). Ten days later, she had finished the work, all 340 pages, as she told her husband. Her response was mixed. A week later in a conversation with William Ellery Channing, she was pleased to learn that he also reacted to the book with decidedly ambivalent feelings. She quoted Channing's words, attempting to report them in sermon-note detail. She concluded her comments on the controversy with Channing's words, telling her husband that she thought he would be pleased "to hear even this much from Dr. Channing" (29 December 1836).

Beginning with the summary of one authority and ending with a quotation from another, Tilden placed her comments within an impeccable frame. Backed by the *Christian Examiner* and the foremost figure in liberal Christianity, she presented herself as a careful reader whose interpretations were conscientiously crafted. In her first letter to Gannett on the question of miracles, she gave a short summary of both the controversy and the work that prompted it. She entered the debate with the following comments:

I have been reading Mr G. Ripley's review of Martineau's Rationale of religion, it has caused much conversation with us, owing to some unpleasant remarks of Mr Norton's concerning it which appeared in the Advertiser, Mr R. has fully answered him. When I read the review for myself it appeared to me that Mr N's remarks were wholly unwarrantable, they seemed to me the effect of rashness and that he did not understand G.R. Mr. Martineau denies the inspiration of the writers of the N. Testament, and also attaches so great importance to a belief in miracles as to make them the exclusive ground of a title to the name of Christian. Now Mr R. does not agree with him in either of these points. In regard to the first (if I understand him) he thinks the writers were partially inspired, and that their inspiration does not necessarily imply infallibility, and to the second topic he does not consider the belief in miracles *necessary* to the title of Chr. but that a man may be a good Chr. without this belief. I believe I have concisely stated the grounds of difference. I do not object to free discussion but if it is to continue I trust there will be no bitterness in it. Mr Norton was much too sharp—I was extremely interested in the review, especially as it gives copious extracts from Martineau which are very beautiful. I long to get the lectures and read them for myself. The portions on the "Uses of the Bible" and the principle [*sic*] events in the "Life of our Saviour" are exquisite. I should dissent from Mr M. on the same topics which Mr R. does but I don't feel now prepared to say that I fully agree with all which Mr R. says concerning miracles, but that he did not merit Mr N's observations. (11 November 1836)

Beginning and ending with reference to Norton's comments, Tilden marked out her own approach as clearly different from his. Unlike Norton, she would draw no hasty conclusions. Pointedly aware of his failings, she guaranteed that no one could level the charge of "rashness" against her. She clearly established the grounds of her commentary. Based on her own reading ("When I read the review for myself"), she substantiates that reading by her own summary of Ripley's main points. Where, in her estimation, Norton had written without understanding what Ripley meant, she would demonstrate the extent of her comprehension and willingly acknowledge its limits. While she felt comfortable stating the points of difference between Ripley and Martineau, she was not ready to assess her own differences from Ripley. That would require another reading of his review, and until then she would reserve judgment. Whether her position on miracles was the same as Ripley's remained to be seen.

At this point, what she could assert without hesitation was her criticism of Norton's approach. Looking back to where she began her comments, it would appear that Tilden attributed the atmosphere of controversy largely to Norton's article. His "unpleasant remarks" had prompted "much conversation" about Ripley's review. From Tilden's perspective, Norton's mistakes made Ripley's or Martineau's negligible. His error of method created a far more serious problem than any particular position on the question of miracles or inspiration. Not only had he acted too quickly, but he had introduced a tone that would flaw any interpretation. His "bitterness" weakened the credibility of his remarks. What Tilden advocated was "free discussion."

Her comments on the nature of productive debate suggest both the source and the legitimation of her own aesthetic of frankness. In his review, Ripley lauded Martineau for his "spirit of frank discussion" and adapted this "spirit" to his own comments.[26] In disagreeing with Martineau, he distinctly stated that he had no interest in fomenting controversy. He spoke in the "spirit" of suggestion, not contention. Ripley's approach was by no means unique to him. Unitarian ministers had defined themselves in contrast to the rhetorical flamboyance of their orthodox counterparts. In the emergence of an identifiable Unitarian Church in the United States, the conflicts had been undeniably bitter, characterized more by Norton's style than by Ripley's. Unitarian ministers soon assessed the damages to their position caused by this rhetoric and by the second decade of the century were advocating a less contentious tone in their comments, whether from the pulpit or in the religious journals where the wars were being waged.

William Ellery Channing was at the forefront in this effort of style. In his 1819 sermon "Unitarian Christianity," delivered at the ordination of Jared Sparks, he had called for the warfare to end and for discussion to begin. Championing "free and frank" inquiry, he maintained that his fellow ministers had no interest in cultivating an inflammatory style either in or out of the pulpit.[27] His colleagues took heed. A stock item in the pulpit repertoire was the sermon on the importance of avoiding divisions within the church. Always good material for pulpit exchanges, such sermons unfailingly called attention to how a discussion was framed.[28] These sermons preached the practice of open discussion identified by a carefully considered prose.

Tilden's aesthetic of frankness was firmly grounded in this Unitarian ideal. Not only did it sanction the "plain speaking" she valued, but it offered her the context in which such directness would not be seen as inappropriate. Unlike the early moments in family conversation where outspokenness was defined as temper, discussion of religious topics called for frank expression of her ideas. She could speak her mind as long as her words were characterized by the "spirit of frank discussion." She was clearly aware of the precedents for her approach. In late December, when she quoted Channing's response to Furness's controversial *Remarks on the Four Gospels*, the words she chose to remember had more to do with the reader's approach than the writer's argument. In her quotation, Channing speaks with the spirit of magnanimity. Tilden's prose furnished him with the following words: "When a writer gives us so much that is good we ought not to find fault with him because we don't agree with him. There is much to like" (29 December 1836).

Two weeks earlier, Tilden had applied her own version of generous reading in her initial response to Furness's book. Clearly disagreeing with the way in which he naturalized Christ's miracles, she framed her difference from Furness with praise. While she questioned the authority of his interpretation, she nonetheless admired what stood behind the author's work. Committing an intentional fallacy of a new order, she focused on the "great feeling" with which the work was written before she registered the particulars of her disagreement.

> Last evening I finished reading Mr Furness book "Remarks on the four Gospels." What shall I say of it—as yet I hardly know. Certainly some of it is beautifully true, I feel that my faith and interest in Christ are quickened and enlivened by it. It is written with great feeling and shows a hearty interest in religion. Humanitarians must be delighted with the work—But I cannot wholly agree with him. Some expressions startle, offend me. He is really ingenious in his explanations of Scripture, *I* do not *see* his *authority* for all of them. His view of the Miracles is altogether new and strange to me. He quotes Dr. Channing largely on the Miracles, but if I understand Mr F. he wholly disagrees with him. According to W.F. I do not see why any one with superior moral excellence and *faith* may not perform miracles as well as the "*Man* of *Nazareth*" The whole book (340 pages) shews a heart full of a most affectionate interest in Jesus, it is written with much simplicity of style, but now & then I think with some carelessness also. I am grateful for the confirmation it has afforded my own faith not by what he says of the miracles however. I think it will lead to much discussion, but as yet I have scarcely heard an opinion concerning it. (15 December 1836)

Two weeks later she would have the chance to test her own opinion against Channing's when he paid one of his pastoral visits. For Tilden, the point most in need of discussion was Furness's position on the miracles. Calling his position "altogether new and strange," she added the qualifying phrase "to me." Guiding her comments by her model of frankness, she acknowledged that Furness's position might, in fact, not be entirely new. She would

claim only its newness to her. What troubled her in Furness's discussion
was how utterly common miracles became. By turning them into expressions of exemplary character, Furness separated them from a power unique
to Christ. She clearly saw the implications of this position. If character made such all-powerful action possible, then she did not see why "any
one with superior moral excellence and *faith* may not perform miracles."
The possibility was opened to all, and in consequence, Jesus became
simply human. As her underlining reveals, Furness's commentary on the
miracles firmly tied Jesus' identity to the human realm. He was "the '*Man
of Nazareth*.'"

From Tilden's perspective, Furness's work was saved by its tone. Because
it conveyed "a most affectionate interest in Jesus," she could bracket its
comments on the miracles and concentrate instead on her response. As her
opening and closing remarks suggest, reading the book proved to be a valuable experience. Her faith and interest were "quickened and enlivened."
And despite—or perhaps because of—her disagreement with his treatment of the miracles, she had found her own position confirmed by reading his work.

That she would find little to agree with in Furness's discussion of the
miracles comes as no surprise. Two weeks earlier, having reread Ripley's review, she was ready to state her own position on the miracles. It differed
from both Martineau's and Ripley's, but she did not consider such difference disagreement. At the same time, it was not quite agreement, as her
phrasing suggests. Beginning her comments on her second reading of
Ripley's review, she noted that she "like[d] it better than [she] did at first"
and that there was "*very very* little that [she] should not quite agree with."
She measured her disagreement in terms of agreement and presented the
disparity as inconsequential.

The "very very little" of her assessment, however, opened ample space
for her statement of difference. Departing from both the book and its reviewer, she revised their positions to produce her own interpretation.

I cannot in my mind separate the miracles from Chty. for they are so
necessary to the unity the completeness of our religion. Many minds
are more convinced by them than by any other argument; though to
me the truth and moral beauty, the adaptation of Christ's character
and instructions to my own soul, to the wants of the universal world
in all states and ages, is a conclusive argument for its divine character.

Nothing would tempt me to give up the miracles, they are such a beautiful and strong confirmation of our Saviours claim as the Son of God, we could not part with them they are *necessary* to complete the chain of evidence, they are a keystone to the arch of the Chr[istian] faith. (4 December 1836)

From her perspective, the miracles were necessary. She could not "separate" them from Christianity itself. Their necessity, however, did not match Martineau's argument. Where he maintained their importance to the individual believer, she identified them with Christianity as a whole. In this way, her interpretation paralleled Ripley's. In his argument, a belief in miracles could never be made a test of an individual's faith. An individual could believe in Christianity independently of the miracles, and such belief should in no way be deemed inferior. Tilden adopted a similar stance. She saw a "conclusive argument" for the "divine character" of Christianity in its perfect adaptation to human character. She was convinced by its "truth and moral beauty" rather than by the miracles themselves. With Ripley, she saw Christ's miracles as a proof of his authority, but at this point, she parted company with the reviewer. Having followed his authority in her summary of his remarks and in the very phrasing with which she praised the extracts from Martineau's work, she would in the end come to a different conclusion. Where Ripley relegated the miracles to a secondary position, she would argue for their primacy, not in Martineau's manner, but in her own. In her reading, they were essential to Christianity as a system. They guaranteed its "unity" and furnished its completeness. Presenting them as one link in the "chain of evidence," she changed her image and elevated their importance. The miracles were a "keystone to the arch of Christian faith." While an individual, like herself, might well be faithful without them, they held the very structure of religion together.

What held Tilden's interpretation of the miracles together was its response to and revision of authority. When read as a whole, her letters from late 1836 delineate a method of interpretation she could authentically claim for herself. It was grounded in a firm alliance with the recognized authorities of her world. William Ellery Channing, the congregation of the Federal Street Church, a reviewer for the *Christian Examiner:* she framed her comments as response to their words. She would, at times, even borrow their words, but the loan always resulted in revised repetition. Taking the authority's words out of context, she re-placed them in her own and provided them with her own meaning. When she quoted authority or appealed to it, the language was evocatively vague. Channing's response to Furness is a case in point. It sums up his method of interpretation, not the interpretation itself. What Tilden adopted was a style, a style she could well craft to her own and different ends. The same could be said of a reference she made to Gannett as her guide in interpretation. Lamenting his absence, she told him that she looked forward to when they could again read together. Until that time, she substituted another source. She turned to "*his* Scriptural Interpreter." Her reference was to the religious publication of that name.[29] Gannett had served as its editor for five years. It included numerous articles on biblical interpretation, some written by him, many solicited from other contributors. Taking it as her nominal guide, she provided herself with the sanction of Unitarianism without demanding a specific interpretation. Gannett's literal presence might well force her to take his reading as her own. His "Scriptural Interpreter" could enforce no such demands. She was free to respond to its authority in her own way.

What characterized this interpretive response was its tone. Reclaiming the frankness she had once had to forfeit, she revised it into the direct assertions of her letters. Modeling her comments along the lines of a "free and frank" discussion, she presented her ideas as convictions carefully created. Guarding herself from the charge of "rash" response, she emphasized her "calm and quiet" mind. In contrast to the earlier association of this phrase with a silencing of thought, she here revised it to mean a thorough, painstaking process in which all thought passed before the mind's eye. If certain thoughts were left unsaid, such silence represented the individual's clear choice.

Throughout her 1836 letters to Gannett, Tilden presented herself as an exemplary character. Drawing on the Unitarian belief that the interpretation was only as good as the interpreter, she carefully crafted a persona whose position could be accepted on the authority of its character. That her attempts did not go unnoticed or unrewarded emerge from Gannett's side of the correspondence. He termed her "an example of hope." Not only recognizing her as exemplar, he accepted her counsel and praised her judgment, which, as he had earlier told her, he had "learned greatly to respect" (7 May 1836).

Tilden virtually created an exemplary character in her own image. In contrast to her earlier efforts at shaping herself into the minister's mold, she exercised the prerogative of the novelist creating both a character for herself and a narrative in which to act. As late as January 1837, two weeks before she sailed for England, she would not know just how plot-driven this narrative would become. Writing to Gannett on 4 January 1837, she anticipated no change in their circumstances. She wrote in response to the best information she had. Having received only one letter from her husband, little change seemed likely. His letter suggested that he was slowly improving and would continue to improve. The word from early November, however, was not the same as the news from midmonth, when Gannett's English doctor, Francis Boott, decided that Tilden must, if possible, join her husband. Writing to Channing and to Bigelow, Boott asked if such a precipitate journey were possible for Tilden. Relying on their wisdom, he did not approach Tilden directly, and he advised the same to his patient. He agreed to let Gannett write to Tilden but stipulated that the letter be sent to Channing. In consequence, Gannett wrote two letters, one begging Tilden to come, the other giving a simple, noncommittal recitation of his experiences in London. Channing, after reading Boott's letter and consulting with Bigelow, was then to decide which letter Tilden would receive.

From Tilden's next letter to Gannett, written after her arrival in Liverpool, it is not clear whether Channing gave her either letter.[30] She commented only on Boott's words and made no mention of Gannett's. It appears that the only information she was given before she left for England came from Boott's letter and her conversation with Channing. Her response was immediate. Demonstrating the "exemplary character" she had created for herself, Tilden received the news of Gannett's continuing decline with characteristic decisiveness. In a matter of days, she left Boston for New York, where she would sail on the next packet for England.

In the words she left behind, Tilden illustrated the authority she had learned to claim as her own. Characterized by directness, her words were also marked by sympathetic understanding. To her sister and mother, she sent words of comfort and embodied them in her enclosures of pressed flowers. Although she was identifiably the individual in need of comfort, she herself turned comforter. In a note to her mother she wrote, "You dear Mother, *have* sent me heart's ease long ago. Can't I send it to you now" (14 January 1837). The understanding that yielded comfort, however, also produced criticism. One feature of direct statement was its considered frankness. Writing to Channing after their conversation in Boston, Tilden politely indicated her displeasure at how the situation had been handled. Reminding him of her own agency as an individual, she demonstrated her

CHAPTER SIX

Claiming Authority: The "I"
of the Sympathetic Seer

Tilden left Boston for New York on 12 January 1837. She arrived on the 14th, stayed with her sister Catherine for two days, and sailed for England on the 16th. It was little more than a week, if that, since she had received the news about Gannett's alarmingly poor health.[1] Two weeks after Tilden left New York, her sister Mary began a letter by singing her sister's praises. In the events surrounding her hurried departure, Anna had finally been given the narrative in which she could embody the part of the exemplary character. Commenting on the news in Boston, Mary remarked, "There is no end to the enquiries about your departure, and [to] the praises, that are sounded from all quarters about your courage and determination" (29 January 1837). With her unwavering certainty and calmly directed decisiveness, Tilden had established an identity unassailable in her congregation's eyes.

In the months that separated her from her congregation, Tilden continued to establish this identity through her letters. As she had discovered in her correspondence with Gannett, this particular form opened the freest space for self-representation. Writing from England or the Continent, sending letters primarily to her mother but also to her sisters, she cast herself as an individual integrally part of two worlds. In her travel letters home during her eighteen months abroad, she was the responsive observer carefully cultivating the common ground she shared with her correspondents. Taking their words, she imagined "home." Taking her words, she shaped the uncommon ground of her travels into a setting her readers could readily imagine.

In her descriptions from both home and abroad, Tilden drew on conventions of representation, both verbal and visual, well known to her readers back in Boston. Immediately at her disposal was a wide range of travel writing. Whether travel letters of instruction like Orville Dewey's *The Old*

World and the New or tour books like William Gilpin's *Observations on the River Wye*, Tilden and her family were well acquainted with the "moral" and "picturesque" aspects of travel.[2] She read sermons, if not in stones, then in sunsets and valleys and mountain passes. At the same time, she borrowed the visual elements of pictorial representation to compose her verbal landscapes. Although she herself lacked the training that would have enabled her to sketch the sites she visited, she knew the principles of picturesque composition and did not hesitate to apply them to her prose descriptions.[3]

Tilden was well versed in the difficulties of representing the visual solely by means of the verbal. Where her words failed, she turned to other sources of representation with which she knew her correspondents would be familiar. Tilden's descriptions frequently revolved around lines from poems and incidents from novels. To bring places home to her correspondents, Tilden called on the experienced eye of the reader. What her mother and sisters had seen in Wordsworth's poems or Scott's novels could be used to portray what their fellow reader saw in England and Scotland. The literary setting served as guide to the physical place. It also allowed both letter reader and letter writer to remain an active presence in the letter's world of representation. By virtue of their common reading, Tilden's mother and sisters were included despite their absence. And Tilden herself avoided the depersonalized voice of the travel narrator. The tone of observing critic was a familiar feature of travel narratives, but in the descriptions Tilden crafted, she was preeminently the daughter and sister who had read particular works with a particular group of readers.[4]

Tilden's descriptions are shaped in accordance with the roles she envisioned both for herself and for her correspondents. Never at ease in the position of distanced observer, she preferred letters to journals, framing her observations as responses rather than self-contained judgments. In contrast to the standard voice of criticism used by the travel narrator, Tilden departed from convention to develop a speaking persona based on a carefully considered evaluation of the places she visited. As in her letters over the Norton-Ripley debate, she guarded herself against premature criticism. No charge of rash judgment would mar the observations she offered. She refused to cultivate the tone of detached observer for another reason as well. Wanting to remain imaginatively connected to her "home" identity, she cultivated the familial relationships she had defined most readily for herself, extending them into the new world of epistolary conversation. She sought a different way of collapsing the distance between herself and home. Casting her correspondents as her representatives, she asked them to stand in her place and speak her words where she could not.

IMAGES FOR HOME: TILDEN'S EUROPE LETTERS AND THEIR READERS

Tilden looked to two of her correspondents in particular to serve as her representatives back home in Boston. Writing to her mother and to her older sister Catherine, she provided them with detailed information about Gannett's health and with an interpretive framework within which to present it.[5] Fearing that the Federal Street Church would judge her husband and herself unfavorably for their extended stay in Europe, Tilden attempted to circumvent any criticism from the congregation. With one notable exception, her comments on Gannett were carefully qualified. While reporting improvement in his health, she made it clear that he was still far from a full recovery. Only once, in the brief euphoria after her arrival, did she represent Gannett's condition as irreversibly improved. Her perception changed almost immediately, for in their first few days together in London, she quickly learned how problematic his health remained. Two days after her arrival, she notes in her journal, "Mr G. was not well. I fear he is not so much better as I had supposed" (10 February 1837).

At this point, "not well" meant a profound disturbance of mind. The smallest degree of uncertainty sent Gannett into despair. If he could not decide what pair of boots to purchase, if he felt that he had breached etiquette with an acquaintance or had not been fully engaged in conversation, he returned to their lodgings so visibly upset that hours passed before he was once again calm. Two weeks into their stay in London she reported the following incident: "Mr G. returned about 5 o'clock very ill & thinking he had not done right towards Campbell, he continued so sick all the evening that at 10 o'clock I sent for Dr. Boott, he came immediately, & in the course of an hour he was much relieved" (20 February 1837). On the facing page, she added, "He had done quite right in regard to C. but nothing which could be said would make him think so." Events like these made her exceedingly cautious in her reports on Gannett's condition. Haunted by her initial words of encouragement as well as those sent back to Boston by Gannett's casual acquaintances, she feared the misunderstandings that would arise if, and finally when, Gannett was unable to resume his duties as originally planned. Her letters to her mother and to her sister Catherine thus became her vehicle for explanation. Both women were long-standing and well-respected members of the church. Catherine had taught in the Sunday school since its founding. Zebiah Brown Tilden had not only housed the minister for many years but had served as an adviser, often conveying the congregation's concerns to him in the privacy of a letter.[6] Both Zebiah Tilden and her daughter Catherine were church members to whom the congregation listened, and thus, when Anna wrote to them about her husband, she knew she was giving the information a potentially public audience.

She also knew that she was presenting her views to two individuals who would use her comments with discretion. If, in writing to Catherine, she lodged a complaint against "our blessed talking city of Boston" (20 August 1837), she could guarantee that her words would remain solely the province of her private reader's knowledge. At the same time, she trusted her correspondents to use what they chose from her letters. Her description of Gannett's health would be judiciously represented when her mother or sister spoke with members of the congregation. Her comments would be received as the authoritative interpretation.

Reminiscent of her correspondence with Gannett during the previous spring, these letters carry out an extended work of persuasion. Where the earlier letters focused their effort directly on the correspondent, the letters from Europe assumed the correspondents were in agreement. Her mother and sister required the materials of persuasion and not persuasion itself. They needed the information to convince others that Tilden's letters provided the only trustworthy report on the minister's condition. In large part, her task lay in creating a credible, but flexible, representation of Gannett's health. She sought to present Gannett's condition in a way that would neither alarm nor encourage. On the one hand, she made clear that he was, in fact, better. On the other, she emphasized how much "better" he would have to be before he could once again serve as minister to the Federal Street Church. She walked the fine line between reassurance and request. Wanting the congregation to feel itself justified in its expense, she at the same time did not want their expectations of recovery to exceed their generosity. After her first letter home, her message was consistent and clear: Gannett's health, although improving, was still precarious. Full recovery remained imaginable but only with the greatest care and the greatest patience. A long period stretched between improvement and recovery; Tilden and Gannett's doctors were the only ones close enough to the situation to make certain that the former was not prematurely identified as the latter.

Tilden's comments were phrased in the simple, direct manner she had developed in her correspondence with Gannett. Writing to her mother in June, she tempered exclamation with a sobering declarative statement: "How much Mr G. is changed for the better—he is another man—and yet not a strong or well one" (4 June 1837). Three and a half months later, the refrain was the same. Gannett was better but with no guarantee that his improvement would be permanent. Almost a year after his departure for England, their travel plans were still painstakingly shaped by his unstable condition. In September 1837 she writes, "We are still obliged to move cautiously and slowly, in order to keep what health and strength Mr G. has gained. We expected to have left Birmingham at 5 o'clock this A.M. but are detained until 2 at least, if not all day, as Mr G. is not well enough to leave." After giving a general summary of how their travel was arranged, she explained the particular reason for their delay. After a month's stay in Vichy, France, packing was an extensive project that overly fatigued Gannett. Stressing his newly acquired virtue of prudence, she cites his willingness to delay their departure for England as a sign of improvement. At the same time she made clear that it was a hard-learned lesson. His prudence arose from the "dread" he felt at the prospect of one of his "ill turns."

Her carefully qualified assessment extends throughout the passage. Her description balances encouragement against caution. Giving the reason for their initially unplanned stay in Vichy, she sang the praises of the place as far as she could but then clearly stated their limitations. Vichy's famous waters had been duly and dutifully taken by Gannett with promising, yet incomplete, results. She writes, "The waters of Vichy have been of great service to him in many respects, but especially in regard to that sad habit of constipation, from which he has now for so long a time, been a constant sufferer. In this, he is also much better but yet *very* far from right." Once again improvement is presented as limited and uncertain yet not quite matter for discouragement. She provides one area in which his progress seemed inarguable. Indecision no longer plagued him. His mental health had prospered, although his physical condition continued to be a source of uncertainty. Immediately after her comments on the partial relief provided by Vichy's waters, she continued with a statement of firm reassurance. "As for *depression* of spirits, we have both of us forgotten there is such a thing, he has quite recovered from it. It would delight you to see the cheerful, vigorous tone of his mind."

The final portion of this passage raises questions about how the recipient would have used her correspondent's words. Which parts of the letter would Zebiah Tilden have quoted directly, which would she have presented only in their general outline? Which would have been omitted altogether? While Tilden balanced her descriptions with an eye to their potential audiences, she also authorized her initial audience, her addressed correspondents, to represent her words as they saw fit. Tilden termed her style "plain speaking" and recognized how problematic such a style might be. *All* of what she said could not be repeated verbatim to the congregation. She trusted her correspondents to revise her words as necessary. They would *not* misrepresent her, and perhaps could not, for she believed that the "plain" character of her words would guarantee their faithful representation. What her initial reader changed for subsequent audiences would by no means mistake the purpose of her descriptions.

Tilden's extended description of Gannett's health from her September letter provides a case in point. Its careful balance between realistic assessment and guarded optimism permeates the whole. At the same time the balance is tilted ever so slightly toward reassuring the congregation. She ends her description of Gannett's progress with the unqualified words about his mental health, and she concludes the passage by celebrating the congregation itself. In its entirety, the conclusion of the passage reads as follows:

> As for *depression* of spirits, we have both of us forgotten there is such a thing, he has quite recovered from it. It would delight you to see the cheerful, vigorous tone of his mind. Oh if he could only have physical health restored him—! if this could but be granted to us—but I must, I ought cheerfully to say 'Thy will be done' Oh dear Mother if you only knew, if you could imagine how 'good' Our Father has been to us amidst all the suffering we have been called upon to endure, and the disappointments of our lives which have not been few—yet I am sure we can see and feel that *He* has watched over us—What friends what true friends have been raised up for us, in foreign and strange places, who have opened to us sources of pleasure and happiness, and have helped us in sickness or trouble. How much we have been allowed to

enjoy *together,* both of nature and art, what beautiful weather and seasons we have had for every thing. And what friends we are blessed
with at home—God bless and keep you all—

Zebiah Tilden faced an interesting process of revision in sharing this report
with the congregation. Would the first two sentences have been read directly to interested individuals? Or would only the last of these sentences,
with its invitingly plural "you," have signaled Tilden's approval for direct
quotation? Her prayer for his complete recovery might well have passed
uncensored, but the doubting "ought" that follows would most likely have
been omitted. In the mother's public representation of her daughter, Anna
Gannett the minister's wife might have, without hesitation, cheerfully proclaimed "Thy will be done" as she unreservedly affirmed God's goodness.
Their sufferings would have been highlighted, but not from the daughter's
perspective. What the daughter acknowledged directly ("the disappoint-
ments of our lives which have not been few") the mother might well have
tempered by claiming such a perspective as her own, and by implication, as
the congregation's. Together they could exclaim over the extent of the Gannetts' trials, since by the rules of exemplary character, the sufferers were not
supposed to announce their own sufferings. Tilden's gratitude would have
been highlighted but references to "pleasure and happiness" left out. Her
final comment would have been appropriate for full quotation, for the passage ends with a celebration of home that would have been highly reassuring to any listener's ears.

Tilden's letters reflect a keen sense of audience. In writing home, she knew
that the arrival of her letters would be heralded as a public event, especially
since Gannett wrote so little in her first several months abroad. A letter potentially had many audiences, and she was well aware of the differences
among them. This awareness is seen most distinctly in three letters written
within days of each other to three different correspondents—the first to
her mother, the second to Catherine, the third to her youngest sister, Zebiah. Written shortly after Tilden and Gannett decided to remain abroad
several months longer, these letters differ precisely according to their correspondents. The letter to her mother provides a lengthy account of the
doctors' advice; to Catherine she sends an exhaustive history of Gannett's
health since her arrival in England. She also includes some private complaints about the public lives led by ministers' wives. For Zibby, she tells a

very different story, presenting a collection of traveler's tales designed specifically for her particular reader. Through her words, she offered her sister places to imagine as well as preparations to be made for this imagined voyage.

In her letters to her mother and older sister, Tilden's imagination pointed in a far different direction. Concerned that the decision to spend an extended period of time in Vichy would be perceived as an excursion for pleasure, she wrote to both correspondents in the hope that any such misinterpretation would quickly be corrected. In her 14 August letter to her mother, she admitted her concern and provided a message for her mother to convey as necessary. Tilden remarked, "I trust none of our many friends will think that we came to Vichy to lengthen our time in Europe, or that either of us have [*sic*] the *least desire* to remain here another winter. I have been a little afraid *some* might think we were having a good time here, & so liked to stay away. I can only say that such a thought would be not only unkind, but *wholly untrue.*" Concerned that the congregation would mistake desperation for pleasure, Tilden included the annotated version of their decision. From what Gannett had previously written, she feared that their excursion to Vichy would in all probability be misinterpreted. After reading Gannett's letters to his close friend Samuel Torrey and to Jacob Bigelow, his Boston doctor, she felt that he had unwittingly omitted the most important information. He had consulted physicians in Paris; they advised him to extend his stay. He reported their advice as a "plain statement of fact" but failed to mention his own preference in the matter. Initially believing that the doctors' advice was in fact moot because he simply would not be able to act on it, he did not bother to include their disappointment over a delayed return to the States. When he wrote to Bigelow and Torrey, Gannett had given no serious thought to implementing the doctor's recommendation. Tilden then supplied her mother with the rest of the story. Speaking once more with the Paris physicians, Gannett was "strongly advised" to make the unplanned trip to Vichy as a last resort. The only other choice was to return home "justly discouraged" over the prospects of any lasting improvement in his health.

In this section of the letter, Tilden carefully underlined the authority on which they based their decisions. The Paris doctors were "*able physicians*" who did not casually suggest, but "strongly advised," the visit to Vichy. She concluded the passage by arguing the wisdom of their decision from the point of view of the congregation. Preaching a sermon on wise stewardship, she maintained that their primary motivation was grounded in faith and sanctioned through experience: "We had left home, and friends & spent much money in pursuit of health, and having done so much, it seemed foolish and wrong to throw away what seemed to us to be a last chance. The event has proved that we were right to come here, whether the good will be permanent or not, we can't tell, but we must live in Hope." To prove the value of the congregation's investment, Tilden emphasized their industry. Having "done so much," they chose to do more in the hope that the last chance would prove the best. She immediately validated their decision but predictably qualified its outcome. Gannett, she said, was much improved, but there was still no guarantee of permanent recovery.

A week later, she wrote a second letter from Vichy, this time to Catherine (20 August 1837).[7] Still worried that Gannett's letter would have been taken as an accurate representation of his health, she devoted two-thirds of this letter to a painstaking record of Gannett's progress since he left the United States and of the varying accounts that had made their way back to Boston. Appearances, she maintained, were deceptive. What others saw as real improvement she alone knew to be transient. Returning to one of the first reports from England, she firmly distinguished appearance from reality: "During the latter part of his voyage he *appeared* as Mr Field[s] & others wrote home, to be much better, but they did not understand him. . . . This entire rest did do him a little good for the time, but produced no radical change either in body or mind." Privileging her own perception, she implied that the earliest accounts were invariably misleading because no one who wrote about Gannett "understood" the complexity behind the seemingly simple appearance.

The letter proceeds by way of minute detail, painting a grim picture of continuing decline. She carefully documents the costly mistakes that had limited improvement to a marginal hope. Combining exercise with economy, Gannett insisted on walking everywhere. He wanted to "save the expense of riding." Tilden pointedly calls attention to this measure of economy and its attendant expense. He had severely fatigued himself, forfeiting any strength he had gained on the relatively restful voyage to England. By her account, Gannett's health in the months before her arrival was increasingly uncertain. The "change of scene" provided by Paris and his brief trip to Holland did him some good, but the benefit was of short duration. In her description of the days following her arrival, she again preached the fallacy of judging by appearance: "He returned to London the last of Jan, in a much better state than when he left it, & he was kept up tolerably well by the expectation of my arrival, so that when I first saw him the 5 of Feb, I thought him for the *first day* only, to be *very* much better than he really was. The day after my arrival in London we wrote home, giving too good, and not true accounts of his health, as I soon learnt to my sorrow." Admitting that she herself fell prey to misinterpretation, she sounds a cautionary note over her initial credulity. If she herself, in his presence, had been misled, how could anyone who learned the details secondhand assess the situation correctly? Quickly disabused of her mistake, she discovered a different truth than the one she had sent home.

This letter, in effect, sought to set the record straight. It gave the "true account" in contrast to the partial representations that others had sent or that she had mistakenly provided. Characterized by qualified optimism, it did not hesitate to spell out the full nature of Gannett's difficulties. Whether describing his prolonged battle with constipation or his "depression of spirit" and its baffling manifestation in his sometimes thrice weekly "distressed turns," she continued her "plain speaking." By withholding no detail in her description, she sought to gain credibility with her extended audience. The "truth" lay in her account, and in hers alone. This "truth" went beyond her commentary on the past and included her prognosis for the future, a prognosis that reflected directly on the present. Reporting that Gannett had once again been making plans for his renewed work in Boston, she ended with a word for any doubters in the congregation: "I wish you could see him now, he is so bright, so happy & cheerful, his mind is so active again, he enjoys this new feeling of health so much & is making plans in his own mind for the future, as he now dares to look forward to it with hope of usefulness, and service among his people. I believe he is as eager to be at home again as I am." For those who believed the minister and his wife preferred Europe over Boston, Tilden paints a picture of "usefulness" for public consumption, and she in fact tells her sister that the portion of the letter on Gannett's health was more for her mother than for herself. She directed the information to the primary contact with the congregation.

The portion of the letter reserved specifically for Catherine was decidedly private. Although it too voiced homesickness, it also registered a distinct dissatisfaction with certain aspects of home. For Catherine's eyes alone, Tilden recorded her displeasure over what she imagined the home folk would be saying. Unlike the fear she had voiced to her mother, this emotion was much less polite. In fact, it bears nothing of the solicitous phrasing that unmistakably stamps the words of the other letter. There, she had written, "I have been a little afraid," and describes the mistaken judges as "unkind" but gives them no personal presence. In her letter they remain an unspecified "some." To Catherine, she represents a different scene. In contrast to the impersonal, unidentified group, Boston is portrayed as a center of gossip in which "many unpleasant things will be said about [them], for a minister and his wife are always open to observation in our blessed talking city of Boston." Her portrait of Boston is in fact specifically peopled, for immediately preceding this sentence is a reference to one parishioner's comments in particular. She recalls a conversation shortly after her marriage in which a certain unnamed "lady" told her that she would soon become the "*speckled bird* of the parish." She found the representation decidedly unpleasant. She comments to Catherine, "This is just what I dislike. I should be delighted if we were not so dependant [*sic*] upon others." Longing for freedom from others' representations of her, she sounds a familiar note to her sister. Appearances are prey not only to misinterpretation but also to false representation. These words, however, are "spoken" in private. At the end of this passage, she adds in parentheses, "This is to *you Kate* please recollect."

Absent from her letter to Catherine are almost any references to Europe itself. The only comment is a brief description of the view Tilden saw when she raised her eyes from the piece of paper on which she was writing. In this letter, as in her other letters to Catherine, place is notably absent. Wishing her letters could be conversations, she offers no further reminder of the distance that separates them. The letter constitutes its own place in which the correspondents step aside from their different locations and meet in an imagined space carefully insulated from the physical surroundings of both writer and reader. The terrain of the letter becomes the governing geography.

In marked contrast to the abstract surroundings of Anna's letter to Catherine, her letter from Vichy to her youngest sister, Zebiah, privileges particular places on the traveler's itinerary. Gannett's health is not mentioned. At age seventeen, Zibby would have no voice outside the family. Unlike her sister or mother, she did not have to carry the particular burden of serving as her sister's or daughter's representative. Instead, she could receive an image from Anna's present situation as well as a reminder of their shared past. Descriptions of donkeys at Vichy and ruins in Rome frame the letter, and within the frame Tilden provides a single and singular home reference, recalling from the past her very particular relationship with this particular sister.

Nine years older than her youngest surviving sister, Anna attached special significance to this sibling relationship.[8] When she was sixteen and her sister seven, Anna had been given a particular role to fill. She was designated as the "little mother" to this sister who was the adult mother's namesake. Expediency certainly played a part in this decision, given the number of individuals then living under Zebiah Tilden's care.[9] The domestic chores assigned to Anna—keeping the youngest daughter's clothing organized and in good repair, listening to Zibby's recitation of Scripture, putting Zibby to bed—saved time for the mother. Tilden, however, clearly separated these tasks from mundane domestic work, for the mother's charge extended beyond daily physical needs.

Comments in her 1827–28 journal reveal how seriously Tilden took her responsibility. She identified it as a powerful shaping influence for both herself and her sister. At the end of November 1827, newly charged with her task of caretaking, she reflected on its meaning for Zibby's future: "I think I shall take a good deal of care of her, and I [trust] that she will improve, she is a child of very good principles, though she has her faults, of which she seems to be sensible, and I trust that my endeavours to make her better, will succeed. It is one of my greatest pleasures to put her to bed, and I hope she will love me much" (30 November 1827). The passage bears close attention, for it reveals the dynamic by which self-definition proceeded. The self-questioning, self-critical daughter steps aside from her usual self-examination to look instead at her sister. Evaluating this youngest sibling, she cites strengths and weaknesses, though in the most abstract terms. Zibby's principles are "good," and with such a guarantee, her character is essentially sound. Faults, however, exist, though these are immediately diminished by the assurance that she herself knows what they are. In describing her sister, Tilden was essentially describing the image by which she herself would like to have been represented. At the time, such an image may well have seemed within reach, for with the particular opportunity provided for her, Tilden believed she would "succeed," not just in her sister's self-improvement, but in her own.

The opportunity was a welcome one for Tilden, given her unsettled position as the youngest of the family's "almost" adult daughters. It defined a tangible "usefulness" for her days and provided her with a distinct context for practicing the hard work of the exemplary character.[10] It also offered

the hope of an earthly reward. In her journal entries, Tilden clearly identified caretaking with the promise of love: "I hope she will love me much"; "I
want to get to understand her, so that I may manage her in such a way that
she may love & respect & confide in me"; "I want her both to love and respect me and hope to conduct myself in such a manner that she may" (30
November, 1827; 12 May 1828; 10 August 1828). Tilden's position as "little
mother" was thus as much a part of her own formation of character as of
Zibby's. Her pleasures in this task indeed seem genuine, and the apparent
approval she won from her sister make this pleasure no surprise. In this
self-contained world within the household, Anna heard her younger sister's
Bible lessons, conversed with her about principle, discovered a forum
where, for that moment, she was the understanding authority and her sister
the thoughtful pupil.

Tilden apparently never forgot the pleasure she took in these moments,
and they may well have been heightened in memory by her painful experience as a teacher, not of sisters, but paying students. The confident hope of
likely success remained an attractive thought firmly associated with an earlier version of home.[11] Ten years later and thousands of miles away, she
turned back to those moments in her letter to her sister, then a year older
than Anna had been when she received the title "little mother." In this letter, Tilden reminded her sister of the particular parts they had played when
Zibby was seven and Anna sixteen. "You see I have not forgotten that in
former times I was called your 'little mother'" (23 August 1837). This remark appears at the end of a page of advice. Although she began the letter
with references to the particular customs of Vichy, she quickly moved into
questions about Zibby's life at home. Wondering how her sister spent her
days, she offered the very advice she had been given when she was her sister's age. Regardless of domestic chores, she trusted that Zibby had arranged
her days in the interest of her studies. The amount of time, she assured her
sister, was not an issue if she used that little time well. Similarly, the absence
of formal instruction was not presented as a major obstacle. She wrote,
"Even if you cannot have the advantage of masters any longer, you can improve yourself greatly, by the care and pains which you can take. If you have
but little time to devote to these things, give that little to thorough work."
Her own experience spoke through these words, validating her past, yet
presenting a slightly different future for her sister.

Tilden offered her sister a significantly different narrative from the one
she herself had lived. Although she brought questions of character firmly

into play in the context of further study, she allowed her sister a greater freedom than she herself had obtained. "The truth is," she wrote, "I love you so much that I long for you to be all that is good and excellent, and weal or woe for your future course, will depend more than you are aware of upon the character you choose to make for yourself now." Her words are marked by a notable absence. God is nowhere mentioned in her advice. Character depends fundamentally on the individual who herself forms it. While the individual's choice profoundly affects her future life, the future is as much a part of *this* world as of the next. And the desirable attributes of character belong to both the mind and the soul: she wants Zibby to be both "good" and "excellent." A distinction in fact separates the two: Tilden reserved "good" for moral questions, "excellent" for intellectual ones.

Tilden's advice to her sister is framed by lively descriptions of her travels. Unlike other letters in which references to home frame the news from abroad, this letter places home in the context of travel. Perhaps remembering her own sense of entrapment in late adolescence, Tilden predicts that Zibby herself would some day "cross the ocean." [12] She tailors her descriptions to her sister's interests and offers a sweeping glimpse into one traveler's experience. Beginning with an anecdotal style reminiscent of the children's literature she would have read to her sister, Tilden represents herself as a comic character mastering the difficult art of making a donkey canter: "You don't know what sort of noises the Donkies make, or what is necessary to say to them, to induce these obstinate creatures to canter. When I went to Randan a few days ago, I tried to imitate the *awful sound* the boys make to these animals, and I succeeded pretty well in uttering the *H e,e,e* of the country. At all events it produced the desired effect." With a storyteller's eye and ear for detail, she sketches this slight vignette, presenting both the problem, making a donkey canter, and the solution, providing the appropriately awful sound. The rest she leaves to her sister's imagination, succinctly activated through her wry comment: "it produced the desired effect."

Following this opening humor, Tilden keeps the noise level high and responds to her sister's question about the children's "clattering sabots." Assuring her that the clatter had by no means been exaggerated in the telling, she promises to bring home a miniature pair of wooden shoes as a souvenir for her sister. With this mention of home, the content of the letter also turns in that direction. Tilden offers her advice to Zibby and ties both her correspondent and herself into a shared past and shared home. Advice to her sister, however, readily merges with descriptions from abroad. In her final suggestion to Zibby about her studies, she imagines her sister traveling to Europe and counsels her on what preparations she could *now* make. She encouraged Zibby to continue drawing even though the family could no longer afford lessons for her. Anna lamented her own lack of skill in this area. While the existence of a single drawing of a tulip signed "Anna Linzee Tilden" indicates that Tilden herself may have begun drawing lessons while still in school, she apparently felt that she had not progressed far enough to transfer her rudimentary skills into landscape sketching. "It is delightful too," she told her sister, "to be able to make little sketches of the scenery about you; how often I have wished that I could do so, when I have seen others with their drawing books, taking views of beautiful falls, temples and ruins." Case in point was her experience in Rome. During a visit to the Colosseum, her companions "happily . . . employed themselves in sketching some of the beautiful objects before them."[13] Tilden's sketch could only appear in words, and as she frequently reminded her readers, verbal descriptions made the work of representation that much more difficult for the correspondents. Not only did the writer have to translate the visual into the verbal, but the reader had to practice the same alchemy in reverse.

In her letter to Zibby, Tilden chose to describe two settings from Rome, both in reference to the artistry of visual representation. This emphasis was chosen with an eye to her reader. Knowing Zibby's enjoyment of the visual arts, she presented a Rome markedly different from the one she had described to her mother. Where her mother's interest lay in assessing Catholicism through the events of Holy Week, her sister's curiosity was sparked by the secular world of painting and sculpting. Tilden encouraged her sister to hone her drawing skills so that she might one day sketch the Colosseum, and she described in detail her visit to the sculptor Thorvaldsen's studio and the process by which his works were produced.[14] Even the particular work she highlights takes account of her sister's background. Responding to Zibby's own musical interests, she evokes the family as a whole when she describes Thorvaldsen's *Apollo among the Shepherds*. What better image to represent the family than this scene of individuals grouped together as listeners. Evoking the pleasant evenings during Bryant Tilden's time at home between voyages, Anna calls to mind the gatherings in which the father would play clarinet while daughter Mary sang and the oldest daughter Isabella accompanied both on piano. Zibby would then have been a small child, and fittingly in Tilden's description of Thorvaldsen's work, her first attention is to the listening child: "The different attitudes of attention in the

various groups is [*sic*] admirably done, a child by the side of Apollo is perfect, he is resting against a rock—a boy with two lambs, one of them in his
arms is beautiful—an old man and child listening to the music—a boy
with his dog—oh these are exquisitely executed." After giving this description, she assures her sister that this is only one of many works she could
have chosen to portray. That her choice was for the musical gathering
speaks not only to home but of it.

In her letters, Tilden unfailingly conjured up images of home. If she was
writing on Sunday, she imagined her correspondents in church, and on the
first Sunday of the month, she lovingly called attention to its special
significance as the Sunday for the communion service. She frequently described family groups in her letters, imagining the familiar gatherings that
occurred with weekly regularity. She as frequently presented home settings
from abroad. The scenes she imagined of family gatherings in Boston were
mirrored in the scenes she represented of herself and her husband. At times
she described evenings spent in the homes of friends, but most often her
descriptions were of Gannett and herself alone in their rooms. In addition
to these brief hearthside scenes, Tilden devoted large sections of her letters
to the news from home. She encouraged her correspondents to write often
and extensively. Lamenting a period in which she had not heard from
home for several months, she recommended her practice of letter writing
to her readers: "I wish somebody at home would take as large a sheet of paper as this, and write as closely as *I* do upon it, just add a few lines every day
as you have time for it. You don't know how precious every word from
home is. Tell us about every thing" (10 December, 24 December entry, 1837).
Her letters consistently request more news: "Tell us about every thing"; "I
want to hear all about everything" (19 November); "tell me *every thing* exactly" (23 October). And whenever letters arrived, her first written words
were always in response to what she had learned. Regardless of the length
of time that separated her correspondents' words and her own, she suspended this passage of time and wrote to the moment of their concerns.
Especially in her correspondence with her mother and Catherine, she reserved her first comments for the individuals at home. News of births and
deaths prompted expressions of joy or consolation. Reports of deepening
economic distress yielded concern and fear. Her letters were framed by
home references. They appear at the beginning, responding to the news of
family events. And at the end, her final words are those that speak directly
to home.

She constructed a framework of home for her words from abroad. Certain references to home were clearly strategic. In the context of the decision to delay their return to the United States, her longing words for home formed part of her argument. Not trusting to an unannotated statement of fact, she made certain to include their particular feelings. It was not enough simply to repeat doctors' advice. The manner in which this advice was received and the regret with which it was taken had to be included as well. Concern over the congregation stood behind many of Tilden's references to home but by no means behind all of them. When she brought to mind a scene from home or provided her correspondent with its domestic equivalent abroad, she sought to collapse the distance and difference separating her world from her correspondents'. Thousands of miles stretched between them. Months separated their exchange of words. Even with a short ocean passage, a letter traveled for a month before reaching its recipient. A reply by "return mail" invariably involved a period of waiting. Two weeks might well pass before the next packet sailed. With poor winds, three weeks would lapse before the Atlantic was crossed. Further delays accompanied the letters sent from Boston, for several weeks might pass before Tilden and Gannett themselves arrived in the city where they had directed that their mail be sent.[15]

The distinct reality of transatlantic correspondence in the nineteenth century effectively meant that a report from one writer's present was profoundly a word from the past by the time the reader received it. Reading a letter thus created an odd sense of displacement. The writer writes in the present, knowing the reader will not read these words until they are long past. The reader reads in the present, reading of the writer's present, all the while knowing that the writer's present is past. The reader's and writer's "present" can never be simultaneous. They can, however, be made to correspond by creating the illusion of a shared present. Tilden's home references function precisely in this way. Presenting images of home, whether set in Boston or Glasgow, she brackets the distance between them by highlighting what is common to both places. To the mind's eye she offers a scene that is independent of any particular location. It is also a scene that is contained by the present, set apart from any reference to time passing. Her sketches of home settings are defined by presence: a group of individuals sitting together. They also evoke a continuous present: the gathering associated with no distinct moment, a gathering that occurs frequently, regularly, predictably. When she introduces these settings, her language evokes immediacy. "I wish I could just look in upon you now," she writes, or, "I

wish *you* could just peep in upon us at this moment" (4 June, end of 11 June
entry; 10 December, end of initial entry). Calling attention to the moment
in which she writes, Tilden attempts to make that present available to her
reader. The "now" of her descriptions is designed to suspend the literal
"now" in which each correspondent lives.

Tilden prolongs the letter's present time by focusing on the act of letter
writing itself. She calls attention to the very moment in which she writes.
The letter is as much about how and when it was written as it is about particular information or particular sites. Before describing the places she has
visited, she prefaces them with remarks about the scene then surrounding
her. Writing to Catherine, she extends the dateline to include a description
of the day itself: "This is a beautiful bright morning, & I am writing to you
from my pleasant, *plain*, little room, on one side I look upon the yellow
fields & green walnut trees, and before me is a glass with beautiful flowers
which Mr G. has brought me before breakfast. He has now gone to the baths,
after breakfast he is going to a town about 12 miles from Vichy" (20 August,
beginning of 23 August entry, 1837). Her words are insistently present: "this
is," "I am writing," "I look." Even in the detail that marks an action that
had already occurred, she remains in a form of the present: "has brought"
rather than the "brought" of the simple past. Any hint of the past is quickly
erased, for her sentence on Gannett's plans for the day makes it clear that
she is still in the ongoing moment "before breakfast."

Tilden shapes the form of the letter itself into another element in the
shared verbal present of correspondence. She turns her letters into journals. Rather than writing a letter at one sitting, she writes over a period of
days. Each day is duly marked with the characteristic spacing she used in
her journals. The date, underlined, is placed at the left-hand margin of the
paper regardless of where the previous words ended. The letters indeed
look like a journal, and Tilden refers to them as just that. To her mother she
calls her correspondence her "letter journal," an "odd sort of journal," she
says, which she keeps as much for her mother as for herself. Sending her a
gathering of her days, Tilden compresses the passing of time into a single
space. The letter is perceived as a whole, no matter how many parts compose it. At the same time, the present-mindedness of the journal entry
keeps both reader and writer focused on the events of the day as they happen. The relatively short entries convey a sense of immediacy that would be
lost were the letter written in retrospect. Rather than reflecting back on
what had happened, she presents what had only just happened or was in
fact happening, even as the writer wrote.

In her pursuit of immediacy, she even learned to embrace interruption. Her letters chronicle the moments in which she stopped writing. Rather than a silencing disruption, these moments became yet another way to maintain the illusion of a continuous present. When she was unable, for any number of reasons, to continue putting words on the page, her letter records the pause in her prose. Instead of silently editing out the circumstances of her writing, she lets such interruptions stand as further evidence of the present she maintains in and through her words. In an entry from Switzerland, Tilden reports the effect of Gannett's return from the post office:

> I only wish [Gannett] could get quite well—Whilst I am writing Mr G. has come in, having put his letters in the office he went to see the Eng. papers and has brought home such sad news of troubles in America that we hardly know what to do, it has thrown such a cloud over our travelling—we hardly know how to be happy when you are all in so much distress, what is to become of our country? she will be a bankrupt—Before writing this last sentence I was going to say . . . (4 June 1837, June 14 entry)

In this entry, Tilden could well have chosen to finish her thought before reporting Gannett's return. Instead, she makes the interruption the topic of her comments, following her thoughts as they occurred. Rather than reserving her remarks on the dismal economic news for later in her letter, she lets her response break in on her comments about Gannett's health. Interruptions remain, reported as they occur. The journal entries of her letters give precedence to the "now" of the letter writer's experience. She chooses not to revise them into the past.

Attempting to create an illusory present that collapsed distances of both time and place, Tilden turned to her descriptions of home as the single location in which the absent could imagine meeting. Although she made clear that their domestic settings abroad were never to be those in Boston, they were nonetheless the equivalent of that "blessed home" she had left behind. Regardless of their literal location—whether France, Scotland, England—they offered familiar territory to both sides of the correspondence. The feelings associated with home did not change with change of location, nor did the language of their expression. Despite literal reminders of difference in setting, the gathering of family in one place paralleled that in another. Writing to her mother from Switzerland, Tilden introduces the gathering she imagined among family members at home by first bringing them into her present: "It is *storming hard* now, and I hardly think we can descend the mt. tomorrow the path will be so broken and muddy. Here we are 5,220 feet above the sea among the high and glorious Alps, isn't it grand to be here?" Calling attention to the "here" and "now" of her setting, she invites her correspondent into her room in the Alps. She brings them in out of the storm and offers the shelter of an exclamation that includes them by implication. Immediately following this evocation of presence, she turns to her Boston home: "I suppose you have been to church to day, I wonder whom you have heard—I wish I could just look in upon you now, I fancy that I should see Uncle Tilden, Aunt Sally, Mr Brown & Isabella with you. I think you have a warm summer evening whilst we are within 3 feet of snow."

Her first thoughts of Boston are of a shared activity and one that was central to the family's life. She imagines them attending church and wonders who preached the sermon. The question of minister addresses both their past and present, for in her days at home, the members of the Tilden household were always eager to find out who the minister would be if neither Channing nor Gannett was scheduled to be in the pulpit. In this case, however, the very uncertainty about the minister speaks directly to the present situation. Gannett's extended absence raises the question of preacher for those both at home and abroad. Tilden then turns to the particular individuals who would have gathered at her mother's in the evening. She marks this thought with difference—their summer evening juxtaposed against her proximity to snow—but concludes with a passage that once again diminishes distance. Ending this entry with a prayer, Tilden writes what could have been spoken by any one of their family group: "Good night dear Mother. May the blessing of Heaven rest upon us all, and let us once more meet in health and happiness. Oh may He give us strength for all our future trials. I feel as if they are in store for us, yet we need not be discouraged for verily trials are blessings, though hard to call them so at the moment we are enduring them.—" (4 June 1837, end of 11 June entry). The first part of the prayer takes the form of benediction. The sense of distance lingers, for the words of this benediction remind their recipients of parting. At the same time, such a prayer would fit readily into a family's evening devotions, as family members parted for their separate households. The second half of the prayer, however, makes no reference to the family's separation. The request for strength and the acceptance of suffering ring with phrases long in use within the family. Tilden ends her evocation of home with the language so familiarly spoken within its walls.

LITERARY LANDSCAPES AND PICTURESQUE TRAVEL:
TILDEN'S FAMILIAR GEOGRAPHY

Tilden's use of well-known phrases and familiar images not only connected her with the home from which she was absent but enabled her to represent the unknown and unfamiliar in a descriptive style that her correspondents could easily imagine. Her travels through Great Britain and the Continent took her to places to which her correspondents had never been. Within the family, traveling had been reserved for business and health, and rarely had there been an opportunity to send the daughters or the mother farther than New York State. Tilden herself had been the recipient of this particular journey, traveling to Saratoga Springs, Lake George, and as far as Niagara Falls in the summer of 1835. Maria, constantly in poor health, was not well enough to travel and was lodged instead in the then rural setting of Groton.[16] Catherine had been sent to Santa Cruz for her health once the school was closed, but no one besides Anna had visited Europe.

Images of Europe, however, held a considerable place in each family member's imagination. Through their reading, they had visited these "foreign" sites many times, and frequently in each other's company. Given the shared reading within the household, family members had often traveled together in prose where Anna now visited in person. The places on Tilden's and Gannett's itinerary were familiar by more than name. They had imagined them as the scenery in which Sir Walter Scott's characters acted or as the setting described by their favorite poet, Wordsworth. If not associated with a particular poem or novel, the sites were known through the history they had read or could be envisioned through the conception they shared about the representation of nature.

To present these known, imagined, but unseen sites, Tilden drew on both literary allusion and pictorial convention. She filtered her descriptions through lenses familiar to her audience. She could count on her correspondents for a ready facility with settings rendered verbally. The Tilden household was decidedly a place that traded actively in words. The family members read fiction and poetry, sermons and journals. They recorded their ministers' words, preserving them for future consideration. They read each other's actions and rendered their responses in carefully measured conversation or questioning, private prose. They read without words, praising the impromptu musical sessions they enjoyed during the father's brief times at home. And they read what had not been written, viewing the wordless text of nature as both the evidence of divinity and the responsive power of humanity.

Writing from Europe, Tilden drew on the verbal common ground on which they had stood for as many years as she could remember. Their shared reading of Wordsworth and Scott became her way of representing the landscape they knew intimately as settings. Her descriptions of the Birmingham Music Festival or of the Freiborg organ played into the music they held in common. And where there were no particular texts readily available, she turned to the vocabulary they had developed for expressing an always capitalized nature. Whether describing a star-punctuated sky in Boston or a sunset in rural Waltham, the Tildens shared a language for representing an otherwise unwritten scene. By no means original to them, this language drew heavily from the eighteenth-century writings on the sublime and the picturesque. What they borrowed they borrowed freely. They were less interested in identifying themselves as followers of Edmund Burke or William Gilpin than in using their terms to evoke the feelings associated with a particular place. Re-creating a place for the mind's eye required a clear rendering of the viewer's response.

When presenting scenes from abroad, Tilden provided her correspondent with a highly charged vocabulary. Her adjectives would have been readily recognized by her reader, not as the vague descriptors a modern reader might imagine, but with an evocative precision. In Tilden's scene painting, views were "glorious," mountains "magnificent," landscape "grand." The individual viewer experienced "awe" before the works of nature and turned this awe frequently into reverence for the God who made nature his work. Her descriptions from England and Europe echo her earlier journals, where nature was presented as a challenge for verbal expression and often celebrated with an overlay of natural theology. And her journal comments echo the language other family members used in their attempts to create a verbal representation of what they saw.

This shared vocabulary borrowed heavily from the widely known concept of the picturesque. Developed by William Gilpin, largely in response to Burke's division of the beautiful from the sublime, the "picturesque" provided another way of viewing the landscape and its effects on the viewer. Burke emphasized the different emotions evoked by different situations. An experience of the sublime resulted from a setting defined by an unremitting intensity. What characterized the sublime was massive size, extremes of light, sharp demarcations in sense impression (loud or sudden sounds, powerful odors), a repetition of forms that left the impression of infinity. It evoked the "most powerful passions" from the viewer, identified by Burke as varieties of pain and terror. "It is productive of the strongest emotion which the mind is capable of feeling. ⟨I say the strongest emotion, because I am satisfied the ideas of pain are much more powerful than those which enter on the part of pleasure⟩."[17] In contrast, the beautiful was largely what the sublime was not. Burke associated it with pleasing variety, an eminently human scale, mild coloration, smooth surfaces, and only the most gradual change in any of its elements. The viewer responded accordingly, with pleasure.[18]

Gilpin focused on a different aspect of the viewer's perception. Rather than emphasizing the viewer's initial response, he focused on the activity of the viewer's imagination. Whether the individual felt soothing pleasure or sheer terror mattered less than how the individual translated response into representation. In viewing one's surroundings, the individual turned creator, seeing more in the land than simply met the eye. Landscape, in Gilpin's terms, provided a "stimulus to the imagination." Were the situation one that might merit Burke's term "sublime," the individual would be struck by a seemingly endless extension of form. Gilpin termed this "simple grandeur" and identified it with "a *uniformity* of large parts, without *ornament,* without *contrast,* without *variety.*"[19] For landscapes defined by variation, Gilpin saw a different kind of "grandeur" and envisioned a different reaction from the viewer. Where "simple grandeur" prompted a mimetic response, the grandeur that accompanied variety invited the individual to treat all variations as malleable. Representation became the viewer's own theme on variation.[20]

Interested above all in pictorial representation, Gilpin set forth his principles of "picturesque composition" as a guide for both the viewing artist and the artistic viewer. Maintaining that nature as a whole was beyond human comprehension, he saw the artist's task as one of skillful selection and revision. To create an image that would be seen by the human eye as a "harmonious whole," the painter could not simply copy the scene but in fact had to rearrange it. Such rearranging, however, was carefully ordered, both in what the individual chose to represent and how he chose to represent it. Drawing on eighteenth-century beliefs about the structure of perception, Gilpin advocated a three-part composition that would readily direct the eye to the "leading subject" of the middle ground. The diagonal winding of a river, the juxtaposition of foreground shade leading to middle-distance light, the carefully placed vertical screens on either edge of the picture: Gilpin taught his readers how to direct their eyes across the landscape and urged them to duplicate this in their own sketches. To prevent structure from hardening into stasis, Gilpin encouraged his readers to concentrate on the variations within the landscapes. He prized what he called "roughness," both in nature and in its sketched representation, for through this inclusion of irregularity, the imagination remained active. The artful inclusion of the varying surface invited the viewer to participate in its continued representation.

Participation, in Gilpin's schema, was key. Viewing a landscape required an active engagement on the viewer's part. It demanded flexibility of mind. The individual moved back and forth between the objects he saw and those he had seen. To represent the "view," memory came into play, and for memory to contribute its full share, the individual engaged in activity of another kind. It was not simply a matter of mastering a few techniques for sketching landscape; the artist succeeded only if the imagination saw more than met the eye. From Gilpin's perspective, the visual image was only a tool serving a different arena of representation. He writes, "The picture is not so much the *ultimate end,* as it is the *medium,* through which the ravishing scenes of nature are excited in the imagination."[21] The sentence occurs in an essay about a particular kind of excursion. Gilpin designated this activity "picturesque travel" and praised its benefits.[22] The traveler of the picturesque mold gained an inexhaustible resource for the future, for he returned with "many delightful scenes stored in his memory." He could afford to stay home, for the best scenes were not the ones he visited but those he imagined.

Gilpin devoted a series of "tour books" to his concept of the picturesque. Extremely popular in both England and the United States, they took as their topics particular regions of Great Britain.[23] Gannett mentions reading Gilpin's *Observations on several parts of Great Britain particularly the Highlands of Scotland* during their visit to Scotland. A version of Gilpin's *Observations on the River Wye* appeared in 1834. Titled *The Wye Tour, or Gilpin on "The Wye"*, it boasted "picturesque additions" and "archeological illustrations" and was clearly marketed for the tourist. When Tilden wrote to her mother that they had gone to see "the beauties of the Wye" (23 September 1837), her phrasing suggests familiarity both with Gilpin and with his concept of the picturesque.[24]

The only surviving letter from Tilden's 1834 excursion to New York State demonstrates that familiarity also meant influence. Written during her visit to Lake George, it reflected the eminently "picturesque" nature of her travels. The moment that prompted her to write could, in fact, not have been more "picturesque." The dateline reads "Sunrise on Lake George" (22 August 1834). Under Gannett's guidance, the traveling party duly boarded a steamship before 5 A.M., suitably availing themselves of the ideal opportunity for "taking the views." Once on board, Tilden positioned herself both to observe the scene and to record her observations. Her verbal description pays careful attention to Gilpin's rules of composition. She frames her picture with vertical side screens; she calls attention to the variety created by the different heights of the hills; she illuminates the center of this verbal canvas, bringing the light of the sunrise directly into the middle distance of her description. Her picturesque rendering of the landscape reads as follows: "Surrounded by hills, thickly wooded, which are in the most lovely *irregular succession* the mist is rising from the Lake and the rays of the early sun, shining through it forms the most bewitching clouds half way up the mountains" (Tilden's emphasis). Tilden's underlining emphasizes the precise terms of Gilpin's picturesque. He had praised "irregularity" in the "succession" of a landscape; so too did Tilden.[25] Her interpretation of the scene reflects a similar emphasis. Borrowing his vocabulary, she concludes her description by privileging the private imagination. "The *beautiful*," she writes, "does prevail in nature, and language is too poor and feeble to tell *how* beautiful, but our hearts and souls can tell to ourselves if we cannot to others." Like Gilpin, she was not able to subordinate the "beautiful" to a less powerful or dominant position. In her words, beauty was consonant with a strongly affective power. She could fill her letter, she tells her mother, with "the touching glories of the present hour." The absence of the most extreme emotions by no means diminished the effect of the experience.

Her one difficulty, however, lay in the area of representation. Words were poor tools. Although they could announce "beauty," they were "too poor and feeble" to illustrate it. The verbal picture she sketched for her mother could provide no more than an outline and in fact offered a clearer representation of the viewer's state of mind than of the landscape itself. If it served to stimulate the reader's imagination, its purpose was served, but she would lay no claim to its pictorial power. It could indicate beauty but could not picture its distinctive extent: it could not say "how" beautiful the setting was because language was not specific enough to portray the variation in natural forms.

Discussions about the limitations of language figured prominently in both Burke's sublime and Gilpin's picturesque. The experience of the sublime was in fact closely associated with the loss of language. If words could describe a setting, then in all probability the setting was not sublime. The signature of the sublime appeared in the viewer's speechlessness. Rendered silent before the appearance of infinity, the individual could only say how inexpressible the experience was. What Burke reserved for the sublime, Gilpin adapted to the picturesque. Here, the difficulty was not one of power. The individual's failure with verbal description was due to the failure of language itself. "Words," Gilpin wrote,

> may give the great outlines of a country. They can measure the dimensions of a lake. They can hang its sides with wood. They can rear a castle on some projecting rock: or place an island near this, or the other shore. But their range extends no farther. They cannot mark the characteristic distinctions of each scene—the touches of nature—her living tints—her endless varieties, both in form and colour.—In a word, all her elegant *peculiarities* are beyond their reach. (*Observations on Several Parts of England*, 2:10)

Words could quantify, but they could not express qualities with any degree of accuracy. They could list the features of the landscape, but they could not, according to Gilpin, translate the verbal into the visual.

Gilpin's privileging of pencil over pen comes as no surprise. Defining himself as an artist of sketches, he gave pride of place to the form he sought to claim as his own. Tilden's apology for the limitations of language strikes a different note, since her only available tools of representation were words. Language was unwieldy for the work she sought to do, yet it was all she had. Her task was to craft a method of representation that would overcome the limitations so readily associated with words. Combining the conventions of the picturesque and the sublime, she alternated between descriptions of place and of person. When language failed to convey what she saw, she could describe the seer instead. In so doing she sought to create a bridge between herself and her correspondent. If she could not say what she saw, she could tell what she felt. By expressing her experience of a particular place, Tilden hoped to place her particular correspondent at home within it.

Her description of their visit to the glaciers near Grindelwald, Switzerland, illustrates how she worked out this combination of the picturesque and sublime. The setting would have been seen as a textbook case of the sublime: a massive expanse of ice, striking coloration, a clear sense of unbroken uniformity.[26] Tilden's description, while drawing on elements of the sublime, in no way reproduces this as her experience. She carefully embeds the description within a general description of the Alps. By contextualizing the glaciers, making them part of a larger whole, she breaks the illusion of infinity. Though large, the glaciers are brought down to perceivable size. She further breaks the element of unbroken vastness by introducing elements of the picturesque. She calls attention to the wildflowers that grow "almost to the very verge" of the glacier. She also keeps the reader's eye fully drawn to the figures of Gannett and herself in the landscape. She describes their meal of bread and wine before they venture on their excursion. She follows their progress on horseback over the "rocky and steep but quite safe" path. She notes their change of guides, describes the "sharp pointed poles" they were given to use as staffs, and remarks that the exertion of the walk only added to its enjoyment. Unlike the difficulty associated with the Burkean sublime, Tilden's experience yields pleasure. Far from being distanced or alienated, Tilden feels herself entirely a part of the landscape. "The whole scene was like enchantment," she tells her mother, and she follows this with a description of dazzling light that in other hands would have produced a frisson of terror. She, however, was "perfectly bewitched" under a spell of delight that connects her to the "immense" scene before her. Her description follows:

This week we have enjoyed a great deal having been to the beautiful vallies [*sic*] of Lauterbrunnen and Grindewald [*sic*]. The ride from Interlaken to Lauterbrunnen was the most beautiful, the very finest I have ever had—The scenery wild and grand—Nature's own work is here. The numerous cascades, many of them formed by the melting of the snows were constantly adding to the beauty and variety of the scenery. Sometimes from 4 to 6 in sight at once and rushing from an immense height, they seem to leap down the mts as if eager and joyous to meet the swift rivers below, they do indeed appear *glad* to join them—The beauty of the valley and the Fall of the Staubbach are the great wonders of this place—passed the night here & the next morning left for Grindewald where after taking a lunch of bread and wine, we set off on horseback to see the *Glaciers!* The horse path is very narrow, & in many places rocky and steep but quite safe, crossed noisy rushing streams, forded one—When near the Grand Glacier (whose exquisite colours had been delighting us all the way) we alighted from

our horses and were joined by another guide who gave us long sharp
pointed poles and he carried a pick axe to cut the Ice. In a few minutes
we were at the foot of the Glacier. Wild flowers grow almost to the
very verge of it. It is an immense mass of ice broken up into ravines or
gulfs and many fine pyramids. With the aid of our trusty poles we
walked with perfect ease or had only enough of difficulty to make it
the more delightful—The deep *blue* colour of the ravines is exquisitely beautiful—There are two Glaciers at Grindewald and both de-
scending from the same Mer de Glace, this latter is an immense *plain*
of ice on the top of the mts. One Glacier descends between the Wel-
terhorn and the Mettenberg, the other which we saw but did not go
to, is between the Mettenburg [*sic*] and the Great Eiger—These three
mts. make a grand & stupendous appearance. Immense masses of
rock and earth are pushed forward every year into the valley by the
force of the Glaciers—The whole scene was like enchantment. The
sunlight breaking upon the snow and giving yet greater clearness and
light to the fine colour in the recesses of these beautiful Glaciers—I
was perfectly bewitched by the scene—How beautiful is Switzerland!
Notwithstanding all I had anticipated here the reality has far surpassed my expectations—Returned by the same route to the Inn—
stopped a few moments at a little plain Protestant church in the valley—It was beautiful to see this, and to feel that the calm and holy
light of Christianity had pierced these mountain summits as well as
the glorious light of nature—I don't see how people can help being
good in these secluded yet beautiful and magnificent places. (4 June,
entry for 9 June 1837)

The description carefully places the sublime within imaginative reach of
home. Not only is their visit to the glaciers framed by home references (the
shared meal and the "plain, Protestant church"), but the letter writer remains clearly visible through the details of her prose. Before she describes
the glaciers themselves, she gives a brief sketch of the seasonal cascades created by melting snow. Although her language borrows slightly from the
picturesque and the sublime ("rushing" and "immense," respectively), the
personification in effect personalizes the description. The torrents "leap
down the mts as if eager and joyous to meet the swift rivers below, they do
indeed appear *glad* to join them." Gannett's journal identifies the conceit as
distinctly Anna's response.[27] Reporting the same scene, Gannett attributes
the personification to his wife: "The melting of the snows causes numerous

cascades wh[ich] are leaping & hurrying over the mountains, as if, Anna says, 'glad to contribute their supply to swell the rivers'" (4:89). The emphasis she places on the word "glad," underlining it in her letter to her mother, suggests that the thought was not new to her when she offered this image. "They do indeed appear *glad*," she writes, as if the thought still rings true upon reflection.

Tilden left her signature on this description in more ways than one. It reappears in her reference to the wildflowers and once again in her comment about the effect of place on character. The words identify their writer. Known in the family for her interest in flowers, she leaves her mark on the immense expanse of glacier by singling out what is small and distinct. Her vision, at this moment, borrows decidedly from the picturesque, for her mention of "ravines," "gulfs," and "pyramids" draws directly from Gilpin's suggestions of how to re-create the impression of irregularity in a landscape.[28] What she saw of the glaciers she reports almost entirely in the language of the picturesque. Although the word "immense" suggests the sublime, she uses this word primarily for what she herself did not see—the Mer de Glace and the "immense masses of rock and earth . . . pushed forward . . . by the force of the Glaciers." Her final description evokes the sublime in the image of bright sunlight on ice, but once again, the sublime merges with another way of seeing the setting. She consistently balances her representation, guaranteeing that the landscape will not overwhelm its reader.

As she comments, there was just "enough of difficulty to make it the more delightful." The site pleases; it does not terrify—or rather, she will not let herself be terrified. Her experience of the sublime is markedly picturesque. The words she uses belong to the vocabulary of the picturesque: the scene is "like enchantment," and she finds herself "bewitched." That she draws on the picturesque is by no means surprising. To have adopted the manner of expression associated with the sublime would have emphasized the very distance between herself and her correspondent that she sought to collapse. She wrote to her mother with the express purpose of making visual and accessible the places she saw, no matter how immense or inexpressible the setting or experience in fact was. At the conclusion of the entry for the day of the glacier excursion, she exclaimed, "I wish I could tell you so that I could make you *see too,* all we have enjoyed."

A style that emphasized inexpressibility hardly answered her needs. She sought to create the illusion of a commonly experienced present in her descriptions of place. The rhetoric of the sublime, with its insistence on the isolation of the viewer, undermined her project. She needed a language that invited its readers to become part of her experience rather than one that privileged it as inaccessible. Her own experience in the Alps did not meet the classic lines of the sublime. Unlike the expected sense of disorientation and alienation, Tilden never felt more herself. Describing their crossing of the Simplon Pass, she had written, "I never am so well as when among the mountains" (31 May 1837). The rugged challenge of walking in the Alps attracted her. She would have readily repeated the four hours they spent walking their first day. Identifying so closely with the place itself, she could not experience the isolation by which the sublime was defined.

The picturesque, however, also fell prey to certain limitations. While it offered a way of reclaiming beauty, it lacked the moral overtones Unitarianism had so readily associated with the sublime. As Gilpin pointed out, the interests of the picturesque were not necessarily coincident with a moral order. He cited the example of lounging workers. In a sketch they added a pleasing variety; they were a highly desirable aspect of the scene. Outside the picture's frame, however, the virtue of these picturesque figures quickly turned into the vice of idleness. The sublime, by comparison, was easily associated with the "higher" concerns of life. With the emphasis on vastness and immensity, it was readily appropriated by religion. The infinite God, the miraculous creator, was seen in the works of nature and seen most powerfully in those that were most overwhelming to human perception. The sublime offered the prospect of moral value, and for that very reason, it was worth incorporating into any system of representation. In this passage, Tilden saves the connection for the very end. In her comment about the effect of place on person, she reweaves the sublime back into her picturesque. Magnificence in the setting yields the corresponding effect in the character. Her exclamation about character extends her home reference to the Protestant chapel. The short sermon she preached would have sounded a familiar note to the reader in red brick Boston. The "sublime" in Tilden's use is brought directly to the reader through its familiar meaning. What a visit to an Alpine valley yielded was an observation readily applicable to home.

In the Alps, Tilden's descriptive focus remained nature itself, but on their return to England and their travel both to the Lake District and to the Highlands of Scotland, a different possibility came into play. Visiting places described in some detail by her family's favorite writers, she drew on allusions to, and at times quotations from, Wordsworth and Scott. Their words offered imaginative possibilities that once again played on the importance of familiarity. To describe a place to which one had never physically been, Tilden turned her readers back to their reading. In rereading an author's words, they would perform a small miracle of memory. They would be able to "remember" a place they had seen only in their mind's eye.

The physical place inhabited by distinctly living human beings often merged into the well-known and well-loved setting. When a common text was available, Tilden worked it directly into her representation of the sites they visited. By connecting the writer's "scene" with the traveler's "place," she situated her singular experience within the context of the familiar. The best-loved passages from her family's reading served as the guide for her travels. Tying directly into the community of readers within the Tilden household, she referred them to Scott's novels and Wordsworth's poems.

> Ask Catherine if she remembers the residence of the Solitary [from Wordsworth's *Excursion*]. (19 November 1837)
>
> Ask Zibesis if she remembers my quoting the "Lay of the Last Minstrel" to her. (19 November 1837; 26 November 1837)
>
> Scott places his story of the Lady of the Lake among these very mountains and Lochs (we have been reading it to day). (10 December 1837; 13 December entry)
>
> Scott mentions the Cathedral in his Rob Roy. (10 December 1837; 24 December entry)
>
> We took a boat up Loch Katrine for 8 miles, (stopping at Ellen's beautiful Isle). (10 December 1837; 24 December entry)

In her descriptions of place, Tilden asks her correspondents to remember their reading. Her purpose was twofold. Not only would the readers be given a familiar frame of reference, but the familiarity itself would enable them to place the letter writer within their imagined setting. Their sister/daughter traveling through England and Scotland appeared in the verbal settings they remembered and read back in Boston.

Tilden's reference to Wordsworth's poem *The Excursion* displays the two-way traffic Tilden established between living human beings and verbally constructed characters. Writing to her mother during her excursion to the Lake District in mid-November 1837, she included the message for her sister Catherine about a particular section from Wordsworth's poem. Her reason for making this reference is clear: Wordsworth's description provides the best representation of what they saw. She writes, "Ask Catherine if she remembers the residence of the Solitary. Wordsworth has in this exactly described a scene which we saw in going through Langdale by Blea Tarn. The lines begin in this way 'We scaled, without a track to ease our steps &c'" (19 November 1837).[29] In Tilden's description physical place becomes a function of fictional setting. She sees situation in terms of "scene" and casts herself and Gannett as figures within another writer's words.[30] The particular spot in Langdale was a scene Wordsworth had "exactly described." At the same time, Tilden's quotation of the specific lines she had in mind from the poem suggests a further crossing of actual experience with its imagined counterpart. If Wordsworth's lines described what they saw, the line she quotes effectively describes what they did. The "we" of "we saw" and the "we" of "We scaled" are virtually indistinguishable. As Wordsworth's scene moves out of the poem and into the physical reality of Langdale, Tilden and Gannett step into the imagined reality of the poem. They enact what both they, and their correspondents, have read.

Tilden and Gannett's travel through the Lake District and into the Highlands of Scotland was clearly a literary tour and distinctly embraced as such. Tilden had taken her volume of Wordsworth's poetry, given to her by Gannett early in their engagement, with her to England. They picked up copies of Scott's poems and novels along the way, reading the appropriate work at the appropriate site.[31] In her letters, Tilden frequently mentions their pleasure at visiting places that already carried deep meaning for them. Concluding her comments on their visit to Abbotsford, the home of Sir Walter Scott, she writes, "You may well suppose we enjoyed this visit much, it was so full of interesting associations, and so is Scotland. I am glad we are here, at almost every step is something dear to me from either being connected with history or celebrated in the Songs, poems and ballads of Burns, Scott, Ramsay &c" (19 November 1837, 26 November entry). Her response to the Lake District in England had been very much the same: "Many places here are doubly dear and interesting to us from being some of the very scenes described in the Excursion, which you know we both like so much. I never go from home without taking it with me." Carrying her copy of Wordsworth with her, she saw the landscape in terms of the words she had read. In this case, language betrayed no limitations. Unlike her experience in the Alps where words could not describe the setting, the situation in the English and Scottish countryside was quite different. There, where words had preceded her, she could call on them as the familiars that would indeed conjure up the most palpable image of the landscape.

For Tilden, representation finally depended less on physical description than on a combination of shared memory and feeling. To convey a place home to her correspondents, she emphasized her experience of being in that place. Through this emphasis she could draw on the family's past experiences, evoking their presence by remembering the books they had read together. At the same time, she kept herself distinctly present in her descriptions. Prefacing her description of the physical objects in Scott's study at Abbotsford, she told her mother, "Yes, dear mother, *I* have been in Walter Scott's study" (19 November 1837; 26 November entry; Tilden's emphasis). In contrast to the masking of identity she had contemplated two years earlier, she developed a style in her letters that allowed the representer to remain clearly visible through the representation. By highlighting *her* experience, she offered her readers a sense of place directed toward active participation. Presenting herself "there," she enabled them to imagine themselves in the scenes she described.

TRAVELING CRITIC OR SYMPATHETIC EYE: DEFINING THE TRAVELER'S ROLE

When writing to each of her correspondents, Tilden often practiced this exercise of the imagination. In her letter to Zibby, she took her youngest sister into Thorvaldsen's studio in Rome. "How much you would like to visit some of the ateliers in Rome," she commented. She transported her mother to the Swiss Alps: "Isn't it grand to be here." Writing to her sister Catherine about their mother, she longed for her mother's presence, both as parent and teacher: "I often think how much she would enjoy in Europe, and fancy her with her love of the beautiful, looking at Raphael's and Titian's pictures, and a thousand other things here, oh how much I should enjoy studying with Mother, she has such fine powers, such a quick keen relish for knowledge and excellence" (23 October 1837). When she thought of her correspondents, she imagined them with her. Her prose lingers on these moments. In this passage, she thinks of herself studying art with her mother; in other letters she imagines herself in conversation with her absent family members. Each example sought to bridge the literal distance between herself and her readers. Imagined presence filled the place of absence.

The tone of her letters reflects this connection of writer and reader. Her remarks were rarely critical about the places they visited. She registered few complaints. What she placed before her reader was defined by positive attributes: beauty, powerful affect, amazement, enchantment. Unlike the common tone of criticism that characterized the bulk of travel writing in this period, her travel letters are markedly free from the critic's voice. Her stance as responsive observer found little that was useful in the observing critic's armory of analytical tools.

The travel writer was known for his or her harshly discerning comments. As an outside observer in a "foreign" place, she or he capitalized on detachment, using this distance as a platform for interpretation. One could claim a greater authority precisely because one stood outside the situation. It guaranteed a clearer perception, so the argument went, of what was actually there. As Christopher Mulvey has shown, travel writers in the nineteenth century based their right to write on the very nature of their distance from the places they described. Because they did not belong, they could see what the inhabitants themselves could no longer discern.[32] Whether this meant social criticism, as in the case of Harriet Martineau, or aesthetic appreciation, as with Henry James, remained largely the signature of the particular writer's preference. In either case, the traveler claimed authority by asserting the superiority of his or her interpretive skills.

The hallmark of the traveling critic was comparison. No place could be described without reference to another, and most commonly the comparison worked to one site's disadvantage. Comparison often took the form of matching experience against expectation. What travelers had previously heard about a place shaped their response once they arrived. And if one could claim disappointment, then the particular individual claimed a more discerning eye than those of other travelers who had been too impressed by too little. Gannett himself had mastered this technique, planning as he was to cull a publishable travel narrative from his journals on his return home.[33] Describing their visit to the Isle of Wight, he registered disappointment. Quick to note that they had "visited the best part of the Island," he asserted the credibility of his criticism. His comments, he maintained, were based on a fair survey. He writes, "Still the Isle of Wight rather disappointed me. I had heard so much of its beauty that I expected more. It is pretty, the landscape neat and fertile, but it is never grand, except at Black Gang Chine & the scenery is not often even *beautiful*. . . . We admired the thatched cottages, covered with rosebushes—the monthly rose and the myrtle in flower—" (7:77). Tilden's description of the same visit is tellingly different. She writes to her mother: "This is a very beautiful and picturesque place; the pretty hedges, rich verdure of the fields, the neatly thatched cottages, covered with roses and jessamine, climbing to the very roof and in full blossom, also the myrtle with its dark glossy leaves and pretty white flowers, delighted us. . . . We passed a delightful day, and saw what is best worth seeing on the island" (23 September 1837). Gannett found "neatness" disappointing; Tilden equated it with the picturesque. His afterthought was her primary interest. Where he adds a brief mention of flowers at the end of his entry, she devotes most of her description to the flowers themselves. She not only names them but gives careful attention to their appearance. Gannett provides little for a reader's eye to see: the cottages are indiscriminately covered with rosebushes, and the plants are simply "in flower." Tilden's version is indeed much more "picturesque," inviting the reader to see the climbing roses, the sheen of the leaves, and the contrast formed by dark green against white. Her description takes beauty as its province and underscores its effect on the viewer: her word for their experience was "delight."

When Tilden built a description around comparison, she used it to connect rather than divide. She was less interested in showing how places were distinguished from one another than in illustrating their similarities. To her sister Catherine she wrote, "It does us all good to see more of mankind, and the world, it teaches us that we are 'brethren all'" (23 October 1837). She preferred to remark on settings in which her expectations had been surpassed rather than emphasize situations that had disappointed her. Even when her comments hinted at criticism, she was careful to include praise. Describing Holy Week services during their stay in Rome, Tilden gave a decidedly ambivalent response. In this case, prior expectations came into play, for as a good Protestant in Catholic Rome, she had come, as had her husband, with a full measure of distrust toward anything Catholic. Gannett never let his distrust waver. He dutifully attended the Miserere on two consecutive days, first at St. Peter's, then in the Sistine Chapel.[34] Of the first day's experience, he wrote bluntly, "I was not affected by it." On the second day, he admitted that "the music was softer and more impressive than yesterday at St. Peter's, but still was wonderful rather than affecting." On the third day he stayed at their lodgings and took a bath. His final assessment of Holy Week in Rome was, as was to be expected from a good Unitarian minister, highly critical: "Holy Week has passed, and been a week

of excitement and gratification, and yet of disappointment. The ceremonies
that I have witnessed have been puerile, in no instance satisfying me by
their pomp or impressing me by their solemnity—" (3:33).

Unlike her husband, Tilden attended all three settings of the Miserere.
She went to the services Wednesday, Thursday, *and* Friday. In his journal,
Gannett noted the difference in their Good Friday afternoon activities: "In
the P.M. Anna went to the Sistine Chapel to hear the 3d Miserere. I took
a warm bath and remained at home" (3:41). Although Tilden's version
shared some of the same critical tone of Gannett's, she painted a quite different picture for her mother, who had specifically asked her daughter to
describe this event in particular. Tilden wrote, "You ask me how I liked the
Miserere at Rome—I never heard more perfect harmony in my life, the music is wholly *vocal*, but it sounds like the finest toned organ—I had no conception that the human voice could be made to produce such a wonderful
effect—Still on the whole I was disappointed, there was a want of *feeling* in
it on the part of the performers, it certainly was not as touching though
more wonderful than I had expected—" (31 May 1837). Tilden's description
begins with unqualified praise. She exclaims over the musical aspects of the
performance. Choosing the very element that would most interest her family members, she focuses on the sounds she heard. She here draws on a
comparison that is entirely to the advantage of the event being described.
The massing of human voices duplicates the sound of the "finest toned organ." The effect, she says, is "wonderful."

As in the passages about the Isle of Wight, Tilden and Gannett use words
to opposite effect. For Gannett, "wonderful" was a term of criticism. He
found the second day of the Miserere "wonderful rather than affecting."
Tilden's version abandons this distinction. There is no opposition between
"wonder" and "affect," but the "wonderful" was indeed "affecting." It produced the particular effect over which she marveled. She does not, however,
leave this praise unqualified. Her final comments with their emphasis on
disappointment and limitation echo Gannett's position. They may well have
arisen from his particular response. Tilden wrote her letter to her mother
in late May, a month and a half after their Holy Week experiences in Rome.
What she herself wrote in her journal is unknown, since her comments
would have appeared in one of the lost journals. The authority of Gannett's
position would undoubtedly have weighed heavily with Tilden. His province was religion, and while she could claim a clearer understanding of music, it was more difficult to maintain a competing version of theology in his

presence. She did, however, change the terms of his criticism. His comments point to the limitation of the service as a whole. In his estimation it evoked little worthwhile religious sentiment, a clear indication that the service itself was the problem. Tilden's critical statements are far more tolerant of the event itself. What she criticized was the performers and not what they were performing. And her final comment reincorporated the initial response of praise: the Miserere had exceeded her expectations. She concluded her description by repeating the word "wonderful."

In this setting Tilden's prose shows the influence of her husband's authority. Several months later such influence is more difficult to discern. Her letters and his journals reveal increasingly disparate accounts of what they saw. In taking the tour of Holyrood House, home to Mary, Queen of Scots, he did not quarrel with the guide's insistence that certain stains on the floor were left by the actual blood shed during the murder of Mary's secretary and adviser, David Riccio. Willing suspension of disbelief seemed an honorable act in this case. He comments, "The stain on the floor why not believe" (7:163). Tilden refused any such "romantic" credulity. She wrote to her mother, "The stains on the floor are yet pointed out by the guide, but it requires more faith than I have to believe them" (10 December 1837). She was well aware that her "disbelief" was her own. In this sentence, she had originally written "we," the first-person plural occurring automatically from her frequent use of it, but she had then crossed it out and substituted the decidedly singular "I."

Differing in what they chose to credit, Tilden and Gannett also differed on the more substantive questions of art and its representation of character. On their visit to Windsor Castle, she praised the monument to Princess Charlotte.[35] Four months pregnant at the time, Tilden focused on the subject of the work, a subject with which she could readily identify. The cenotaph represented the princess's death in childbirth. Tilden called the work "beautiful and touchingly interesting" and provided her mother with a detailed description: "She is represented as having just expired, whilst above, is her spirit ascending, and accompanied by two angels, one of whom bears the little infant in her arms. Around the body of the Princess are four draped figures, weeping. The design is beautiful, & in general extremely well executed" (8 October 1837, 11 October entry). Tilden's description focuses the reader's attention on the woman and her "ascending" spirit. She is at the center of Tilden's words, the subject clearly emphasized by the smaller accompanying figures. Tilden termed this design "beautiful." Gannett, on the other hand, gave only qualified approval. To his eyes, the figures were poorly balanced. Although he admired the work "on the whole," he found fault with the central figure:

> The Princess is representing [*sic*] as having just expired.[36] She is lying on her side, with one hand thrown over the side of the bed, and just appearing below the drapery; this I did not like. Her spirit is leaving the body, and is represented as another human figure, quite large; this too was disagreeable, it was coarse, not etherial [*sic*]. Two angels standing one on each side seem ready to attend the spirit to heaven; one bears the *new born* babe in its arms; the expression of their faces is admirable—sad, yet tranquil. Two figures sitting, and two kneeling are both enveloped in drapery as if to cover their sorrow too big for utterance; their attitudes are very good. The design of the monument is admirable. (6:174)

His criticism points in the direction of abstraction. He would have preferred a more idealized portrayal, one in which the woman's body was fully covered and her spirit cut down to size. His objections center on the representation of the dead princess's spirit: it was both too large and too human. For the surrounding figures, however, he had nothing but praise. He only wished that the woman and her spirit had been tastefully contained by the draped figures surrounding her.[37]

Differences surface again in their responses to a painting seen in the Ashmolean Museum at Oxford. They both describe the same work, a painting by eighteenth-century portrait artist Allan Ramsay, but each description bears only faint resemblance to the other.[38] That they viewed it from a different frame of reference appears in the very titles they gave the work. The painting itself was a portrait of Flora Macdonald, the "Jacobite heroine," as she was invariably designated, who helped Prince Charles Edward, the "Young Pretender," escape to the Continent after his failed attempt to claim the throne in 1746.[39] Sixty years later, as Scott's subtitle reminds his readers, Sir Walter Scott took the Jacobite rebellion as his context for the eminently successful, eminently popular novel *Waverley*. Within it, he transformed Flora Macdonald into Flora MacIvor, a character defined by the traits for which her historical prototype had been known.

When Tilden and Gannett describe Ramsay's portrait of the historical Flora Macdonald, they differ on what figure they are really seeing. Tilden refers to the work as a painting of *Flora MacIvor*, her underlining evidently included to let her mother see Scott's character as well as the literal subject

Cenotaph for Princess Charlotte by Matthew Cotes Wyatt.
Courtesy John Harrington, *St. George's Chapel, Windsor*
London: Sampson Low, Marston, and Low, and Searle, 1872

Painting of
Flora Macdonald
by Allan Ramsay.
Courtesy Ashmolean
Museum, Oxford

of the portrait. Gannett also includes both designations, but he sees the portrait first as Flora Macdonald, and only then—and parenthetically—as Flora MacIvor. Tilden frames the painting with fiction. Gannett places fiction in parentheses and, in fact, sees little to praise. He gives no description of the portrait itself and says only the following: "a fine but rather hard looking woman" (6:163). Tilden's version is much more visually descriptive, and it sees a strikingly different expression in the figure's face. She writes to her mother, "*Flora Mc'Ivor,* painted with her Highland plaid, her hair is short and curled in the neck, with a rose on one side, her forehead is a fine, high one, and the countenance very bright and intelligent" (8 October 1837, 11 October entry). What to Gannett was a "hard looking woman" to Tilden was the very image of intelligence. She notes the high forehead, the ready shorthand for impressive intellect. The painting represented what Tilden admired most. As she would write to her sister two weeks later, this time in reference to her mother, "She has such fine powers, such a quick keen relish for knowledge and excellence" (23 October 1837).

In her first year abroad, Tilden continued to develop the responsive authority she had begun crafting during Gannett's illness. The letter itself offered the structure for such an endeavor. Premised on response, it remained firmly tied to images of community. Between salutation and signature, it offered a space in which ideas could be voiced without interruption but also without isolation. What was written in Tilden's letters was written in response to some prior exchange—whether in the past of her daughterly family life or in the more immediate present of news conveyed from her Boston home. And her letters offered their readers the similar opportunity for response, whether to her descriptions or to her queries. What she valued above all in her letters was the freedom of expression the form provided for her ideas. Even when writing to her mother, she did not feel the need to be self-censoring. With her mother as her representative in Boston, she could trust that any thoughts she had included would be wisely edited for public consumption.

Life abroad became itself an image of freedom. In her letters Tilden periodically praised the freedoms she experienced in her life away from Boston. Writing from Vichy, she celebrated the absence of prying eyes. "I like one thing in Europe very much," she commented, "and that is the perfect freedom that subsists in regards to dress and little matters. Nobody stares and wonders why you don't do this or that, you can do as you please, and it is no one's business" (14 August 1837). Reminiscent of her 1827 criticism of etiquette, her words celebrate a particular liberty—the freedom to shape one's action by the actual circumstance rather than by a general rule. There, the issue had been the propriety of taking the arm of a young gentleman, even when midwinter's slippery ground lay underfoot. Here, her comment was prompted by the simple freedom of taking a walk without wearing a bonnet—and without raising the congregation's collective eyebrows. She relished the opportunity to do "just as she pleased."

Six months later, writing from Scotland, she notes a similar pleasure in the freedoms offered abroad but not at home. Praising the Scottish Unitarians' practice of open communion, she told her mother that she wished the practice could be adopted back in the Federal Street Church. She wrote,

I have been to meeting all day, the services have been most interesting. In the A.M. we had both a doctrinal and practical sermon from Mr H[arris] on Election, and the P.M. was devoted wholly to the Communion service. I like this plan much better than ours, and also that any one may remain who wishes, without *any* previous form of admission. I am quite sure that no one can find any words of Jesus which justifies our present custom in regard to the Lord's Supper, he leaves it free to all, and surely it is a matter between God and our conscience alone. Oh I do wish we had more freedom among us.— (31 December 1837)

As with the previous passage, Tilden extends the illustration of a particular freedom to include a more wide-ranging definition. In the words from France, she focused on self-selected action, doing as one pleases. Here, she wishes more expansively for a new world of "more freedom." In this case, such freedom was tied to individual conscience. The individual alone knew best what course of action to take. How others interpreted this action or her appearance might well be a misrepresentation of her reality. Returning once again to the deceptive power of appearance, Tilden sought a way to disarm this power and replace it with her own freedom.

To practice such freedom at home among mother and sisters and congregation and minister-husband was another matter. In letters she could represent a painted figure's expression as "bright with intelligence." If she attempted to embody that expression at home, her appearance might well be judged "hard looking." The difference between her image of Flora MacIvor and her husband's comment on Flora Macdonald reveals the limitations of the freedom Tilden had gained for herself. She had earned the freedom of fiction: only as an imaginary character could she claim an appearance that was not misinterpreted. Returning to Boston, she resumed her mask. Minister's wife, devoted mother, increasingly silent and invalid woman: her final years remain to be represented on her own terms and in her own story.

Epilogue:
Epitaphs, Obituaries, and Memorials

Near the highest point on Oak Avenue, overlooking Auburn Lake, in the oldest section of Mount Auburn Cemetery, three grave markers stand at the back left-hand corner of plot #1374. The stones are well weathered. The years between their placement and our present have nearly claimed the clarity with which they once indicated the lives they marked. On the right-hand stone, the most recent, the initials "E. S. G." are faintly visible. Beneath is the date of death: "Aug. 26, 1871." Two markers away, the initials are yet more faint. To see what they once were, fingers are necessary, feeling out the "H. T. G." of Henry Tilden Gannett's name, the son who died as suddenly as did the mother, almost six years to the day after her death. His is the only one of the three with an epitaph: four lines that yield their words after a time-consuming, patience-trying process of looking and feeling.

In the middle is a tombstone on which no letters seem to have been engraved. For all the eye can see, the marker silently records a life whose name was never written into the stone. It appears to be a blank slate on which the gravestone-loving lichens have written a self-perpetuating record. Such apparent blankness, however, offers its own lesson about interpreting appearances. What initially seems to be an uninscribed surface yields a different story to the finger. There are letters on the apparently blank surface, but the stone is now so worn that even the sense of touch questions its ability to feel out the markings that once identified the person buried beneath them. The left-hand slant of a letter "A," the vertical line of an "L," the curve of a "G," and beneath them a letter that feels like a lowercase "d." Blank smoothness follows; then a more distant "2," the top portion of a "5," and a year that remains only in fragments: "1," the next digit entirely worn smooth, the last two yielding the upper part of a "4" and the lower part of a "6." From that blank surface can be read

A. L. G.
dec 25, 1846

Were Tilden's grave marked only by this one stone, it would virtually be impossible to make out her initials or the date of death. The sense of touch alone could not feel the letters back into clear existence. What the finger learns to read appears in another part of this cemetery plot. Centered toward the front is a simple granite block set on a slightly larger stone pedestal. Both now serve as a base for what first captures the attention in this otherwise undecorated plot. Centered on the top of the rectangular granite structure sits a mass of pink quartz displaying the name "WELLS" on a bronze plaque. The first grave markers to catch the eye are the two directly to the left of this quartz-topped base. Of polished granite, the names on them are firmly distinct: Louisa Appleton Wells, 1872–1945, and Catherine Boott Gannett Wells, 1838–1911.

The firstborn daughter took the family plot as her own. Her grave marker and her daughter's are the most prominent in the lot. Her stone sits directly next to the base now announcing her married name. But this "base" was once a monument in itself. It commemorated a particular life, as the words engraved on it reveal. A lengthy inscription appears on the side of the monument that faces the road. Like its counterparts in the back, it too has become difficult to read. In puzzling out the words one Indian summer day in 1993, three pairs of eyes were required to discern the letters slowly worn away by time: the daughter and her mother and her aunt on hands and knees despite the 160 years shared among them. Daughter, mother, aunt puzzling out, struggling to reclaim the words written about a daughter, mother, sister, aunt some 150 years earlier.

The inscription runs nine lines; 115 words inscribed on an otherwise undecorated block of stone. It pays tribute to an exemplary "Christian mother and wife" and celebrates a "true and noble minded woman." The words, crafted by friend and prominent fellow parishioner George Ticknor, tell a story their subject had rarely thought herself entitled to claim. Written by the congregation of which she was a part, first as child, then as young woman, then as church member and minister's wife, they embody her in the powerful conventions of the time. Remembered for her "domestic virtues" and "devotion to . . . duty," she appears in their words as a "constant example."

In this spot consecrated by the gratitude of the Society of Christians worshiping God in Federal Street Boston, as a Burial place for the

Family of EZRA STILES GANNETT their faithful Pastor, rest the mortal remains of ANNA LINZEE, his wife born July 13, 1811 died Dec 25 1846 whose domestic virtues and devotion to all religious truth and duty acted as a constant example on many far beyond the circle of loving friends in which she moved and whose early and sudden death fell as an unspeakable sorrow on those to whom she was more intimately known as a true and noble minded woman and as a tender, firm and Christian mother and wife.

Recording the mourners' "unspeakable sorrow," the inscription remembers a period of time for which we have little record. Tilden's years as "mother and wife" are by far the least chronicled of any she lived. After their return from Europe, her writing virtually ends. Journals may well have existed, but they have been lost. A two-and-a-half-page description of her children is all that remains. Titled "Some Recollections of My Children" and written as journal entries, it focuses on the children's development of character and her own role as teacher. If an extensive correspondence with her sister Sarah, then living in St. Louis, bridged the distance, none of these letters survives. Between their arrival in Boston in July 1838 and her death on Christmas Day, 1846, there are five letters: two to her father, three to her husband, one of which was written in the voice of their two-year-old daughter to accompany a New Year's gift. In the eight remaining years of her life, her few extant words speak only fragments of her perspective.

What survives are the public remembrances written after her death. The public records of her life's end tell various stories, offering narratives that read uneasily against her own words. Five sources exist. Each addresses a different audience, though these audiences would certainly have held members in common. They range from the most identifiably public to the most definably private. There was the official notice of death in various Boston newspapers, the most public and least personal. There were the terse entries in the Massachusetts Vital Records Office. The "personal public" received its words from a different source: the minister in his pulpit. Shortly after Tilden died, Gannett offered a three-paragraph eulogy for the woman who had been part of the church since her birth. The church offered its own memorial in the form of its grave-site inscription, words that would speak to those who had known their fellow member as well as to the anonymous public who wandered through Mount Auburn for moral instruction in an aesthetically pleasing location. And the chief mourner, who would visit Mount Auburn frequently, gathering flowers from her grave and arranging them carefully in his journal, would create a separate journal devoted entirely to her memory. Or rather, to his.

In the *Boston Evening Transcript* for Saturday, 26 December 1846, a pointing hand directs the reader's attention to the following information: "Rev Dr Gannett's second lecture announced for tomorrow evening will be deferred until further notice." The reason for the cancellation is to be seen in a one-line listing under "Deaths": "Last evening, suddenly, ANNA, wife of Ezra S. Gannett, D.D. 33." The same notice appears in the *Boston Daily Advertiser* and the *Christian Register*. The only words that change are the ones that reflect the different publication date of each paper.[1] The notice follows the standard form for announcing a woman's death: the date, the woman's first name, the rest of the woman's named identity given by reference to her husband or father, her age, and, perhaps, some indication of the cause of death. The form for men differs in one single, significant aspect. Men's names are never divided. First and last read together; the life is identified as its own, by itself.

In Tilden's case, the notice belongs as much to her husband as to herself. Reference to him fills half of the single line. The information about her is sparse—and inaccurate. Her given age is wrong: she was thirty-five, not thirty-three, when her life ended. And we learn very little about the cause of death. Only one word is offered: "suddenly." Beyond the unexpected occurrence of death, nothing else is said. Silence was by no means the customary practice: other "sudden deaths" included further information. A brief glance through the papers yields several examples. The *Evening Transcript* attributed the unexpected death of William Parsons to a "fainting fit." The *Daily Advertiser* offered the following description for the "very sudden" death of sixty-three-year-old Timothy Mayhew: "He was at work in his blacksmith shop, and while at work fell down, and instantly expired."[2] Tilden's death, however, is left a public cipher, defined solely by its unexplained suddenness.

The explanation appears in two separate entries in the Massachusetts Vital Records Office. There were two deaths in the Gannett household on December 25, "sudden" in the sense of unexpected, yet unexpected only in the limited sense of individual hope. What ended Tilden's life was part of the all too familiar narrative for women in the nineteenth century. The public records speak the common, stark reality in terse terms: "Child of E. S. Gannett, Still Born," "Anna L. Gannett, Childbed." She had survived three pregnancies and three childbirths, but the fourth proved fatal to both mother and child. The Vital Records Office duly reported both deaths; the newspapers would note only one.

Neither the *Daily Advertiser* nor the *Evening Transcript* included obituaries on any regular basis. Only when dignitaries died was a full account written and the individual celebrated for *his* contributions. For other lives lost in death, public remembrance was limited to a few lines at most. Given this paucity of specific information, the modern-day reader searches the papers for other details, looking for some slight indication of how a particular life might have been perceived by the newspaper-reading public. What else did Gannett's colleagues or parishioners see when they read the news of Tilden's death? For example, the issue of the *Daily Advertiser* in which Tilden's death was reported also included a small announcement for a new collection of sermons entitled "Christian Consolation," written by Gannett's fellow Unitarian minister Andrews Preston Peabody. Did Gannett receive a copy from his friend or from one of the members of his church? Did he purchase the book for himself, seeking the consolation in which, as a minister, he was supposed to be well practiced?

Later in the same issue, a large advertisement invites the reader to add another useful volume to her collection. Written by the "Author of 'Women in America,'" this new work promised a familiar species of female biography.[3] A group of sketches, it balanced its verbal portraits between exemplary models and cautionary tales. It took as its province the imagined entirety of a woman's life. Titled *Girlhood and Womanhood,* it announced as its purpose: "[to] prove the natural connexion that exists between these two important periods." The author's source was key. As the subtitle of the book, "Sketches of my schoolmates," indicated, the moral tales included in the volume derived from the writer's own experience, stemming from the time when she herself was a girl at school. And the reader, it is assumed, would find these stories most suitable for her own instruction.

The advertisement lists several of the choices to be found within the book. The selection is daunting: "Anna Percival, or the Maniac Mother— Emily Howard, or the Gentle Wife—Amanda Malvina Burton, or Fashionable Ambition—Margaret Etherington, or Family Pride—Mary and Ellen Grovsenor, or The Two Sisters—Elizabeth Harrington, or the History of a

Coquette—Amelie Dorrington, or the Lost One—Matilda Harwood, or the Imaginary Invalid—Sarah Sherman, or The Mechanic's Daughter." The prospects for a woman's life look exceedingly grim. The tales to be told are primarily cautionary ones. The reader could expect a lesson in how to avoid behavior that her society had labeled "ambition," "pride," and "coquetry." She could read the graver tale of the fallen woman in the story of Amelie Dorrington, the "Lost One." She could learn how to separate the "imaginary invalid" from the "real" one, how to distinguish between the "Two Sisters," one exemplary, the other not, and how to keep herself from becoming that horrifying failure, the "Maniac Mother." What was left was a single story, the only one whose title endorsed it as a wholly desirable choice: "Emily Howard, or the Gentle Wife." In its abbreviated form, for the public eye, it read as follows: "25th inst. suddenly, Anna, wife of Ezra S. Gannett, D.D. 33."

The only "obituary" available to a woman like Anna Tilden in publications like the *Advertiser* or the *Transcript* came indirectly in the form of advertisements or excerpts. Tribute was paid in ambivalent terms: poems lamenting the "Many sudden deaths of the young which have lately occurred in our community," articles on the "education of Females," or advertisements for books on female character such as *Girlhood and Womanhood*.[4] The particular lives were kept private, carefully subsumed under the husband's or family's name. The one exception belongs to the Unitarian weekly newspaper, the *Christian Register*. Unlike the daily papers, it frequently printed extensive obituaries, not of public officials, but of wives and mothers and daughters. Women were celebrated for their life's work as it was defined by their family and friends. Take the example of Mrs. Elvira Harris:

> Died in Jacksonville, Mich., on the 10th of December, of consumption. Mrs. Elvira Harris, wife of the late Daniel Harris, formerly of Worcester, Mass., aged 33 years.
>
> During her painful and protracted sickness she manifested uncommon patience and calm resignation to the will of God, and as the time of her departure drew near with a bright hope of blessed happiness beyond the grave. She calmly and even joyously remarked to her friends, that she was going to die and with a welcome smile on her countenance, she quietly and calmly resigned her spirit to him who gave it.
>
> She has left an orphan daughter and a numerous circle of relatives and friends to whom she was greatly endeared, to mourn her loss, and

long will they remember her many virtues, cheerful disposition, and pleasant voice, which has so often lit up with joy the hearts of a large domestic circle, and never will they forget the bright example of her faith, humanity, patience, and resignation in sickness and in death. (*Christian Register,* 27 February 1847)

Remembered as a patient sufferer, this woman lives on as the exemplary figure. She is the minister's illustration brought to life in her death. Unlike the minister's weekly examples, however, she was a particular person, a young woman of thirty-three with a daughter, a person who had made the long journey from Massachusetts to Michigan. And yet, the obituary clearly tells us less about the individual and much more about an ideal. Elvira Harris died the "beautiful death" so highly valued by the nineteenth century. Her "calm resignation" was undeniably familiar to readers who had never known of her existence. Her "uncommon patience" was rendered common by the praise lavished on all who exhibited this virtue. When her particular friends "remember[ed] her many virtues, her cheerful disposition, and pleasant voice," or when they recalled her "even joyous" knowledge of imminent death, they celebrated the qualities that were the long-standing abstractions of virtuous womanhood.

As another obituary for another woman notes, "Her life and death were full of salutary lessons."[5] Individual women's lives became a means by which to instruct others. To learn the lessons they offered, the unique was transformed into the universal. Particular women became general examples. Whatever distinguished one woman's life from her female contemporaries was subordinated to the common virtues they shared. The tribute submerged the specific life of the woman in the standard it was made to uphold. Her life became exemplary precisely because it had been carefully separated from the elements belonging solely to it. Where men's lives could remain both morally instructive and distinctly individual, the exemplary figure known as the "Christian woman" was built on the suppression of such detail.

Even though obituaries for women were common in the *Christian Register,* none exists for Tilden. The absence is curious. As Gannett's wife and an active member of the Federal Street Church, she was a suitable subject for the pages of this Unitarian periodical. Gannett himself had been instrumental in its founding. His lectures were frequently reviewed by and his sermons occasionally published within it. In connection with his wife's death, however, all that appeared was the same notice included in the *Advertiser* and the *Transcript*. The space for published tribute went unfilled. Did Gannett feel himself too closely associated with the paper so that any notice of his personal life might be perceived as a self-interested advertisement? Or did the reason lie elsewhere, in Gannett's own clearly defined sense of separate spheres for men and for women? A wholehearted believer in keeping women out of the public eye, he may well have rejected the idea of a published obituary on grounds of "principle." He would not present even the most abstracted version of his wife's life in the public domain of a weekly publication for fear that such notice would compromise (even after death) her "womanly nature."[6]

Although Gannett did not commit his wife's life directly to print, he did provide a spoken memorial. When he returned to the pulpit three weeks after Tilden's death, he offered a three-paragraph eulogy as part of his sermon. Each paragraph spoke to a different attribute; each offered one piece of an exemplary whole. The words in which he embodied her life were words largely familiar to his congregation. In describing Anna Linzee Tilden Gannett, he used the vocabulary of Christian character. The story he told was the one she had struggled over in the years when "girlhood" changed to "womanhood." He offered the following description of his wife to the personal public of his—and her—congregation.

> The strength of her character lay in its moral integrity. Her devotion to the right was almost marked with the certainty of an instinct. It had the force of a law which might never be broken. What was right must be done, cost what it would. This was the deepest and steadiest conviction of her soul. To this she clung through sickness and health, through hope and fear, in every season and under all experience. She dreaded nothing in herself so much as a departure from rectitude. She shrank from nothing in others with such an instant disapprobation as from a similar departure. Falsehood of every kind was so much her aversion, that she would rather disappoint or offend by honesty than conciliate by the slightest compromise of truth. In every exigency I knew she could be trusted, even as we trust the unchangeable laws of the Creation amidst the strains which overwhelm the earth.
>
> To this firmness of moral purpose was united an extreme gentleness of mind. The masculine in expression belonged not to her. She was a *woman* in her whole constitution and being. The delicacy of her sensibilities was such as could be seen, I think I may say, only in one of her

sex. Her affections were deep and true. Where she bestowed her love, she gave all her heart. Yet even her most partial or intense affections could not make her swerve from the path of duty. I know she would have died for them who were dear to her; but I do not believe she would have done what her soul told her was wrong, even to gain their fondest gratitude. She saw their faults, for the purity of her moral sentiment reflected the images which fell upon it in their real character; and they affected her with the most painful emotions which she ever experienced.

In her religious character there was much to interest as well as to satisfy those who enjoyed her confidence. With a natural inclination to the side of doubt rather than of faith, she had looked at the great truths of religion with the eye of an anxious curiosity. Years ago her mind took hold of the questions which lie at the foundations of all belief, the mighty questions of God and revelation. She had toiled through those questions, till her faith stood in the conclusions of the understanding, and not in the simple assent of the feelings. From these questions she advanced to others of less magnitude, but of deep importance. Providence presented to her view a scene which at once perplexed and exercised her mind; but the progress which she was making through all its difficulties was most beautiful to observe. By sure steps she was reaching that solution of the great problem of life which so many never think of attempting, and so few approach, which harmonizes all apparent discordance, and leaves the soul free for other inquiries,—a solution which can be reached only by patient thought.

Of her domestic life I dare not trust myself to speak. (Quoted in William Channing Gannett, *Ezra Stiles Gannett*, 242–43)

The first two paragraphs celebrate Tilden for the strength of her moral character. Gannett describes her as an individual who always acted on principle, who would never do "what her soul told her was wrong" even if such "wrongdoing" meant an apparent act of protection for one she loved. "She dreaded nothing in herself so much as a departure from rectitude," he maintained. In his characterization, she was an individual distinguished by an unwavering "firmness of moral purpose."

Celebrating her "moral integrity," he nonetheless qualified it, giving it a peculiar definition that carefully safeguarded his notion of "true womanhood." In a single moment of emphasis, he called her "a *woman* in her whole constitution and being." His descriptions follow suit, consistently separating Tilden as agent from the effect of her actions. In Gannett's representation, her unwavering "devotion to right" was more an involuntary response than a willed action. It acted as an "instinct" and behaved as one of the "unchangeable laws of the Creation." By his account, Tilden remained passive even when identified with the most active of attributes. He accorded her the woman's "safest" success by connecting her action with a fulfillment of "duty." She did not, he told his congregation, "swerve from [its] path." Her principled action was placed within the framework of "delicacy." She was never seen in action: "What was right must be done, cost what it would."

The cost, at one level, was figured in the kind of representation she received. In Gannett's paragraph on Tilden's "religious character," her past was revised into an acceptable present. As with the issue of "rectitude," the question of religious inquiry was carefully fitted into its proper narrative. By his account, she addressed the fundamental questions of faith but always with the "delicacy" he ascribed to "woman." Fully granting her his own "inclination to the side of doubt," he made it clear that her faith was built in an admirable fashion. She had not simply taken religious belief for granted, nor had she confused a vague "religious feeling" with a sound system of belief. In his words, "her mind took hold of the questions which lie at the foundations," and she did not rest once the answers were reached. He praised her for her continued effort. After working through one set of questions, she had not made the mistake of thinking that religious inquiry was at an end. He characterized her final years as ones spent studying "the great problem of life," examining the apparent inequities that punctuated human existence.[7] She engaged in the intellectual work that few even attempted, and he maintained that her work was not in vain. By his estimation, she was making "beautiful" progress toward a solution.

The adjective raises uneasy questions. Like its counterparts—"anxious curiosity," "toiled," "perplexed," and the earlier verbs "clung," "dreaded," "shrank"—it confines her thought to an acceptable realm of "womanly" effort. She made progress through "patient," not "ardent," thought. Her doubts were characterized as a type of "curiosity" rather than as a life-determining struggle. Her progress was "beautiful." Had she been a man and a public figure, it would most likely have been "powerful."

Describing her spiritual crisis, Gannett portrayed it within his own bounds. He even changed the nature of her uncertainty. In his version, she considered the "mighty" but vague "questions of God and revelation." Any number of items might fall under these headings. She could be considering the "nature of God": How did the believer reconcile the "God of wrath" with the "God of love"? Or she might be addressing the interpretation of Jesus' relation to divinity. Was he God or man? "Revelation" offered a variety of topics as well. She might be questioning the specific issue of miracles or focusing on the best methods for interpreting Scripture. Gannett's vague categories suggest several laudatory items for the Christian woman to address. They also conceal the less acceptable nature of Tilden's questions, for her own crisis of faith had not focused on issues of "how" but on questions of "whether." She did not study the nature of God but doubted his very existence. How to interpret the Bible mattered less to her than whether immortality existed anywhere but in the mind's desire. Her spiritual crisis offered a far more radical challenge than Gannett's description suggested.

Gannett concluded his remarks by telling his congregation what he could not say. He fell silent when he came to the topic of "domestic life." Her daily life went unchronicled, left to the audience's imagination. Thirty years later, the same course of memory was repeated. William Channing Gannett included these paragraphs from his father's sermon in the biography he wrote shortly after his father's "sudden death" in a train accident.[8] The biography offers another public record of Anna Tilden's life, but only as her life was part of her husband's. As the son himself admits, the mother existed primarily in the category of imagination known as "memory." She was kept alive by the father's words. Raised by Anna's sister Catherine, the children called Catherine their "mother-aunt." William Gannett dedicated the biography to her, and in the few pages on his mother's death, he acknowledged that the aunt's presence filled the mother's absence. He writes, "All through the shaping years the mother's sister so filled the empty place with loving care that [the children] hardly knew their loss" (246).

The mother, however, was anything but forgotten, for Gannett kept an image of her alive in a memorial book of recollections he wrote for himself and for his children.[9] Her presence also lingers in volume upon volume of his daily journal. As in the sermon, this presence is evoked by attributes of character. His journal entries contain few references to the particularities of Tilden's daily life. He rarely recalls what she did or said. She is remembered as a force, an influence that is increasingly turned into an exemplary figure against which Gannett judged himself. In his entries, Tilden is never named. When he refers to her, it is always by pronoun. "Anna" appears for the last time in the journal entry for 23 December 1846, the last entry he wrote before her death: "Came home in 8 o'clk omnibus—found Anna sitting in the parlour, writing at her work table, bright and cheerful" (vol. 40). Visiting Trenton Falls three years later, he summarized his trip by remembering her presence but marking her absence. He writes, "But the visit derived its special interest from the recollection of her who so loved these true friends & so delighted in this spot. She was continually before me, and gave a sacred joy to the days I now passed here" (vol. 43, 29 September 1849). Anna Tilden Gannett had become the unnamed influence whose power was felt but whose person was unseen. His memory of her sanctified his experience: recollection conferred "sacred joy."

For Gannett, such moments of presence were closely tied to place and invariably ended in self-examination. Whether in this visit to Trenton or in the family's yearly stay at Rockport, he found "her" present. Continuing a tradition begun before Tilden's death, Gannett and his children returned yearly to summer on the Massachusetts coast. His visits brought Tilden vividly to his mind, but the image he records says little about Tilden herself. His associations were distinctly private: "every spot [connected with the "Old Farm"] seemed dear & sacred" (vol. 44, 4 July 1850), but beyond "the window at which *she* loved to sit, & the beautiful, quiet bay wh[ich] she so much admired" (vol. 45, 8 August 1851), no mention is made of Anna's particular words or work during their earlier days in Rockport. Similarly, his "memorial book" speaks much more distinctly for the writer than about the person remembered. Begun at Rockport, this "book" continued with entries written every Christmas Day. In 1848 Gannett devoted the entry to his own doubts about immortality. The year 1851 saw him wondering over the "completeness of the separation" that death had effected between himself and his wife. In this entry Anna became the inspiring example, prompting him to self-improvement. Reminding himself of his failures, he wrote, "Why am I not more as she would wish me to be, if she were here? Let me act more under the persuasion of her love and her life. She loathed all insincerity: let not me deal dishonestly with others or with myself. She was faithful in the discharge of every duty: let me not be dilatory or neglectful" (quoted in William Channing Gannett, *Ezra Stiles Gannett*, 245). Identifying her with a flawless performance of duty, he chastises himself for falling short of the mark. To remember "her" becomes a means toward (re)formation of his character. What began as Gannett's "recollection of her last hours" and a collection of "memorials . . . of those who loved her" (ibid., 241) became a work of self-examination in which the nominal subject was meta-morphosed into the governing standard.

Tilden's transformation into an unchanging example is best seen in the Mount Auburn monument and the story behind it. The day after her death, Tilden was interred in the burial ground on Boston Common. The location was expedient: what Gannett could afford and what was immediately avail-able.[10] It was hardly a location that either Gannett or Tilden would have chosen as their final resting place. Tilden had long been an admirer of Mount Auburn Cemetery, the gardenlike memorial ground where sermons could be read in both stone and flower. That Jacob Bigelow, her husband's longtime physician, was the driving force behind the cemetery certainly added to its significance. And her own delight in nature and the opportuni-ties it provided for meditation made it a highly desirable place for contem-plative walks. She was a frequent visitor to Mount Auburn and a firm sup-porter of its goal. The founders planned the cemetery as a place of "natural" consolation. Within its borders, the "joint influence of art and nature" worked together to comfort the mourner and remind the visitor that the dead and the living remained connected through nature.

Such ideas echo in Tilden's remarks written after her visits to the ceme-tery. In her 1834 journal, she records at length her first trip to Mount Auburn. Visiting the grave of a school friend, she felt privileged to have been asked by the mother to accompany her to this "sacred spot." Tilden writes, "To me there is something delightful in this place having been se-lected as a 'home for the dead.' I think it must do good to the hearts of all who visit such a holy and consecrated place. It is beautiful to go *there* and think of those who have left us" (1 May 1834). She then quotes several stan-zas of a poem by the popular magazine poet Harriet Gould. Titled "The Voice from Mount Auburn," it celebrates a multivocal chorus. In Gould's poem, the voice of nature speaks through the birds and the "whispering" trees. Mount Auburn's "voice" is also heard in the language by which the "living . . . commune with the dead." Tilden became a firm advocate for this type of "communion." Three years later in a letter to her husband, she celebrated the cemetery for the messages it made possible. Commenting on the recent death of a young father, she remarked, "Dr R[obbins] had re-quested that he might be buried at Mt Auburn. I am very glad this is to be done, I think it must be always a pleasant thought to Eunice that his body even, is in such a beautiful abode, and how many touching and instructive lessons may she give her children at their fathers resting place—There they may be taught the truths of Heaven, and there learn to feel and own a *Fathers* love, even in their sorrow—" (2 June 1836).

When Tilden died, a similar opportunity for her children seemed impossible. Burial in Mount Auburn was undeniably expensive. Lot prices in the 1840s had been raised from the original fee of sixty dollars (still a goodly sum). The expense would be difficult, but it was one difficulty Gannett would not have to face. Shortly after Tilden's death, a group of individuals from the Federal Street Church raised the money required. To translate "heartfelt sympathy" into action, they provided the funds for a lot, an iron fence, and a monument.[11] In the letter informing him of the congregation's offer, the gift was extended as a means of consolation: they "[knew] of nothing they [could] offer which would be more consoling . . . than a Lot at Mount Auburn." It would provide him with the place where the dead and the living could meet "naturally" in thought. Clear subscribers to the belief that pastoral settings brought comfort, they offered nature, enhanced by the work of art, as a promised image of immortality. Anna made a slight appearance in the text of the letter itself. She is referred to as their minister's "morning and evening Star." Their image speaks comfort: hers is a returning presence. It also shapes the identity of the dead: in their representation, Tilden's life reflected and revolved around Gannett's.

Gannett responded to his congregation's offer without hesitation. Unlike the awkwardness he felt over other demonstrations of his congregation's generosity, he experienced no difficulty in accepting this gift. He thanked the givers for their kindness, praising their action for both its sensitivity and its power. He commented, "The Friends whom you represent, could have signified their wish to soothe my grief in no other way at once so delicate and so effectual." He made clear that a major part of the gift's "effect" lay in its close match to his wife's own desire. Again, Tilden is unnamed. Gannett writes, "I know that if she whom God has so suddenly taken from me could have selected her own grave it would have been amidst the shades of Mount Auburn." He concludes the letter by licensing the givers to carry out their intention without his intrusion. He tells them to select the monument and compose the inscription, but does not leave their choice entirely free. He establishes a single, significant criterion. He asks them to "study that simplicity which alone would be emblematical of her character" (December 1846).

Gannett's response to the resulting memorial is cryptic. In his journal, after visits to Mount Auburn, he notes that his "plot looks well," but he says nothing about the particular form of the monument erected in Tilden's memory or of the words written on it. The only comment appears on the envelope of the letter to Gannett that enclosed a copy of the inscription. These words are in the son's hand: "Discovers he chose a very expensive monument." Expense would not be known by appearance. It is certainly less decorative than many, simple in its unbroken series of rectangular shapes, no ornament but the words themselves. These words are direct: in them, Tilden becomes the "true Christian character," remembered for her "devotion to all religious truth and duty." Combined with her "domestic virtues," this devotion created a "constant example." Through the congregation's words, she displayed the "simplicity of character" available only to the exemplary figure.

Such "simplicity" seems a long way from the character of Tilden's last letters. Different personae speak in each: the daughter writing to the father as a comical reporter of daily news; the mother writing for the daughter, giving words to a two-year-old that convey the mother's message of concern; the wife writing to the husband, safeguarding her interests by calling them his amusements. What emerges from these letters is a tone of canny self-irony. The letters are marked by moments of flamboyance that laughingly call attention to their own exaggeration. Writing to her father after the birth of her second child, her first son, she claims for the newborn the title of "best" but immediately cuts the superlative down to size. He is, she says, "to say the *least,* the best boy we've got" (28 April 1840). And "only boy" rings through the "least" that she says. Enclosing a note with the two-year-old daughter's New Year's gift for her father, Tilden created a voice for the daughter that could also speak for the mother. Behind the words of the child and their breathless diminutives lies the continued concern about an unresolved problem. Under the guise of "Kitty," Tilden wrote, "And I hope you will try to be well, and live a great many years to take care of little brother, and myself. . . . So pray do remember your two babies" (1 January 1841). Europe finally failed to provide the cure; Gannett's health remained perpetually problematic. His journal entries note ongoing complaints about his body and articulate returning despair over his spiritual and mental well-being. Behind the mother's words for the daughter stood a reminder of the father's duty.

Tilden's own health was uneven, and she spent time away from Boston every summer hoping to regain the strength she invariably lost during the winter. In her surviving letters to Gannett, she presented a domestic idyll of her own construction. References to her children or to Gannett's longed-for presence serve as the safe frame within which she could voice her own thoughts, whether they centered on a sermon or on the books she hoped to read. Writing from Princeton the summer after her second child was born, she made scant mention of her reason for being away. Three pages into the letter, she admitted that she had "not felt any better" and implied the opposite was in fact true. She mentions her eyes, noting that she "dare not use them [in the evening] either to read or write." She went to bed "very early, *by dark*," turning the hours she could not use into her best attempt to "get rest and strength." Comments about her own health, however, were quickly bracketed by references to the children. Responding to Gannett's ongoing concern for their health, she merged the remarks about her own physical struggle with reassurances about the children's well-being. His letters regularly expressed fear for his sons and daughter. Not a letter was sent without an urgent request that Tilden contact him immediately if anything seemed wrong. In this letter of 2 August 1840, her concern was clear. Fearing that he would have heard reports of scarlet fever in the nearby town of Hubbardston, she assured him that no signs of the disease had been reported in the area around Princeton where they were staying.

This letter plays out an extended sequence of self-assertion and self-effacement. Whether hiding her own poor health behind her children's well-being or presenting her own critical report of a sermon, she repeatedly steps away from her perspective and back into his. In each case, however, her deference does not wholly efface her comments. The wit of her statements endures, even after she has bowed deftly to another's authority. Her comments on hearing an orthodox sermon are a case in point. She weaves her small narrative well. The letter opens by painting a happy scene of mother with children: "It is Sunday afternoon dear Stiles, I have just returned from church, and placed myself at the beautiful end window of our room to say a few words to you. Dearest Kitty is busy by my side, with a pencil and paper, and darling little Willie is asleep. I assure you it is refreshing to be situated just as I am at this moment." Only after the image is established does she explain its particular meaning. The family idyll is "refreshing" not simply because it typifies the domestic setting her husband loved but primarily because it relieves the dreariness of the morning's sermon. She wrote, "It is refreshing to be situated just as I am at this moment after hearing such an orthodox sermon as I have been listening to."

Describing the sermon, she cultivates a tone of mild satire. Not wanting to fault the young minister's earnestness, she cannot help laughing at the machinations required to sustain his topic. "It really seemed to me," she writes, "that he had to work hard to make out an argument even to his own mind. He took the rebellion of this country from England for a grand explanation and *plain illustration* of total depravity! He was honest enough to say that he did not bring infants into the case at all, they were 'pure as their Creator made them' and whatever 'God made was *right*' but this innocence lasts only till the moment their moral nature begins to act." She dispenses with the minister's "grand explanation" by her emphasis and exclamation. She finds his "*plain illustration*" humorously obscure and calls his argument immediately into question. A long-standing listener of sermons, Tilden knew that the best arguments of the day were transparent; they appeared without heavy labor on the minister's—or the congregation's— part. The sermon's plain example grows murkier as she pokes fun at the minister's inconsistency. In this sermon on "total depravity," she wonders about the meaning of the phrase. Responding to the exception he makes for children, she writes, "I don't know what dictionary he looks in for the meaning of the word *total*."

In the next moment, the tone of her comments quickly changes. She turns the satire on herself, imagining the reader smiling at both the tale *and* its teller. "You will be amused I dare say," she tells Gannett, "at my being so much interested in Orthodox preaching." Her "interest" is no more than his "amusement," a light diversion from his own deep involvement in the debate over truth played out between "Liberal Christians" and their "Orthodox" counterparts. She does not, however, allow his imagined laughter to stand as the final remark. Switching completely away from satire and self-irony, she concludes this portion of her letter with a small statement of her own truth. Her interest represents a larger concern. She writes, "The truth is, I have heard so little of it [Orthodox preaching], that I am glad of a chance to know something more about it." Behind the mother creating domestic images for the father and witty satire for the minister is the woman attempting to learn from whatever her circumstances offer.

That circumstances away from Boston were more congenial appears in one slight moment of laughing self-characterization. Returning to her tone of self-irony, she laments her husband's absence but rationalizes it through

the work she imagines him accomplishing in Boston. "I dare say you find
that you can do ten times as much in a day without as with us." In their
company, she acknowledges, distractions would be plentiful. The "babies"
offer him the pleasure of play; the wife, in her own words, the "pleasure
also of hearing me fret." She paints an image of grumbling discontent, do-
mesticated by the unlikely attachment of pleasure and complaining. She
also extends a different prospect for the future, one that seemed justified by
the present. She writes, "Perhaps one of these days I shall leave off fretting.
I haven't fretted but *very little* all this week that I can remember, very much
owing I suspect of my being released from the charge of Master Bellamy's
dusting." With domestic chores at a minimum, she is freed from the complaints that accompanied them. Sounding like anything but an embodiment of domestic virtue, she here celebrates her release from its duties. Like
her younger self, she still preferred reading.

Behind the fretting woman stood the reader whose frank outspokenness
had once been called temper and later reclaimed as courage. The "true and
noble-minded woman" memorialized in Mount Auburn for her "devotion
to all religious truth and duty" had worked out her own truths in her journals and letters. Sometimes that truth spoke plainly, often it spoke from behind a mask, but her voice, seeking its audience, would finally not silence
itself. What silence it encountered was imposed, not embraced. Behind the
congregation's monument, marking the place where Tilden was buried in
the Mount Auburn plot, the individual tombstone offers its own comment
on her life. The appearance that meets the eye yields a misleading interpretation. What was apparently left blank reveals a different story. Beneath the
seemingly uninscribed surface lie the initials by which Tilden named herself: A[nna]. L[inzee]. G[annett]. And behind that name are various words
crafted for a variety of audiences. These words, long forgotten, speak once
again, the unknown voice now known, addressing an unknown reader in
an unforeseen correspondence.

Notes

1. See also Joanne Dobson, *Dickinson and the Strategies of Reticence: The Woman Writer in Nineteenth-Century America* (Bloomington: Indiana University Press, 1989); Constance D. Harsh, *Subversive Heroinism: Resolutions of Social Crisis in the Condition-of-England Novel* (Ann Arbor: University of Michigan Press, 1994); and Joyce Warren, ed., *The (Other) American Traditions* (New Brunswick, N.J.: Rutgers University Press, 1993). Dobson places Dickinson's life and work in the context of other American women writers (Catharine Sedgwick, Lydia Sigourney, Fanny Fern, E. D. E. N. Southworth, Alice Cary, Elizabeth Stoddard), illustrating the ways in which privacy became a public and publishable issue. In her study of the condition-of-England novel, Harsh argues that the power embodied in the domestic settings created by British novelists in the 1840s modeled a type of social change that, with the economic resurgence of the 1850s, became a path not taken. Although the essays in Warren's collection do not focus exclusively on the vexed question of "the senti-mental," Warren does provide a useful definition in her introduction. Discussing why the concept fared so poorly in the earlier version of an American literary canon, she writes, "Sentimentality requires an awareness of other people, a mental dialogue or displacement. The person who observes the sentiment-provoking situ-ation must identify with or at least sympathize with the unfortunate person(s) whom he/she observes. The dominant American literary tradition, which reflects the individualism of American culture, focuses on the solitary male individualist" (11). I write "earlier" American literary canon with some doubt, since this version certainly remains *the* version in many high school and college curricula: a few writ-ers added but no fundamental change to the "classics."

2. Foster makes this remark in reference to Maria Stewart in her opening chapter on African American women writers of the eighteenth and nineteenth centuries (*Written by Herself: Literary Production by African-American Women, 1746–1892* [Bloomington: Indiana University Press, 1993], 4). Addressing the "overwhelming [critical] silence" of the 1980s, Foster calls for the kind of work that will shatter such silence. She writes, "The problem of discovering the stories previously unheard requires that we look beyond what has been preserved as the official or privileged realities. We must become literary anthropologists, looking underneath the stated ideas and events to see what is not shown. We must discover and understand the

251

context of the fragments left by those whose words were not valued or were deval-ued" (9). Noting that individual African American women established an authori-tative voice early in the history of the American colonies, she discusses how these writers combined a variety of genres to create words that would be heard and enacted.

William Andrews has worked steadily on African American autobiography for the past two decades. His introduction to the spiritual narratives of Jarena Lee, Zilpha Elaw, and Julia Foote gives a masterful overview of the ways in which the evangeli-cal conversion narrative offered women—black and white—a form in which they could claim and act from an "authentic, individually authorized selfhood" (16). See *Sisters of the Spirit: Three Black Women's Autobiographies of the Nineteenth Century* (Bloomington: Indiana University Press, 1988).

Joanne Braxton's *Black Women Writing Autobiography: A Tradition within a Tra-dition* (Philadelphia: Temple University Press, 1989) was the first full-length study of African American women's autobiographical writing. The work covers a wide range of writers from the early nineteenth to the late twentieth century. Looking at the changes in form and focus, she separates her study into three distinct periods (narratives from the period of American slavery, autobiographical writing from the post-Reconstruction era, and literary autobiography from the twentieth century) yet illustrates the common personae of "outraged mother" and outspoken vision-ary that unite these varied writings.

3. Nina Baym's *Woman's Fiction: A Guide to Novels by and about Women in Amer-ica, 1820–1870* (Ithaca, N.Y.: Cornell University Press, 1978) was the first book to give serious attention to "forgotten" works of nineteenth-century women writers. Virtually opening a new field for study, she provided an overview of the dozens of writers and hundreds of works produced in the fifty-year period she had chosen. In 1984 Baym shifted her focus to the audience who read these works. Her *Novels, Readers, and Reviewers: Responses to Fiction in Antebellum America* (Ithaca, N.Y.: Cornell University Press, 1984) is an invaluable study of reviews and what they re-veal about the novels' various readers.

Mary Kelley looks at the role of the woman writer as defined by six of the most prominent authors of the mid-nineteenth century. Her *Private Woman, Public Stage: Literary Domesticity in Nineteenth-Century America* (New York: Oxford Uni-versity Press, 1984) clearly delineates the economic hardships under which women wrote as well as the problematic households in which they defined themselves as woman and writer. Cathy Davidson's *The Revolution of the Word* (New York: Ox-ford University Press, 1986) extended this work back into the eighteenth century, focusing on a number of eighteenth-century American women writers whose works shaped the American novel. Most recently, the essays collected in Warren's *(Other) American Traditions* address a wide-ranging group of nineteenth-century women writers. In her introduction, Warren continues the work from her earlier study, *The American Narcissus* (New Brunswick, N.J.: Rutgers University Press, 1984).

Focusing on the centrality of community in novels written by women, she directs attention to their sometimes implicit, often direct, critique of individualism. The essays themselves address both individual writers/works and their place in a shared community of expression.

4. Baym's bibliography lists forty-eight different writers and 132 titles.

5. Patricia Meyer Spacks, *The Female Imagination* (New York: Knopf, 1975); Elaine Showalter, *A Literature of Their Own* (Princeton: Princeton University Press, 1977); Rachel Brownstein, *Becoming a Heroine: Reading about Women in Novels* (New York: Viking Press, 1982); Ellen Moers, *Literary Women* (Garden City, N.Y.: Doubleday, 1976); Sandra Gilbert and Susan Gubar, *The Madwoman in the Attic: The Woman Writer and the Nineteenth-Century Literary Imagination* (New Haven: Yale University Press, 1979). Little need here be said of these groundbreaking works except to note (some) of the studies built on their foundations: Alison Booth: *Greatness Engendered: George Eliot and Virginia Woolf* (Ithaca, N.Y.: Cornell University Press, 1992); Margaret J. M. Ezell: *Writing Women's Literary History* (Baltimore: Johns Hopkins University Press, 1993); Susan Fraiman, *Unbecoming Women: British Women Writers and the Novel of Development* (New York: Columbia University Press, 1993); Joanne S. Frye, *Living Stories, Telling Lives: Women and the Novel in Contemporary Experience* (Ann Arbor: University of Michigan Press, 1986); Susan Rubinow Gorsky: *Femininity to Feminism: Women and Literature in the Nineteenth Century* (New York: Twayne, 1992); Susan K. Harris, *Nineteenth-Century American Women's Novels: Interpretative Strategies* (Cambridge: Cambridge University Press, 1990); Gaye Tuchman and Nina E. Fortin, *Edging Women Out: Victorian Novelists, Publishers, and Social Change* (New Haven: Yale University Press, 1989); Patricia Yaeger: *Honey-Mad Women: Emancipatory Strategies in Women's Writing* (New York: Columbia University Press, 1988).

6. Jill Ker Conway's anthology *Written by Herself: Autobiographies of American Women* (New York: Vintage, 1992) provides a notable example. A selection from twenty-five women's autobiographies, the book was designed for a "crossover" market. Published by Random House's Vintage Press, it was packaged less as a textbook for women's studies courses than as a book for the "general" reading public. Its appeal was immediate. When I ordered it in November 1992 for my course on women's autobiographical writing, it was already out of stock. The *Norton Book of Women's Lives*, edited by Phyllis Rose (New York: Norton, 1993), focusing entirely on twentieth-century women, expands the notion of "autobiography" to include journals, letters, and memoirs. Like Conway's book, it is targeted for an audience beyond the academy.

I pause here and reflect on this recent interest *and* its marketing: in a world where the old equations still hold, the publication raises troubling questions. Many of the excerpted autobiographies in Conway's anthology probably would not win republication on their own. Of the twenty-five she includes, thirteen are no longer in print. In a review of the *Norton Book of Women's Lives,* the reviewer termed the women represented in the volume "vulnerable." And the title of this collection it-self suggests how far there is to go: "The Norton *Book of Women's Lives*" rings un-easily against Norton's other anthology titles. The book contains women's *writings*—constructions of women's lives—but still the old stereotype persists. Women live lives while men write works—artistry once again subordinated to "being."

In addition to Conway's and Rose's volumes was the early collection edited by Mary Jane Moffat and Charlotte Painter (*Revelations: Diaries of Women* [New York: Vintage, 1974]). Now out of print, it announced a new field of study: "a literature so vast and varied that many shelves of anthologies would not exhaust the subject" (4). Ten years later the Feminist Press published Margo Culley's excellent anthology of women's autobiographical writing (*A Day at a Time: The Diary Literature of Ameri-can Women from 1764 to the Present*, 1985). Her introduction remains a superb re-source for those teaching and writing about women's autobiographical work.

Almost contemporary with Culley's work is another anthology of diary literature packaged for the industry's notion of a decidedly "popular" audience: *Private Pages: Diaries of American Women, 1830s-1970s*, edited by Penelope Franklin (New York: Ballantine Books, 1986). Its cover design gives a flowery evocation of the stereo-typed diary. The word "private" is written in the script recognizably associated with romance novels; the colors of the cover are beige, blue, and pink with an attempt to make the cover, with its decorative border of flowers, look like the inside cover of the diaries sold for girls in early adolescence. The back cover mentions "entries . . . telling of love, marriage, and motherhood," and the introduction opens with a sen-sational appeal to the violation of privacy in which the diary is figured as an alarm-ingly female object: "It's happened to all of us: we find unguarded, abandoned on a desk, by a bedside, or in an attic—someone else's diary. It lures us seductively" (xiii). Books, however, need not be judged by their covers or by the opening lines of their introductions. The selections are fascinating and valuably long (one difficulty with Conway's and Culley's anthologies is the brevity of the excerpts) and the introduction to each figure useful.

7. Liz Stanley, *The Auto/Biographical I: The Theory and Practice of Feminist Auto/biography* (Manchester: Manchester University Press, 1992); Sidonie Smith, *A Poet-ics of Women's Autobiography: Marginality and the Fictions of Self-Representation* (Bloomington: Indiana University Press, 1987) and *Subjectivity, Identity, and the Body: Women's Autobiographical Practices in the Twentieth Century* (Bloomington: Indiana University Press, 1993); Françoise Lionnet, *Autobiographical Voices: Race, Gender, Self-Portraiture* (Ithaca, N.Y.: Cornell University Press, 1989); Braxton, *Black Women Writing Autobiography*; Felicity Nussbaum, *The Autobiographical Subject: Gender and Ideology in Eighteenth-Century England* (Baltimore: Johns Hopkins University Press, 1989); Domna Stanton, *The Female Autograph: Theory and Practice of Autobiography from the Tenth to the Twentieth Century* (Chicago: Chicago University Press, 1984); Estelle Jelinek, ed., *Women's Autobiography: Essays*

in Criticism (Bloomington: Indiana University Press, 1980), and Jelinek, *The Tradition of Women's Autobiography: From Antiquity to the Present* (Boston: Twayne, 1986); Margo Culley and Leonore Hoffmann, eds., *Women's Personal Narratives* (New York: Modern Language Association, 1985), and Margo Culley, ed., *American Women's Autobiography: Fea(s)ts of Memory* (Madison: University of Wisconsin Press, 1992).

Stanley, Smith, Stanton, Lionnet, and Nussbaum focus on theorizing autobiography. By far the most innovative and experimental, Stanley's work breaks apart the "academic" structures that govern (most) scholarly work. Departing from the traditional chapter organization, she blends anecdotal sketches with direct address to the reader, précislike statements with extended discussions in essay form. Enacting her own definition, she terms feminist autobiography a form that calls attention to "the process of construction . . . characterised by its self-conscious and increasingly self-confident traversing of conventional boundaries between different genres of writing" (255).

Nussbaum's focus on the eighteenth century addresses autobiographies written by both men and women. Studying the "politics of subjectivity," she examines a range of autobiographical texts to illustrate how these "first-person texts disseminate a regimen that enables the production of a particular kind of self"—and not only disseminates but enforces (xvii).

In her two books, Smith calls attention to the problematics of the "universal" (i.e., male) subject: "the 'normative' generic definitions that in their very conceptualization preclude both aesthetic appreciation and sophisticated reading of works by women" (*Poetics*, 15). Through her work, she provides readers with a new framework for reading, one that concentrates on the series of negotiations women autobiographers undertake in writing their lives.

Crossing centuries and cultures in her study, Lionnet applies the notion of *métissage* to the understanding of autobiographical writing. This "braiding of cultural forms" (4) serves as a signal and powerful strategy for writing outside the dominant discourse while still remaining in conversation with it.

Braxton examines the tradition of autobiography developed through the writings and conversations of a long line of African American women. Opening with an autobiographical introductory essay, she reminds her reader that life stories are told in many forms but always with a particular audience and purpose in the storyteller's mind. Her work covers a variety of autobiographical forms—from the spiritual autobiographies of Jarena Lee and Rebecca Cox Jackson to Charlotte Forten Grimke's diaries to the literary autobiographies of Zora Neale Hurston and Maya Angelou.

Jelinek and Culley, allied more closely with Anglo-American feminist criticism, center their work on the recovery and discussion of particular texts. Culley is best known for her role as editor—of both autobiographical writings and essays about them. Her *American Women's Autobiography* is indeed the feast its subtitle announces with its fourteen essays on a wide-ranging group of autobiographical writings. Following in the footsteps of Jelinek's earlier collection of essays (1980), it offers its readers a variety of approaches on a variety of writers. In addition to her work as editor, Culley has used her essays within these collections to lay the foundation for studies both of the tradition of women's autobiographical writing and of methods for reading these traditions and the works within them. Jelinek's *The Tradition of Women's Autobiography* examines the elements that can be identified specifically with autobiographical writing by women. Seeking to illuminate the differences between life writing by men and by women, she articulates a tradition of women's autobiography in which the episodic takes precedence over the chronologic narrative and the individual's affiliation with the "world of their times" plays a minor role in comparison with the rich world of personal relationships.

8. In the past several years, a number of women's diaries have been published or reissued, in many cases under the auspices of the "regional interest" they were seen to address: for example, *The Log of the Skipper's Wife,* edited by James W. Balano (Camden, Maine: Down East Books, 1979); *The Captain's Best Mate: The Journal of Mary Chipman Lawrence on the Whaler Addison, 1856–1860,* edited by Stanton Garner (Hanover: University Press of New England, 1986); *Down the Santa Fe Trail and into Mexico: The Diary of Susan Shelby Magoffin, 1846–1847,* edited by Stella M. Drumm (New Haven: Yale University Press, 1962; Lincoln: University of Nebraska Press, 1982). With Joanna Stratton's *Pioneer Women: Voices from the Kansas Frontier* (New York: Simon and Schuster, 1981) and Sandra Myres's *Westering Women and the Frontier Experience, 1800–1915* (Albuquerque: University of New Mexico Press, 1982), interest turned, in particular, to women who chronicled their experiences in the West. Civil War diaries, especially those kept by women in the American South, have also experienced something of a renaissance of interest. Mary Chestnutt's diary is, of course, the best-known example.

What remains largely unpublished are women's diaries and journals from the early nineteenth century. Beacon Press has recently published selections from Elizabeth Cabot's diary (*More than Common Powers of Perception: The Diary of Elizabeth Rogers Mason Cabot,* ed. P. A. M. Taylor, 1993). More attention has been given to women's letters from this period, though here the publications reflect the woman's "fame" (Margaret Fuller, Louisa May Alcott, Elizabeth Peabody). Little has been said about the correspondence of women who had no "public" identity.

9. So much so that it has become a topic of discussion in *PMLA,* the most established of literary journals. The October 1996 issue (vol. 111, no. 5) devoted its guest column to the "Place of the Personal in Scholarship" with essays by Michael Bérubé, Cathy N. Davidson, Sylvia Molloy, and David Palumbo-Liu. Diane P. Freedman, Olivia Frey, and Frances Murphy Zauhar, eds., *The Intimate Critique: Autobiographical Literary Criticism* (Durham, N.C.: Duke University Press, 1993),

provide a thought-provoking collection of essays about the constraints of traditional criticism and the power of the "personal" to break such constraints. The authors not only question the old forms but pioneer new ones: letters, polyphonic interchanges of "academic" prose and anecdotal sketch, third-person distancing of first-person observation, essays written as a combination of related, not argued, paragraphs. As the editors note in their introduction, "In putting this volume together, we encouraged writing that challenged argument as the preferred mode for discussion, questioned the importance of the objective and impersonal, and, rather than aiming for a seamless, finished, 'product,' characteristically made direct reference to the process by which it was accomplished" (2–3).

10. "'That Profoundly Female, and Feminist Genre': The Diary as Feminist Practice," *Women's Studies Quarterly* 3–4 (1989): 6–14.

11. Stratton's and Myres's studies of women on the various American "frontiers" followed this method, as did Patricia Caldwell's study of seventeenth-century conversion narratives, *The Puritan Conversion Narrative: The Beginnings of American Expression* (Cambridge: Cambridge University Press, 1983). On the smaller scale of the essay, Hilary Hinds addresses the boundaries broken by Quaker women writing in seventeenth-century England. See her essay, "'Who May Binde Where God Hath Loosed?': Responses to Sectarian Women's Writing in the Second Half of the Seventeenth Century," in *Gloriana's Face: Women, Public and Private in the English Renaissance*, ed. S. P. Cerasano and Marion Wynne-Davies (New York: Harvester Wheatsheaf, 1992), 205–27.

12. Carolyn Heilbrun, *Writing a Woman's Life* (New York: Norton, 1988). Stuart, Stanley, and Barry in Teresa Iles's *All Sides of the Subject: Women and Biography* (New York: Teachers College Press of Columbia University Press, 1992).

Feminist criticism sharply delineates the problems associated with a "traditional" approach to biography. The individual as a readily isolatable entity is a highly problematic construct given its source in a patriarchal structure. As Nancy Chodorow has shown in *The Reproduction of Mothering: Psychoanalysis and the Sociology of Gender* (Berkeley and Los Angeles: University of California Press, 1978), individuation is differently experienced by male and female infants. In the case of boys, self-definition can be said to proceed by "difference from," whereas girls, identifying with their mothers, experience themselves as distinct selves within the context of "likeness to." To be individual is to be like the mother. From this angle of vision, a life is less an insular experience of separate self than the relation of individuals connected within and by community. The recent work of Carol Gilligan and her research group at the Center for the Study of Gender, Education, and Human Development at the Harvard Graduate School of Education has expanded this notion of the connected self well beyond infancy and traced its imprint on female adolescence and adulthood. The question of moral development highlights the difference: the "traditional" model of justice in which the individual "appeals" to a standard of "fairness" and the "care" model in which decisions center on the preservation of relationships. See Carol Gilligan, Nona P. Lyons, and Trudy Hanmer, eds., *Making Connections: The Relational Worlds of Adolescent Girls at the Emma Willard School* (Cambridge: Harvard University Press, 1990); Carol Gilligan, Janie Victoria Ward, and Jill McLean Taylor, eds., *Mapping the Moral Domain: A Contribution of Women's Thinking to Psychological Theory and Education* (Cambridge: Center for the Study of Gender, Education, and Human Development at the Harvard Graduate School of Education, distributed by Harvard University Press, 1988); Carol Gilligan and Lyn Mikel Brown, *Meeting at the Crossroads: Women's Psychology and Girls' Development, 1992* (Cambridge: Harvard University Press, 1992); and Carol Gilligan, D. Kay Johnston, and Barbara Miller, eds., *Moral Voice, Adolescent Development, and Secondary Education: A Study at the Green River School* (Cambridge: Harvard University Press, 1987).

With the emphasis shifted away from the isolated individual, the representation of "a life" marks a quite different process. Heilbrun's *Writing a Woman's Life* called eloquently for a new kind of biography that would represent women's lives on their own terms. Wary of standardizing any one approach, scholars working on feminist biography describe their work in a variety of ways. Sara Alpern and the other editors of *The Challenge of Feminist Biography: Writing the Lives of Modern American Women* (Urbana: University of Illinois Press, 1992) term their book a "workshop in print" (2), explicitly rejecting any attempt to produce a definitive version. "Our goal," they write, "was not to set down rigid guidelines about how such questions should be answered or to force a template onto women's biographies. We wanted, rather, to contribute to the ongoing discussion of the nature and practice of feminist biography and to assist and encourage others in their own projects" (13).

An active part of this discussion, the contributors to Iles's *All Sides of the Subject* speak to the vexed question of multiple subjectivities: the subject writing, reading, represented. Citing the distortions created by a genre focused primarily on "uniqueness," the articles present biographical subjects that the long-standing tradition of biography would never have considered. The very notion of the "unique" or "exceptional" comes into question, providing a tool by which we can, as Rachel Gutiérrez says, "understand social injustices" and their powerful reliance on stereotypes that determine who can or cannot be "exceptional" (54). Throughout these various essays, one emphasis remains common: the importance of keeping the biographer's process clearly visible. Summing up the elements she finds common to feminist biography, Liz Stanley suggests the following: "an a priori insistence that works of biography should be treated as composed by textually located ideological practices . . . an analytic (not just descriptive) concern with the specifics of how we come to understand what we do, by locating acts of understanding in an explication of the grounded contexts these are located in and arise from; a rejection of the spotlight approach to a single individual" (115). Preceding the collections of Iles and Alpern et al., Carol Ascher, Louise DeSalvo, and Sara Ruddick's *Between Women: Biographers, Critics, Teachers, and Artists Write about their Work on Women* (Boston: Beacon Press, 1984), together with Heilbrun's *Writing a Women's Life*, could well be said to have gotten our thinking about feminist biography fruitfully under way.

13. The comment appears in the opening entry for the journal Tilden kept from 20 April 1834 to 1835.

14. The Houghton Library of Harvard University holds all but two pieces of Tilden's known writing. These include a book of sermon notes, 1824–31 (bMS Am 1888.4 185); her first journal, kept from January 1827 to mid-September 1828 (bMS Am 1888.4 186); an 1834–35 journal from her period of spiritual crisis (bMS Am 1888.4 187); and one volume of the journal from her European trip (bMS Am 1888.4 188). In addition to the journals there are eighty-three letters: fifty-nine to Ezra Stiles Gannett, her minister and, later, husband (bMS Am 1888.4 26); fifteen to her mother (bMS Am 1888.4 143); five to her sisters (bMS Am 1888.4 144–45); two to her father (bMS Am 1888.4 142a); and one letter to William Ellery Channing (bMS Am 1888.4 142). A single letter to her sister Catherine is held by the Massachusetts Historical Society in the Gannett Collection, and a brief description of her children is housed in the Gannett Collection at the University of Rochester.

In all probability, the Houghton's holdings represent only a portion of what Tilden wrote. For example, Tilden refers to "volume II" and "volume 5" of her "Europe journal." The Houghton has only the first volume. Tilden's correspondence may also have been yet more extensive than the extant letters show. Her sister Sarah moved to St. Louis in the late 1830s, but no letters to Sarah have surfaced. Tilden's sister Catherine spent a significant amount of time in New York City. Only a few letters to Catherine have been located.

Given the frequency of quotation from Tilden's letters and journals and from Gannett's letters to Tilden (bMS Am 1888.4 87), the Houghton Library shelfmarks are given here and in the bibliography.

15. I edited her sermon notes for publication in the 1989 volume of *Studies in the American Renaissance* (hereafter cited as SAR 1989): "'Most Glorious Sermons': Anna Tilden's Sermon Notes, 1824–1831," 1–93.

16. Writing to her minister, Tilden's mother called Anna her "dear blind girl" and described her daughter's slow and uncertain recovery: "I wish I could give you better accounts of Ann, the most I can say in her favor is, that she is not any worse. Dr Gorham said this much [:] he thought her a little better & that her recovery would be very slow. I think, myself it will be many weeks before she quits her chamber. . . . She sits up only long enough for her bed to be made, & her room is darker if possible than when you left her, she expects a long confinement, & is not only submissive, but reasonable & cheerfull [*sic*]. Tomorrow I shall put a close stove into our

chamber which will warm it without the light affecting her eyes" (Zebiah Tilden to Ezra Stiles Gannett, 17 November 1828, bMS Am 1888.4 67, Houghton Library, Harvard University).

17. Manuals for letter writing were common in the nineteenth century, reflecting their long history and continued popularity since their first appearance in the mid-sixteenth century. Organized by types of letters, the letter-writer offered its reader a number of models to follow for (seemingly) any occasion. In his monograph on letter-writers written and/or published in America, Harry B. Weiss lists 27 different titles and 127 different editions published between 1698 and 1835. Originally designed as a "secretary's guide," these books branched into all areas of correspondence, or as one of the more popular versions advertised itself: "*The Universal letter-writer* [1808]; or, Whole art of polite correspondence; containing a great variety of plain, easy, entertaining, and familiar original letters, adapted to every age and situation in life, but more particularly on business, education, and love. Together with various forms of petitions, suitable to the different wants and exigencies of life" (in Weiss, "American Letter-Writers, 1698–1943" [New York Public Library, 1945], 33).

18. Tilden's 1827–1828 journal mentions the following collections of letters: Elizabeth Hamilton's *Letters on the elementary principles of education* (1801; Boston: S. H. Parker, 1825) and Hester Chapone's *Letters on the Improvement of the Mind Addressed to a Lady* (1773; New York: Evert Duyckinck, 1826). Ten years later, she retained her interest in conduct books, even though she was no longer the audience for which they were nominally written. In 1836, she commented favorably on Eliza Farrar's *The Young Lady's Friend* (Boston: American Stationers' Co., 1836), despite the criticism it had received from certain "delicate" readers.

CHAPTER 1: DAUGHTER, SISTER, MOTHER, WIFE

1. "Naming" my subject raises a host of questions, some distinctly theoretical, some decidedly practical, some a curious mixture of the two. The easiest was the decision not to use "Gannett": not only would confusion result over which "Gannett" I meant, Anna or Ezra, but I did not want to identify my subject solely by her married identity. I also readily chose not to use first names because of the presumption it signaled and the anachronism it invited. I was not on a "first-name" basis with these individuals; I could not claim to "know" them in the way we know the individuals we call by first name. I was working with their words and their representations of themselves, in a time very different from our own, and I wanted to maintain that sense of difference for my reader. Nor did I want to perpetuate the condescension associated with the once (still?) common practice of referring to figures by their first name if they are women. First names appear only when it would otherwise be unclear to which of the Tildens I was referring.

The power associated with naming and particularly the power to name oneself are concerns within any discussion of identity. My subject was variously named and named herself variously. Before her marriage she signed herself Anna L. Tilden or Anna Linzee Tilden; after marriage, Anna L. Gannett. "Linzee," a family name on her father's side (her father's sister Eliza married John Linzee, and her favorite cousin Susan shared the same middle name with Anna) was the one constant in a realm of shifting names. Within her own experience, even the first name was subject to change. Following the common practice of the time, she was given several nicknames. In addition to Anna, she was also "Ann," "Nan," and "Nanny"—the latter, interestingly enough, after her marriage and the birth of her children. The diminutive became the name applied to her adulthood.

While an argument could be made for the use of "Linzee," I was uneasy with its disconnection from any public identity. As the middle name, it was virtually bounded by the private life. I have instead chosen the name "Tilden," both for its public acknowledgment and its private significance. It clearly frees her identity from being merged in marriage yet retains the connection with a publicly acknowledged family name. At the same time, it raises questions about the roles scripted for her: for the first twenty-four years of her life, she was one of the "Tilden daughters"; only in the last eleven years was she "Mrs. Gannett." "Tilden" calls attention to the terms on which she was asked to construct her life and suggests that she altered these terms even while adopting them. The name becomes a marker for autonomy within constraint.

2. Tilden sailed from Boston to Charleston on 5 January 1800 but would never reach his destination. The ship, the captain, and its crew were all lost at sea. That the oldest son and namesake would become a prominent member of the Massachusetts Hospital Life Insurance Company seems hardly coincidental. In the Tilden family genealogy, the following description of the elder Tilden's possessions is given: "pew in the Old Brick Meeting House; half of house, land stores and wharf in Battery March [*sic*] Street, house and land in Milk Street" (Tilden ms genealogy, in the John W. Linzee Papers [SG/Til/7–7b #139], compiled by John W. Linzee, box 1, fifth generation, New England Historic Genealogical Society, Boston).

3. In 1990s dollars that figures something on the order of $440,000.

4. Joseph Tilden held a subscription to the Boston Athenaeum and was actively involved in its early years. Tilden served as treasurer from 1811 to 1815, trustee from 1816 to 1822, and proprietor from 1815 until his death in 1853. Anna Tilden may also have been able to borrow books under Samuel Torrey's name. Torrey was the husband of Tilden's cousin Susan, who, like her father, Joseph, served as a family benefactor.

5. In an entry from late November 1827 Tilden writes, "There was pleasant and entertaining conversation such as I like to hear even if I do not take a part in it." Individuals in early-nineteenth-century England and the United States took a

decided interest in studying conversation. It was identified as one of the activities in which an individual displayed his or her character, and conduct books invariably devoted a chapter to discussing the elements of "good conversation." See Lydia Sigourney's chapter on conversation (Letter 12) in *Letters to Young Ladies* (New York: Harper & Brothers, 1836), 173–88, and Farrar's discussions in *Young Lady's Friend*, 271–73, 299–301. Farrar combined education with conversation, commenting, "Well-educated girls have a wide range of topics, which afford plenty of agreeable and useful discussion, between them and their gentlemen friends; and it is much better to talk with them, and with your female friends, of things than of people; of books, pictures, and the beauties and wonders of nature, than of Miss A——'s spoilt complexion, or Mr B——'s broken engagement, or of the quarrel between C—— and D——. If you are familiar with the works of great minds, and spend much time in reading them, or if you love nature and scientific researches, you need not be told to avoid gossip, you will have no relish for it" (299).

Ministers found conversation a useful sermon topic, and lyceum lectures often featured it as well. As Lawrence Buell has noted, it became a genre of its own, most clearly associated with Margaret Fuller, though Bronson Alcott also gave "conversations" with lesser success (See Buell's *Literary Transcendentalism: Style and Vision in the American Renaissance* [Ithaca, N.Y.: Cornell University Press, 1973], 77–101). In Fuller's case, the choice of the form is telling: her conversations are closely allied with education, designed for women who, like Tilden, had received some years of private school education but whose formal study had been curtailed by their domestic duties. Tilden's school friend Ellen Sturgis did in fact attend Fuller's conversations, and Tilden herself would have been a likely participant; however, the Federal Street Church's weekly lectures ran opposite Fuller's conversations, and Tilden's loyalty was dictated by the church and her minister-husband.

6. In 1793, Bulfinch drew up plans for converting part of the still marshy South End into a fashionable district. Proposing a crescent-shaped street fronted by sixteen connected red-brick houses, he divided the crescent at the midpoint with an arch leading through the buildings to the newly created, aptly named Arch Street. On the other side, the crescent was separated from Franklin Street by a small oval park that Bulfinch designed, complete with urn brought from Europe, as a memorial to Benjamin Franklin. In his *Boston: A Topographical History* (Cambridge: Harvard University Press, Belknap Press, 1968), Walter Muir Whitehill has called the Tontine Crescent Bulfinch's "most original contribution" to Federalist Boston (52).

7. In order of birth, the children of Bryant and Zebiah Tilden: William Brown (1804–5), Elizabeth Isabella (1806–84), Catherine Brown (1807–82), Sarah Storrow (1809–?), Anna Linzee (1811–46), Maria Dall (1813–89), Mary Appleton (1815–85), Bryant Parrott (1817–59), Zebiah Brown (1820–47), Harriet Parkman (1824–25). Tilden ms genealogy, box 2, seventh generation.

8. When her grandmother's death seemed imminent, Tilden and her sisters set to work on their sewing. On 12 February 1827, Tilden writes, "We have heard from Grandmother to day, and she may continue for some time or she may die very suddenly. . . . Sarah and self have been working on our black gowns to day." The work was timely, but perhaps not timely enough, for Tilden's entry records that the news of her grandmother's death came that very afternoon. "In the afternoon Prudence the girl who lives at Grandmother's came into the room and told Aunt Brush that they wanted her and mother to go down there directly, so they got ready and went as soon as possible. A little time after Charles Tilden came in and soon as he saw Catherine he said, 'She's gone'" (12 February 1827).

Six months later, Tilden commented on the conventions of mourning, turning (economic) necessity into virtue. After the death of her friend Ellen Sturgis's brother William, Tilden noted her approval of the family's decision about dress: "The girls will make but little alteration in their dress, which I think is a very good plan. I do not think that deep mourning is at all necessary" (12 August 1827).

9. In the early nineteenth century, comments on the use of time and the control of temper punctuated both public and private writings directed toward young women. Whether such comments came in the form of a conduct book's warning against time wasted (particularly in reading novels) or a mother's injunction to the daughter about her errant temper, young unmarried daughters were advised to concentrate on improving their usefulness and calming their disposition. For representative comments on the use of time, see Lydia Sigourney's first letter, "The Value of Time," in her *Letters to Young Ladies* and Farrar's chapter "On the Improvement of Time" in *Young Lady's Friend.* The most famous of fictional heroines cited for her unwieldy temper is Louisa May Alcott's Jo March. Alcott's mother had found the same fault in her daughter.

10. In a journal entry for 20 October 1827, Tilden had written, "I [heard] from Ellen [Sturgis], who I wish I knew whether she had the same feelings towards me that I have had for her. She is kind when I see her and she writes me but her notes are not just what I wish they were. I should like to find in her a friend whom I might talk to the same as I would write to a sister, and upon any subject I pleased and have it rightly understood."

11. In his biography of Emerson, Ralph Rusk outlines the school's curriculum, suggesting that Emerson drew on his Harvard assignments for the pupils in his classroom. See Rusk, *The Life of Ralph Waldo Emerson* (New York: Columbia University Press, 1949), 90 – 91.

12. What *is* certain is that this difficulty with her eyesight never ended. She experienced the same problem, of a comparable severity, during the three-week sea voyage to England in 1837. Consulting a physician in London, she was told that nothing could be done for her. She accepted the verdict with equanimity and wit,

offering a few dry remarks on how little "scientific men" could do and how much they charged to do it. She commented, "In the A.M. went to Lawrence's a celebrated Oculist & a very scientific man, to consult him about my eyes. After having examined them carefully he said there was nothing could be done for them. So we paid him a *guinea* for the information only" (Europe journal, 16 February 1837).

13. From the afternoon sermon, 3 May 1829 (SAR 1989, 50). Examples of the sermons' disconcerting inconsistencies and their disturbing representations of human nature are numerous. From a sermon she heard on 18 October 1829, Tilden records Gannett's strong insistence that the biblical writings were written by men and not by direct inspiration. The sermon, as she records it, did not support its own argument. At the end, Gannett apparently told the congregation that it was better to believe in such inspiration (whether true or not) than treat the Scriptures with indifference (65–66). Three months later, Gannett cited the death of infants as proof of immortality. Any other conclusion, he maintained, would be unthinkable and unacceptable. Gannett's support for his claim is uneasy at best: "The death of an infant is a proof of the immortality of our natures, for though a skeptic would say that when an aged person dies his capacities decay as [does his] body, and that in middle age has answered the purpose of his existence, or that if he has not, from a long continued habit of neglect he never will improve more, what can he say of the child who dies before its powers and capacities have been unfolded, before it is scarcely conscious of its humanity. It is one of the laws of God that moral agents act upon and influence each other" (10 January 1830, 67–68). Some weeks earlier, a similar evidence had been offered when Gannett cited Christianity's ability to meet the needs of the time as a powerful proof of its "divine" truth (6 September 1829, 59).

The representation of humanity in Gannett's sermons from this period was consistently critical. The listener was addressed as "sinner" and "thou guilty one" (13 September 1829, 61). Images of a self-created hell were vividly portrayed: "Can we behold without shuddering the wretch, who sinks deeper and deeper in sin, till at last he leaps in mad defiance the barrier which [word omitted] from time into eternity? What agonies and remorse await him! I look through the vista of futurity and see the misery of such as these" (20 September 1829, 63). Sin was "universal" (62); "unutterable woe" (64) threatened every life, and the individual was alone to blame: "Those who do not obey this warning voice of Jesus cannot enter the kingdom of heaven, they will bring upon themselves woe, unutterable woe, in eternity! and all this they may be saved from by their own exertions" (11 October 1829, 64).

14. See Cott's *The Bonds of Womanhood: 'Woman's Sphere' in New England, 1780–1835* (New Haven: Yale University Press, 1977), chap. 4, and her article "Young Women in the Second Great Awakening in New England," *Feminist Studies* 3 (Fall 1975): 15–29.

15. A number of sermons from this period counseled the listeners to "govern" their passions (6 September 1829, 11 October 1829, SAR 1989, 59, 64). Gannett charged the congregation with moral intemperance. Tilden records, "There is a large class who want the habit of self denial, they ascribe their faults, and want of virtue, to outward circumstances, to do so is unjust for every man has the capacity of doing right. If *he wills* to do right, *he can* do right. . . . We have every means within our selves (if we would but call them forth) to meet and overcome these trials" (March 1830, 69). Gannett preached an active self-denial, praising the "self-conquered man" as the desired result (13 June 1830, 72).

16. His response was composed of two letters, one dated 25 February 1835 and apparently written immediately after reading Tilden's packet of letter, journal, and sermon commentary (also dated 25 February). The second of Gannett's letters was written two days later, after he had "tested" himself to make certain that his affections were singly focused on Tilden. Both letters were sent together.

17. Of the authors in her first study, Baym writes, "They were profoundly Victorian in that they had an oppressive sense of reality and its habit of disappointing expectations. . . . Although they identify [the protagonist's] treatment and training by society in the shape of powerful others as responsible for her damaged self-esteem and consequent impoverished personality, they separate cause from effect and insist that in nineteenth-century America women have the opportunity and responsibility to change their situation by changing their personalities. . . . The end of change, finally, is a new woman and, by extension, the reformation of the world immediately around her as this new person calls out different relations and responses from her environment" (*Woman's Fiction*, 18–20).

18. From Margaret Fuller, *Summer on the Lakes*, reprinted in *The Portable Margaret Fuller*, ed. Mary Kelley (New York: Penguin, 1994), 89–90.

19. What twentieth-century critics of nineteenth-century women have all too often failed to talk about is the amount of expressed ambivalence toward marriage. Although we continue to cite the nineteenth century for its celebration of marriage, there was far more criticism than we've heard. With studies like Mary Kelley's *Private Woman, Public Stage* and Lee Virginia Chambers-Schiller's *Liberty a Better Husband: Single Women in America: The Generations of 1780–1840* (New Haven: Yale University Press, 1984), we have begun to reconfigure our conception of how women viewed marriage: whether and when they saw it as the "one thing needful," how they described the changes it brought to their lives, and what images they drew on to redefine themselves. We need to look again at what women themselves said about marriage, both in forms designed for public audiences and those addressed to private. And we need to look at the intersection of these forms: how novels and essays figure in letters and journals and how letters and journals become defining forms for the female protagonists of nineteenth-century novels.

20. Gannett's health difficulties were of a twofold nature: severe depression and chronic constipation. His contemporaries would not have separated these disturbances into distinctly different diseases. In their assessment, Gannett's "natural disposition" resulted in a dual manifestation of a single problem. He had not learned the self-control that led to a "regular" life. The consequent "irregularity" was jointly physical and mental. The perpetually late hours (sermons were rarely finished before 2 or 3 A.M. Sunday morning) and the number of projects he pursued (editing and writing for a number of religious periodicals, in addition to the weekly sermons, vestry lectures, Bible study classes, and Sunday school work) left him exhausted. In 1828, only four years into his ministry at the Federal Street Church, Henry Ware Jr. warned him, "I have long been concerned at your mode of life, which appears to be a careless, reckless throwing away of a chance for longevity. And, since I have been suddenly cut off in the midst of a similar career, I have thought of you much. . . . Want of method, late and irregular hours, neglect of regular exercise of body to balance every day the fatigue of the mind . . . no constitutions can stand such a life" (quoted in William Channing Gannett, *Ezra Stiles Gannett: Unitarian Minister in Boston, 1824–1871* [Boston: Roberts Brothers, 1875], 149).

Ware was not the only one to express concern. A year earlier, in April 1827, Tilden's mother had written, "Your duties as a Christian minister I cannot think require so much of your devoted attention as to undermine your health" (bMS Am 1888.4 67, Houghton Library, Harvard University). In addition to the irregular hours he kept, Gannett suffered from chronic constipation. While this complaint in our day has become the substance of jokes and the province of advertisers, the early nineteenth century saw danger where the public now sees comedy. Gannett tried any number of cures, ranging from a series of medical preparations (a list of these, carefully written out by Tilden, accompanied him on the trip to Europe) to any number of water cures in any number of resorts (from upstate New York to England to France).

21. This and the following quotation of 21 April form part of the notes "On Illness" in the Gannett papers at the Houghton Library, Harvard University (bMS Am 1888.4 190). Professor at the Harvard Medical School, known for his medical lectures as well as for his botanical studies, Jacob Bigelow (1787–1879) was one of the most renowned doctors in nineteenth-century Boston. Emphasizing the body's own powers of recovery, Bigelow argued against the common practice of prescribing high dosages of the drugs then available. In Gannett's case, Bigelow kept medication to a minimum, putting the greater weight on rest and a complete change of daily routine. Bigelow was also instrumental in the founding and design of Mount Auburn Cemetery. Praised by Tilden for its moral instruction, it was a site she visited whenever possible. Eventually she would become one of its "permanent visitors," buried there in June 1847, six months after her death.

22. Born in Boston and educated at Harvard, Francis Boott (1792–1863) entered medical study with John Armstrong in London in 1820, receiving his degree from Edinburgh in 1824. With his connections in Boston, London, and Edinburgh, he became the doctor of choice for many American travelers in the 1820s and 1830s. In addition to his medical practice, he was, like his American colleague Jacob Bigelow, an ardent and accomplished botanist, fellow of the Linnaean Society.

Boott served as doctor for Gannett and Tilden, continuing to advise Gannett after their return from the Continent in the fall of 1837 and seeing Tilden during her pregnancy. When the child was born, she bore the name of her parents' doctor: Catherine Boott Gannett. The families remained close, exchanging birthday remembrances, and Gannett carefully updated Boott on the changing nature of his family. With every birth of a child, he notes in his journal that a letter was sent to the Bootts describing "Anna's confinement."

23. Anna Eliot, daughter of Boston merchant Samuel Eliot, married George Ticknor (1791–1871), then Harvard's inaugural Smith Professor of French and Spanish, in 1821. Mother of four children, two of whom survived to adulthood, she became a close friend of Tilden's during Gannett and Tilden's stay in Rome in 1837. The Ticknors had settled in Rome shortly after Ticknor resigned his Harvard professorship in 1835, a resignation prompted partly by Harvard's refusal to implement Ticknor's suggested reorganization of the university along departmental lines. After his resignation, Ticknor spent the better part of a decade working on his three-volume *History of Spanish Literature*. Published in 1849, it was literally a life's work. Ticknor continued to work on the project after the appearance of its first edition. Revised editions were published in 1854 and 1863, with the "definitive edition" published in 1872, a few months after his death.

24. At the time, Gannett was one of the editors of the *Christian Examiner*. Gannett had long been active in fostering the various Unitarian publications of his day. He edited the *Scriptural Interpreter* and was a frequent contributor to the *Christian Examiner* as well as to the *Christian Register* and *Monthly Miscellany of Religion and Letters*. With its emphasis on defining a practical Christianity for the laity, the latter was extremely important to him. He served as editor for several years until the late 1840s. Having assumed the editorial duties for the *Christian Examiner* as well, he found it impossible to serve as editor for both publications. See William Channing Gannett's *Ezra Stiles Gannett*, 216.

25. From the letter offering Gannett a cemetery plot in Mount Auburn (December 1846, in Gannett Collection, Massachusetts Historical Society). Gannett's brief remarks about his wife in the summer and fall journal entries silently fulfill his standard of reticence. Where he would record his wife's "confinements," noting the childbirth itself, this unexpected labor did not follow previous patterns. There is no way to know when the birth was expected. His journal entries give no clear indication, and her only written comment from 1846 is a notation of her sons' birthdays.

26. Catherine and Zebiah Tilden to Bryant P. Tilden, 29 December 1846–1 January 1847, collection of Michael R. Gannett.

27. The phrases appear in a letter of condolence written by Gannett's good friend and colleague Orville Dewey shortly after Tilden's death (letter of January 1847, Gannett Collection, Massachusetts Historical Society). Dewey had preceded Gannett as colleague pastor to William Ellery Channing at the Federal Street Church.

28. Harriet Martineau to Catherine Tilden, 1836, bMS Am 1888.4 155, Houghton Library, Harvard University; Mary A. Tilden to Anna Tilden, 1837, bMS Am 1888.4 169, Houghton Library; Zebiah Tilden to Bryant P. Tilden, 29 December 1846– 1 January 1847, collection of Michael R. Gannett.

CHAPTER 2: EXEMPLARY LIVES

1. It might well be said that *all* Unitarian sermons were sermons on "character." Ministers played seemingly unending variations on this theme. In particular, see Henry Ware Jr.'s two-part sermon "Sources of Moral Weakness and Moral Strength" (*The Works of Henry Ware, Jr., D.D.* [Boston: James Munroe and Co., 1846–47], 3:178–201) and his sermons "The Doctrine of Probation," "The Doctrine of Probation, a Key to the Mysteries and Doctrines of Revelation," and "The Doctrine of Probation, a Key to the Mysteries of God's Dealings with Man" in the same volume (407–17, 418–29, 430–44); Emerson's sermons 24, 27, 36, 54, 58, 68, 87, 115, 144, 146, 164, and 169 (*The Complete Sermons of Ralph Waldo Emerson*, ed. Albert J. von Frank et al. [Columbia: University of Missouri Press, 1989–92], and William Ellery Channing's "Likeness to God" (291–302), "Character of Christ" (302–10), and "Self-Denial" (Second Discourse, 343–47).

2. Tilden's sermon notebook is decidedly "homemade." No standard description will quite fit. A collection of the assorted notes she accumulated in a seven-year period, it reflects the idiosyncracies of Tilden's weekly habit of writing down what the minister said. Her 1827–28 journal regularly refers to her note taking but says nothing more descriptive than, "I wrote some of the sermon." It is not clear when these notes were gathered into one book. The notebook is relatively small, only slightly larger than pocket size: the cover measures 16.8 x 11 cm, with a spine of 1.6 cm. It consists of twenty gatherings of three different types: (1) two booklets of fifteen sheets each, sewn together with white thread; (2) twelve gatherings of two sheets each, folded together, unsewn; (3) six gatherings of singly folded sheets. The gatherings are tied into the cover by white thread sewn through the notebook pages and then knotted underneath four white cloth thongs. These thongs are glued to both front and back covers. Once separate booklets, the first two gatherings were tied into the cover at the same time. However, this occurred after the notes had been written, for needle holes pierce words at the inside margins. The last sixty sheets pose a more difficult problem. They were apparently sewn together as a whole and

then tied into the previous gathering; however, thread is missing, and what remains is so tightly tied that to determine the method of sewing would be to take the notebook apart.

3. See Winifried Herget's "Writing after the Ministers: The Significance of Sermon Notes," in *Studies in New England Puritanism*, ed. Winifried Herget (Frankfurt: Verlag Peter Lang, 1983), 113–38.

4. See SAR 1989, 1–93.

5. Henry Ware Jr., *Formation of the Christian Character* (Boston: American Unitarian Association, 1883), 130.

6. The story of American Unitarianism's emergence has been often and well told. What follows in this chapter is a brief overview of the main issues that would most directly affect Tilden's own debate over liberal Christianity.

For histories of Unitarianism in America, see Conrad Wright, *The Beginnings of Unitarianism in America* (Boston: Starr King, 1955); idem, *The Liberal Christians: Essays on American Unitarian History* (Boston: Beacon Press, 1970); idem, ed., *A Stream of Light: A Sesquicentennial History of American Unitarianism* (Boston: American Unitarian Association, 1975); and idem, *American Unitarianism, 1805–1861* (Boston: Northeastern University Press, 1989); and David Robinson, *The Unitarians and the Universalists* (Westport, Conn.: Greenwood Press, 1985). Robinson's book is useful as well for its biographical information on individuals who figured prominently in both Unitarianism and transcendentalism. Unitarianism's sociocultural context is discussed in Daniel Walker Howe, *Unitarian Conscience: Harvard Moral Philosophy, 1805–1861* (Cambridge: Harvard University Press, 1970), and its influence on literary expression in Buell, *Literary Transcendentalism*. For Emerson's relation to the Unitarian Church, see his *Sermons*. David Robinson's introduction in the first volume of the *Sermons* (1–32) provides an overview of early-nineteenth-century Unitarianism and Emerson's place within it. See also David Robinson, *Apostle of Culture: Emerson as Preacher and Lecturer* (Philadelphia: University of Pennsylvania Press, 1982), Wesley T. Mott, *The Strains of Eloquence: Emerson and His Sermons* (University Park: Pennsylvania State University Press, 1989), Mary Kupiec Cayton, *Emerson's Emergence: Self and Society in the Transformation of New England* (Chapel Hill: University of North Carolina Press, 1989), and Susan L. Roberson, *Emerson in His Sermons: A Man-Made Self* (Columbia: University of Missouri Press, 1995). See also my entry on Unitarianism for the *Encyclopedia of Transcendentalism* (Westport, Conn.: Greenwood Press, 1996), for which this bibliography was written.

7. The quotation is taken from "The Connection between the Duties of the Pulpit and the Pastoral Office" (1830), Ware's inaugural address as Harvard's first Professor of Pulpit Eloquence and Pastoral Care (*Works*, 2:175–200).

8. Emerson's emphasis on the individual here exposes the all too troubling implications of self-reliance. In this situation, the person who lives in poverty is essen-

tially overlooked. The "beggar" is situated in a position from which there is seemingly no escape. Instead, he serves his ephemeral benefactor by providing the
almsgiver with a chance to strengthen himself.

9. In his *Strains of Eloquence*, Mott looks specifically at Emerson's representation
of Jesus for what it reveals about Emerson's uneasiness toward his own achievements. Mott argues that Emerson saw in Christ an analogue to his own situation.
Presenting Christ as the individual whose success was measured by the verdict
rendered against him during his life, Emerson created a standard of achievement
against which he could favorably judge himself. See chap. 1, "'Christ Crucified':
Christology, Identity, and Emerson's Sermon No. V," 9–33.

10. Emerson delivered this sermon fifteen times over an eight-year period. For
information on where and when this sermon was preached, see *Sermons*, 1:179.

11. Journal entries for 23 January 1828 and 16 December 1827. Her decision to
wear her hair in the fashion of Quaker practice suggests a particular issue. The
carefully pulled-back style accentuated the forehead, at the same time accentuating
the feature associated with intellect.

12. Tilden clearly looked forward to the prospect of assuming full responsibility
for a Sunday school class. On the few occasions when she substituted for her older
sister Catherine, her journal entries record just what importance she placed on this
particular "woman's work": "I have been much pleased with my days duties in the
school, so much so that I really wish I had a class for myself, these schools I expect
will do much good" (11 May 1828).

13. The sermon in question was preached on 9 April 1826. In her notes, Tilden
cites the familiar "idols" of power and wealth but concludes with a less likely candidate for idolatry—love of one's children (SAR 1989, 29).

14. An example appears in Tilden's entry for 10 January 1830, recording a sermon
preached by Gannett: "We can at once see the advantages of sickness when a child is
old enough to understand its purposes, but how can a little child be benefitted by it?
by the increase of care that is required from the mother, it is perhaps kept from
many dangers, and this attention that is given creates in her a more tender, though
not a more sincere love for the sufferer, than for the rest of her children, and thus
balances the pain and care by pleasure. . . . When the mother looks upon the face of
her loved little one, so beautiful in death, she clings to the belief that it lives, and she
is made more interested in a future life, her heart is drawn nearer to her Heavenly
Father, her imagination pictures to her her child in the abode of angels, that it is
under their guidance, that it will be educated by them, that it will not have to en-
counter the troubles, and temptations of this life, and that its spiritual instructors
will do more far more for it, than her tenderest care could suggest" (SAR 1989,
67–68).

15. In all likelihood, the person in question is Horace Appleton, one of Gannett's
parishioners. Gannett visited him regularly during the summer and was with him
when he died in early fall. On the following Sunday, Gannett preached a memor-

ial sermon at the Federal Street Church. In her sermon notes, Tilden reports: "Mr Gannett has been really great in his discourses to day. The morning sermon was upon the cross of Christ and it was most excellent. In the afternoon it was appropriate for H[.] Appleton's death, giving an account in the most delicate manner of a part of his last hours. It was an affecting sermon, and one calculated to do good, and make an impression on the heart and mind of all present" (7 September 1828, SAR 1989, 44).

16. From one of Gannett's sermons, preached in June 1830. In her sermon notes, Tilden writes, "Our respect is great for the self-conquered man" (SAR 1989, 72).

17. The passage appears in her sermon notes in an entry from 6 September 1829. The sermon took its text from Acts 17:23, "To the unknown God." By her account, the sermon was about the knowledge of God—what it meant to "know" God and what stood in the way of such knowledge. In the sentence immediately preceding the one quoted, Tilden writes, "The mind that is disturbed and harassed by evil passions that have been allowed to grow up and choke it, it cannot understand God" (SAR 1989, 59).

18. Tilden was not alone in her concern over apparently minor transgressions. Ministers frequently preached on the dangers of "small sins." The phrase is Henry Ware Jr.'s, used as the title for an immensely popular sermon published in 1827 (*Works*, 3:231–41). See also Emerson's Sermon 44 (*Sermons*, 2:25–29) and Charles Brooks's "On Procrastination" in the *Liberal Preacher* 3, no. 7 (1830): 89–104.

19. For entries on Christ, see 6 March 1824 (SAR 1989, 21), 26 February 1826 (26), 5 March 1826 (27), 10 February 1828 (39), 8 June 1828 (43), 7 September 1828 (45), 1 March 1829 (46), 5 April 1829 (47), 12 April 1829 (47), 16 August 1829 (56), 13 September 1829 (62), 7 March 1830 (69).

20. The identity of Christ was undeniably a problematic issue for Unitarian ministers. While they firmly argued that Christ was not God, it was also clear that Christ was not man. They granted him a special status, a "double capacity," in Ezra Stiles Gannett's words, on the border and maintaining the border between divinity and humanity. The phrase appears in *The Christian Ministry*, Gannett's ordination sermon for Andrew Preston Peabody (Portsmouth, N.H.: J.W. Foster—J.F. Shores, 1833), 11.

21. *The Unitarian Conscience: Harvard Moral Philosophy, 1805–1861* (Cambridge: Harvard University Press, 1970), 151–60.

22. The titles of the sermons are as follows: "Christ the Foundation," "Jesus the Messiah," "Sufficiency and Efficacy of Faith in the Messiah," "Jesus the Mediator," "Jesus the Savior," "Jesus the High Priest," "The Atonement by Jesus Christ," "Jesus the Intercessor," "Christ the Judge of the World," "On Honoring the Son," "The Example of Our Lord." First published in 1825, the volume merited a second edition the following year and was reprinted in 1846 as part of the collected works.

23. Take for example the individual who described her own humility. She would readily be open to the charge of pride. How "cheerful" does contentment sound

when it becomes the focus of a conversation? Fortitude is measured by the silence of the sufferer.

24. The sermon in question is number 76, preached a total of eight times between 1830 and 1836. In the sermon, Emerson reminds the listener that Jesus' authority stemmed solely from his allegiance to "moral truth"—a truth, he assured his congregation, that was equally available to all: "The same truth will have the same effect from whatever lips. . . . Jesus hath it, but he has not monopolized it. . . . At last, when truth has had its whole effect on our minds, it will gain its fulness of authority by becoming to us simply the echo of our own thought" (*Sermons*, 2: 193–95).

25. Both were issued by the same firm in Philadelphia: Cary, Lea, and Blanchard.

26. Anna Tilden Gannett to Ezra Stiles Gannett, 16 December 1836.

27. Asking Channing's opinion on Furness's book, Tilden reports to Gannett, "I was surprised to see how far our opinions coincided" (letter of 29 December 1836).

28. See Robinson's *Apostle of Culture*, 31–32.

29. Journal entry for 21 February 1828. In her journal, Tilden records attending several of Ware's lectures on the Holy Land (entries for 24 January 1828, 14 February 1828, 18 February 1828, 21 February 1828, 28 February 1828). Designed to raise money for Harvard's Divinity School, these lectures were a marked success.

30. From Robbins's funeral sermon for Ware: *A Discourse before the Second Church and Society in Boston in commemoration of the life and character of their former pastor, Henry Ware, Jr., D.D. on Sunday October 1, 1843* (Boston: James Munroe and Co., 1843), 22–23.

31. One of the many charitable organizations in Massachusetts, the Marblehead Female Humane Society worked specifically with the individuals—wives, children, mothers—who lost their means of support with the deaths of their seafaring husbands and sons.

32. This forms a marked contrast to Emerson's criticism of benevolence work in his Sermon 19. That Ware and Emerson would position themselves differently on many aspects of religious belief would become increasingly clear in the 1830s. In the late 1820s, the "future" differences are readily seen in their differing emphases: Emerson preferring the abstract principle and its significance for the individual, Ware focusing on the practical and communal.

33. Ware's choice of this example is curious. Using it to illustrate a seemingly insignificant act of charity, he has clearly freed it from its original context. In the biblical version, the woman's action is identified as a wildly extravagant one, less an act of minuscule charity than of the most luxurious magnanimity. This is, of course, also the conversation in which Christ tells his disciples, "The poor you have with you always"—a sentiment that fits awkwardly with Ware's emphasis on diminishing, if not eradicating, poverty.

34. Those who did were, in the words of one journalist of the day, "fair game." Notoriety was the best they could hope for, and as the following description of Frances Wright indicates, the woman who spoke in public in the first decades of the nineteenth century had little hope that what she said would be heard. The audience was far more interested in her position on the platform than the position she chose to argue. "Miss Wright as public lecturer is fair game. . . . Considered as a lady, agreeable to the conventional proprieties of civilized society [she] has with ruthless violence broken loose from the restraints of decorum, which draw a circle around the life of a woman; and, with a contemptuous disregard for the rules of society, she has leaped over the boundary of feminine modesty, and laid hold on the avocations for man, claiming a participation in them for herself and her sex. . . . Miss Wright stands condemned of a violation of the unalterable laws of nature which have created a barrier between the man and the woman" (from the Louisville newspaper the *Free Enquirer,* 10 December 1828, quoted in Lillian O'Connor's *Pioneer Women Orators* [New York: Columbia University Press, 1954], 49).

35. Emerson's Sermon 19 and Ware's benevolence sermon form a revealing diptych. Ware emphasizes the charitable deed; Emerson, the doer. The difference is largely explained by the different circumstances in which these sermons were delivered: Emerson spoke to his weekly congregation, Ware for a special service dedicated to the support of a particular charitable organization. But whether the emphasis fell on deed or doer, both ministers left their female listeners in a decidedly uncomfortable place. Emerson downplayed the kinds of action available to women (Sunday school work, Missionary Society); Ware valued the work Emerson diminished but made the worker disappear, separating the individual from her action. Emerson's emphasis on principle defined the individual as male; Ware removed the question of individuality from charitable work by rendering the women invisible members of an unseen group. Neither minister reflected the experience of women who did the work available to them or those who longed for a different kind of work altogether.

36. Reporting Horace Appleton's death, Tilden writes a sermonic eulogy in her journal: "We heard that Horace Appleton died at 6 o'clock this morning, his hours last evening some of them were delightful. In his death he fully shew the power of the Christian religion, he was perfectly aware of his situation, having asked the physician himself if he could live through the night—It was a calm though sad scene. His Mother is a fine woman and bears it as a Christian does the will of her *Heavenly Father*[.] Appleton was an uncommon fine young man both in his Moral and Intellectual character, and it was his prayer 'to do good in his death.' He had a high part among the exercises at Commencement this year, but at 10 o'clock on that day he felt himself too unwell, and gave up going, at 10 on the next Thursday, his bright soul had left this world, for higher spheres and greater enjoyments, than it is possible for him to have had on earth—" (4 September 1828).

37. Journal entry for 1 March 1827. No context is given. There is only a brief reference to Aunt Mary's presence at tea. Although none of their conversation is reported, it is not difficult to surmise that its topic was the particular hardships in this particular woman's life.

38. She writes, "All her daughters were much afflicted, though they all behaved with the propriety and calmness which might be expected from the example they had had from their excellent mother" (12 February 1827).

39. In particular, see Carroll Smith-Rosenberg, "The Hysterical Woman: Sex Roles and Role Conflict in Nineteenth-Century America," in idem, *Disorderly Conduct: Visions of Gender in Victorian America* (New York: Knopf, 1985), and Diane Price Herndl's *Invalid Women: Figuring Feminine Illness in American Fiction and Culture, 1840–1940* (Chapel Hill: University of North Carolina Press, 1993).

40. The Tildens' difficulties were by no means unusual. In the late 1820s, Boston's economy suffered a series of reversals. Whether in the textile industry or in the shipping trade, Boston merchants found it difficult to remain solvent. Describing the situation of the 1820s, Jane and William Pease write, "Wherever one looked, to whomever one spoke, times were bad, money was tight, interest rates high, dividends low, businesses failing, and unemployment pressing hard on the poor" (*The Web of Progress: Private Values and Public Styles in Boston and Charleston, 1828–1843* [New York: Oxford University Press, 1985], 23).

41. The uncle in question is Joseph Tilden (1779–1853), firstborn son of Sarah Parker Tilden and Joseph Tilden. Active in state government, an actuary in the Massachusetts Hospital Life Insurance Company, president of the Columbian Bank of Boston and superintendent of manufactures at Lowell, he figured prominently in the Boston community (Tilden genealogy, box 1, fifth generation, and box 2, sixth generation, New England Historic Genealogical Society).

42. Emerson taught in William's school from 1821 through 1824. Tilden mentions both William and Waldo Emerson as her teachers, and so her attendance would have spanned more than the year 1824 when Emerson taught alone during William's absence in Germany. What remains of Emerson's school records show as well that several of the Tilden daughters were pupils in the Emerson school. The notebook that later became his "Preaching Record" originally served as the attendance record for the school. Although the pages with the students' names were subsequently cut out, enough of these pages remains to identify Tilden as one of the students. "A. Tild" is clearly legible on one of the cut pages (bMS Am 1280.H 96, by permission of the Houghton Library, Harvard University and by the Ralph Waldo Emerson Association).

43. Journal entries for 17 August 1827, 13 August 1827, 12 August 1827.

44. In addition to the numerous privately run "Schools for Young Ladies," Boston's short-lived experiment with publicly sponsored high school education for young women was in its second year of operation.

45. As the title suggests, Tilden's "fascinating" book is a gothic novel. First published in 1796, *Children of the Abbey* by Regina Maria Roche was immensely popular, remaining in print throughout the nineteenth century and into the twentieth.

46. With her emphasis on intention, Tilden seems to have here crafted her own version of Emerson's emphasis on principle in Sermon 19.

47. A sermon like the one recorded on 11 October 1829 (SAR 1989, 64) spoke directly to her situation. All she need do was look at the sermonic example of the individual who placed "no restraint upon his angry feelings" to read the consequences she wished to avoid. The example's "ungoverned feelings" disrupted the "quiet and harmony of a family." She saw herself doing the same, and thus her charge to herself that she "overcome" her temper.

48. After the word "me" and before the period, Tilden drew two small open circles; she then followed with her resolution "to try and not answer back."

CHAPTER 3: IN SEARCH OF AN AUDIENCE

1. Regular weekly sermons rarely singled out young, unmarried women as examples, good or bad. Their appearance was more likely to occur in occasional sermons, though as we have seen, Ware's sermon for the Marblehead Female Humane Society drew no distinctions among women before it rendered them invisible. The young, unmarried woman, however, made her appearance in sermons on female education. These pieces were more often published than preached and more typical of the late eighteenth century than the third and fourth decades of the nineteenth century. After midcentury, as women increasingly pushed the boundaries of their conventional roles, a number of sermons on the "influence of woman" appeared, often by that title and generally upholding the belief that woman's work was best done by indirection.

2. In her biography of Edgeworth, Elizabeth Harden writes, "In the autumn of 1782, [Richard Edgeworth] had set Maria the task of translating Madame de Genlis's *Adèle and Théodore,* but she had completed only one volume when Thomas Holcroft's translation appeared. Working on the translation, however, brought her into direct collaboration with her father for the first time and established him in the role of editor and literary adviser" (*Maria Edgeworth* [Boston: Twayne, 1984], 11).

3. Harden notes that this book "established Maria Edgeworth as the leading writer for children of her day" (28).

4. Quoted in Harden (75) from a letter by Maria Edgeworth to her friend Sophy Ruxton, 20 February 1805.

5. The work in question is David Hume's exceedingly popular and widely used *The History of England from the invasion of Julius Caesar to the Revolution of 1688* (written in the years 1754–62). Given the numerous editions of this work, it is not clear which one Tilden would have used and whether she was working from Tobias

Smollett's continuation of Hume's work (*The History of England from the reign of William and Mary to the death of George II, designed as a continuation of Mr. Hume's History*, 1785). She may have been using an even more recently updated (and also abridged) American version (1826) edited by the Reverend John Robinson that extended the history to the coronation of George IV.

6. Tilden was in good company. Louisa May Alcott reflected the importance she gave to Edgeworth in the novels she gave her characters to read. Marmee reads Edgeworth to her daughters in *Little Women* (New York: Penguin Classics, 1989, 76). In *Little Men*, Meg's son Demi Brooke pleads with Professor Bhaer for more fiction, justifying his request by citing Edgeworth's "Harry and Lucy" and "Frank" stories (*Little Men* [New York: Puffin Books, 1995], 50). Worth noting, however, is that none of the characters reads Edgeworth exclusively, and each often chooses the sensation novel over the moral tale.

7. Tilden's journal references suggest that both were part of the household library. Rereading a group of fictions designed for somewhat younger readers, Tilden mentions the characters that appeared in several of the stories in each volume. She exclaims, "I have been reading some of Miss Edgeworth's Rosamond, if there are any works which I really love it is her's. Even Frank and Rosamond I can read many parts over and over again and yet return to them once more with real pleasure" (9 November 1827). For Tilden, the value of these books lasted well into adulthood. Learning of her sister Sarah's pregnancy in 1837, Anna contemplated a variety of gifts but finally settled on *The Parent's Assistant*, Maria Edgeworth's first collection of "moral tales" for children.

8. The following are the titles that were specifically defined as religious fiction: *Mary Hollis* (1822), published by the New York Unitarian Society and reprinted twelve years later as one of the "tracts" in the series sponsored by the Union Ministerial Association; the short story with its telling title "The Deformed Boy" (1826); *Home* (1835), published in Munroe's series of "Scenes and characters illustrating Christian truth"; *The Poor Rich Man, and the Rich Poor Man* (1836); *A Love token for Children* (1837), advertised as a collection "designed for Sunday-school libraries."

9. Sedgwick, *The Life and Letters of Catharine Maria Sedgwick*, ed. Mary L. Dewey (New York: Harper & Brothers, 1871), 94.

10. On 3 November 1836, Tilden wrote, "This afternoon I am going to obtain Miss Sedgwick's new story 'The poor rich man & the rich poor man,' it is highly spoken of and I wish much to read it." A week later, having read the short fiction, she sang its praises: "Miss Sedgwicks little story 'The rich poor man and the poor rich man' is very good and must do good. One sentence has forcibly struck me dear Stiles and I know that it will you. When Susan the poor man's wife is debating within herself about some kind deed, she resolves to do it, saying to her husband '*God gives the opportunities*' These few words are a sermon in themselves, I

have thought of them again and again, I think they will strengthen me" (11 November 1836).

11. In the preface to the first edition, p. x. This and subsequent quotations are taken from the "author's revised edition" published in 1856: *Redwood: A Tale* (New York: George P. Putnam & Co.).

12. At the end of her chapter on reading, Child gives a number of reading lists divided according to the age of the intended readers. The following (complete with Child's annotations) are the books Child recommended for fifteen- and sixteen-year-olds:

Mrs. Chapone's Letters.
Watts on the Improvement of the Mind.
Taylor on Self-Cultivation.
Abbott's Letters from Cuba.
The Modern Traveller. With Maps and Engravings. These volumes are published in a series intended to comprise all the best books of travels in various countries. The volumes are sold separately if desirable.
Selections from Fenelon. By a Lady.
Rhoda.
Isabella. By the same Author. I think these are the purest and best works of fiction that can be put into a woman's hand.
The Lady of the Manor. By Mrs. Sherwood. Having intended to avoid everything sectarian, I am puzzled about Mrs. Sherwood's books. She is a zealous Episcopalian, and she never writes anything that is not very strongly tinged with her own doctrines. But there is so much power and tenderness in her appeals to the heart, her characters are so true to life, and there is so much earnestness and sincerity in her religious views, that I cannot omit her name in a list of good books. The same remarks are true with regard to her numerous little books for children; they are all natural, interesting and pure—but full of Calvinism and abstract questions of theology.
Things by Their Right Names.
Discipline.
Self-Control.
Temper, or Domestic Scenes. By Mrs. Opie.
Redwood. By Miss Sedgwick.
Hope Leslie. By D[itt]o.
Clarence. By Do.
Tales of Fashionable Life. By Miss Edgeworth.
Belinda. Do.
Castle Rackrent. Do.

Patronage. By Miss Edgeworth.

The Absentee. Do.

The Sketch Book. By Washington Irving.

Life of Columbus. By Do. This has been published in an abridged form, for young people.

Life of Ledyard. By Jared Sparks.

Life of Lord Collingwood. The lessons conveyed by this book are full of all that is noble and estimable in human character.

Marshall's Life of Washington.

Lives of the Novelists. By Walter Scott.

Lives of Painters and Sculptors. By Allan Cunningham. Forming a part of the Family Library.

Travels of Anacharsis in Greece.

Rollin's Ancient History.

Goldsmith's History of England.

The Family Shakspeare. To be read in connexion with history.

All the WAVERLEY NOVELS. Valuable as distinct pictures of human nature in all its varieties, and as charming historical records.

Robertson's History of Charles Fifth.

Robertson's History of Scotland.

Robertson's History of America.

POETRY

Milton's *Comus* and *Lycidas.* I mention these in preference to Paradise Lost, because I think very few young people can enter heartily into the sublime beauties of that magnificent poem. Comus is a most pure and beautiful model for forming the youthful taste.

Cowper's Poems.

Wordsworth's Poems.

Sir Walter Scott's *Lady of the Lake.*

Marmion. Lay of the Last Minstrel.

Thomson's *Seasons.*

Campbell's Poems.

Mrs. Heman's Poems.

Bernard Barton's Poems.

Bryant's Poems.

Mrs. Sigourney's Poems.

13. The book in question would have been one of the many editions of *Letters on the elementary principles of education.* It was originally published in London in 1801;

the third American edition appeared under the auspices of the Boston firm of S. H. Parker in 1825. An education essayist and sometime poet, Elizabeth Hamilton (1758–1816) published several volumes of essays on education, written largely with a female audience in mind. Her commentaries on education were part and parcel of her interest in the structure and development of the human mind. Never married, she appropriated the designation of "Mrs.," using it to her own ends, for her public and publishing persona.

14. The practice of communal reading was a common one. References occur in both the fiction and nonfiction of the period, in writings both public and private. For example, Alcott's Jo March, turned into "Mother Bhaer," asks her son Robby to read while she sews, and later in *Jo's Boys*, the women college students participate in a sewing school in which needlework is accompanied by reading and Margaret Fuller–style conversations (chap. 17).

15. This particular novel was indeed "new," having just been published in 1827. By Robert Plumer Ward (1765–1846), it boasted the subtitle "The man of independence." Tilden apparently did not find its version of independence compelling.

16. In a letter written in 1824 to Hannah Haskins Ladd, one of his former students and one of Tilden's classmates, Emerson had recommended the practice. Responding to her request for suggestions about how she might continue her education on her own, he wrote, "One of these six hours every day [for study] I would give to history So go get Hume, (not the Vol. I) but the reign of Elizabeth & if your sister E will begin it with you, so much the better for both. It is always best to note how many pages you read in an hour & accustom yourself to talk over what you have read, & think (& if possible write too upon it" (*The Letters of Ralph Waldo Emerson*, 10 vols., ed. Ralph R. Rusk [vols. 1–6] and Eleanor M. Tilton [vols. 7–10] [New York: Columbia University Press, 1939–95], 7:156).

17. In her journal entry for 16 November 1827, Tilden wrote, "After breakfast aunts showed me about cutting out my chemise. I sewed some this morning, and in the afternoon also, whilst engaged with my work I learned some lines from Scott's Minstrel."

18. When Tilden's sisters Catherine and Sarah turned "reviewer" and laughingly made the remark that "novel reading would not do" for Anna, their comments suggest just how far the (private reader's) acceptance of novel reading extended. (The public reader known as the "reviewer" maintained a far more critical stance toward fiction.) Losing one's "good nature" to the corrupting power of fiction had been a real question in the mid- to late eighteenth century. For Catherine and Sarah Tilden, their sister's complaint provided them with nothing more serious than a chance to make fun of their sister's passion for reading. They could not pull her away from her book, and when they did so, she lost her temper and was no longer "good-natured." Even her mother's indulgence—allowing her to finish the novel before she left for her sister's house—suggests how large a place novel reading had

won in a daughter's day. The particular novel in question also speaks for the latitude granted in the Tilden household, for Tilden was not reading the exemplary Edgeworth or the instructive Sedgwick but the gothic sensationalist Regina Maria Roche. Her novels depended on the "excitement" so roundly criticized by reviewers.

19. The term *romance,* like the word *sentiment,* has met with a variety of response. The late eighteenth century closely identified the word with an excess of "fancy." The individual who failed to balance an active imagination with a weighty dose of "reason" easily fell prey to the extremes of both emotion and circumstance (two "extremities" that could well be said to define the gothic novel). Today the term lingers, together with its judgmental connotation, in the label "romance novels" and their many series, most notably Harlequin. In her study of the romance genre *Reading the Romance: Women, Patriarchy, and Popular Literature* (Chapel Hill: University of North Carolina Press, 1984), Janice Radway points out the double-edged nature of these fictions. Disturbing in their violence and their acceptance of certain gender roles, they also offer a world in which women remain at the center— both as characters and readers.

In American literary study, the term has long been identified with Hawthorne *and* with Henry James's reading of Hawthorne (and of himself). In his prefaces, Hawthorne maintained that *his* genre was "romance," defining the word to fit the type of fiction he wrote. He distinguished his fiction from the "novelists'": where they dealt in the details of daily life and were accountable to those details, he claimed a freedom from such concerns. He began his prefatory remarks to *The House of the Seven Gables* with the following: "When a writer calls his work a Romance, it need hardly be observed that he wishes to claim a certain latitude, both as to its fashion and material, which he would not have felt himself entitled to assume, had he professed to be writing a Novel. The latter form of composition is presumed to aim at a very minute fidelity, not merely to the possible, but to the probable and ordinary course of man's experience" (Centenary Edition, Columbus: Ohio State University Press, 1965). In this "announcement" he sought to stake a claim for himself against his "competition," the writers of domestic fiction, or as he so peevishly called them, "that damned mob of scribbling women." As critics like Tompkins and Warren have pointed out, Hawthorne's prefatory remarks pointedly address the work of his competition, the writers who built their success out of their canny use of home detail. Unlike Hawthorne, they required no "shadow land" to set their fictional stage.

In his biography of Hawthorne, James readily picked up Hawthorne's statement about fiction and appropriated it to his own use. In his frequently quoted passage on what the United States lacked, James both parodies the cultural one-upmanship associated with the contemporary assessment of fiction ("no sporting class—no Epsom, nor Ascot") and endorses it ("no literature, no novels, no museums, no pictures"). James's own brand of literary realism required a flexibility that played several levels of representation over against each other. In the fiction from the 1870s and 1880s, his characters moved through a world of weighted objects whose dailiness could readily be dissociated from them. One need only think of the various interiors in which Isabel Archer is enclosed to see the ways in which represented space becomes as much metaphor as material, turning the described space from a physical to a psychic setting (the father's library in Albany, Isabel's room in Gilbert Osmond's house).

20. Quotations are taken from the following edition: *Patronage*, introduced by Eva Figes (London: Pandora, 1986).

21. By the early 1800s, the greatest complaint against novel reading was the time it consumed; novels took women away from their household duties. Edgeworth's novels in their anatomy of domestic life escaped even this criticism. When in 1818 Thomas Jefferson replied to Nathaniel Burwell's request for suggestions about "female education," he had nothing good to say about novels but much praise for Edgeworth's fiction. He commented, "A great obstacle to good education is the inordinate passion prevalent for novels, and the time lost in that reading which should be instructively employed. When this poison infects the mind, it destroys its tone and revolts it against wholesome reading. Reason and fact, plain and unadorned, are rejected. . . . This mass of trash, however, is not without some distinction; some few modelling their narratives, although fictitious, on the incidents of real life, have been able to make them interesting and useful vehicles of sound morality. . . . Such are the writings of Miss Edgeworth" (*Writings* [New York: Library of America, 1984], 1411–12).

22. *Redwood's* Ellen Bruce is akin to the women represented by Ware in his 1828 sermon on behalf of the Female Humane Society. Ellen is actively engaged in the work of benevolence, and like the figures in Ware's sermon, she attempts to accomplish her good deeds without calling attention to herself. But here the similarities end, for the women of Ware's sermon are truly rendered invisible. No longer identified as persons, they effectively disappear, represented only in actions accomplished by unidentified agents. Ellen Bruce, on the other hand, is never allowed the invisibility she apparently seeks.

23. This power operates within well-defined limits. The reader is granted insight where the characters remain blind. She knows the mind of the central character, having been readily supplied with the narrator's various descriptions. Hers is a privileged knowledge, of greater compass than the fictional characters, yet limited to what the narrator provides. The reader cannot, of course, affect the course of the story, nor does her power of comprehension ("sympathy," as the nineteenth century would say) translate readily into her lived reality.

24. As a reflection of the popularity of the novel, I use the edition of *Children of the Abbey* that I stumbled across in a secondhand bookstore in upstate New York. Poorly printed on poor quality paper, the edition dates from the early twentieth

century. No publication date is given, but the book, a gift to some reader "with Best Wishes" from "Mother Herrick," is dated June 23, 1911. The publishing company, which promises its readers on the title page that this is the "complete edition," was M. A. Donohue and Company of Chicago.

25. Roche portrays Amanda as a solitary. Her chief pastimes place solitude above society: she walks, she reads, she plays the fortepiano. In the narrator's words, "Solitude to Amanda was a luxury, as it afforded her opportunities of indulging the ideas on which her heart delighted to dwell" (155). When not engaged in "lonely rambles," Amanda is often seen reading. The library she frequents at Lord Mortimer's cottage might well have appealed strongly to Amanda's reader: "On one side was a row of large windows, arched quite in the gothic style; opposite to them were corresponding arches, in whose recesses the bookcases were placed; round these arches were festoons of laurel, elegantly executed in stucco-work; and above them medallions of some of the most celebrated poets; the chimney-piece, of the finest Italian marble, was beautifully inlaid and ornamented; the paintings on the ceiling were all highly finished, and of the allegorical kind; and it was difficult to determine whether the taste that designed, or the hand that executed them, merited most praise; upon marble pedestals stood a celestial and terrestrial globe, and one recess was entirely hung with maps. It was a room, from its situation and appearance, peculiarly adopted for study and contemplation; all around was solitude and silence, save the rustling of the trees, whose dark foliage cast a solemn shade upon the windows" (34–35).

26. The challenge to established authority turns on a flawed past embodied in equally flawed fathers. In Sedgwick's novel, the authority of the fathers is portrayed as frequently mistaken and easily set aside. Sedgwick's Ellen Bruce, for example, revises authority in order to make it worth her obedience. For most of the novel, Ellen's only filial duty is to her mother's memory. As long as her father remains unknown, she is not bound to reverence Henry Redwood, an individual whose skepticism and atheism would render her obedience problematic. Once the connection is uncovered, the question of filial duty is redefined. Her duty is not unquestioning obedience but careful reform. Ellen effectively reestablishes her father as the faithful Christian he once was; she redeems his authority by making him worthy of it.

27. In his struggle over who would govern the Massachusetts Bay Colony, Winthrop carefully crafted a definition of "liberty" that firmly supported the governor's (which at that point meant his) "authority." He wrote, "There is a twofold liberty, natural (I mean as our nature is now corrupt) and civil or federal. The first is common to man with beasts and other creatures." The first he readily rejected, associating it with the "natural" man, depraved and tending toward "evil." He endorsed the second definition of liberty and bound it firmly to established authority— whether of the state or in marriage. "The other kind of liberty I call civil or federal,

it may also be termed moral. . . . This liberty is the proper end and object of authority, and cannot subsist without it. . . . [It] is maintained and exercised in a way of subjection to authority; it is of the same kind of liberty wherewith Christ hath made us free. The woman's own choice makes such a man her husband; yet being so chosen, he is her lord, and she is to be subject to him, yet in a way of liberty, not of bondage; and a true wife accounts her subjection her honor and freedom, and would not think her condition safe and free, but in her subjection to her husband's authority." Sedgwick may well have known this passage. It had recently appeared in James Savage's edition of Winthrop's *The History of New England from 1630–1649* (Boston: Phelps & Farnham, 1825–26).

28. In seventeenth-century Puritan Boston, marriage was, of course, a civil act, not a religious one. It was a matter of "contract," distinctly separated from the Church of England "sacrament."

29. The individual in question is William Hubbard (1621–1704), clergyman and historian. Sedgwick's Winthrop describes him in the following terms: "a discreet young man, steeped in learning, and of approved orthodoxy" (154). It is clearly the latter that most appeals to the fictional Winthrop, since Hubbard, at the "time" of this fictional conversation, had not yet published his highly influential *Narrative of the Troubles with the Indians in New-England* (1677). Hubbard's "orthodoxy," as well as his "learning," unmistakably appeared in this history of the first decades of English settlement. In Hubbard's telling, the Pequot Indians were "sullen dogs" doomed by their own "self-willedness and madness" (54). Sedgwick includes this passage in *Hope Leslie,* as a scathing condemnation of the earlier (and in many respects, contemporary) version of the English settlers' relations with the Indians. Hubbard's own version of history was clearly "providential," the type of history so firmly endorsed by the Puritan community of which he was a part. In his most ambitious work, *A General History of New England from the Discovery to MDCLXXX* (published in 1815 for the Massachusetts Historical Society more than a century after his death), he sought to illustrate God's particular role in New England's history. Like his contemporary and colleague Cotton Mather, he defined history as preeminently the illustration of God's enacted will.

Hubbard's conventional stance on history did not, however, prevent him from breaking social and domestic convention. After the death of his first wife, he married his housekeeper and, according to the *Dictionary of American Biography,* "shocked his parishioners . . . because they thought her unfit for the exalted position of minister's wife" (9:333). Whether Sedgwick was aware of Hubbard's personal history is unclear. If she did know this particular story, it would make Winthrop's choice all the more interesting. He would marry Hope Leslie to a person who conserves the past yet at the same time breaks down domestic convention.

30. Quotations are taken from the Rutgers University Press reprint, edited by Mary Kelley (1987).

31. Quotations are taken from the following edition of the novel: *Belinda*, introduced by Eva Figes (London: Pandora, 1986).

32. In late adolescence, Tilden hoped that Sturgis would become the friend who would "rightly understand her." Her entries praise Sturgis for her intellect and its expression. Referring to Sturgis and her sister Ann, she commented, "Both the girls have minds that might be made very fine, if they are not so already" (6 August 1827). Two weeks later, Tilden noted "proof" in writing of her observation: "Ellen lent me a composition book of hers to read, the pieces are some of them excellent" (23 August 1827). Tilden's assessment was not unfounded. Sturgis's poetry would later be celebrated by Emerson and Fuller. A regular member of Fuller's conversations, Sturgis remained actively a part of the transcendentalist circle until her marriage, but like Tilden, she found that her husband's expectations did not merge easily with the "newness" articulated by Emerson and his contemporaries.

CHAPTER 4: LOSING FAITH AND FINDING FICTION

1. bMS Am 1888.4 91, Houghton Library, Harvard University. This is the figure Anna Tilden gave in her 1834–35 journal; the tuition in 1830 may well have been lower.

2. Catherine returned to teaching in 1838, much to her sister's concern. Writing from Switzerland, Anna lamented the economic necessity that took Catherine back to the classroom. The school was in full operation upon Gannett and Tilden's return from Europe. Catherine Tilden remained actively involved in women's education for the rest of her life, branching out from the "school for young ladies" to women's colleges. Her grave marker in Mount Auburn remembers her as "A Pioneer in the Extension of College Education to Women."

3. Gannett's use of the words *sensibility* and *sympathy* reflects the Unitarian adaptation of eighteenth-century distinctions. From Gannett's usage here, it is clear that he had in mind the by then familiar definition of *sensibility*. Defined against the term *sense,* with which it was almost invariably paired, it signaled a heightened responsiveness to the expression of emotion. Where "sense" was governed by "reason" and "judgment," "sensibility" responded to "feeling" and "imagination."

Sympathy held greater currency with the Unitarians, mostly through their attempts to change its meaning. Ministers' sermons advised their listeners to a selfless version, presenting it as a wise understanding extended toward another individual, a display of "disinterested affections." If carefully controlled, "sympathy" became the appropriate channel for sensibility, but as Gannett here warns, it required regulation and, in Catherine's case, diminution. Behind Gannett's comment is an underlying endorsement of the regulating mechanism—what the eighteenth century called sense, what Gannett and his colleagues called reason. Their notion of rational thought—considered, careful inquiry in which the individual set personality aside—was the core of their belief system. They prized balance in individual character and measured it by the equanimity of emotion with which individuals met unsettling circumstances.

4. Worth noting is the value Anna (and presumably her sister Catherine) placed on this attribute of sympathy. Far from an unruly aspect in need of careful regulation, Anna viewed it as one of the most desirable elements of character. In 1827, commenting on her cousin Charles Tilden's performance at the yearly Harvard Exhibition, she had written, "I like him better than ever since I heard him on exhibition day, for I find that he really does seem to have some enthusiasm about him, and I do dislike to have person[s] never excited or deeply interested and shewing no sympathy with others. I love sympathy dearly and like to feel it for others." After this assertion, she ends her entry by demonstrating the quality she had just praised: "I wonder what they are all doing at home this evening?" (16 July 1828).

5. By 1830, the concept of "fashionable education for young women" had long been a target for American criticism. Emphasis on the traditionally designated accomplishments (painting, music, dancing, French, fancy needlework) was seen as a relic from a less principled, less practical Old World. What young women in America required, it was argued, were lessons in "useful knowledge," a category that comprised many possibilities (reading, writing—both a "fair hand" and also a good essay—bookkeeping, history, moral philosophy, natural theology, geography, sewing, household management) but finally centered on the role of women as mothers, wives, and potential teachers of children.

6. In 1830, the advent of the normal school, designed to train young women as teachers, was still a decade away. The Tildens' decision to set up a school in their home was the rule at this point, not the exception.

7. In Boston, public education was divided into primary, grammar, and high school. At the primary level (ages four to seven), classes were coeducational, but in the grammar schools classes were segregated by sex. This division extended beyond the formal policy regarding the students to the informal policy regulating teachers. Women taught in the primary, men in the grammar and high schools. One qualification needs to be added: women did, in fact, work in grammar schools but only as "assistants." The practice was supported by its economic advantage. Grammar and reading masters earned twelve hundred dollars a year, female assistants two hundred a year. See Jane H. Pease and William H. Pease, *Ladies, Women, and Wenches: Choice and Constraint in Antebellum Charleston and Boston* (Chapel Hill: University of North Carolina Press, 1990), 69.

Primary schools taught reading, its attendant skills (spelling, handwriting), and elementary arithmetic. Grammar schools continued the emphasis on reading and arithmetic but added geography and history. For the older students, certain "optional" subjects were available (for example, natural philosophy, geometry, and algebra). See Mary Ann Connolly's doctoral thesis, "The Boston Schools in the New Republic, 1776–1840," Harvard School of Education, 1963.

At the primary and grammar school levels, the curriculum was not officially divided along gender lines, but in practice, the gender divide indeed shaped the course of study. Girls were expected to accomplish various sewing tasks after (and in some cases while) they learned their lessons. Primary schools apparently prided themselves on the amount of domestic work completed by the female students. Connolly quotes school reports in which teachers enumerated a variety of their pupils' "accomplishments": "twenty-six girls (aged four to seven) were said to have made 'thirty shirts, twelve pairs of sheets, six pairs of pillow cases, twenty-six pocket handkerchiefs, eight cravats, ten infants' frocks, five coarse bags, four dozen towels, four pairs of socks, three pairs of mittens and a number of small pieces of work'" (184).

At the high school level, the curriculum itself reflected the different understanding of "appropriate" course work. While the High School for Girls entirely dispensed with the traditional "accomplishments" (the only "drawing" included was an elective in "the principles of perspective"), the subjects were tellingly different from those at the English High School. For example, the English High School emphasized various forms of public speaking ("declamation," "forensic discussion"); given the taboo against women speaking in public, this aspect was entirely absent from the High School for Girls. The boys studied the various branches of "natural philosophy" ("including Astronomy, Moral and Political Philosophy"); study of philosophy for the female students was centered on religious and moral aspects. Where boys spent all three years in "exercises in criticism," girls practiced "writing from dictation." For the curriculum, in full, of each school, see Connolly: p. 142 for the High School for Girls, and p. 222 for the English High School.

8. A simple matter of numbers suggests the high degree of competition for the relatively few places at Boston's Latin and English High Schools. In 1829, there were fifty-seven primary and nine grammar schools operating in Boston (Pease and Pease, *Web of Progress,* 108). Even factoring out the female students ineligible for admission to the boys' high schools, there were far fewer slots at the high school level than there were potential students. To give some indication of the numbers involved: in 1829, the English High School enrolled 114 students (Connolly, "Boston Schools," 301).

9. Quincy's argument was not supported by the students' previous educational experience. Their schooling divided almost equally between private and public. Connolly reports the following figures: "In 1826, 72 pupils prepared in private schools, 61 in public; in 1827, 62 prepared in private schools, 59 in public" ("Boston Schools," 230). Regardless of the interest in and success of the High School for Girls, Quincy closed the school in order to channel existing funds into the education of

boys. His reason reflects his contemporaries' belief in educational utility. Seen as essential preparation for a profession, boys' education was considered a pressing public concern. To equip its future citizens, here defined by their economic role in the workforce, Boston educated its young men. Pease and Pease write, "Quincy led the fight to close the recently opened girls' high school in 1829 on the grounds that because girls were not being prepared there for future occupations or professions, it was 'impracticable' for the public to fund their education beyond grammar school levels" (*Web of Progress*, 113).

Tilden would have been eligible to attend the High School for Girls during its three short years of existence. No record remains of whether any of the Tilden daughters sought to be admitted. The odds would have been against them. In the first year, the school could accommodate 133 students; 286 young women applied (Pease and Pease, *Ladies, Women, and Wenches*, 67). At the end of 1827, there were 427 applicants for 200 places (Connolly, "Boston Schools," 228).

10. Tilden may well have read Ware's work, though this is difficult to document because no letters or journals are extant from this period. First published in 1831, *Formation of the Christian Character* (hereafter cited parenthetically in the text as "*FCC*") quickly went through several printings. Given the friendship between Gannett and Ware, Gannett would, in all likelihood, have owned a copy. It would have been part of his study in the Tilden household, a study that served as a sort of lending library for the family.

11. Tilden had learned the ministers' methods well. Drawing on their etymological framework, she questioned the meanings associated with particular words. If the nineteenth-century assurance of eternal life, she argued, rested on a word that connoted a limit to its length, then the evidence was questionable, as every thinking believer should see.

12. For example, in a sermon on the doctrine of probation, what Ware calls "this final good" is figured in decidedly commercial language. The individual looked forward to the "final adjustment" (*Works*, 3:310). When character successfully met circumstance, "it is one more item toward the total of our great account" (3:417). In the "immortal ages," Ware envisioned "endowments, gifts, and advantages" (3:437), and the individual, by Ware's advice, could maintain a certain type of ownership if he used his possessions well. The prosperous individual, whose "account" had been approved, was the most blessed in heaven, receiving the "final good which God bestows on his accepted children" (3:440).

13. After his graduation from Harvard, Ware taught school, as did his younger colleague Emerson. Whereas both Ware and Emerson were sons of an earlier generation of liberal Christian ministers, Gannett stepped aside from his father's Calvinism to become a Unitarian, as had the much admired Joseph Stevens Buckminster before him. Catharine Sedgwick's "conversion" to Unitarianism occurred from a similar dislike for the religious doctrines of her childhood faith.

CHAPTER 5: ASSUMING AUTHORITY

1. What also comes to mind are the life stories of women whose fictional counterparts were not featured in the domestic fiction of the day. In her narrative *Incidents in the Life of a Slave Girl* (New York: Oxford University Press, 1988), Harriet Jacobs reminds her readers of the different "plot" her life had followed. Her concluding comment—"My story ends with freedom; not in the usual way with marriage" (302)—is a double-edged phrase, distinguishing her from her white audience and their "usual way" and at the same time privileging her conclusion over theirs—freedom over marriage.

2. In her book *Liberty, a Better Husband*, Lee Virginia Chambers-Schiller discusses the role of the unmarried woman in the fiction and nonfiction written particularly for a female audience. She writes, "The Cult of Single Blessedness upheld the single life as both a socially and personally valuable state. It offered a positive vision of singlehood rooted in Protestant religion and the concepts of woman's particular nature and special sphere. It promoted singlehood as at least as holy, and perhaps more pure, a state than marriage" (18). The concept of "single blessedness" was a malleable one, lending itself as readily to the criticism of marriage as to the celebration of woman's purity. Any number of writers and works come to mind: Margaret Fuller's *Woman in the Nineteenth Century* (1845), Fanny Fern's *Ruth Hall* (1855), Catharine Sedgwick's *Married or Single?* (1857), Louisa May Alcott's *Work* (1873), and Gail Hamilton's, Fanny Fern's, and Marietta Holley's satirical pieces.

3. The outstanding examples in the mid-1830s would have been Ruth Gibbs Channing and Mary Pickard Ware. Mary Ware, Henry Ware Jr.'s second wife, would in fact become something of a Unitarian saint, praised for her ready willingness to stand in the shadow of the first wife, celebrating the woman whose place she filled. She was acclaimed for becoming "mother" to Ware's children, for supporting Ware during his protracted illnesses, and for her "joint ministry" with her husband during his years at Harvard.

She defined her role as minister's wife with sobering seriousness and stunning self-denial. Writing to her closest female friends in January 1827, six months before her wedding, Mary Pickard, soon to become the second Mrs. Henry Ware Jr., described the changes in identity under which she was laboring: "Instead of the self-dependent, self-governed being you have known me, I have learned to look to another for guidance and happiness; and, more than that, have bound myself, by an irrevocable vow, to live for the future in the exercise of the great and responsible duties which such a connection inevitably brings with it" (*Memoir of Mary L. Ware* [Boston: Crosby, Nichols, & Co., 1853], 182). With the future framed by an "irrevocable vow" to the ever pressing demands of duty, she studied a new identity. No longer "self-dependent" and "self-governed," she was now a follower who would be guided by her husband.

With what difficulty Pickard learned the lesson of self-denial is unclear, but a hint emerges in a letter of the same date written to a different friend. She writes, "I have taken upon myself great and unknown duties for which I feel incompetent." She believed that her "feeling of distrust and fearfulness [would] soon pass away," largely by virtue of an active self-suppression. Once "duty" assumed its dominant role, her fears would subside, but at the same time she would no longer hold the power to shape "the direction of events" in her life (183).

When the *Memoir of Mary L. Ware* was published in 1853, shortly after her death, it quickly sold out. There were three printings in the first year alone and almost yearly reprintings during the 1850s.

4. When Gannett left for England in the fall of 1836, he followed a well-worn path. A long line of ailing ministers preceded him: Joseph Stevens Buckminster, William Ellery Channing, Henry Ware Jr., Orville Dewey, Ralph Waldo Emerson.

In his study of travelers and their writings, Christopher Mulvey gives the traveling ministers their own category. Calling them "recuperative clergymen," he notes the frequency with which they published some form of their journey after their return home. See *Anglo-American Landscapes: A Study of Nineteenth-Century Anglo-American Travel Literature* (Cambridge: Cambridge University Press, 1983), 7–8, 83–92, and chap. 4.

5. Letters have received a significant amount of critical attention in recent years. Studies of the novel continue to examine the use of the letter in and as fiction; numerous works have addressed the narrative structures created when the letter becomes the governing form. See Linda Kaufmann's *Special Delivery: Epistolary Modes in Modern Fiction* (Chicago: University of Chicago Press, 1992). Janet Altman's *Epistolarity: Approaches to a Form* (Columbus: Ohio State University Press, 1982) provides a more theoretical discussion of the letter. The framework, however, remains the letter's role in fiction.

Outside the framework of fiction, letters have received a moderate attention from recent theorists. Most notable, of course, is Jacques Derrida with his play on one particular form of correspondence (*La Carte Postale: De Socrate à Freud et au-delà* [Paris: Flammarion, 1980]). In 1986, *Yale French Studies* devoted an issue to the discussion of letters with an emphasis on the influence wielded by published letters over their contemporary and latter-day readers. See "Men/Women of Letters," ed. Charles A. Porter, *Yale French Studies*, no. 71 (1986).

More recently, the interest in women's autobiographical writing has prompted a variety of works on a variety of letter writers. See Elizabeth Goldsmith, ed., *Writing the Female Voice: Essays on Epistolary Literature* (Boston: Northeastern University Press, 1989), a volume of essays ranging widely between centuries and genres. Discussion of letters also figures prominently in Culley and Hoffmann, *Women's Personal Narratives;* Shari Benstock, ed., *The Private Self: Theory and Practice of Women's Autobiographical Writings* (Chapel Hill: University of North Carolina Press, 1988); and Bella Brodzki and Celeste Schenck, ed., *Life/Lines: Theorizing*

Women's Autobiography (Ithaca, N.Y.: Cornell University Press, 1988). In particular, see Patricia Meyer Spacks's "Female Rhetorics," in Benstock, *Private Self,* 177–91, for discussion of women writing letters and the conflict presented by this form. In the same volume, see Deborah Kaplan's article on Jane Austen's letters. Kaplan reads the letters as letters, on their own terms, rather than as texts to be mined for "interpretation," either of Austen's novels or of her life ("Representing Two Cultures: Jane Austen's Letters," 211–29). Katharine Goodman's discussion of Elisabeth von Stageman foregrounds letters written precisely for the purpose of autobiography ("Elisabeth to Meta: Epistolary Autobiography and the Postulation of the Self," in Brodzki and Schenck, *Life/Lines,* 306–19).

6. In his essay "Authorial Self-Consciousness in the Familiar Letter: The Case of Madame de Graffigny," *Yale French Studies,* no. 71 (1986): 113–30, English Showalter Jr. discusses the letter's allusiveness in a different context, concentrating on the outside reader rather than on the correspondents themselves. In his argument for letters as "literature," he uses "allusiveness" as the evaluating criterion. He writes, "Perhaps one could argue that letters are literature only to the degree that the former tendency ["allusiveness"] makes itself felt, thereby situating the letter in a genre, imposing a form, catering to a public; and perhaps also the most engaging letters are those in which the literary impulse most effectively makes accessible the invisible private world of the writer and gives readers the feeling of having grasped secret allusions" (123).

7. In recent discussions of letters, attention has been carefully drawn to the "object status" of this genre. Showalter writes, "With letters, the material object and the text inscribed thereon cannot be separated at the origin, and the presence of the original object continues to radiate throughout the correspondence that follows" (ibid., 127). In his introduction to this issue of *Yale French Studies,* Charles Porter writes about the letter as "potential fetish." He also points out the disarming difference between the letter that is sent and the letter that is published (5, 7).

8. By 1843, when the *Boston Almanac* devoted a special section to churches and their buildings, the "liberal" and "orthodox" Christians, with their roots in the original Puritan congregations, no longer dominated the religious life of the city. The Congregational Church, of which both Unitarian and Trinitarian churches were members, was officially disestablished in 1833. By the 1840s Congregationalism, of both Unitarian and orthodox varieties, constituted less than half of the Boston churches. The denominations that fared best were of a decidedly evangelical bent. The *Almanac* for 1843 lists an addition of nearly one thousand members to the Methodist ranks in the one-year period from July 1841 to July 1842. Membership figures are noticeably absent from the *Almanac's* description of the older Congregational churches, particularly those of Unitarian leanings. While the Baptists and the Methodists could boast of church membership doubling in as many years,

the long-established, and decidedly nonevangelical, churches apparently had no such good news to report.

9. In the sermon outlining his objections to the continued observance of communion, Emerson told his congregation: "I am not engaged to Christianity by decent forms; it is not saving ordinances, it is not usage, it is not what I do not understand that engages me to it—let these be the sandy foundation of falsehoods. What I revere and obey in it is its reality . . . the rest it gives to my mind, the echo it returns to my thoughts, the perfect accord it makes with my reason" (*Sermons*, 4:193).

The particular issue of the Lord's Supper has long been seen as secondary in Emerson's decision to leave the ministry, a convenient item around which to shape his resignation. This simplifies the complexity of the question, for Emerson's resignation from the Second Church did not coincide with his departure either from preaching or from the ministry. He continued to preach until the late 1830s; the most powerful example is his address to the Harvard Divinity School in 1838. There, he again preached a doctrine of change as he had six years earlier to his own congregation. In both cases, change was rejected, but "rejection" occurred on a remarkably different order of magnitude. After his resignation and before his departure for Europe, Emerson preached, as frequently as health permitted, for the Second Church. After his address at the Divinity School, he was not asked to speak at Harvard for thirty years.

10. "Free and frank" discussion is a ubiquitous phrase in Unitarian writings; no single source can be credited with its origin. It appears in Channing's, Buckminster's, Ware's, and Ripley's sermons and articles. Borrowing the late-eighteenth-century call for free inquiry, the Unitarian ministers expanded their predecessors' words to emphasize an uncompromising standard of truthful expression.

11. Highly popular and firmly endorsed, reading societies were advocated for middle- and upper-middle-class young women who were no longer in school but not yet married. The "course in reading" extended over several weeks; the meetings were devoted to the discussion of a particular book and directed by a "reading master." In some cases, discussion meant "monologue," the silent readers listening to the "master's" commentary. Tilden attended one such course from late December 1827 to early March 1828. Her response was mixed. Excited by the prospect, she looked forward to the weekly meetings only to find them less stimulating than she had hoped. Although she consistently recorded how "pleasant" the meetings were, her final comments questioned the value of this pleasure: "It has certainly been very interesting to me going there, but as for the benefit which I have derived from it I cannot say much" (3 March 1828). Despite her disappointment, she faithfully attended the six-week session of the course, grateful to her uncle for his gift of tuition.

12. Tilden's influence extends to Gannett's theological positions, as well. In his letters from abroad during the time Tilden was with him and in the sermons after

their return to the United States, Gannett increasingly preached a God of mercy and adopted a more tolerant attitude toward the past.

13. Tilden had voiced her concern as early as 1834. Writing in her journal shortly after her father left on the trading voyage that would keep him out of the United States for almost two years, she phrased her thoughts as a prayer: "Oh may our Heavenly Father, *guide* and *guard* him, may he see things as he ought, and may he be the noble creature, he was made to be" (30 November 1834). Shortly after his next departure, Tilden registered relief. Writing to Gannett, she comments, "Father actually *sailed* yesterday, and we were very glad, I think he has not been so well and happy for this many a year. How much we have to make us grateful about him. He has again proved himself the noble, generous, liberal minded man of our *good old times. . . .* I am so glad we have *reason* to feel proud and happy again" (2 June 1836). As in her earlier journal entry, she leaves unspoken the specific nature of her father's moral failings.

14. Tilden expressed concern to Catherine over their mother's health in a letter written shortly after Zebiah Tilden agreed to accompany her daughter and son-in-law to the New York State health resort. Tilden writes, "Mother's spirits were getting so much depressed that I can't but think this little journey will do her good, change her thoughts and rest her" (10 June 1836).

15. News traveled swiftly in Boston. Waldo Emerson was born on 30 October 1836, just six days before Tilden reported what, by then, had apparently become the favorite phrasing for the news.

16. Martineau's depiction of United States society rendered many of its members critical, if not hostile. Her unwavering condemnation of slavery, her representation of women's intellectually impoverished circumstances, her criticism of religion, and the always present sore point of American "vulgarity" produced a range of return criticism from her readers. Writing directly to Martineau, Margaret Fuller criticized what Tilden would later criticize about Andrews Norton's response to Ripley's review. Both cited the writer's failure to produce a measured prose for conveying a carefully balanced critique. Fuller told Martineau that her work was marred by an "intemperance of epithet" and faulted the book for a "want of soundness, of habits of patient investigation, of completeness, of arrangement" (*The Letters of Margaret Fuller,* ed. Robert N. Hudspeth [Ithaca, N.Y.: Cornell University Press, 1983–94], 1:309). Public reviewers were yet more critical. The *North American Review* (45 [October 1837]: 418–60) faulted Martineau for inaccuracy, inconsistency, and confusion. Characterizing her as a nominal radical who had finally revealed her aristocratic leanings, the reviewer spent much of the essay discrediting the writer. She was credulous to a fault, accepting at face value the caricatures various Americans had fed her. Her tone was offensive: a combination of "ignorant flippancy" and tiresome conceit. In the reviewer's estimation, her two volumes

were filled with "rash and worthless judgments" (424) and gave the reader no more than "tangled ravellings of thought" (421).

All response was not so disparaging. Emerson praised the work for its outspokenness. Writing in his journal, he commented, "She gives that pleasure which I have felt before, when a good cause which has been trampled on is freshly & cheerily maintained by some undaunted man of good sense & good principle." His praise, however, was qualified by a decidedly gendered condescension. He applauded the "man of good sense" for her "respect for principles," but he failed to see the value in her representation of domestic settings. He commented, "The *woman* is manifest, as she seems quite willing, in the superfluous tenderness for the fine boy & the snug farmhouse & other privacies" (*The Journals and Miscellaneous Notebooks of Ralph Waldo Emerson*, ed. William H. Gilman et al. [Cambridge: Harvard University Press, 1960–82], 5:354–55; hereafter cited as *JMN*).

17. When Eliza Farrar (1791–1870) published *The Young Lady's Friend* in 1836, she was already well known and highly respected for her books for young readers. In 1830 she had published a version of Robinson Crusoe for children (complete with a reformed Crusoe) followed by a biography of Lafayette in 1831 and, two years later, a life of John Howard, the acclaimed British prison reformer. The latter was written at the request of Henry Ware Jr. as part of his series The Sunday Library for Young Persons. In 1834 Farrar published *The Youth's Letter-Writer*, an instruction manual structured as a series of stories. Immediately successful, it went through three editions in as many years. *The Young Lady's Friend*, equally as successful, was not universally championed. Public reviews were highly favorable. The *Christian Examiner* praised its "great directness and simplicity" and its attention to immediate application. Criticism was also forthcoming, but according to Elizabeth Schlesinger, in her article on Farrar ("Two Early Harvard Wives: Eliza Farrar and Eliza Follen," *New England Quarterly* 38, no. 2 [1965]: 147–67), the negative comments were voiced in private. As witnessed by Tilden's remark in her letter and by Farrar's letter to her publisher (quoted in Schlesinger), some readers found the book's frankness offensive. Farrar writes, "[I] do not regret that it contained passages which offended some, since I have no doubt it has been the more read on that very account" (154).

Tilden not only admired Farrar's work but found her friendship invaluable. Like Tilden, Farrar was married to an individual whose mental health was precarious. Her husband, John Farrar, one-time professor of mathematics at Harvard, left his position in 1836, and both husband and wife were soon in Europe, pursuing the "cure" on which Gannett would shortly embark. Tilden saw Farrar frequently while she and Gannett were in Paris. In her journal, Tilden writes, "I had much interesting conversation with Mrs F. about her book, right & wrong, the will of God etc. I like her very much" (3 March 1837), and a day later, "she has been most truly kind to us & proved herself a good friend." On leaving Paris, Tilden commented, "What a valuable friend Mrs F. has proved herself to me. I must always count her acquaintance as one of the pleasantest circumstances of my coming to Europe" (5 March 1837).

18. The short work was extremely well received, as Sedgwick records in a letter to her niece Kate: "Mr. Joseph Curtis came to see me last evening, and told me that, in all his experience, he had never witnessed so much good fruit from the publication of any book as from that of the 'Poor Rich Man.' This *pleased me.* I knew he would not flatter, and that, though he might overestimate its merit, he did not grossly misjudge" (*Life and Letters,* 260). The *Christian Examiner* praised it lavishly, seeing in it a powerful remedy for an ailing society. Although the economic upheaval of the late 1830s had not yet unsettled Boston with its full force when the review appeared in January 1837, difficulties were widespread, and instability was increasingly the word of the day in commerce and banking. The reviewer for the *Examiner* championed the book: "The book is, or ought to be, in everybody's hands." Praising the book's potential effect on its readers, he commented, "[The author] has a clear perception of what the people need, a keen feeling of the errors which prevail in our social order, a perfect understanding of the remedies which are demanded, a hearty longing for the best pattern, and an exquisite tact in setting forth, in a graphic, attractive, and convincing form, the truths which she wishes to convey. There is a charm about her lessons which makes it pleasant to listen to her, and a persuasion in her voice which converts her listeners into disciples" (21, no. 3 [1837], 398).

19. James Martineau (1805–1900), minister and lecturer, was a well-known figure among the Boston Unitarians. Brother to Harriet, he was respected by the Boston circle for his emphasis on the authority of human intellect. Encouraging each individual to study Scripture and doctrine as thoroughly as possible, he firmly supported the contextualization widely used by his American counterparts. He was also praised for his ability to combine natural and revealed religion into a harmonious unity.

Gannett and Tilden visited the Martineaus with some frequency during their stay in England. Gannett devoted pages of his journal to reprising James Martineau's sermons as well as their conversations. His assessment was highly critical—both of the minister's meaning and of his manner. On the sermons, Gannett commented, "The first half was beautifully written, but wearied me by its elaborateness and richness of expression. I longed for something said simply and naturally. The last half, on miracles, was written in a plainer style, but the reasoning seemed to me obviously fallacious. On the whole I was disappointed and felt that though unbelievers might be reconciled to revelation by such views, they were untenable and would do no good to a Christian audience." Conversation left Gannett even more critical—of both Martineaus: "I was not pleased with the tone of conversation around the table. It was confident and arrogant. Spiritual pride was charged upon others as freely as they ever charged heresy upon us—and a sort of intellectual self love seemed to me the fault of this gentleman and his sisters" (entry for 24 September 1837, vol. 6, 105). In a letter to her mother, Tilden records the same visit but gives it only one sentence, saying little about either sermon or conversation. She writes, "In the evening we went to Mr Martineau's lecture, and afterwards returned home with him, & passed an hour or more with his family" (23 September 1837).

20. Ripley was not alone in his assessment of an ailing religion. Emerson is by far the more famous commentator on the "corpse-cold" nature of Unitarianism (*JMN*, 9:381). His descriptions of the faith he had once preached are literally chilling. In 1842, he referred to the "icehouse of Unitarianism" (*JMN*, 8:182). In the late 1850s, Unitarianism fared no better: "'Tis here a mere spec of whitewash, because the mind of our culture has already left it behind" (*JMN*, 14:283). The Unitarian was a mere mannequin, clothes with no emperor: "See the poor Unitarian with his dreary superficiality. He is a bare coat & pantaloons" (*JMN*, 14:299). His most famous (or infamous) statement occurs, of course, in the Divinity School address with his description of the "spectral preacher": "A snowstorm was falling around us. The snowstorm was real; the preacher merely spectral; and the eye felt the sad contrast in looking at him, and then out of the window behind him, into the beautiful meteor of the snow. He had lived in vain. . . . If he had ever lived and acted, we were none the wiser for it" (*The Collected Works of Ralph Waldo Emerson,* ed. Alfred R. Ferguson et al. [Cambridge: Harvard University Press, 1971–], 1:84–85).

21. While Unitarians often cited the essential agreement of the synoptic Gospels as further evidence for Christianity, certain differences between the Gospels and between the Gospels and other books of the New Testament remained problematic. The Ascension, for example, was variously associated with Easter Sunday and with the fortieth day after Easter (the first reported in Luke, the second in Acts: two books traditionally attributed to a single author).

22. Some, like Tilden, saw this "consistency" as highly problematic, questioning whether the "clear" proofs were none other than wishful thinking. Take, for example, Emerson's comments on God's existence and the soul's "immortality": "That is a great part of the argument in every mind for the being of God and the immortality of the soul, that it is very desirable those facts should be true; that nothing can be conceived which is so urgently demanded by the desires of the mind as these facts. And this is an argument which continually persuades us" (*Sermons,* 4:168). As Tilden's doubts demonstrate, the argument was not always as persuasive as the ministers claimed. Her own experience had thoroughly taught her a different "truth." What the mind wanted and what the life offered were often two very different things.

23. Ripley argued that as long as one individual accepted Christianity without relying on the miracles, the miracles were peripheral to faith. Norton countered that the miracles were essential and that without them, believers had the ground of their

faith pulled out from under them. Discarding the centrality of the miracles would, in Norton's view, have only one effect: "to destroy faith in the only evidence of Christianity—as a revelation" (quoted in Ripley's reply to Norton, reprinted in Perry Miller, *The Transcendentalists* [Cambridge: Harvard University Press, 1971], 161). Norton's letter in the *Boston Daily Advertiser* appeared on 5 November 1836.

24. William Henry Furness (1802–96) served out a long pastorate for the Unitarian Church in Philadelphia. His active ministry lasted fifty years (1825–75), and he remained closely involved with the church as pastor emeritus until his death two decades later. His long-standing position within Unitarianism suggests his ability to turn potentially controversial material into acceptable speculation. While he agreed with Emerson in the miracles controversy, unlike his good friend, he voiced his rejection of the miracles in an acceptable form. His voluminous studies safeguarded him from the type of criticism his former colleague received.

Furness was also a good friend to Gannett, a frequent visitor in the Tilden household in the 1820s and a continued and welcome visitor in the Gannett home after their return from Europe.

25. A few months later, Tilden had the chance to read *The Rationale*, when she and Gannett read it together in England. Her comments, however, only note their reading; she records neither her reaction nor her husband's.

26. Tilden heard Ripley's tone as one of frank and generous inquiry. Later readers, however, have seen condescension where Tilden saw open-mindedness. Perry Miller's account in *The Transcendentalists* has largely shaped the way a more recent audience has understood the story. Characterizing the theological debate as the "war in New England" (158), Miller drew the lines as if for battle. The quotations he includes from Ripley in fact appeared in the *Boston Daily Advertiser* as part of Ripley's response to Norton's criticism. Miller includes no quotations from Ripley's review essay itself, only from the defense of his position offered to the Boston public after Norton's highly critical letter appeared. Ripley's *Advertiser* response clearly pays no compliments to Norton and virtually calls Norton to account for the method of his criticism and the motives behind it. Ripley's refrain remains the call to "scientific inquiry and discussion," a call he faults Norton for ignoring.

27. In the final section of the sermon, he expands his discussion of Christ to include what he calls "the benevolent virtues." For the minister, such virtue is to be practiced from the pulpit. He comments, "We can hardly conceive of a plainer obligation on beings of our frail and fallible nature, who are instructed in the duty of candid judgment, than to abstain from condemning men of apparent conscientiousness and sincerity, who are chargeable with no crime but that of differing from us in the interpretation of the Scriptures. . . . Charity, forbearance, a delight in the virtues of different sects, a backwardness to censure and condemn, these are virtues which, however poorly practised by us, we admire and recommend" (*Works,* 382).

28. Examples include Henry Ware Jr.'s "The Divine Government—Character, Progress, and the Consummation of Christianity" (*Works,* 3:67–80) and "The

Christian Conjunction:—Liberty and Authority, Reason and Faith, Liberality and Zeal" (*Works*, 3:202–19); Orville Dewey's "On Sectarianism" (published in the *Liberal Preacher* 2, no. 10 [1829]: 127–44); John Brazer's "Christian Unity" (*Liberal Preacher* 2, no. 6 [1828]: 59–76). Concluding a sermon in which he acknowledged the inevitability of division (looking forward to his later articulation of the "party of youth" and the "party of age"), Emerson called his listeners to a Unitarian type of transcendence: "Every man ought carefully to ponder the evils of party spirit, that he may be a partisan, when he must be, without them. I do not think it is possible entirely to keep aloof from these communities of opinion. When a persecution arises against an opinion which you hold, you must avow your sentiment, and join the weaker party in their defence. We are to use all our means to spread the knowledge of true religion, and we must unite with others to make our efforts of any avail. But let us cleave, in the midst of parties, to an independence of party" (*Sermons*, 2:190).

29. Published monthly, the periodical was designed for the conscientious church member who sought to supplement Sunday sermons with daily study. Gannett authored the idea for this particular publication and served as the journal's editor from its inception in 1831 until 1835 when Theodore Parker took over editorial duties.

In the biography of his father, William Channing Gannett cites this periodical as the forum in which individuals like Parker and Furness were able to formulate their later, controversial positions. In his editor's introduction for the first number, Gannett promised his readers a rather different prospect. Offering them the means of "*popular* instruction," he promised to "avoid controversy." "I shall," he wrote, "aim to make the Bible better understood, more diligently studied, more seriously regarded, more gratefully loved, and more cordially obeyed" (*Scriptural Interpreter* 1, no. 1 [1831]: 3).

30. It is not clear *when* Tilden read Gannett's two letters. At the time of their arrival, Channing may well have shown her only the letter he received from Boott or may have communicated Gannett's circumstances to her through conversation alone. In such a case, she may not have "received" Gannett's letters until their return from Europe, one and a half years later. Her silence to Gannett about his letters suggests that she had not read them, but such silence could also have stemmed from her attempt to leave the past in the past. Given Gannett's tendency to agonize over past action, Tilden's decision not to mention his letter(s) would clearly have served as a strategic attempt to keep Gannett focused on the present.

CHAPTER 6: CLAIMING AUTHORITY

1. The exact date is not known. On 2 January, Tilden had written to her sister Catherine, reporting her receipt of letters from Gannett, the first she had received since his departure. Written and sent before Boott's mid-November determination

to send for Anna, these letters described Gannett's seeming improvement. Tilden's letter to Catherine, filled as it is with "reassuring" news about her husband's health, thus predates her conversation with Channing about Boott's firm suggestion that she join her husband. William Channing Gannett places Tilden's departure two days after she received the news of her husband's continuing decline. In the biography, he writes, "A wondering letter sped across the Atlantic, declaring that the wife must come at once. In two days she was on the way" (*Ezra Stiles Gannett*, 160). The extant documents give no such precise indication of how much time elapsed between the arrival of Boott's letter and Anna's departure.

2. Orville Dewey (1794–1882), who preceded Gannett as colleague pastor to Channing at the Federal Street Church, had taken the "travel cure" some years earlier. On his return, he worked up his traveler's observations into a book for American readers. Titled *The Old World and the New* (New York: Harper & Brothers, 1836), it contained a long section comparing American and British societies. The conclusions were hardly surprising. Although Dewey granted England superiority in transportation and praised the English for their sturdier health, such small concessions did not touch his unwavering emphasis on the failings of the British political structure. The chapter subheadings give the game away: "The aristocratic System—Its essential Injustice" and "The republican System—The tendency to it irresistible" (2:viii).

Well acquainted with the Tildens and a good friend of Gannett's, Dewey saw Tilden off when she sailed for England in January 1837. Gannett mentions Dewey's book in his journal and apparently had a similar project in mind when he began his travel journal on board ship. Although the book was never written, Gannett did work up a lecture on London, delivered several times after his return.

The full title of Gilpin's work announces its affinity for the travel genre and the direction of its observations: *Observations on the River Wye and Several Parts of South Wales, & Relative Chiefly to Picturesque Beauty; Made in the Summer of the Year 1770* (Richmond, Surrey: Richmond, 1973). Gilpin was to aesthetics what Hume was to history. Highly popular, his works provided the common reader with guidelines both for observing the landscape and for traveling through it. Well into the nineteenth century, even after the advent of the ever successful Murray handbooks, Gilpin's works remained a guidebook of choice among those individuals who styled themselves travelers and not tourists. For a lively discussion of this distinction and its long-standing history, see James Buzard's *The Beaten Track: European Tourism, Literature, and the Ways to Culture, 1800–1918* (Oxford: Oxford University Press, 1993). Buzard gives the fullest account of travel writing to date. His work discusses a wide range of travel writing—from Baedeker guides to Henry James's essays—examining the roles these texts played and the ideologies they upheld.

Mulvey has also commented on the tourist/traveler distinction in his *Anglo-American Landscapes*. His study centers on the expectations travelers carried with them and how such expectations were used to shape the locations American and British travelers described in their accounts.

3. In a letter to her youngest sister, Zebiah, she lamented this weak spot in her education, encouraging her sister to gain the skill she had never acquired. For discussion of this letter, see "Images for Home: Tilden's Europe Letters and Their Readers" (pp. 201–6) in this chapter.

4. The first person was everywhere in evidence in early nineteenth-century travel literature. This writing "I" appropriated omniscience as one of its attributes. It spoke as an authority, resting its claim on its position outside the surroundings it observed. What the inhabitants could not perceive, immersed as they were in their daily lives, the visitor saw with "clarity," or so the premise ran. Examples such as Dickens and Trollope or Emerson and James come to mind.

Mulvey calls attention to the traveler's self-conscious privileging of his or her observations, pointing out their assertions of superiority: the traveler alone could "appreciate" what the inhabitants daily took for granted (*Anglo-American Landscapes*, 63, 70, 265). Buzard also addresses this in his discussion of the troubling ethical implications of the tourist's assessment of any given place (*Beaten Track*, 182–209).

Buzard gives a rather different emphasis to this observing "I." Arguing that writers sought to distinguish their work from "mere guide-books," he sees these writing travelers highlighting their idiosyncratic natures. Each gave his or her "personal impression." For Buzard's discussion of writers' attempts to distinguish their narratives from those written by traveling "tourists," see chap. 3: "A Scripted Continent: British and American Travel Writers in Europe, c. 1825–1875."

The form of these impressions, however, suggests that the personal perspective was designed to become the common view. The first person supported an idiosyncratic plural: what the writer said, the reader was expected to see.

5. Catherine's circumstances at this time were highly unsettled. Still subject to the uncertainties of teaching positions, she had, in the mid-1830s, moved back and forth between Boston and New York but had returned to Boston sometime in the spring of 1837.

6. Ten years earlier, she counseled him against instituting yet another discussion group within the church. She commented, "It appears to me there are but few at present who would feel sufficient confidence to ask questions, or make observations, without that unhappy sort of embarrasment [*sic*], which might throw a chill over the whole surface & congeal those very feelings you would want to invigorate." She went on to suggest a few changes in his ongoing vestry lectures, based apparently on conversations of which she had been a part: "I also propose to you to

shorten the minutia of little things in your expositions of the Bible on Tuesday eve[nin]gs. We have sometimes thought them too lengthy & too particular unless for a younger class than those who attend" (April 1827).

7. This is the single letter from Tilden held by the Massachusetts Historical Society.

8. Tilden's youngest sister, Harriet, had died in infancy eleven years earlier, when Tilden was fifteen and Zebiah six.

9. At this point, the household totaled nine members: sisters Catherine, Sarah, Anna, Maria, and Zibby; brother Bryant, mother Zebiah, the children's cousin Cornelia, and the minister Gannett. In less than a month the number increased to ten with the return of husband and father, home from his failed voyage. The homecoming did not lighten the burden. Bryant Parrott Tilden felt the failure keenly, according to Anna's journal account. On 7 July she wrote in her journal: "Oh how much I wish that Father had some steady employment even though he may not derive but little profit from it." Four days later she revealed more of what lay behind her "wish." She commented, "Father came home, he says he has no home or friends and is miserable, poor man" (11 July 1828).

10. In mid-May, she praised the situation but questioned her performance: "I feel that much may be done by my own conduct in setting her an example, & I wish that I gave her a better one, but I must *try to be good* & I may possibly in a degree succeed" (12 May 1828).

11. This hope, as we have seen, was short lived. By the early 1830s, the relationship between sisters had radically changed. Anna could no longer afford to be "little mother" to her youngest sister, but instead, the two worked side by side with older sisters Catherine and Sarah as teachers in their school.

12. The prediction never passed from the imagined future into the realized present. Zebiah Tilden, the daughter named for the mother, died at age twenty-seven, just a few months after her sister.

13. In this case, Tilden's companions were Anna Eliot Ticknor and her daughter. The daughter of a prosperous Boston merchant, Anna Eliot would have received the full complement of education for young women, as would her daughter. Both not only would have learned the rudiments of drawing but would have taken their studies beyond basic skills under the tutelage of a drawing master.

14. Widely acclaimed in his day for his devotion to the statuary of the classical world, Bertel Thorvaldsen (1770–1844) and his studio were prominent features on the traveler's Rome itinerary. Emerson mentions visiting the sculptor's studio, as does Dewey. Thorvaldsen had settled in Rome in the late eighteenth century and worked there for close to forty years before returning to his native Copenhagen in 1838.

15. Measuring the time between letters in increments of weeks was by no means the norm of Tilden's experience. Letters and notes posted in and around Boston generally traveled quickly from writer to recipient. During Gannett's stay in Leices-

ter, for example, Tilden could, almost unfailingly, count on next-day delivery, although as we have seen in the case of one crucial letter, expected delivery provided no guarantee (see Chapter 5). And, of course, apart from letters, "news" in Boston traveled swiftly. With the occupation of visiting so integrally part of the day's work, word of mouth rapidly conveyed information about events both within the domestic circle and beyond it.

16. Maria Tilden boarded with Margaret Fuller's mother for an extended period of time. The relation apparently went beyond a medical and financial one. Writing to her mother in September 1837, Margaret Fuller requested, "Mention the Tildens when you write. I do hope the journey will benefit poor Maria" (*Letters*, 1:302). In her letters from the fall of 1837, Tilden expressed an ongoing and deep concern about Maria's health. Fearing that the family would not tell her the full story, she had begged Catherine, "I am only the more anxious and unhappy not to hear, than to hear, all about Maria" (23 October 1837).

17. Edmund Burke, *A Philosophical Enquiry into the Origin of Our Ideas of the Sublime and the Beautiful* (New York: Columbia University Press, 1958), 39.

18. Discussions of "the sublime" betray a long and weighty history. Whether one looks to Longinus or to Edmund Burke, the debate turns on perception and the meaning and value we accord to it. A clear hierarchy operates, placing certain responses at the apex of the structure and diminishing others. Discussions of the sublime categorize experience and, at the same time, categorize the individual, describing him (generally) as a distinctly separate being. One condition of the sublime is an intense sense of isolation from others. The experience of the sublime occurs for the individual, not the group, and could well be said to depend on this distinction. Only in isolation could the full force of an experience be felt, and thus, communal situations (for example, domestic settings) were by definition excluded from the category of the sublime. From here, it is easy to see the ways in which such concepts were as distinctly gendered as they were hierarchical.

Critical attention has again been drawn to the eighteenth-century sublime given poststructuralist interest in moments when a seemingly stable meaning is radically disrupted. See the special issues of *New Literary History* ("The Sublime and the Beautiful: Reconsiderations," 16 [Winter 1985]) and *Studies in Romanticism* ("The Sublime: A Forum," 26 [Summer 1987]). See also *The End of the Line: Essays on Psychoanalysis and the Sublime*, ed. Neil Hertz (New York: Columbia University Press, 1985); Joanne Feit Diehl's *Women Poets and the American Sublime* (Bloomington: University of Indiana Press, 1990); and Rob Wilson's *American Sublime: The Genealogy of a Poetic Genre* (Madison: University of Wisconsin Press, 1991).

Literary criticism has had less to say about the picturesque, an absence that clearly reflects the assumptions on which Burke's sublime was built. With its evocation of habitable space, its welcoming invitation to enter its represented world, its association with shared (as opposed to individual) experience, the "picturesque" failed to meet a standard of excellence defined by individuality and inaccessibility. Like its counterparts in fiction ("sentimental" novels) and poetry (the popular "fireside" poetry of Longfellow and Whittier), it has until recently been dismissed as a lesser method of representation. Its complexity, however, deserves much closer study. Buzard focuses on the appropriating nature of the "picturesque," emphasizing the way in which the viewer was licensed to rearrange the landscape to improve its "composition" (*Beaten Track*, 15–16). As Buzard notes, the individual who traveled with the picturesque as his guide practiced the equivalent of "air-brushing out" the aspects of the inhabitants' lives that were (from the traveler's perspective) deemed undesirable.

19. From Gilpin's *Five Essays*, quoted in Carl Barbier's *William Gilpin: His Drawings, Teaching, and Theory of the Picturesque* (Oxford: Oxford University Press, 1963), 112.

20. In "The Art of Landscape Sketching" (1792), Gilpin wrote, "I do not so much mean to exact a liberty of introducing what does not exist; as of making a few of those simple variations, of which all ground is easily susceptible, and which time itself indeed is continually making" (quoted in Barbier, *William Gilpin*, 122).

21. From Gilpin's *Western Tour*, quoted in Barbier, *William Gilpin*, 143.

22. Defining picturesque travel as the pursuit of beauty, Gilpin listed the advantages it brought to the traveler. "The expectation of new Scenes" satisfied the individual's "love of novelty" ("Essay on Picturesque Travel," in *Three Essays: On Picturesque Beauty; On Picturesque Travel; and On Sketching Landscape* [London: R. Blamire, 1794], 47–48) and provided an ample collection of observations. Given the addition of "*new objects*" and the combination of new objects with old, the traveler grew more "learned in nature" (50). The benefits were not, however, simply ones of acquisition, for the greatest boon of picturesque travel was the opportunity it offered the traveler's imagination. Whether displayed in recollection of scenes visited or prompted by the ever evocative "roughness" in a natural landscape, the imagination was the most active traveler in the scenes it surveyed.

Gilpin's concept of picturesque travel was thoroughly put into practice by eighteenth- and nineteenth-century travelers. Elizabeth McKinsey discusses the phenomenon in connection with Niagara Falls in her extensive study of North America's "natural wonder," *Niagara Falls: Icon of the American Sublime* (Cambridge: Cambridge University Press, 1985), 57–62. Beth Lueck looks at the politics of the picturesque tour in her study of American nationalism in the early nineteenth century, "James Kirke Paulding and the Picturesque Tour: 'Banqueting on the Picturesque' in the 1820s and '30s," *University of Mississippi Studies in English* 9 (1991): 167–88.

23. Noting Gilpin's popularity with an American audience, McKinsey discusses his influence on representations of Niagara Falls. Niagara was hardly a subject for the picturesque: its scale was announcedly the sublime, and as McKinsey notes, the use of Gilpin's compositional principles brought order to the visual image but often

at the expense of expanse. In "picturesque" representations, the size of the falls was diminished to accommodate human figures (*Niagara Falls*, 61–63).

24. How much of Gilpin's work Tilden or her family members had read remains unknown. Their descriptions of nature, however, are clearly influenced by notions of the picturesque. Gannett was reading Gilpin's *Observations on Several Parts of England, Particularly the Mountains and Lakes of Cumberland and Westmoreland, Relative Chiefly to Picturesque Beauty, Made in the Year 1772*, 2 vols. (London: T. Cadell and W. Davies, 1808) while he and Tilden were touring the Lake District. Since Tilden's journal from this period has been lost, the question of her reading is intriguing but can be answered only by speculation.

25. In his writings, Gilpin emphasized the importance of "roughness" or "irregularity" (words he used synonymously). At the same time he praised "variety" or "succession" in a landscape. Integral to his emphasis on the viewer's imagination, these characteristics guaranteed that the individuals would be actively engaged by and in what they saw (*Observations on the Several Parts of England*, 2:74; *Observations on the River Wye*, 21). For example, describing the scenery around Ullswater in England's Lake District, he praised the succession of forms created by the changing character of the landscape: "We now re-entered Gobray park; which afforded us, for near three miles, a great variety of beautiful scenes on the left, composed of rocky, and broken-ground, forest-trees, copse-wood, and wooded hills: while the lake, and mountains, whose summits were now glowing with the full splendor of an evening sun, were a continued fund of varied entertainment on the right. The eye was both amused, and relieved by surveying the two different modes of scenery in succession: the broad shades, and bright diversified tints, of the distant mountains, on one side; and the beautiful forms, and objects of the foreground, on the other" (*Observations on the Several Parts of England*, 2:74). Twenty years later in his "Essay on Picturesque Beauty," he outlined the connection between "roughness" and the picturesque: "Turn the lawn into a piece of broken ground: plant rugged oaks instead of flowering shrubs: break the edges of the walk: give it the rudeness of a road; mark it with wheel-tracks; and scatter around a few stones, and brushwood; in a word, instead of making the whole *smooth*, make it *rough;* and you make it also *picturesque*" (*Three Essays*, 8).

26. Gannett treated the excursion as a failed attempt, as had his fellow Unitarian minister Orville Dewey before him (see Dewey's *Old World and the New*, 1:236: "And now, if I could say that these glaciers were stupendous mirrors, in which the mountains are reflected, it would doubtless be presenting a picture of unequalled splendour and sublimity. But alas! nothing could be farther from the truth"). The sublime of their expectations was not met by the landscape they visited. In his journal, Gannett writes, "The view did not repay us for the trouble. . . . The mer de glace seems of much narrower dimensions at this distance than it is in truth and the glaciers were not beautiful. Mont Blanc did not appear so high as some other peaks" (4:65).

27. I make no claim for the originality of this response. Her personification is undoubtedly conventional. My point here is that within Gannett's and Tilden's representations of the particular event, personification was peculiarly her device, not his.

28. Assuring his readers that he meant "liberty," not "license" (*Observations on the Several Parts of England*, 1:xxxvi), Gilpin advocated highlighting particular shapes in the landscape and in fact encouraged the viewer to alter them when need be. In the preface to his *Observations on the Several Parts of England*, he cites the problem created by the relatively straight banks of a river. "Would the truth of portrait be injured, in painting this subject," he asks, "if trees were planted to hide the deformity; or a small turn given to the river, to break it's disgusting regularity" (1:xxviii). Among the natural formations Gilpin found the most conducive to the picturesque were "jutting promontories" (here seen in Tilden's "pyramids"), any variety of valley and waterfall (Tilden's ravines and gulfs). For Gilpin's views on altering the landscape in its representation, see *Observations on the Several Parts of England*, 1:127; *Observations on the River Wye*, 18–19; and "Essay on Picturesque Beauty," 7–8, 17–18. In his remarks on revising the landscape, Gilpin is probably best remembered for his suggestion that someone take a hammer to Tintern Abbey to improve its appearance as a "ruin" ("a number of gabel-ends hurt the eye with their regularity; and disgust it by the vulgarity of their shape. A mallet judiciously used [but who durst use it?] might be of service in fracturing some of them; particularly those of the cross isles, which are not only disagreeable in themselves, but confound the perspective") (*Observations on the River Wye*, 33).

29. Tilden was not simply quoting Wordsworth but quoting Wordsworth quoting himself. In his *Guide through the District of the Lakes in the North of England* (Malvern: Tantivy Press, 1948), in all probability a book well used by Tilden and Gannett in their "tour" (the "definitive" edition had appeared in 1835), Wordsworth cited particular lines from *The Excursion*. Tilden's comment clearly echoes Wordsworth's words. He had written, "Then proceed to Colwithforce, and up Little Langdale to Blea Tarn. The scene in which this small piece of water lies, suggested to the Author the following description, (given in his Poem of the Excursion) supposing the spectator to look down upon it, not from the road, but from one of its elevated sides" (viii). At this point, he quotes several lines from Book 2 of *The Excursion* (ll. 327–48). Tilden began the reference some lines earlier, apparently wanting to direct her reader's attention to the barrenness of the climb rather than solely to the valley below. The portion included by Wordsworth picks up in the fifth line with the word "behold":

> We scaled, without a track to ease our steps,
> A steep ascent; and reached a dreary plain,
> With a tumultuous waste of huge hill tops
> Before us; savage region! which I paced
> Dispirited: when, all at once, behold!

Beneath our feet, a little lowly vale,
A lowly vale, and yet uplifted high
Among the mountains; even as if the spot
Had been from eldest time by wish of theirs
So placed, to be shut out from all the world!
Urn-like it was in shape, deep as an urn;
With rocks encompassed, save that to the south
Was one small opening, where a heath-clad ridge
Supplied a boundary less abrupt and close;
A quiet treeless nook, with two green fields,
A liquid pool that glittered in the sun,
And one bare dwelling; one abode, no more!
It seemed the home of poverty and toil,
Though not of want: the little fields, made green
By husbandry of many thrifty years,
Paid cheerful tribute to the moorland house.
—There crows the cock, single in his domain:
The small birds find in spring no thicket there
To shroud them; only from the neighbouring vales
The cuckoo, straggling up to the hill tops,
Shouteth faint tidings of some gladder place.

30. In her letter, Tilden borrows Wordsworth's language for more than the description of the landscape. Using his word "scene" from the *Guide,* she adopts it for her own representation of what they saw en route through Langdale.

Raising questions of perspective as it does, the word "scene" is worth consideration. The distinction here is between "scene" and "situation." An individual's daily experiences provide a continuum of events. Each event occurs within a particular situation that the individual may or may not remark. When event becomes "scene," however, a particular transformation takes place. A "scene" is a construct reflecting the conventions of a certain genre. Most literally, scenes occur in plays. They are a function of theater. Less rigorously they serve as synonym for "setting," sometimes with, sometimes without, action implied—a scene in Wordsworth's poem, a scene in Scott's novel. Tilden's descriptions of place clearly reflect the reader's eye.

31. By the 1830s, the literary tour had become a popular piece in the traveler's repertoire. As Buzard points out, the romantic poets were quickly packaged in guidebook format for the individual who sought a text-directed excursion. Byron was perhaps the most popular of these literary tour guides, but Wordsworth came in a close second (see Buzard, *Beaten Track,* 113–30). Literary pilgrimages were all the fashion, and few travelers passed up the opportunity to visit Wordsworth or to pay homage to the memory of Sir Walter Scott at Abbotsford. See also Mulvey's

discussion of the requisite pilgrimage to Stratford in *Anglo-American Landscapes,* chap. 5: "Stratford-upon-Avon: Blessed beyond all other Villages," 74–92.

32. Mulvey, *Anglo-American Landscapes,* 265. See also Buzard's comments on John Murray's rationale for his travel guides (65–76). In the preface for his *Handbook for Travellers on the Continent,* Murray privileges his work over "local histories, written by residents who do not sufficiently discriminate between what is peculiar to a place and what is not worth seeing, or may be seen equally well or to a greater advantage somewhere else" (quoted in Buzard, *Beaten Track,* 70). From Murray's vantage point, as a well-seasoned traveler he alone could make the comparison that would yield the "peculiar" features of a place.

33. Although the book was never completed, Gannett drew a lecture on London from his journal observations. Gannett records repeating the lecture several times, complete with a map of London initially drawn for him by Anna's sister Maria. The results were mixed. After its first delivery, an extemporaneous performance, he records discomfort: "The lecture lacked neatness and composure" (vol. 12, 5 February 1839). At the next delivery, for the Salem Mechanics' Association, he complained about the lecture hall and his performance: "a bad room, full, but not large—very hot, and I was tired and uncomfortable—did not satisfy myself" (14 February). Five days later, he presented a revised version of the lecture in Charlestown, shortened by fifteen minutes, down from the original hour and a half. The following night he reports his greatest satisfaction with the lecture at the Suffolk Street Chapel, a building known for its "spacious" vestry (*Boston Almanac* 1843, 126) and its affiliation with Boston's "Ministry-at-Large" (the association, pioneered by Joseph Tuckerman, designed for relief work with the poor). In his journal, Gannett comments, "the best I have given" (20 February). Gannett's final reference to the lecture occurs on 5 March, when, on short notice, he substituted for the abolitionist Wendell Phillips at the East Cambridge Lyceum. The experience left him disgruntled, not because of the room, the audience, or his performance. The problem was the pay—or its absence. In his journal, he complains, "W Phillips shd have lectured this eveg but was prevented, and this morning Green came to get me to take his place. No pay—this is not right. Lecturers shd be paid as well as any other workmen. They consume time in preparing a lecture, and strength in delivering it."

34. During Holy Week, different musical settings of the Miserere (51st Psalm) were traditionally sung in the churches of the Vatican. Holy Week services rated prominently among the tourist attractions of Rome, as did the services associated with Christmas and Epiphany. Emerson, for example, on his first trip to Europe, spent Holy Week in Rome. In a letter written before he left Naples, he notes the common track being beaten by foreign visitors and separates himself from them. Writing to his future sister-in-law Susan Haven, he comments, "Every body is crowding to Rome just now, for the Holy Week begins on the 1st April & that is the

season of the great annual pomp of the Catholic Church. I follow the multitude & yet without much curiosity. . . . Perhaps I shall think differently when I see the purple & gold, & hear the Pope & his monks chaunt the 'Miserere' in St. Peters" (*Letters,* 1:368). Emerson did "think differently" about the experience itself. Quite unlike the thinly veiled scorn for the Holy Week "spectacle," he registers a powerful (for Emerson) response to hearing the Miserere. Describing not only the reputation of the service but the service itself, he concludes his journal entry with praise: "The sight & the sound are very touching[.] Every thing here is in good taste. The choir are concealed by the high fence which rises above their heads. We were in a Michel Angelo's chapel which is full of noblest scriptural forms & faces" (*JMN,* 4:155). The next day he returned, hearing the Miserere in the venue of St. Peter's. As with Gannett, the setting diminished the service, but unlike Gannett, Emerson found the building well worth the impression it left. He commented, "To night I heard the Miserere sung in St Peter's & with less effect than yesterday. But what a temple! When night was settling down upon it & a long religious procession moved through a part of the Church[,] I got an idea of its immensity such as I had not before. You walk about on its ample marble pavement as you would on a common[,] so free are you of your neighbors; & throngs of people are lost upon it. And what beautiful lights & shades on its mighty gilded arches & vaults & far windows & brave columns & its rich clad priests, that look as if they were the pictures come down from the walls & walking" (*JMN,* 4:155).

35. The work of Matthew Cotes Wyatt (1777–1862), this piece of marble statuary had received widespread attention for both its subject matter and its execution. Princess Charlotte (1796–1817), only daughter of George IV and potential heir to the throne, spent most of her life estranged from her father and separated from her mother. Her parents separated shortly after her birth, and her father seems to have been interested mainly in keeping her out of sight and off the throne. She clearly saw herself as a possible monarch and broke off the engagement favored by her father because the marriage (to William of Orange) would require her to leave England. She married Prince Leopold of Saxe-Coburg in 1816 and died nineteen months later in childbirth. Her loyalty to England, the treatment by her father, and the drama of her death combined to make her a popular heroine, greatly mourned by her potential subjects. A national subscription raised a handsome fifteen thousand pounds, and Wyatt was commissioned to design and execute the cenotaph in St. George's Chapel at Windsor.

Completed in 1826, it won a carefully qualified approbation, which Gannett's assessment essentially repeats. Praised for its execution but condemned for its design, this monument met with resistance for its bare-breasted figure of the ascending Princess Charlotte, as well as for the draped figure of the corpse with the fingers of one hand clearly visible from beneath the drapery and looking indeed as if the death grip were upon it.

The work was a common item on the traveler's itinerary and frequently described by travelers in their narratives. Naval chaplain Charles Stewart (1795–1870) records his impression of Wyatt's work, even giving a chapter subtitle to the monument. His description suggests that he had learned to see the site well before he arrived. Writing about his visit to St. George's Chapel at Windsor, he comments, "It is also adorned by many fine monuments, among which, that of the Princess Charlotte is the most striking. As a whole, this has been objected to by connoisseurs, as complex and incongruous—representing her, at the same time, in two distinct personifications. In one, as on the couch of death, just as the spirit has taken its everlasting flight; and in the other, as a glorified being, crowned with immortality, and rising in triumph to the regions of the blessed. Separated, either would have been appropriate and beautiful—particularly that which, by the breathless, yet scarce lifeless, form beneath the sheet of death, tells the tale of grief which has prostrated, in sorrow, the exquisitely chiselled forms grouped around. This, by itself, is a masterpiece; proving, at a moment's glance, the power of art to make even marble speak, with an overwhelming eloquence. It is by Wyat [sic]; and no one, having the soul of a man, can stand and gaze upon it, without a touching and profitable recurrence in thought, to the brief life and affecting death of the amiable and interesting subject of the sculptor's skill" (*Sketches of Society in Great Britain and Ireland* [Philadelphia: Carey, Lea, & Blanchard, 1834], 2:198).

36. The last three words of this sentence are written above the line, replacing Gannett's first choice, "dying." Tilden's use of the revised phrase suggests several possibilities. In writing to her mother she may well have consulted Gannett's journal for details, borrowing some of his interpretations and rejecting others. His revision, however, may also have resulted from his conversation with Anna. Her use of "ascending spirit" fits nicely with the tone of "having just expired" (in contrast to his "leaving the body").

37. One might well say that his objections were a luxury he could afford. His body would never feel the threat of the particular death represented so graphically in the memorial to Princess Charlotte, a memorial in which all pregnant women could find themselves represented.

38. Allan Ramsay (1713–84), renowned portrait artist of the eighteenth century, capped his long career as "Principal Painter in Ordinary to Their Majesties" (George III and Queen Charlotte). By 1767, the time of this appointment, he was fully established as the preeminent portrait painter of his day and an active participant in debates over aesthetic theory. His 1755 *Dialogue on Taste,* cast in the popular form of the conversation between allegorical mouthpieces (Colonel Freeman and Lord Modish), champions the individual's role. Distinguishing objects of "taste" from those of "reason and judgment," Ramsay termed the former "relative to the person only who is actuated by them, who is the sole judge whether those feelings may be agreeable, or otherwise." The individual alone could determine what he

likes; taste is a matter of "private opinion" (quoted in Alastair Smart's *Allan Ramsay: Painter, Essayist, and Man of the Enlightenment* [New Haven: Yale University Press, 1992], 140).

39. Ramsay's portrait of Flora Macdonald was painted only three years later, in 1749. At the time of the portrait, Flora Macdonald was residing in London, actively sought for the fame she had won from her role—not in aiding insurrection, but for enacting self-sacrifice in the cause of love. The painting enjoyed as widespread a popularity as its subject and was widely reproduced as an inexpensive engraving. See Smart, *Allan Ramsay*, 89–90.

EPILOGUE

1. The phrasing for the date of death depends on when the newspaper appeared; thus the *Boston Evening Transcript* for 26 December reads, "Last evening, suddenly, ANNA, wife of Ezra S. Gannett, D.D. 33"; the *Boston Daily Advertiser* for Monday 28 December reads, "25th inst. suddenly, Anna, wife of Ezra S. Gannett, D.D. 33"; and the *Christian Register* (published weekly) for 2 January 1847 gives, "On Friday evening, suddenly, Anna, wife of Ezra S. Gannett, D.D. 33."

2. *Boston Evening Transcript*, 14 January 1847; *Boston Daily Advertiser*, 28 December 1846.

3. Little is known about the author, "Mrs. A. J. Graves." She makes no appearance in *Notable American Women* or in the nineteenth-century biographical dictionaries such as *American Women*. The National Union Catalogue lists only her initials and gives neither birth nor death dates. More can be gleaned about her two books, *Girlhood and Womanhood* and *Women in America*. The latter was first published in 1841, warranted a new edition for four consecutive years, and was reprinted as late as 1855. It offered, as announced by its subtitle, "an examination into the moral and intellectual condition of American female society." Her second book did not meet with quite the same popularity: it yielded only three editions.

Baym briefly discusses *Girlhood and Womanhood* in *Woman's Fiction*. Citing the book as "one of the most technically accomplished of the morality fictions so common in the late thirties and early forties," she points out the sharp contrast the book draws between "single blessedness" and unhappy marriage. Summing the women's stories, Baym comments, "Only two of ten schoolgirls make happy marriages; for the rest marriage is a brief, convulsive nightmare from which they awaken when they are widowed or abandoned to build life anew with other stranded women—sisters, friends, or mothers" (77–78).

4. An article on education for women appeared in the *Boston Evening Transcript* on 9 January 1847. Commenting on the satirical outpourings that greeted the proposal for a women's college in Paris, the *Transcript* offered its own version of "female education": "The woman best qualified to please [this in response to

comments about "woman's purpose"] is she who possesses the greatest versatility of mental acquisitions; the most nobly educated woman is she who scorns not to darn a stocking whilst conversing with her husband or friends."

The anonymous poem appeared in the *Boston Daily Advertiser* for 13 January 1847. Fifteen quatrains of iambic tetrameter, it takes as its topic the sharp contrast between human assumption and human experience, punctuating its stanzas with grim, and somewhat sensational, reminders of death's reality. For example, "Blind, we surmise not that beneath / The glossy rind a worm is hid; / Or that the eyeball froze in death, / Lies veiled by youth's just-slumbering lid."

5. Obituary for Eliza Sanger in the *Christian Register,* 13 February 1847.

6. In a sermon published in 1832, he had identified women as "the delicate sex . . . excluded from the competition and toil of political or mercantile life" (p. 44 in "The Claims of Religion on the Female Sex," *Liberal Preacher* 2, no. 3). He championed their "influence" but made it clear that such influence worked best when the woman herself was absent. He praised women's "silent efficacy." Their influence, he told his audience, "is felt through society, felt where they are never seen" (47). Twenty-five years later his perspective had not changed. In a sermon titled *The Influence of Woman* (Boston: John Wilson and Son, 1857), he again celebrated the unseen agents for their effect on a society in which they made no appearance. He criticized those who had "undertaken the office of champion in her behalf," maintaining that attempts to establish women's rights on firmly acknowledged public ground endangered the powerful and mysterious "right" of woman's "moral nature." He remained a champion for "the numberless indirect agencies which she consciously or unconsciously use[d]" and for "the indescribable but undeniable sympathy" that she embodied (11). Her "influence," he claimed, depended on her invisibility. Little wonder that Gannett's daughter Kate Gannett Wells became an active member in the antisuffrage movement.

7. As defined by Gannett, this "great problem" was none other than the age-old "problem of evil." Gannett presents it from a particularly Unitarian slant. Less concerned with the source of evil and its repercussions for Deity (could a good God create evil? but if not of God's creation, did the existence of evil limit God's power?), the Unitarians focused instead on its appearance in and purpose for human lives. Relying heavily on their doctrine of probation, Unitarian ministers cast evil as good in the making. Apparent inequity (i.e., circumstantial differences) mattered less than the individual's use of his or her particular situation.

8. Tributes poured in following Gannett's death. In his biography, William Channing Gannett notes, "On the next Sunday [after his father's death], in many a church,—and not in Unitarian churches only,—the sermon touched on the ideal of character just passed from sight" (*Ezra Stiles Gannett,* 380). William Gannett includes several of these tributes: sixteen from ministers, two from judges. A plaque was placed in the Arlington Street Church (the name changed when the church

moved to its new building in 1859), where it can be read to this day. Praising Gannett as an "eloquent and logical preacher" and "devoted pastor," it celebrates the minister's "self-sacrifice" in the "discharge of duty" and memorializes him for his "untiring activity for the moral and social elevation of the community" (*Ezra Stiles Gannett*, 413).

The biography also describes and gives an illustration of an elaborate carved monument "near his grave" in Mount Auburn: a stone cross in the same form as one that Gannett had designed for his church, an open sermon case on which were inscribed the texts for his first and last sermons, and his two canes. No evidence of this monument remains, except for two telltale slots cut into the granite block on which Tilden's memorial lines are inscribed. The fate of Gannett's memorial remains unknown, whether deterioration required its removal or whether the daughter (or her children) removed it to make room for the quartz family marker that now sits where Gannett's cross may once have stood.

9. Although William Gannett quoted from this book in the biography of his father, its location is unknown. It is in neither the father's nor the son's papers.

10. The *Boston Daily Advertiser* for Monday, 4 January 1847, records the date of interment as 26 December. Given New England winters and the impossibility of in-ground burial, it was common practice to store bodies in the Boston Common Burying Ground vault until the ground thawed. Burial could take place on the Boston Common itself and would have been a possible choice for Gannett given the inexpensive cost of the plots.

11. They left the design of the monument to their bereaved minister, but he in turn gave that task back to the members of his congregation. The letter offering Gannett the plot in Mount Auburn is a draft of the letter sent to the minister. On the letter, William Channing Gannett indicates only that it was returned to him long after it was written. He notes, "The gift of the Mt. Auburn lot at the time of Mother's death, Xmas 1846. Letter of the parish friends and Father's reply sent me by Jennie Chapman, April, *1920!*"

Selected Bibliography

SOURCES

Bigelow, Jacob. *History of Mount Auburn Cemetery.* Boston: James Munroe and Co., 1859.

Boston Daily Advertiser, 1846–47.

Boston Evening Transcript, 1846–47.

Burke, Edmund. *A Philosophical Enquiry into the Origin of Our Ideas of the Sublime and the Beautiful.* New York: Columbia University Press, 1958.

Cabot, Elizabeth Rogers Mason. *More than Common Powers of Perception: The Diary of Elizabeth Rogers Mason Cabot.* Edited by P. A. M. Taylor. Boston: Beacon Press, 1993.

Channing, William Ellery. *Channing's Works.* New Complete Edition. Boston: American Unitarian Association, 1885.

———. Letters to Ezra Stiles Gannett, 1825–35. Massachusetts Historical Society, Boston.

———. Letter to Anna Tilden (n.d.). Massachusetts Historical Society.

Chapone, Hester. *Letters on the Improvement of the Mind Addressed to a Lady.* 1773. New York: Evert Duyckinck, 1826.

Child, Lydia Maria. *The Mother's Book.* Boston: Carter and Hendee, 1831.

Christian Register, 1847 (Boston).

Dewey, Orville. *The Old World and the New.* 2 vols. New York: Harper & Brothers, 1836.

Edgeworth, Maria. *Belinda.* London: Pandora Press, 1986.

———. *Patronage.* London: Pandora Press, 1986.

Emerson, Ralph Waldo. *The Collected Works of Ralph Waldo Emerson.* 5 vols. to date. Edited by Alfred R. Ferguson et al. Cambridge: Harvard University Press, 1971–.

———. *The Complete Sermons of Ralph Waldo Emerson.* 4 vols. Edited by Albert J. von Frank et al. Columbia: University of Missouri Press, 1989–92.

———. *The Journals and Miscellaneous Notebooks of Ralph Waldo Emerson.* 16 vols. Edited by William H. Gilman et al. Cambridge: Harvard University Press, 1960–82.

———. *The Letters of Ralph Waldo Emerson.* 10 vols. Edited by Ralph R. Rusk (vols. 1–6) and Eleanor M. Tilton (vols. 7–10). New York: Columbia University Press, 1939–95.

—. Preaching Record. bMS Am 1280.H 96. Houghton Library, Harvard University.

Farrar, Eliza. *The Young Lady's Friend*. Boston: American Stationers' Co., 1836.

—. *The Youth's Letter-Writer; or The Epistolary Art*. New York: R. Bartlett and S. Raynor, 1834.

Federal Street Church. Letter to Ezra Stiles Gannett. December 1846. Massachusetts Historical Society, Boston.

Fuller, Margaret. *The Letters of Margaret Fuller*. 6 vols. Edited by Robert N. Hudspeth. Ithaca, N.Y.: Cornell University Press, 1983–94.

Furness, William Henry. *Remarks on the Four Gospels*. Philadelphia: Carey, Lea, & Blanchard, 1836.

Gannett, Ezra Stiles. *The Christian Ministry, A Discourse delivered at the ordination of Reverend Andrew Preston Peabody*. Portsmouth, N.H.: J. W. Foster—J. F. Shores, 1833.

—. "The Claims of Religion on the Female Sex." *Liberal Preacher* 2 (March 1832): 39–53.

—. *The Influence of Woman: A Sermon preached in the Federal Street Meetinghouse, Sunday, July 19, 1857*. Boston: John Wilson and Son, 1857.

—. Journal, 64 volumes, 1836–71. Massachusetts Historical Society.

—. Letters, 1835–45. bMS Am 1888.4 87. Houghton Library, Harvard University.

—. Letters to the Federal Street Church, 1835–46. Massachusetts Historical Society.

—. *Religious Consolation*. Boston: J. Dowe, 1836.

—. *A Sermon Preached in the Arlington Street Church, November 29, 1863, after the death of Mrs. Susan L. Torrey*. Boston: J. Wilson and Son, 1864.

Gannett, William Channing. *Ezra Stiles Gannett: Unitarian Minister in Boston, 1824–1871*. Boston: Roberts Brothers, 1875.

Gilpin, William. *Observations on Several Parts of England, Particularly the Mountains and Lakes of Cumberland and Westmoreland, Relative Chiefly to Picturesque Beauty, Made in the Year 1772*. 2 vols. London: T. Cadell and W. Davies, 1808.

—. *Observations on the River Wye and Several Parts of South Wales, & Relative Chiefly to Picturesque Beauty; Made in the Summer of the Year 1770*. Richmond, Surrey: Richmond, 1973.

—. *Three Essays: On Picturesque Beauty; On Picturesque Travel; and On Sketching Landscape*. London: R. Blamire, 1794.

Hall, Edward B. *Memoir of Mary L. Ware, Wife of Henry Ware, Jr.* Boston: Crosby, Nichols, and Co., 1852.

Hamilton, Elizabeth. *Letters on the elementary principles of education*. 1801. Boston: S. H. Parker, 1825.

Harrington, John. *Saint George's Chapel, Windsor*. London: Sampson Low, Marston, and Low, and Searle, 1872.

Liberal Preacher, 1827–33 (Boston).

John W. Linzee Papers. Tilden manuscript genealogy. SG/Til/7–76 #139. New England Historic Genealogical Society, Boston.

Martineau, Harriet. Letters to Anna Tilden (n.d.) and Catherine Tilden (1836). bMS Am 1888.4 154–55. Houghton Library, Harvard University.

The Picturesque Pocket Companion and Visitor's Guide through Mount Auburn. Boston: Otis, Broaders, and Co., 1839.

Ripley, George. Review of "The Rationale of Religious Enquiry by James Martineau." *Christian Examiner* 21, no. 2 (1836): 225–254.

Roche, Maria Regina. *Children of the Abbey.* London: William Lane printed for Minerva Press, 1796.

Scriptural Interpreter, 1831–35 (Boston).

Sedgwick, Catharine Maria. *Hope Leslie.* Edited by Mary Kelley. New Brunswick, N.J.: Rutgers University Press, 1987.

———. *The Life and Letters of Catharine Maria Sedgwick.* Edited by Mary L. Dewey. New York: Harper & Brothers, 1871.

———. *The Power of Her Sympathy: The Autobiography and Journal of Catharine Maria Sedgwick.* Edited by Mary Kelley. Boston: Northeastern University Press, 1993.

———. *Redwood: A Tale.* New York: George P. Putnam & Co., 1856.

Sigourney, Lydia. *Letters to Young Ladies.* New York: Harper & Brothers, 1836.

Stewart, Charles S. *Sketches of Society in Great Britain and Ireland.* 2 vols. Philadelphia: Carey, Lea, & Blanchard, 1834.

Tilden, Anna Linzee. Journal, 1827–28. bMS Am 1888.4 186. Houghton Library, Harvard University.

———. Journal, 1834–35. bMS Am 1888.4 187. Houghton Library, Harvard University.

———. Journal, 1837. bMS Am 1888.4 188. Houghton Library, Harvard University.

———. Letters, 1832–45. bMS Am 1888.4 26, 142–45. Houghton Library, Harvard University.

———. Letter to Catherine Tilden, 20 August 1837. Massachusetts Historical Society.

———. Notes from Sermons, 1824–31. bMS Am 1888.4 185. Houghton Library, Harvard University.

———. "Some Recollections of My Children." William Channing Gannett Papers, University of Rochester Library.

Tilden, Bryant Parrott. Letter, 1835. bMS Am 1888.4 66. Houghton Library, Harvard University.

Tilden, Catherine Brown. *The First Patient: A Story written in aid of the Fair for the 'Channing Home.'* Boston: J. Wilson and Son, 1859.

———. "For 'Kate' and 'Will.'" Manuscript memoir, unfinished. August 1874. Collection of Michael R. Gannett.

———. Letter to Bryant P. Tilden, 29 December 1846–1 January 1847. Collection of Michael R. Gannett.

———. Letters, 1828–38. bMS Am 1888.4 167–68. Houghton Library, Harvard University.

Tilden, Mary A. Letter, 1837. bMS Am 1888.4 169. Houghton Library, Harvard University.

Tilden, Zebiah. Letters, 1827–36. bMS Am 1888.4 67, 165, 166. Houghton Library, Harvard University.

———. Letter to Bryant P. Tilden, 29 December 1846–1 January 1847. Collection of Michael R. Gannett.

Ware, Henry, Jr. *Discourses on the offices and character of Jesus Christ.* Boston: Office of the Christian Register, 1825.

———. *Formation of the Christian Character.* 1831. Boston: American Unitarian Association, 1883.

———. Letters to Ezra Stiles Gannett, 1825–34. Massachusetts Historical Society.

———. *The recollections of Jotham Anderson.* Boston: Office of the Christian Register, 1824.

———. *The Works of Henry Ware, Jr., D.D.* Boston: James Munroe and Co., 1846–47.

Wordsworth, William. *Guide through the District of the Lakes in the North of England.* Malvern: Tantivy Press, 1948 (facsimile of the 5th ed., 1835).

SECONDARY WORKS

Alpern, Sara, et al., eds. *The Challenge of Feminist Biography: Writing the Lives of Modern American Women.* Urbana: University of Illinois Press, 1992.

Altman, Janet. *Epistolarity: Approaches to a Form.* Columbus: Ohio State University Press, 1982.

Anderson, Linda. "At the Threshold of the Self: Women and Autobiography." In *Women's Writing,* edited by Moira Monteith. New York: St. Martin's Press, 1986.

Andrews, William. *Sisters of the Spirit: Three Black Women's Autobiographies of the Nineteenth Century.* Bloomington: Indiana University Press, 1988.

Ascher, Carol, Louise DeSalvo, and Sara Ruddick, eds. *Between Women: Biographers, Critics, Teachers, and Artists Write about Their Work on Women.* Boston: Beacon Press, 1984.

Backscheider, Paula R. "'I Died for Love': Esteem in Eighteenth-Century Novels by Women." In *Fetter'd or Free? British Women Novelists, 1670–1815,* edited by Mary Anne Schofield and Cecilia Macheski. Athens: Ohio University Press, 1986.

Barbier, Carl. *William Gilpin: His Drawings, Teaching, and Theory of the Picturesque.* Oxford: Oxford University Press, 1963.

Baym, Nina. *Novels, Readers, and Reviewers: Responses to Fiction in Antebellum America.* Ithaca, N.Y.: Cornell University Press, 1984.

———. *Woman's Fiction: A Guide to Novels by and about Women in America, 1820–1870*. Ithaca, N.Y.: Cornell University Press, 1978.

Benstock, Shari, ed. *The Private Self: Theory and Practice of Women's Autobiographical Writings*. Chapel Hill: University of North Carolina Press, 1988.

Bernard, Richard, and Maris Vinovskis. "The Female School Teacher in Ante-Bellum Massachusetts." *Journal of Social History* 10, no. 3 (1977): 332–45.

Blakey, Dorothy. *The Minerva Press, 1790–1820*. London: Oxford University Press, 1939.

Booth, Alison. *Greatness Engendered: George Eliot and Virginia Woolf*. Ithaca, N.Y.: Cornell University Press, 1992.

Boylan, Anne M. "Evangelical Womanhood in the Nineteenth Century: The Role of Women in Sunday Schools." *Feminist Studies* 4 (Fall 1978): 62–80.

———. "Timid Girls, Venerable Widows, and Dignified Matrons: Life Cycle Patterns among Organized Women in New York and Boston, 1797–1840." *American Quarterly* 38, no. 5 (1986): 779–97.

Braxton, Joanne. *Black Women Writing Autobiography: A Tradition within a Tradition*. Philadelphia: Temple University Press, 1989.

Bree, Germaine. "Autogynography." *Southern Review* 22, no. 2 (1986): 223–30.

Brodzki, Bella, and Celeste Schenck, eds. *Life/Lines: Theorizing Women's Autobiography*. Ithaca, N.Y.: Cornell University Press, 1988.

Broughton, Treva. "Margaret Oliphant: The Unbroken Self." *Women's Studies International Forum* 10, no. 1 (1987): 41–52.

Brownstein, Rachel. *Becoming a Heroine: Reading about Women in Novels*. New York: Viking Press, 1982.

Buell, Lawrence. *Literary Transcendentalism: Style and Vision in the American Renaissance*. Ithaca, N.Y.: Cornell University Press, 1973.

Bunkers, Suzanne L. "'Faithful Friend': Nineteenth-Century Midwestern American Women's Unpublished Diaries." *Women's Studies International Forum* 10, no. 1 (1987): 7–17.

Buss, Helen M. "Anna Jameson's *Winter Studies and Summer Rambles in Canada* as Epistolary Dijournal." In *Essays on Life Writing*, edited by Marlene Kadar. Toronto: University of Toronto Press, 1992.

Butler, Marilyn. *Romantics, Rebels, and Reactionaries: English Literature and Its Background, 1760–1830*. New York: Oxford University Press, 1982.

Buzard, James. *The Beaten Track: European Tourism, Literature, and the Ways to Culture, 1800–1918*. Oxford: Oxford University Press, 1993.

Cayton, Mary Kupiec. *Emerson's Emergence: Self and Society in the Transformation of New England*. Chapel Hill: University of North Carolina Press, 1989.

Chambers-Schiller, Lee Virginia. *Liberty a Better Husband: Single Women in America: The Generations of 1780–1840*. New Haven: Yale University Press, 1984.

Connolly, Mary Ann. "The Boston Schools in the New Republic, 1776–1840." Ph.D. diss., Harvard School of Education, 1963.

Cott, Nancy. *The Bonds of Womanhood: 'Woman's Sphere' in New England, 1780–1835.* New Haven: Yale University Press, 1977.

———. "Young Women in the Second Great Awakening in New England." *Feminist Studies* 3 (Fall 1975): 15–29.

Culley, Margo, ed. *American Women's Autobiography: Fea(s)ts of Memory.* Madison: University of Wisconsin Press, 1992.

———, ed. *A Day at a Time: The Diary Literature of American Women from 1764 to the Present.* New York: Feminist Press, 1985.

Culley, Margo, and Leonore Hoffmann, eds. *Women's Personal Narratives.* New York: Modern Language Association, 1985.

Davidson, Cathy N., ed. *Reading in America.* Baltimore: Johns Hopkins University Press, 1989.

———, ed. *The Revolution of the Word.* New York: Oxford University Press, 1986.

Dobson, Joanne. *Dickinson and the Strategies of Reticence: The Woman Writer in Nineteenth-Century America.* Bloomington: Indiana University Press, 1989.

Douglas, Ann. *The Feminization of American Culture.* 1977. New York: Doubleday, 1988.

Eakin, Paul John. *American Autobiography: Retrospect and Prospect.* Madison: University of Wisconsin Press, 1991.

Ezell, Margaret J. M. *Writing Women's Literary History.* Baltimore: Johns Hopkins University Press, 1993.

Fleenor, Juliann E., ed. *The Female Gothic.* Montreal: Eden Press, 1983.

Foster, Frances Smith. *Written by Herself: Literary Production by African-American Women, 1746–1892.* Bloomington: Indiana University Press, 1993.

Fraiman, Susan. *Unbecoming Women: British Women Writers and the Novel of Development.* New York: Columbia University Press, 1993.

Franklin, Penelope, ed. *Private Pages: Diaries of American Women, 1830s–1970s.* New York: Ballantine Books, 1986.

Frye, Joanne S. *Living Stories, Telling Lives: Women and the Novel in Contemporary Experience.* Ann Arbor: University of Michigan Press, 1986.

Gilbert, Sandra, and Susan Gubar. *The Madwoman in the Attic: The Woman Writer and the Nineteenth-Century Literary Imagination.* New Haven: Yale University Press, 1979.

Gillikin, Jo, ed. "Women's Nontraditional Literature." *Women's Studies Quarterly* 17 (1989): 3–4.

Goldsmith, Elizabeth, ed. *Writing the Female Voice: Essays on Epistolary Literature.* Boston: Northeastern University Press, 1989.

Goozé, Marjanne E. "The Definitions of Self and Form in Feminist Autobiography Theory." *Women's Studies* 21, no. 4 (1992): 411–29.

Gorsky, Susan Rabinow. *Femininity to Feminism: Women and Literature in the Nineteenth Century.* New York: Twayne, 1992.

Green, Katherine Sobba. *The Courtship Novel, 1740–1820: A Feminized Genre.* Lexington: University Press of Kentucky, 1991.

Haggerty, George E. *Gothic Fiction/Gothic Form.* University Park: Pennsylvania State University Press, 1989.

Harden, Elizabeth. *Maria Edgeworth.* Boston: Twayne, 1984.

Harris, Susan K. *Nineteenth-Century American Women's Novels: Interpretative Strategies.* Cambridge: Cambridge University Press, 1990.

Harsh, Constance D. *Subversive Heroinism: Resolutions of Social Crisis in the Condition-of-England Novel.* Ann Arbor: University of Michigan Press, 1994.

Heilbrun, Carolyn. *Writing a Woman's Life.* New York: Norton, 1988.

Herget, Winifried. "Writing after the Ministers: The Significance of Sermon Notes." In *Studies in New England Puritanism,* edited by Winifried Herget. Frankfurt: Verlag Peter Lang, 1983.

Holly, Carol. "Nineteenth-Century Autobiographies of Affiliation: The Case of Catharine Sedgwick and Lucy Larcom." In *American Autobiography: Retrospect and Prospect,* edited by Paul John Eakin. Madison: University of Wisconsin Press, 1991.

Howe, Daniel Walker. *The Unitarian Conscience: Harvard Moral Philosophy, 1805–1861.* Cambridge: Harvard University Press, 1970.

Huff, Cynthia. "'That Profoundly Female, and Feminist Genre': The Diary as Feminist Practice." *Women's Studies Quarterly* 3–4 (1989): 6–14.

Huth, Mary M. "Kate Gannett Wells, Anti-Suffragist." *University of Rochester Library Bulletin* 34 (1981): 2–23.

Iles, Teresa, ed. *All Sides of the Subject: Women and Biography.* New York: Teachers College Press of Columbia University, 1992.

Jelinek, Estelle. *The Tradition of Women's Autobiography: From Antiquity to the Present.* Boston: Twayne, 1986.

———, ed. *Women's Autobiography: Essays in Criticism.* Bloomington: Indiana University Press, 1980.

Joeres, Ruth-Ellen Boetcher, and Elizabeth Mittman, eds. *The Politics of the Essay: Feminist Essays.* Bloomington: Indiana University Press, 1993.

Kadar, Marlene, ed. *Essays on Life Writing.* Toronto: University of Toronto Press, 1992.

Kaufmann, Linda. *Special Delivery: Epistolary Modes in Modern Fiction.* Chicago: University of Chicago Press, 1992.

Kelley, Mary. *Private Woman, Public Stage: Literary Domesticity in Nineteenth-Century America.* New York: Oxford University Press, 1984.

———. "'Vindicating the Equality of Female Intellect': Women and Authority in the Early Republic." *Prospects: An Annual of American Cultural Studies* 17 (1992): 1–27.

Kowaleski-Wallace, Beth. "Home-Economics: Domestic Ideology in Maria Edgeworth's *Belinda.*" *Eighteenth Century* 29, no. 3 (1988): 242–62.

———. *Their Father's Daughters: Hannah More, Maria Edgeworth, and Patriarchal Complicity.* New York: Oxford University Press, 1991.

Linden-Ward, Blanche. *Silent City on a Hill: Landscapes of Memory and Boston's Mount Auburn Cemetery.* Columbus: Ohio State University Press, 1989.

Lionnet, Françoise. *Autobiographical Voices: Race, Gender, Self-Portraiture.* Ithaca, N.Y.: Cornell University Press, 1989.

Long, Elizabeth. "Women, Reading, and Cultural Authority: Some Implications of the Audience Perspective in Cultural Studies." *American Quarterly* 38, no. 4 (1986): 591–612.

Lueck, Beth L. "James Kirke Paulding and the Picturesque Tour: 'Banqueting on the Picturesque' in the 1820s and 1830s." *University of Mississippi Studies in English* 9 (1991): 167–88.

Moers, Ellen. *Literary Women.* Garden City, N.Y.: Doubleday, 1976.

Moffat, Mary Jane, and Charlotte Painter. *Revelations: Diaries of Women.* New York: Vintage, 1974.

Monteith, Moira, ed. *Women's Writing.* New York: St. Martin's Press, 1986.

Mott, Wesley T. *The Strains of Eloquence: Emerson and His Sermons.* University Park: Pennsylvania State University Press, 1989.

Mulvey, Christopher. *Anglo-American Landscapes: A Study of Nineteenth-Century Anglo-American Travel Literature.* Cambridge: Cambridge University Press, 1983.

Myers, Mitzi. "The Dilemmas of Gender as Double-Voiced Narrative; or, Maria Edgeworth Mothers the Bildungsroman." In *The Idea of the Novel,* edited by Robert W. Uphaus. East Lansing, Mich.: Colleagues Press, 1988.

———. "Hannah More's *Tracts for the Times:* Social Fiction and Female Ideology." In *Fetter'd or Free? British Women Novelists, 1670–1815,* edited by Mary Anne Schofield and Cecilia Macheski. Athens: Ohio University Press, 1986.

———. "Quixotes, Orphans, and Subjectivity: Maria Edgeworth's Georgian Heroinism and the (En)Gendering of Young Adult Fiction." *The Lion and the Unicorn* 13 (1989): 21–40.

Napier, Elizabeth R. *The Failure of Gothic: Problems of Disjunction in an Eighteenth-Century Literary Form.* Oxford: Clarendon Press, 1987.

Nussbaum, Felicity. *The Autobiographical Subject: Gender and Ideology in Eighteenth-Century England.* Baltimore: Johns Hopkins University Press, 1989.

Olney, James. *Studies in Autobiography.* New York: Oxford University Press, 1988.

Pease, William, and Jane Pease. *Ladies, Women, and Wenches: Choice and Constraint in Antebellum Charleston and Boston.* Chapel Hill: University of North Carolina Press, 1990.

———. *The Web of Progress: Private Values and Public Styles in Boston and Charleston, 1828–1843.* New York: Oxford University Press, 1985.

Personal Narratives Group, eds. *Interpreting Women's Lives.* Bloomington: Indiana University Press, 1989.

Porter, Charles A., ed. "Men/Women of Letters." *Yale French Studies* 71 (1989).

Reuther, Rosemary Radford, and Rosemary Skinner Keller, eds. *Women and Religion in America*. Vol. 1, *The Nineteenth Century*. San Francisco: Harper and Row, 1981.

Richardson, Robert D., Jr. "Emerson's Italian Journey." *Browning Institute Studies* 12 (1984): 121–31.

Richter, David H. "The Reception of the Gothic Novel in the 1790s." In *The Idea of the Novel*, edited by Robert W. Uphaus. East Lansing, Mich.: Colleagues Press, 1988.

Roberson, Susan L. *Emerson in His Sermons: A Man-Made Self*. Columbia: University of Missouri Press, 1995.

Robinson, David. *Apostle of Culture: Emerson as Preacher and Lecturer*. Philadelphia: University of Pennsylvania Press, 1982.

———. *The Unitarians and the Universalists*. Westport, Conn.: Greenwood Press, 1985.

Rotundo, Barbara. "Mount Auburn Cemetery: A Proper Boston Institution." *Harvard Library Bulletin* 22, no. 3 (1974): 268–79.

Rusk, Ralph. *The Life of Ralph Waldo Emerson*. New York: Columbia University Press, 1949.

Ryan, Mary P. "A Women's Awakening: Evangelical Religion and the Families of Utica, New York, 1800–1840." *American Quarterly* 30, no. 5 (1978): 602–23.

Samuels, Shirley, ed. *The Culture of Sentiment: Race, Gender, and Sentimentality in Nineteenth-Century America*. New York: Oxford University Press, 1992.

Schlesinger, Elizabeth. "Two Early Harvard Wives: Eliza Farrar and Eliza Follen." *New England Quarterly* 38, no. 2 (1965): 147–67.

Schriber, Mary Suzanne. "Julia Ward Howe and the Travel Book." *New England Quarterly* 62, no. 2 (1989): 264–79.

Schroeder, Natalie. "The Anti-Feminist Reception of Regina Maria Roche." *Essays in Literature* 9, no. 1 (1982): 55–65.

———. "Regina Maria Roche and the Early Nineteenth-Century Irish Novel." *Eire-Island: A Journal of Irish Studies* 19, no. 2 (1984): 116–30.

Sharf, Frederic A. "The Garden Cemetery and American Sculpture: Mount Auburn." *Arts Quarterly* 24 (Spring 1961): 80–88.

Showalter, Elaine. *A Literature of Their Own*. Princeton: Princeton University Press, 1977.

Showalter, English, Jr. "Authorial Self-Consciousness in the Familiar Letter: The Case of Madame de Graffigny." *Yale French Studies* 71 (1986): 113–30.

Sicherman, Barbara. "Sense and Sensibility: A Case Study of Women's Reading in Late-Victorian America." In *Reading in America*, edited by Cathy Davidson. Baltimore: Johns Hopkins University Press, 1989.

Smith, Sidonie. *A Poetics of Women's Autobiography: Marginality and the Fictions of Self-Representation*. Bloomington: Indiana University Press, 1987.

————. *Subjectivity, Identity, and the Body: Women's Autobiographical Practices in the Twentieth Century.* Bloomington: Indiana University Press, 1993.

Smith-Rosenberg, Carroll. *Disorderly Conduct: Visions of Gender in Victorian America.* New York: Knopf, 1985.

Spacks, Patricia Meyer. *The Female Imagination.* New York: Knopf, 1975.

Spender, Dale, ed. "Personal Chronicles: Women's Autobiographical Writings." *Women's Studies International Forum* 10, no. 1 (1987).

Stanley, Liz. *The Auto/Biographical I: The Theory and Practice of Feminist Auto/Biography.* Manchester: Manchester University Press, 1992.

Stanton, Domna. *The Female Autograph: Theory and Practice of Autobiography from the Tenth to the Twentieth Century.* Chicago: Chicago University Press, 1984.

Tompkins, Jane. *Sensational Designs: The Cultural Work of American Fiction, 1790–1860.* New York: Oxford University Press, 1985.

Trofimenkoff, Susan Mann. "Feminist Biography." *Atlantis* 10, no. 2 (1985): 1–9.

Tuchman, Gaye, and Nina E. Fortin. *Edging Women Out: Victorian Novelists, Publishers, and Social Change.* New Haven: Yale University Press, 1989.

Ty, Eleanor. "Writing as a Daughter: Autobiography in Wollstonecraft's Travelogue." In *Essays on Life Writing,* edited by Marlene Kadar. Toronto: University of Toronto Press, 1992.

Ulrich, Laurel Thatcher. *A Midwife's Tale: The Life of Martha Ballard, Based on Her Diary, 1785–1812.* New York: Vintage, 1990.

Voss, Norine. "'Saying the Unsayable': An Introduction to Women's Autobiography." In *Gender Studies: New Directions in Feminist Criticism,* edited by Judith Spector. Bowling Green, Ohio: Bowling Green State University Press, 1986.

Warren, Joyce. *The American Narcissus.* New Brunswick, N.J.: Rutgers University Press, 1984.

————, ed. *The (Other) American Traditions.* New Brunswick, N.J.: Rutgers University Press, 1993.

Weiss, Harry B. "American Letter-Writers, 1698–1943." New York Public Library, 1945.

Whitehill, Walter Muir. *Boston: A Topographical History.* Cambridge: Harvard University Press, Belknap Press, 1968.

Wider, Sarah Ann. "'Most Glorious Sermons': Anna Tilden's Sermon Notes, 1824–1831." *Studies in the American Renaissance* (1989): 1–93.

————. "What Did the Minister Mean: Emerson's Sermons and Their Audience." *ESQ: A Journal of the American Renaissance* 34, no. 1–2 (1988): 1–21.

Wright, Conrad. *The Beginnings of Unitarianism in America.* Boston: Starr King, 1955.

————. *The Liberal Christians: Essays on American Unitarian History.* Boston: Beacon Press, 1970.

————, ed. *American Unitarianism, 1805–1861.* Boston: Northeastern University Press, 1989.

————, ed. *A Stream of Light: A Sesquicentennial History of American Unitarianism.* Boston: American Unitarian Association, 1975.

Yaeger, Patricia. *Honey-Mad Women: Emancipatory Strategies in Women's Writing.* New York: Columbia University Press, 1988.

Zagarell, Sandra A. "Expanding 'America': Lydia Sigourney's *Sketch of Connecticut,* Catharine Sedgwick's *Hope Leslie.*" *Tulsa Studies in Women's Literature* 6, no. 2 (1987): 225–44.

Zboray, Ronald J. "The Letter and the Fiction Reading Public in Antebellum America." *Journal of American Culture* 10, no. 1 (1987): 27–34.

Index